W9-BPJ-217

HOME COOKING IN MINUTES

Thelma Snyder

•

Marcia Cone-Esaki

SIMON & SCHUSTER
NEW YORK / LONDON / TORONTO
SYDNEY / TOKYO / SINGAPORE

This book is dedicated to our children, Mae, Hana, Suzanne, and David. As they grow up and leave our homes, may they find warmth, love, caring, and satisfaction in their kitchens, wherever they may go.

 SIMON & SCHUSTER
Simon & Schuster Building
Rockefeller Center
1230 Avenue of the Americas
New York, New York 10020

Copyright © 1992 by Thelma Snyder and Marcia Cone-Esaki
All rights reserved
including the right of reproduction
in whole or in part in any form.
SIMON & SCHUSTER and colophon are
registered trademarks of Simon & Schuster Inc.
Designed by Edith Fowler
Manufactured in the United States of America

10 9 8 7 6 5 4 3 2 1

Library of Congress Cataloging-in-Publication Data

Snyder, Thelma.
   Home cooking in minutes / Thelma Snyder, Marcia Cone-Esaki.
      p.   cm.
   Includes index.
   1. Quick and easy cookery.   2. Microwave cookery.   I. Cone-Esaki, Marcia.   II. Title.
TX833.5.S68 1992
641.5'12—dc20   92-17113
ISBN 0-671-62547-0   CIP

Acknowledgments

We'd like to thank Barney Karpfinger, our agent, for streamlining our proposal; Carole Lalli for seeing its potential; Kerri Conan for giving it direction; copy editing for being so thorough; and Toula Polygalaktos for seeing it through to completion.

CONTENTS

INTRODUCTION

We STRONGLY agree with the French saying "Eating well is living well." We both brought memories of our grandmother's kitchens into our own kitchens—memories replete with yeasty home-baked bread, fragrant soups and stews, and cinnamon-y applesauce. The aromas of these daily meals were interwoven with the scents of spices and herbs that would season the preserves, fruit butters, chutneys, and relishes to be put on the pantry shelf for use another day.

We were always assured that there would be food in the larder and someone to share it with. This gave us a great sense of comfort and well-being.

We both wanted our kitchens to have this character and appeal. This may seem like an unattainable dream today, considering the busy lives most of us lead, but we have accomplished it by developing cooking methods that integrate our kitchen appliances. And these are the methods we want to share with you.

This strategy combines a little know-how and a little fun. For example, you can bake a loaf of whole-grain bread in about an hour by using fast-rising yeast, speeding up the rising process even more in the microwave, and baking the loaf to a crusty brown in the conventional oven. While the bread is baking, you can begin sweating the onions in the microwave for a stew that will be completed there just in time to accompany the bread. The applesauce, which you made at harvest time, will be pulled out of the freezer and defrosted in minutes in the microwave.

If you have only twenty minutes, we have tomato sauces that go from the food processor, to the microwave, to your table in the time that it takes to cook the pasta on top of the stove.

This book includes recipes for those best-loved dishes that have been emerging from our family's kitchens for generations—the basics of everyone's collection but with a few minor changes. For example, our versions reflect the latest nutritional studies, which have shown that diets with less fat and more fiber are more healthful. Thus, you'll find low-cholesterol variations in most of the recipes and a listing of how to pair vegetable and bean dishes to create main dishes with more fiber and flavor.

We don't advocate eliminating meat from your diet but suggest that you balance it with a couple of vegetarian meals a week, slowly working your way into better eating habits.

Our pantry is designed the way we wish our grandmother's had been. It includes bottles of vinegars and oils modernized with infusions of herbs and hot peppers that would have set off Grandma's peptic ulcer. We've made a collection of apple and fruit butters, chutneys, pickles, and salsas that can be refrigerated and frozen.

The fixings in "The Well-Stocked Pantry, Refrigerator, and Freezer" are designed to be served with your own recipes or even as accompaniments to something you've brought home from a takeout place, to give it that home-cooked touch.

Now that we've piqued your interest, turn a page to The Integrated Kitchen and learn how to stock your shelves with the appropriate utensils and ingredients. This, along with our revolutionary method of integrating appliances, will make your kitchen experiences easy and fun.

Most of our recipes yield four servings. If you are cooking for one, a general guideline is to cut the ingredients, dish size, and cooking time in half. This will give you at least two meals (half the original servings). With microwave cooking, unlike conventional oven cooking, the less you cook the quicker it goes.

On the other hand, we strongly recommend that you cook the whole recipe and freeze individual portions for later meals. Microwave defrosting takes very little time, so this will give you extra time throughout the week to pamper yourself by making a special salad or dessert if you wish.

KNOW YOUR MICROWAVE OVEN

A range of cooking times is given in every recipe because microwave ovens vary in wattage, or cooking power. Think of these cooking times not as numbers etched in stone, but as guidelines. Begin with the shortest times, check for doneness, and cook for as long as necessary. Do this until you feel that you know your oven well enough to find the proper timing.

Or think of them as movie reviews with one to four stars. In judging your oven you may not always agree with us on the high or low end, but we will always be consistent, so you'll know how to "grade" your own oven.

Here's an easy test to find out how *quickly* your oven cooks: Fill a glass measuring cup with 1 cup cold tap water. Heat it in the microwave oven, uncovered, on HIGH until the water begins to boil.

- If the water boils in less than 3 minutes, you have a 650- to 800-watt oven and should follow the shorter cooking time given in the range of each recipe.
- If the water boils in 3 to 4 minutes, you have a 500- to 600-watt oven and should follow the middle cooking time given in the range of each recipe.
- If the water boils in more than 4 minutes, your oven wattage is less than 500 and should follow the longer cooking time given in the range of each recipe.

Medium power will be 50 to 70 percent of full power, depending on your oven. Full-size ovens generally have MEDIUM at number 5 (50 percent) and smaller ovens have MEDIUM at number 7 (70 percent). Please check your oven manual if you aren't sure.

Defrost power will be 30 to 50 percent of full power, with full-size ovens having DEFROST at number 3 (30 percent) and smaller ovens at number 5 (50 percent).

THE INTEGRATED KITCHEN

The integrated kitchen combines a wide variety of appliances that work together to turn out marvelous home-cooked meals in minutes.

The main player in this cast is the microwave, which not only defrosts and reheats but gets things cooking quickly and speeds up the rising of yeast doughs.

The conventional stove top is used for browning small items and boiling large pots of water for pasta.

The conventional oven is used for baking breads, pizzas, and cakes and for putting the finishing browning and crisping touches to pies and poultry.

The toaster oven accomplishes the same things as the larger oven but is designed for smaller quantities. It also toasts breads and muffins.

The grill adds a barbecue flavor and color to vegetables, meats, and fish that have been precooked in the microwave oven.

The food processor (at least an 8-cup-capacity model) quickly mixes and kneads doughs, whirs out pie crusts, and chops, slices, minces, and mixes ingredients for many other dishes.

The electric mixer combines batters and whips creams.

UTENSIL LIST

Appropriate utensils are one of the keys to putting together meals efficiently. A dull knife will frustrate even the most skillful cook, and a pot too small for the task will cause boilovers, which will necessitate a lengthy cleanup. Here is a list of the minimum requirements for the well-appointed kitchen.

Microwave-safe dishes are called for in all the microwave recipes, but we recommend that you use dishes that can cross over to conventional oven cooking. They should therefore be able to withstand temperatures up to 450° F. This will help you reduce any clutter you might have in your cupboards.

The term *microwave-safe* is a description of the cooking dishes. Materials such as glass and ceramic are ideal for the microwave oven because microwaves can pass right through them to heat the food. Metal dishes should not be used in the microwave. Metal reflects microwaves, and metal trim causes microwaves to couple and spark, which can damage the oven.

- 1-, 2-, and 4-cup glass measures—For measuring, heating, and cooking in the microwave. The handles, which do not get hot, make for easy removal from the oven.
- Four 4-ounce custard cups
- 1-, 2-, 3-, and 4-quart casseroles with lids—The lids make peeking, stirring, and re-covering easier than when plastic wrap is used. Buy casseroles that have fairly wide bottom surface areas so that they can accommodate several large food items in a single layer.
- One 8½-inch round cake dish
- 9- and 10-inch pie plates
- 2 loaf pans (9 × 5 × 3-inch)—dual purpose for microwave and conventional baking.
- One 2-quart rectangular (8 × 12-inch) baking dish
- One 12-inch-diameter circular cook-and-serve dish—For platter meals
- Four 2-cup-capacity soup and cereal bowls.
- 1-, 2-, and 3-quart nesting bowls—For mixing and for raising bread dough. They should be microwave-safe.

FOR CONVENTIONAL COOKING

- One 12-capacity muffin tin (or two 6-cup tins)
- One black cookie sheet (10½ × 5½ × 1-inch)
- One 6-quart metal pot for boiling water
- One 24-inch-diameter heavy metal skillet with lid
- One wire whisk
- One 12-inch-diameter colander
- One 8-inch-diameter fine mesh strainer—To eliminate the use of cheesecloth
- One heavy sharp knife
- One heavy-duty rolling pin

COVERS

The primary purpose of a cover in the microwave is to retain moisture. This adds steam heat to the microwave vibration of molecules so that the total cooking speeds up and causes certain foods to cook more evenly.

Before you cover, you must ask yourself: Will steam heat enhance this food? If the answer is yes, how much steam is beneficial, a little or a lot?

We indicate one of the following terms in our recipes. If no term is indicated, as with sautéing onions or garlic, you can cover or not cover, as you wish.

Cover tightly means to cover with a casserole lid or plastic wrap that has been folded back on one corner. Even a plate that fits the casserole is good for this. Foods that would normally be steamed, boiled, or braised are best cooked with this cover.

It is best to turn back a corner of the plastic wrap to keep the wrap from splitting as steam builds up. This will enable you to use the plastic wrap over again if you need to stir halfway through cooking. When more stirring or checking is involved, as with stews, soups, or pasta sauces, we recommend a lid. Always open a tight cover away from you to prevent steam burns. *Foods that benefit: vegetables, fruits, casseroles, stews, less tender cuts of meat, thick pieces of fish, some shellfish, and soups.*

Cover with waxed paper means to lay the waxed paper loosely on top of a dish. If your oven has a turntable, you may need to tuck the waxed paper under the dish to keep it secure.

Waxed paper aids in the speed and evenness of cooking by keeping in some steam and protects the oven from spatters. Because waxed paper can't be formed to fit the dish, it allows quite a bit of steam to escape, which keeps the food from becoming too soggy. *Foods that benefit: chicken parts, pork chops, individual plates of food to be reheated.*

Cover with paper towel means to lay a paper towel on top of the food in the dish. This, like wax paper, should be tucked under the dish when your oven has a rotating turntable. It tends to fall off the dish, otherwise.

Paper towels absorb extra fat or moisture that comes as a result of cooking certain foods. *Foods that benefit: bacon strips cooked to be dry, some fish fillets and scallops (which exude water), rolls to be reheated (to keep bread surface dry while still retaining some moisture).*

Cook uncovered applies where a drier cooked surface is desired, or when a liquid needs to be evaporated. *Foods that benefit: mushrooms, roast beef, turkey, cakes, and pastry crusts.*

KIDS IN THE KITCHEN   Because we have children of our own, ranging from infant to college age, we wanted to include recipes that would be fun for them to make, too.

Cooking as a family is a form of therapy for us—it gives us time to unwind from our busy days and get reacquainted. It only takes one little task—peeling carrots, for example—to make a child feel that he has "made dinner." And as long as it doesn't matter that the carrots are whittled a bit thin or that the pizza dough is somewhat smaller than it should be because of nibbling, the time spent preparing meals can be what the experts call "quality time." Cooking is a wonderful way to encourage your kids' creativity in small ways that really add up over time.

The recipes that we feel kids would want to make and (depending on their age, of course) could make, with your help, are indicated by the legend "Kids help." Not surprisingly, many of these recipes involve the microwave, which has been touted as a safe appliance for kids because it has no open flame. It *is* safe if properly used; here are a few cautionary notes and guidelines.

- Children under the age of ten to twelve (you know your own) should not use the microwave unsupervised.
- Children younger than ten can assemble precut ingredients on microwave-safe dishes or paper plates. You can do the cooking and then let the kids serve themselves. (Line up ingredients for them so that they can add and mix while you do the cooking.)
- Keep pot holders by the microwave—those dishes can get hot!
- When uncovering a microwave dish that is covered with a lid or plastic wrap, be sure to open it carefully and away from the face, as hot steam will come out.
- After removing food from the microwave, let it stand a little longer than you might normally. If it's a stirrable food, make sure that you stir it before serving, to redistribute heat.
- Beware of heating jelly doughnuts in the microwave. The jelly centers get hotter than the outsides because the microwaves are attracted to the sugar more than to the outside dough.

It takes only 10 to 15 seconds on HIGH power to reheat any of these items. (Wrap each in a paper towel first): 1 jelly doughnut; 1 bagel; 2 slices of bread; 1 large or 2 small muffins; 1 Danish; 1 6-inch pita. If frozen, heat on HIGH for 35 to 45 seconds.

- Sometimes just defrosting frozen foods is enough. Young kids adore partially thawed blueberries, peas, and corn as snacks.

BREAKFASTS

As kids, Thelma and Marcia both spent many summers on working farms, and they remember the second breakfast that was served to the farmhands. Plates of sausages and bacon, baskets of biscuits were passed down long tables while scrambled eggs were spooned out by the hands that made them.

The reason for such abundance was that the workers had been up since 5:30, toiling away after only a cup of coffee and some toast, so a second, more substantial breakfast was required.

Few of us work physically hard enough nowadays to burn up the calories in such a breakfast, but we still like the idea of a long wooden table spread with gingham napkins and a variety of fragrant foods. This is where new country breakfasts come in. Because our tastes have changed, we've trimmed the recipes to satisfy but not overwhelm.

It is now such a special treat to sit down to a leisurely meal and pore over the morning paper that breakfasts have become a new way of entertaining friends. Beyond that, however, those who regularly get their families on the road with a healthy breakfast will reap the rewards for years to come.

Research has shown that it is important to start the day with a good breakfast—and not just any breakfast, but one composed of whole-grain breads, cereals, or muffins, low-fat eggs, and skimmed dairy products. It is this type of meal that will stabilize your blood sugar throughout the morning.

If you are inclined to the doughnut-and-coffee or soft-drink breakfast, your blood sugar will tend to skyrocket, giving you a quick high. But what goes up must come down. After a high-sugar breakfast your blood sugar will plummet to a new low, along with your energy level, resulting in crankiness and fatigue.

There is also evidence that dieters who eat a healthy, substantial breakfast and follow their weight-loss plan for the day tend to lose more weight than their counterparts who skip breakfast but take in the same amount of daily calories.

If we haven't persuaded you yet, just try the Home Fries that are made with only 1 tablespoon of oil. They're delicious! Or keep a jar of the Multigrain Pancake mix on hand and a few Turkey Sausages in the freezer for Sunday brunch or even weekday beginnings.

On weekends we like to feed our fantasies with Country Inn Spoon Bread and Perfectly Poached Pears, which transport us to an old plantation with a porch swing. A breakfast of Grits with spicy Creole Sauce, Frizzled Ham, and Café au Lait, all with a little R & B in the background, puts us on a balcony in New Orleans.

These are the "new" country breakfasts that will make you glad to get up in the morning.

Multigrain Pancakes

MAKES: *4 servings (About 12 4-inch pancakes)*
COOKING TIME: *10 to 12 minutes*

⅓ cup buckwheat flour (see Note 1)
⅓ cup whole-wheat flour
⅓ cup all-purpose flour
2 tablespoons cornmeal
2 teaspoons baking powder
½ teaspoon salt

1. Combine all ingredients in a medium bowl.
2. Pour in 1¼ cups water (see Note 2) and stir until the dry ingredients are just moistened; ignore the lumps.

No fat

SERVING SUGGESTIONS:
Warm maple syrup is the obvious topper for these pancakes, but why not try Warm Blueberry Sauce (page 32), Apple Syrup (page 32), a fruit butter (pages 328–29), or fresh berries?
Or serve these multigrain pancakes as a dinner side dish with grilled chicken or one of the fish recipes.

3. Use a nonstick or well-seasoned skillet or griddle. Heat on top of the stove on medium-high until a few drops of cold water bounce and spatter. If the water just boils, your skillet is not hot enough. If the water vanishes, it is too hot.

4. Pour ¼ cup of the batter for each pancake into the heated skillet. When bubbles appear on the upper surface of the pancakes, they should be ready to turn—this takes about 2 minutes.

5. Cook for about 1 minute on the second side, or until browned and cooked through.

NOTES   Buckwheat flour is available at health-food stores and some grocery stores. If you have made up three or more times the recipe, the ratio is 1 cup mix to 1¼ cups water to serve 4 people. Depending on skillet size, you may cook two to four pancakes at a time.

SINGLE SERVING: Use ¼ cup mix plus ¼ cup plus 1 tablespoon water.

TO THAW
FROZEN JUICE
CONCENTRATE   Remove the metal lid from a 10-ounce can. Microwave on DEFROST for 2 to 4 minutes.

TO HEAT PANCAKE
SYRUP   Pour 1 to 2 cups into a microwave-safe serving pitcher. Microwave on HIGH for 1½ to 2 minutes.

TO REHEAT
PANCAKES   Wrap 2 pancakes in an unrecycled paper towel. Microwave on HIGH for 20 to 45 seconds.

Just as we were starting to pay close attention to cholesterol intake, someone gave us a package of buckwheat pancake mix. The mix required no eggs or milk. This mix encouraged us to try to make one of our own. Now we make up about three times this recipe and store it in a tightly covered jar.

Mixed Winter Fruit Compote

MAKES: *6 servings*
COOKING TIME: *15 minutes*

No fat

SERVING SUGGESTIONS:
This is great served for brunch on a chilly winter weekend with Sautéed Grits (page 120) and Turkey Sausages (page 180). Cook the grits the night before, while cleaning up the kitchen after dinner. The next morning sauté them along with the sausage as the compote cooks in the microwave oven.

The aroma of spices will fill the room, and only a fire in the fireplace will add to the feeling of well-being.

2 cups dry white wine, apple juice, or orange juice
½ cup dark brown sugar
1 teaspoon vanilla
¼ teaspoon ground ginger
1 cinnamon stick or ½ teaspoon ground cinnamon
½ lemon
1 pound mixed dried fruit (prunes, apples, apricots, and pears; usually found together)

1. In a 2-quart microwave-safe casserole, combine all the ingredients except the fruit, stirring well to blend.
2. Stir in the fruit. Cover tightly with a lid or with plastic wrap turned back slightly. Microwave on HIGH for 15 minutes, or until the fruit has plumped, stirring once after 7 minutes.
3. Let stand 5 minutes. Serve warm.

Country-Inn Spoon Bread

MAKES: *6 breakfast servings with syrup and fruit*
COOKING TIME:
12 to 13 minutes

14.7 grams fat per serving

SERVING SUGGESTIONS:
Drizzle with warm maple

3 tablespoons butter or margarine
1½ cups milk
1 cup frozen whole-kernel corn, defrosted (see Note)
½ cup white cornmeal
1 tablespoon sugar
½ teaspoon salt
½ teaspoon baking powder
3 large eggs, beaten

1. Place the butter in a 2-quart microwave-safe casserole. Microwave on MEDIUM for 1 to 2 minutes. (HIGH power makes the butter spatter too much.)
2. Add the remaining ingredients, except the eggs, mixing well. Cover with waxed paper. Microwave on

syrup and flank with Perfectly Poached Peaches (page 240). For a larger-scale brunch, Turkey Sausages (page 180), Frizzled Ham or Canadian Bacon (page 27), or Ham on the Bone (page 162) complete the scene. For an evening meal, this spoon bread is delicious alongside grilled chicken, turkey, or fish.

HIGH for 3 minutes; stir well.

3. Cover again and microwave on HIGH for 3 to 3½ minutes more, stirring every minute, until most of the liquid is absorbed.

4. In a medium bowl, beat the eggs and stir in ½ cup of the corn mixture. Slowly stir back into the remaining mixture. Cover with waxed paper and microwave on MEDIUM for 2 minutes; stir the outer edges into the center.

5. Smooth the top. Cover again and microwave on MEDIUM for 1½ to 2 minutes, or until set. Serve.

TO DEFROST
FROZEN CORN

When guests arrive for the weekend, home becomes a country inn, and it is wonderful to treat visitors with special care. This soft corn bread is one way to do just that.

If stored in a box, remove the outer wrapping and place the whole box in the microwave. Heat on HIGH for 2 minutes. Pour out the 1 cup needed. Put the remaining corn in a sealable freezer bag and place back in the freezer.

If the box is covered with foil, open the box and transfer the contents to a bowl. Heat, uncovered, on HIGH for 2 minutes.

If the corn is in a large bag, remove 1 cup of corn to a bowl. Heat, uncovered, on HIGH for 1 minute to defrost.

Porridge with Brown Sugar, Yogurt, and Dried Fruit

MAKES: *4 servings*
COOKING TIME: *8 to 10 minutes*

No fat

Here is a high-energy breakfast. Be sure to use a large cooking dish to prevent boilovers.

¾ *cup farina or Cream of Wheat, or 1⅓ cups oatmeal, or 1 cup toasted-wheat cereal*
½ *teaspoon salt (optional)*

SUGGESTED TOPPINGS

Maple syrup, brown sugar, date crystals, or molasses
¼ *cup dried fruit, such as raisins, chopped apricots, prunes, or dates*
¼ *cup toasted nuts*
1 cup plain nonfat yogurt or milk
2 cups fresh mixed berries (in season)

1. In a 3-quart microwave-safe casserole, combine the cereal, 3 cups water, and salt. Cover with waxed paper. Microwave on HIGH for 4 minutes; stir.

2. Cover again. Microwave on HIGH for 4 to 6 minutes more, or until all the liquid is absorbed; stir again.

3. Spoon into four bowls and add topping(s) of your choice.

SINGLE-SERVING PORRIDGE: Spoon 2½ tablespoons farina or cream of wheat, or ⅓ cup oatmeal, or ¼ cup toasted-wheat cereal into a 2-cup cereal bowl or measuring cup with ¾ cup water. Microwave on HIGH for 1 minute; stir. Microwave for ½ to 1½ minutes more, or until slightly thickened, stirring every 30 seconds. Stir in additions as above.

TO SOFTEN BROWN SUGAR

Place sugar in a microwave-safe bowl. Add an apple wedge or a slice of soft white bread. Cover tightly with a lid or with plastic wrap turned back slightly. Microwave on HIGH 30 to 40 seconds. Let stand for 30 seconds; stir.

Quinoa and Fruit Breakfast

MAKES: *4 servings*
COOKING TIME: *10 to 14 minutes*

No fat

A nutritious and delicious way to serve a high-protein breakfast.

¾ cup quinoa (see Note)
1¾ cups water
¼ cup raisins or chopped dried apricots
½ teaspoon ground cinnamon
1 apple, grated
Brown sugar, honey, or maple syrup to taste
Low-fat milk (optional)

1. Rinse the quinoa in a small strainer.
2. Combine the quinoa and water in a 2-quart microwave-safe casserole or glass measure. Cover with a lid or with plastic wrap turned back slightly. Microwave on HIGH for 10 to 14 minutes, or until all the water is absorbed and the grains appear translucent.
3. Stir in the remaining ingredients and serve with milk, if desired.

NOTE

Quinoa is a grain that comes from the Andes Mountains. It was one of three staple foods, along with corn and potatoes, of the Inca civilization. Quinoa is a complete protein with an essential amino-acid balance similar to that of milk. It is now grown in the United States and may be purchased in the grains section of health-food stores and many grocery stores.

Egg Custards

MAKES: *4 servings*
COOKING TIME: *8 to 10 minutes*

6.45 grams fat per serving

SERVING SUGGESTIONS:
Custards require a little advance planning, so we make them while cleaning up the kitchen from dinner the night before we plan to serve them. By breakfast time they are chilled and ready to serve with fruit, such as Spiced Plums (page 238). They can also be served warm.

VARIATION

The whole family enjoys egg custards as a special breakfast treat. When people aren't feeling well, this comforting custard can boost their spirits.

1¼ cups milk (we use 2-percent milk)
2 teaspoons vanilla
4 large eggs, beaten
¼ cup sugar
Freshly grated nutmeg (optional)

1. In a 4-cup glass measure, combine the milk and vanilla. Microwave, uncovered, on HIGH for 2 minutes, or until hot but not boiling.
2. Meanwhile, in a medium bowl, beat the eggs and sugar together until frothy.
3. Add the heated milk, pouring slowly and stirring constantly.
4. Pour into four 5- or 6-ounce custard cups. Place the cups around the outer rim of a 10- or 12-inch microwave-safe plate, leaving a space between each cup. Cook, covered with waxed paper, on MEDIUM for 6 to 8 minutes, or until firm, rotating the plate one-half turn after 3 minutes.
5. Let stand 5 minutes. Serve warm, or cover and chill.

PUMPKIN CUSTARDS (1.7 grams fat per serving): Eliminate 1 cup milk and add ¾ cup pumpkin puree to the remaining ¼ cup milk. Cook, uncovered, on HIGH for 2 minutes, or until hot. Add ¼ teaspoon grated nutmeg and ½ teaspoon ground ginger to heated milk. Follow basic recipe, starting with step 2.

Lemon-Scented Cranberry-Bread French Toast

MAKES: *4 servings*
COOKING TIME: *7 minutes, not including baking the bread*

10.3 grams fat per serving

2 large eggs, beaten
½ cup milk
1 tablespoon sugar
½ teaspoon vanilla
½ teaspoon ground cinnamon
4 ½-inch-thick slices Lemon-Scented Cranberry Bread (page 60) or other specialty bread
1½ tablespoons margarine

1. In a pie plate, combine the eggs, milk, sugar, vanilla, and cinnamon; blend with a wire whisk.
2. Slide the bread slices into the mixture and let them soak for about 5 minutes, or until all the liquid is absorbed, turning the bread over once.

Serve this tangy French toast with warm maple syrup or Pink Applesauce (page 239), and Frizzled Ham or Canadian Bacon (page 271). (The applesauce can be made earlier and refrigerated. The Canadian bacon can cook in the microwave oven while the French toast is browning on the stove.)

We like to make this when we have leftover cranberry bread, though we sometimes make the bread specifically for this purpose.

3. Place the margarine in a heavy 12-inch skillet and heat on top of the stove on medium-high for about 1 minute.
4. Add the bread and turn down the heat to medium-low. Cook until crisp and golden, about 3 minutes on each side. Serve immediately.

Scrambled Eggs

MAKES: *4 servings*
COOKING TIME: *2 to 3 minutes*

Low-cholesterol variation

5.6 grams fat per serving

4 large eggs
2 tablespoons water or club soda (makes them even lighter)

1. In a 1-quart microwave-safe casserole, beat the eggs and water with a wire whisk. Microwave on HIGH for 1½ minutes.
2. With a fork, stir the outer, cooked sections into the center. Microwave on HIGH for 1 to 1½ minutes, or until almost set in the center but still moist; stir well with a fork. (They will continue to cook as you are stirring.)

VARIATIONS

We like to serve these with Tomato Chutney (page 333) and Old-Fashioned Biscuits Made Light (page 55) or Salsa Cruda (page 317) and tortillas. For brunch, add Turkey Sausages (page 180) or Frizzled Ham or Canadian Bacon (page 27).

SCRAMBLED EGGS WITH HERBS: Stir in ¼ cup mixed fresh herbs (such as parsley and chives) into eggs before cooking.

SCRAMBLED EGGS WITH CHILIES: Stir 3 tablespoons drained canned mild green chilies into cooked eggs. Serve with tortillas and salsa.

LOW-CHOLESTEROL SCRAMBLED EGGS (1.4 grams fat per serving): Substitute 4 whites and 1 yolk for the 4 eggs. Proceed as above.

Eggs scrambled in the microwave oven require no added fat, and they can be cooked and stirred in one dish. They come out very light and fluffy.

SINGLE-SERVING SCRAMBLED EGGS (5.6 grams fat per serving): Beat 1 egg with 1 teaspoon water in a 6-ounce custard cup. Microwave on HIGH for 35 to 50 seconds, or until slightly puffed up. Stir and break the egg up with a fork. Serve in a warmed tortilla or pita pocket.

Light Omelet

MAKES: *2 servings*
COOKING TIME: *2½ to 4 minutes*

2.6 grams fat per serving.

No shortening is needed to cook this omelet. The single yolk provides the desired flavor and appearance but relatively little cholesterol and fat.
   This is an easy omelet that won't burn or stick to the pan. Prepare the fillings before cooking the omelet.

1 whole egg
2 egg whites
1 cup filling (Choose from Honey-Sherry Onion
    Marmalade (page 321), Mexican Tomato Sauce
    (page 319), Sizzled Peppers and Onions (page
    209), or Lightly Creamed Spinach (page 230)

1. With a beater or whisk, beat the egg, egg whites, and 1 tablespoon of water together in a small bowl.
2. Pour into a 9-inch microwave-safe pie plate. Cover with waxed paper. Microwave on HIGH for 1½ minutes; gently move the cooked outer edges of the omelet to the center, letting the uncooked portions flow to the outside.
3. Cover again and cook on HIGH for 1 to 2 minutes more, or until the center is set but still moist.
4. Spoon the desired filling down the center and using a spatula, fold the omelet in half. Cut in half and serve.

Frizzled Ham
or
Canadian Bacon

VARIATION

MAKES: *6 servings*
COOKING TIME: *3 to 4 minutes*

1.7 grams fat per serving for ham; 2.7 for Canadian bacon

8 ounces lean ham or Canadian bacon, cut into 8
    thin slices

1. Separate the ham and arrange it in overlapping slices around the outside of a 10-inch glass pie plate.
2. Cover with waxed paper. Microwave on HIGH for 2 to 3 minutes, or until heated through, moving the lesser cooked sections to the outside after 2 minutes.

FRIZZLED HAM OR CANADIAN BACON WITH APRICOT GLAZE:In a 1-cup glass measure, combine 2 tablespoons apricot preserves, 1 teaspoon Dijon-style mustard, and 1 teaspoon brown sugar. Microwave on HIGH for 1 minute; stir well. Spoon over uncooked ham or bacon slices, laid out on the 10-inch glass pie plate. Cook as directed above.

Place 4 slices of bacon at a time on a microwave roasting rack or on a microwave-safe plate lined with a paper towel. Cover with a paper towel. Microwave on HIGH for 2½ to 4 minutes, or until cooked. Let stand for 1 minute. Remove the bacon from the rack; pour off the fat or throw away the paper towels that have absorbed the grease. Repeat the process if necessary.

SERVING SUGGESTIONS:
Serve with Scrambled Eggs (page 26), Grits (page 120), and Country-Inn Spoon Bread (page 22), cooking any of these first in the microwave oven, followed by the frizzled ham.

NOTE

Bacon should be slightly undercooked from the doneness that you desire, because it will become a little crisper while standing.

This is a simple way to prepare ham. The pieces curl and crinkle, making the ham look attractive.

A 2-ounce serving contains only 51 milligrams of cholesterol, or one-fourth of what the American Heart Association recommends as a daily intake.

Breakfast Potato Pie

MAKES: *4 to 6 servings, depending on accompaniments*
COOKING TIME: *20 to 25 minutes*

13.3 grams fat per serving for 4; 8.9 grams fat per serving for 6

SERVING SUGGESTIONS:
Served with a fruit salad and hot coffee, this potato pie is a real breakfast treat. For a heartier meal, add

4 small to medium potatoes (about 1 pound), scrubbed but not peeled
2 medium onions, thinly sliced
2 medium green bell peppers, sliced into thin rings
¼ pound lean ham, cut into ½-inch squares.
8 ounces thinly sliced low-fat Muenster cheese
¼ teaspoon freshly ground black pepper
1 large tomato, thinly sliced

1. Pierce the potato skins once on the top and once on the bottom with a fork. Place the potatoes in a circle on a paper towel in the microwave, leaving 1 inch between them. Microwave on HIGH for 10 to 13 minutes, or until tender. Let stand for 5 to 10 minutes.
2. Meanwhile, place the onion and pepper rings in a 1-quart microwave-safe casserole. Cover with waxed paper. Microwave on HIGH for 3 to 5 minutes, or until the vegetables are tender, stirring once.

Old-Fashioned Biscuits Made
Light (page 55) or
Oven-Baked Corn Muffins
(page 61).

Breakfast in a pie plate!

3. Cut the potatoes into ¼-inch slices, leaving the skins on, if desired.
4. Spread one-third of the cooked peppers and onions evenly over the bottom of a 10-inch microwave-safe pie plate.
5. Top with one-third of the potato slices, ham, and cheese slices. Sprinkle lightly with pepper.
6. Repeat the layers two more times. Top with tomato slices.
7. Cover with waxed paper. Microwave on MEDIUM for 8 to 12 minutes, or until the cheese is melted (see Note). Serve in wedges.

NOTE

The pie is cooked on MEDIUM power for even heating throughout. Covering the pie with waxed paper allows it to warm through without getting soggy, as it would with a plastic wrap cover or glass lid.

If you prefer a browned top, run the pie under a preheated broiler for a few minutes just before serving.

VARIATION

SOUTHWESTERN BREAKFAST POTATO PIE: Substitute mild green chili peppers for the green pepper and Monterey Jack cheese for Muenster. Serve with Salsa Cruda (page 317).

Brown Sugar–and–Bacon Tomatoes

MAKES: *4 servings*
COOKING TIME: *3 to 6 minutes*

No-fat variation

5.6 grams fat per serving

SERVING SUGGESTIONS:
Serve with Turkey Sausages
(page 180) and toasted
Old-Fashioned Biscuits Made
Light (page 55). Serve them

Salt and pepper
4 firm ripe tomatoes (about 3 inches in diameter), ½ inch cut from the stem ends
4 teaspoons butter
8 teaspoons brown sugar
2 pieces cooked bacon, crumbled (see Note)

1. Salt and pepper the tomatoes lightly. Top each tomato with 1 teaspoon butter and 2 teaspoons brown sugar. Place each tomato in a custard cup or ramekin, cut-side up.
2. Place the cups around the outer edge of a 10-inch microwave-safe plate (for easy removal), leaving a space between them.
3. Cover with waxed paper. Microwave on HIGH for 3 to 5 minutes, or until heated through. Sprinkle with bacon and serve.

NOTE

for brunch with scrambled eggs or grits. Cook and serve them in individual cups to collect all the juices.

VARIATION

One teaspoon of butter per person makes a difference in the flavor, though it can be omitted in the interest of health.

To cook the bacon, place it on a paper towel on a paper plate or microwave-safe plate. Cover with another piece of paper towel. Microwave on HIGH for 2 minutes. Break up the bacon and throw out the paper towel for dry, crisp, crumbled bacon.

NO-FAT BROWN SUGAR–AND–BACON TOMATOES: Eliminate the butter and bacon.

Home Fries

MAKES: *4 servings*
COOKING TIME: *16 minutes*

No cholesterol

3.4 grams fat per serving

SERVING SUGGESTIONS:
We usually serve home fries on Saturday or Sunday, alongside bowls of yogurt and fresh fruit. They are also great heaped next to eggs with slices of tomato.

If you prepare Brown Sugar–and–Bacon Tomatoes (page 29), you won't be sorry. When fresh tomatoes are not in season, Tomato Chutney (page 333) makes a tangy substitute.

When serving with Turkey Sausages (page 180), cook the sausage first in the same skillet and then transfer it to a plate to keep warm.

This microwave-conventional stove-top method calls for much less oil than would

4 medium potatoes, scrubbed but not peeled
1 tablespoon canola or olive oil
1 medium onion, coarsely chopped
¼ teaspoon paprika
Salt and pepper to taste

1. Pierce the potato skins once on the top and once on the bottom with a fork. Place them in a circle on a paper towel, leaving a 1-inch space between them. Microwave on HIGH for 10 to 12 minutes, or until tender, turning potatoes over once.
2. Cut potatoes into ½-inch cubes, leaving the skins on. Place 1 tablespoon oil in a 10-inch frying pan. On the top of the stove, heat the oil on medium-high until a drop of water spatters when added to the pan.
3. Meanwhile, place the onion in a small microwave-safe bowl. Cover with waxed paper and microwave on HIGH for 1 minute.
4. Add the potato and onion to the hot pan on the stove. Cook for 1 minute on one side; then flip the potatoes over, stir, and cook them for 1 minute more.
5. Turn the heat down to medium-low. (This allows the potatoes to brown slowly without adding extra oil.)
6. Sprinkle the potatoes with paprika, salt, and pepper. Cook about 2 minutes more on each side.

normally be added to home fries because the potatoes and onions are quickly cooked in the microwave and absorb less fat in the frying pan.

Whole-Wheat Breakfast Bread Pudding

MAKES: *4 to 6 servings*
COOKING TIME: *12 to 16 minutes*

6.7 grams fat per serving for 4; 4.5 grams fat per serving for 6

Kids help

SERVING SUGGESTIONS: Serve with sweetened yogurt, fresh berries, a fruit spread, or Pink Applesauce (page 239).

Making this pudding is fun and easy. Marcia's five-year-old daughter especially likes tossing the bread cubes in the warm milk and pushing them under with a wooden spoon.

1½ *cups milk*
¼ *cup honey*
2 *large eggs*
1 *teaspoon vanilla*
6 ½-*inch-thick slices whole-wheat bread, cut into 1-inch cubes*
½ *cup raisins*
½ *teaspoon ground cinnamon*

1. Pour the milk and honey into a 4-cup glass measure. Microwave on HIGH for 2 minutes, or until heated but not boiling.
2. Meanwhile, in a small mixing bowl, beat the eggs and vanilla together.
3. Slowly pour the egg mixture into the warm milk, stirring constantly. Microwave on MEDIUM for 2 minutes, stirring once.
4. Stir in the bread cubes and raisins. Let stand for 5 minutes, occasionally pushing the bread cubes down into the sauce.
5. Pour the bread mixture into a 1-quart glass or ceramic bowl. Sprinkle the top with cinnamon. Cover with waxed paper. Microwave on MEDIUM for 8 to 12 minutes, or until a knife inserted 1 inch from the center comes out clean, rotating the pudding one-quarter turn twice. Let stand directly on the counter for 10 minutes. Serve.

VARIATION PEANUT-BUTTER BREAKFAST BREAD PUDDING (5.5 grams fat per serving for 6 servings, using 2 tablespoons peanut butter): If your youngster likes peanut butter, spread one side of some or all the bread slices with peanut butter before cutting into cubes.

Apple Syrup for Pancakes and Waffles

MAKES: *1½ cups*
COOKING TIME: *3 to 5 minutes*

No fat

SERVING SUGGESTIONS:
Serve over pancakes, French toast, or waffles.

NOTE

This deceptively rich-tasting sauce is a nice alternative to maple syrup. Even if you use frozen waffles, it will give them a "home-cooked" touch and fill the kitchen with a heavenly aroma.

⅓ cup sugar
1 tablespoon cornstarch
¼ teaspoon ground cinnamon
⅛ teaspoon freshly grated nutmeg
⅛ teaspoon ground cloves
1 cup apple juice or cider
1 tablespoon fresh lemon juice
1 medium apple, peeled, cored, and coarsely chopped
¼ teaspoon vanilla

1. In a 4-cup glass measure, combine the sugar, cornstarch, cinnamon, nutmeg, and cloves.
2. Pour in the apple and lemon juices, whisking while pouring. Microwave on HIGH for 2 to 3 minutes, or until boiling; stir well.
3. Add the apple and vanilla. Microwave on HIGH for 1 to 2 minutes more.

Leftover sauce may be refrigerated in a covered jar for 2 weeks and heated on HIGH for 1 to 2 minutes before serving.

Warm Blueberry Sauce

MAKES: *2 cups*
COOKING TIME: *4 to 5 minutes*

No fat

SERVING SUGGESTIONS:
Serve over pancakes, French toast, waffles, or warm cooked cereal.

2 cups fresh or 1 package (12 ounces) frozen unsweetened blueberries or huckleberries
2 tablespoons orange-flavored liqueur or orange juice
1 tablespoon fresh lemon juice

Combine all the ingredients in a 4-cup glass measure. Microwave, uncovered, on HIGH for 4 to 5 minutes, or until just heated through, stirring once. (Frozen berries will take 7 to 9 minutes.)

Old-Fashioned Hot Cocoa

MAKES: *4 servings*
COOKING TIME: *3 to 5 minutes*

Low-cholesterol variation

6.6 grams fat per serving

2 tablespoons unsweetened cocoa powder
¼ cup sugar
3 cups whole milk
½ teaspoon vanilla
Whipped cream or marshmallows (optional)

1. Combine ¼ cup water, cocoa powder, and sugar in a 4-cup glass measure. Microwave on HIGH for 1 to 1½ minutes, until boiling. Stir well to make a smooth mixture.
2. Add the milk, stirring well to mix. Microwave on HIGH for 3 to 5 minutes, or until heated through, stirring once. *Do not boil.*
3. Stir in the vanilla. Beat with a whisk to make mixture foamy. Pour into individual cups and top with whipped cream or marshmallows, if desired.

SINGLE-SERVING COCOA: In a microwave-safe cup or mug, combine 1 heaping teaspoon unsweetened cocoa powder and 2 teaspoons sugar. Pour in 1 tablespoon milk and stir well until smooth. Add milk to fill. Stir well. Microwave on HIGH for 1½ minutes, or until hot but not boiling. Stir well, testing to see that the cocoa is not too hot to serve.

VARIATION   LOW-CHOLESTEROL OLD-FASHIONED HOT COCOA (2.3 grams fat per serving): Substitute 1% milk for regular.

Café au Lait

MAKES: *4 servings*
COOKING TIME: *2 to 3 minutes to heat the milk, plus the coffee brewing time*

Low-cholesterol variation

3.0 grams fat per serving

VARIATION

Marcia spent some of her student life in Paris. Before

1½ cups milk
1½ cups freshly brewed coffee
Sugar to taste

1. Pour the milk into a microwave-safe pitcher. Microwave on HIGH for 1 to 3 minutes, or until bubbles start to form around the edges of the pitcher.
2. Beat with a whisk to make the milk slightly foamy.
3. Pour the warm milk and coffee into cups in equal parts. Stir in sugar as desired.

LOW-CHOLESTEROL CAFÉ AU LAIT (0.9 gram fat per serving): Substitute 1% milk for regular.

classes began in the morning she always stopped at a corner café to read the paper and have a café au lait—not a cappuccino with lots of foam, but simply warm milk and coffee. It was such a simple pleasure, and it is one that can be easily produced at home.

Lemon-Honey Cream-Cheese Spread

MAKES: *About 1 cup*
COOKING TIME: *1 to 2 minutes*

2.3 grams fat per tablespoon

VARIATION

SERVING SUGGESTIONS:
Spread on toasted breads, bagels, and muffins

TO HEAT A BAGEL, MUFFIN, OR ROLL

1 package (8 ounces) cream cheese
3 tablespoons honey
1 teaspoon grated lemon rind
1 teaspoon vanilla

1. Unwrap the cream cheese and place in a medium microwave-safe bowl. Microwave on DEFROST for 1 to 2 minutes to soften.
2. Beat in the remaining ingredients. Spoon into a serving dish. Refrigerate until serving time.

ORANGE-HONEY CREAM-CHEESE SPREAD: Substitute grated orange rind for lemon rind and ½ teaspoon ground cinnamon for vanilla.

Wrap in a paper towel (to absorb the excess moisture). Microwave on HIGH for 15 to 20 seconds (longer will result in the "hockey puck" syndrome). If heated from a frozen state, wrap and heat for 35 to 45 seconds.

BREADS

We ARE passionate about the scent and flavor of freshly baked bread. The aroma is incomparable. It is enough to soothe the savage breast (husband's and children's included) and make all seem right with the world. Once we became hooked on our own bread, nothing else could quite take its place.

We hear protests of "With my busy schedule there's no time to bake yeast bread!"—but not to worry. By keeping rapid-rise yeast in the refrigerator and frozen bread dough in the freezer, you can employ our combination method of food processor, microwave, and conventional oven to produce excellent breads quickly. Be prepared for compliments when you serve the lightest walnut bread you've ever tasted, a grainy and wholesome wheat bread, and cinnamon rolls worth rolling out of bed for on your day off.

There are times when quick breads fit the bill, and those are the times when you might turn to light Blueberry Muffins, Jalapeño Corn Bread, or a malty Beer Bread that is unbelievably easy to make.

We also include breads that are fun for family or guests to make, such as Garlic Knots, Parmesan Bread Sticks, and Soft Pretzels. And finally, if you want to make a really good impression, try one of our easiest breads—the Pleated Cheese Bread.

BASIC INFORMATION FOR
BAKING OUR QUICK YEAST BREADS

We have given recipes for three types of bread. One is made with purchased frozen bread dough that is defrosted in the microwave and baked in the conventional oven. The second is made with quick-rise yeast that is accelerated even further in the microwave before being baked conventionally. The third relies on a double rise, the second of which accommodates anyone's schedule because it can be left in the refrigerator for 2 to 24 hours.

FLOUR All recipes call for unsifted flour. When we call for all-purpose flour, we suggest you use the unbleached variety because it has slightly higher protein content and it retains the vitamins leached out during chemical whitening. It also gives baked goods a creamier color.

YEAST We use dry yeast and prefer the rapid-rise variety, except for Refrigerated Shredded-Wheat Bread, in which regular yeast also works well. These finely ground granules are mixed first with dry ingredients so that the water added is between 120 and 130°F. Too much heat (140°F) will kill it while too little (below 80°F) will inhibit growth. Always check the expiration date on the package, too, to make sure the yeast is reliable.

HOT WATER We've suggested using a food sensor, which comes with some microwave ovens, to obtain exactly the right water temperature. If you don't have a food sensor, you can simply use hot tap water. (It should be too hot to leave your finger in it for more than a second.)

Defrosting, Raising, and Baking Purchased Frozen Bread Dough

MAKES: *1 loaf bread, 16 slices*
COOKING TIME: *Defrosting and rising time: 39 minutes; baking time: 30 to 35 minutes*

2 grams fat per slice

SERVING SUGGESTION:
Make a soup or stew in the microwave, while the bread is baking in the conventional oven.

Family and guests feel pampered when greeted by the aroma of freshly baked bread. But some days, mixing and kneading bread, even with our rapid method, takes too much time. On those days we turn to our freezer for purchased frozen bread dough. With our combination microwave–conventional oven technique we have delicious bread in less than an hour.

TESTING THE OVEN POWER

1 frozen bread loaf (1 pound)
2 tablespoons butter or margarine, plus extra to grease dish

1. Place 2 tablespoons butter in a 1-cup glass measure. Microwave on MEDIUM for 1 minute. (Butter will spatter if heated on HIGH power.) Brush the butter all over the loaf with pastry brush.
2. Place the dough in a microwave-safe loaf dish. Place the loaf dish in a 2-quart microwave-safe rectangular dish holding 2 cups boiling water. Cover both dishes loosely with waxed paper. Microwave on HIGH for 2 minutes.
3. Turn the dough over. Cover again and microwave on DEFROST for 8 minutes, turning the dough over every 2 minutes for even heating. (The bottom of the dough becomes warmer than the top.) Rotate the pan if you see that one end or side of the bread is becoming warmer than the other. Let sit, covered, for 10 minutes.
4. Remove the defrosted loaf of bread from the loaf dish and grease the loaf dish with margarine or other solid shortening. Place the thawed dough in the loaf dish, and place that dish in a 2-quart rectangular microwave dish holding 2 cups boiling water. Cover both dishes loosely with waxed paper.
5. Microwave on WARM (10 percent power) for 4 minutes. Let sit 15 minutes.
6. Repeat the two procedures in Step 5 two to three times more, or until the dough has doubled in bulk.
7. Meanwhile, preheat the conventional oven to 375°F.
8. Remove the loaf dish with risen dough from the water bath. Bake in the preheated oven for 30 to 40 minutes, or until golden brown.

It is critical that bread dough be raised on very low power. Even a slightly higher power will kill the yeast and keep it from rising. We call for WARM power, but since each oven manufacturer gauges its ovens differently, you should make sure that the lowest power setting on your oven is satisfactory for this delicate procedure. Follow these instructions:

- Place 2 tablespoons refrigerated butter in a custard cup.
- Microwave on WARM (lowest power setting on oven) for 4 minutes.
- If the butter has melted completely in 4 minutes, the power is too high and may kill the yeast. If butter has partially melted, but some chunks of butter still remain, the power will be perfect for raising bread dough.

Pleated Cheese Bread

MAKES: *1 large loaf, 16 slices*
COOKING TIME: *Defrosting and raising time: 39 minutes; baking time: 25 to 30 minutes*

Low-cholesterol variation

11.5 grams fat per slice

SERVING SUGGESTIONS:
Serve for brunch, as a first course, with a salad for lunch, or coupled with vegetable soup for dinner.

This filled cheese bread looks like a beautiful, string-drawn purse. For the holidays or any celebration, tie a ribbon around the top knot; then sit back and enjoy the raves.

2 tablespoons butter or margarine, plus extra to
  grease dishes
1 loaf frozen purchased bread dough (1 pound)
1 pound Muenster cheese, grated
2 eggs, lightly beaten
½ teaspoon dried dill
½ teaspoon dried thyme
¼ teaspoon freshly ground black pepper

1. Place the 2 tablespoons butter in a 1-cup glass measure. Microwave on MEDIUM for 1 minute. (Butter will spatter if heated on HIGH power.) Brush the butter all over the loaf with a pastry brush.
2. Place the dough in a microwave-safe loaf dish. Place the loaf dish in a 2-quart microwave-safe rectangular dish holding 2 cups boiling water. Cover both dishes loosely with waxed paper. Microwave on HIGH for 2 minutes.
3. Turn the dough over. Cover again. Microwave on DEFROST for 8 minutes, turning the dough over every 2 minutes for even heating. (The bottom of the dough becomes warmer than the top.) Rotate the dish of water if you see that one end or side of the bread is becoming warmer than the other. Let sit, covered, for 10 minutes.
4. Remove the defrosted loaf of bread from the loaf dish and grease the loaf dish with margarine or other solid shortening. Place the thawed dough in the loaf dish, and place that dish in a 2-quart rectangular microwave-safe dish holding 2 cups boiling water. Cover with waxed paper. Microwave on WARM (10 percent power) for 4 minutes. Let sit 15 minutes.
5. Meanwhile, in a medium bowl, combine the cheese, 1 egg, dill, thyme, and pepper.
6. Preheat the conventional oven to 375°F.

7. Grease a 9-inch pie plate well with solid shortening or margarine.

8. With a rolling pin and then with greased fingers, gently push and smooth the dough into a 16-inch circle, being careful not to tear the dough. Gently roll the dough up onto the rolling pin and slide the pie plate underneath. Unroll the dough, letting any excess hang over the sides of the plate.

9. Spoon the cheese filling onto the center of the dough, mounding the center slightly. Gather the dough up gently toward the center of the dish, pleating it as you go, in loose, even folds. When all the dough is pleated around the filling, twist it gently into a knot on top.

10. Brush the entire top surface of bread with 1 beaten egg mixed with 1 tablespoon water. Bake for 25 to 35 minutes, or until golden. Let cool in pan for 10 minutes; transfer to a serving board. Serve hot, cut into wedges.

VARIATIONS PLEATED CHEESE BREAD WITH A KICK: Eliminate the dill. Add 2 tablespoons chopped jalapeño peppers to the cheese mixture.

LOW-CHOLESTEROL PLEATED RICOTTA CHEESE BREAD (5 grams fat per slice): When raising the bread, brush it with 1 tablespoon olive or canola oil; grease the pie plate with oil as well. Eliminate the Muenster cheese filling and instead combine 1 container (15 ounces) reduced-fat ricotta cheese, ¼ cup grated Parmesan (optional), 2 lightly beaten egg whites, 2 tablespoons chopped fresh parsley, 1 teaspoon each grated lemon peel and oregano, ½ teaspoon salt (optional), and ¼ teaspoon ground black pepper in a medium bowl. Spoon onto the bread dough and fold up as directed.

Brush the bread with 1 beaten egg white combined with 1 tablespoon water. Sprinkle with 1 tablespoon poppy seeds and bake as directed.

Cinnamon Rolls

MAKES: 16
COOKING TIME: *Defrosting and raising time: 39 minutes; baking time: 25 to 30 minutes*

5.15 grams fat per roll

Kids help

SERVING SUGGESTIONS: Serve as an addition to a brunch or breakfast or as a snack with tea.

These fragrant rolls can be prepared and baked in just about 1 hour.

¼ cup (½ stick) butter or margarine, plus extra to grease dishes
1 loaf frozen purchased bread dough (1 pound)
¾ cup brown sugar
⅓ cup coarsely chopped pecans or walnuts
1 teaspoon ground cinnamon

1. Place 2 tablespoons of the butter in a 1-cup glass measure. Microwave on MEDIUM for 1 minute. (Butter will spatter if heated on HIGH power.) Brush the butter all over the loaf with a pastry brush.
2. Place the dough in a microwave-safe loaf dish. Place the loaf dish in a 2-quart microwave-safe rectangular dish holding 2 cups boiling water. Cover both dishes loosely with waxed paper. Microwave on HIGH for 2 minutes.
3. Turn the dough over. Cover again. Microwave on DEFROST for 8 minutes, turning the dough over every 2 minutes for even heating. (The bottom of the dough becomes warmer than the top.) Rotate the dish of water if you see that one end or side of the bread is becoming warmer than the other. Let sit, covered, for 10 minutes.
4. Remove the defrosted loaf of bread from the loaf dish. Rub the dish with margarine or other solid shortening. Place the thawed dough in the microwave-safe loaf dish, and place that dish in a 2-quart rectangular microwave-safe dish holding 2 cups boiling water. Cover with waxed paper.
5. Microwave on WARM (10 percent power) for 4 minutes. Let sit 15 minutes.
6. Meanwhile, in a bowl, combine brown sugar, nuts, and cinnamon.
7. Preheat the conventional oven to 375°F.
8. Grease an 8½- or 9-inch round baking dish well with margarine or solid shortening.
9. Place the remaining 2 tablespoons butter in a 1-cup glass measure and microwave on MEDIUM for 1 minute.
10. With a rolling pin, gently roll the dough into an 8 × 16-inch rectangle. Brush with melted butter. Sprinkle with brown-sugar mixture.
11. Roll dough up, jelly-roll fashion, from the 16-inch side. Pinch edges firmly to seal. Cut into sixteen equal slices.
12. Arrange slices, cut sides down, in prepared round pan.

13. Bake for 25 to 30 minutes, or until golden.
14. Let stand for 5 minutes. Invert onto a serving dish. Serve warm.

VARIATION CINNAMON-RAISIN ROLLS (3.3 grams fat per serving): Substitute raisins for chopped nuts.

Refrigerated Shredded-Wheat Bread

MAKES: 2 loaves, 16 slices each
COOKING TIME: 40 MINUTES

1.6 grams fat per slice

A friend of Marcia's, Sheree Peery, from Pittsburgh, said she had a whole-wheat bread recipe that we had to try. She claimed her bread was easy, could be made 2 to 24 hours in advance of baking, and best of all was delicious. She was right! Marcia fiddled with it to fit her own family's tastes, and so we have a couple of variations.

This is the only bread in this book that takes more than an hour from start to finish, but it is no more labor intensive than our other breads. The real advantage is that it can be mixed up the night before for baking the next day. The second rise is designed for the refrigerator (so don't let it overrise at room temperature), and it produces a nice high loaf.

2 regular shredded-wheat biscuits, broken up
⅓ cup molasses
1 tablespoon sugar
3 tablespoons butter or margarine, cut into pieces
1 tablespoon salt
3 cups all-purpose flour
3 cups whole-wheat flour, plus additional for kneading
1½ packages dry yeast (regular or fast-rise)

1. Pour 2½ cups water into a 4-cup glass measure. Heat the water to 130°F in the microwave using the food sensor that comes with the oven, inserting the sensor end into the water. (If you have no food sensor, use very hot tap water.)
2. Meanwhile, in a small bowl combine the shredded wheat, molasses, sugar, margarine, and salt. Add the hot water and stir to dissolve the salt and melt the margarine.
3. In a large bowl, combine 2½ cups of the white flour with the yeast. Pour the hot-water mixture on top and beat with a mixer for 2 minutes on medium speed, scraping the bowl occasionally.
4. Stir in remaining all-purpose and whole-wheat flour to make a stiff dough.
5. Turn dough out on a lightly floured counter and knead until smooth and elastic, about 8 to 10 minutes.
6. Cover dough with plastic wrap. Let rise for 20 minutes.
7. Divide the dough in half. Stretch each half into a 14 × 9-inch rectangle. Roll up the short side to form a loaf; repeat the process with the other half. Place the loaves in two greased 9 × 5 × 3-inch loaf pans. Brush the loaves with oil and cover with plastic wrap. Refrigerate for 2 to 24 hours.

8. When ready to bake, remove from the refrigerator and uncover the dough, letting it stand for 10 minutes. If it has not risen enough, let it sit for 1 hour or more in a warm place to double in size. Puncture any gas bubbles that may have formed on top of the bread with the point of a knife.

9. Preheat the conventional oven to 400°F. Bake for about 40 minutes (the bread will appear fairly dark on top). Remove from the oven and immediately tap the loaves out of the pans and let them cool on a wire rack. The bread will have a crispy crust; if you like it softer, brush the bread with a little butter or margarine while still warm.

VARIATIONS

SHEREE'S BREAKFAST BREAD: Add ⅓ cup sugar with the molasses. The bread will be slightly sweeter and will be particularly nice when toasted for breakfast.

MULTIGRAIN WHEAT BREAD: Add ½ cup rye or wheat flakes, or a combination, with the shredded wheat.

Fast-Rise Whole-Wheat Shredded-Wheat Bread

MAKES: *1 loaf, 16 slices*
COOKING TIME: *Rising time: 15 minutes; baking time: 15 to 18 minutes*

No cholesterol

2 grams fat per slice

Kids help

1¼ cups all-purpose flour
1¼ cups whole-wheat flour
2 shredded-wheat biscuits, broken up
2 packages rapid-rise yeast
2 tablespoons brown sugar
1½ teaspoons salt
2 tablespoons lightly flavored olive oil or canola oil, plus 1 teaspoon for greasing pan.

1. Place the flours, shredded wheat, yeast, sugar, and salt in the bowl of a food processor. Pulse on and off a few times to mix well.

2. Place 1 cup water in a 1-cup glass measure. Heat the water to 130°F in the microwave using the food sensor that comes with the oven, inserting the sensor end into the water. (If you have no food sensor, use very hot tap water.)

3. With the processor running, pour the water and oil

Cook a quick soup or stew in the microwave while the bread is baking in the conventional oven. This loaf makes particularly delicious sandwiches. Try it toasted and spread with honey for breakfast.

Most people who claim not to like whole-wheat bread love this.

This loaf can be made in about 45 minutes, leaving just enough time to whip up a quick soup or stew—a nutritious meal with little fuss!

into the bowl through the feed tube. Process until a soft dough forms and pulls away from the sides of the bowl. Add an additional 1 to 2 tablespoons warm water if necessary.

4. Scoop out the dough and knead it lightly, by placing it on a counter that has been sprinkled with *2 tablespoons* flour. Push the dough down, fold it over, and turn it about 20 times, until it is shiny and elastic.

5. Form a loaf about 2 inches high, 3½ inches wide, and 7½ inches long. Grease an 8½ × 4½-inch glass or ceramic bread dish with 1 teaspoon olive oil. Place the formed dough in the dish.

6. Place the loaf dish into a 2-quart rectangular glass dish holding 2 cups of boiling water. Cover both dishes with waxed paper. Microwave on WARM (10 percent power) for 3 minutes; let stand for 12 minutes, or until the dough rises above the top of the dish. (Note: If your oven doesn't have a WARM power setting, place the bowl in the hot water and cover it with a cookie sheet for 30 minutes. In this case, a metal loaf pan may be substituted.)

7. Meanwhile, preheat the conventional oven to 400°F.

8. Gently remove the bread dish from the water bath and bake in the center of the preheated oven for 15 to 18 minutes, or until the loaf sounds hollow when tapped on top. Turn the loaf out onto a rack and let it cool for at least 15 minutes before cutting.

Walnut Bread

MAKES: *1 loaf, 16 slices*
COOKING TIME: *Rising time: 15 minutes; baking time: 15 to 18 minutes*

5.3 grams fat per slice

SERVING SUGGESTIONS:
This versatile bread complements anything from a

2 cups all-purpose flour
¾ cup whole-wheat flour
2 packages fast-rising yeast
2 tablespoons brown sugar
1½ teaspoon salt
2 tablespoons Walnut-flavored Oil (page 304), plus 1 teaspoon to grease the dish
¾ cup coarsely chopped walnuts

1. Place the flours, yeast, sugar, and salt in the bowl of a food processor. Pulse on and off a few times to mix well.

summer salad to a soup or stew. We especially like it with cheese or sliced chicken for a tasty sandwich. Try thin slices spread with jam or honey—perfect with afternoon tea.

You'll love the wonderful flavor of this bread, and a loaf makes a great hostess gift.

2. Place 1 cup water in a 1-cup glass measure. Heat the water to 130°F in the microwave oven using the food sensor that comes with the oven, inserting the sensor end into the water. (If you have no food sensor, use very hot tap water.)

3. With the processor running, pour the water and oil into the bowl through the feed tube. Process until a soft dough forms and pulls away from the sides of the bowl. Add 1 to 2 tablespoons warm water if necessary.

4. Scoop out the dough and sprinkle it with the nuts. Knead it lightly, by placing it on a counter that has been sprinkled with *2 tablespoons* flour. Push the dough down, fold it over and turn it about 20 times, until the nuts are incorporated and the dough is shiny and elastic.

5. Form a loaf that is about 2 inches high, 3½ inches wide, and 7½ inches long. Grease an 8½ × 4½-inch glass or ceramic bread dish with 1 teaspoon walnut oil. Place the formed dough in the dish.

6. Place the loaf dish in a 2-quart rectangular glass dish holding 2 cups boiling water. Cover both dishes with waxed paper. Microwave on WARM (10 percent power) for 3 minutes; let stand for 12 minutes, or until the dough rises above the top of the dish. (Note: If your oven doesn't have a WARM power setting, place the bowl in the hot water and cover it with a cookie sheet for 30 minutes; in this case, a metal loaf pan may be substituted.)

7. Meanwhile, preheat the conventional oven to 400°F.

8. Gently remove the bread dish from the water bath and bake in the center of the oven for 15 to 18 minutes, or until the loaf sounds hollow when tapped on top. Turn the loaf out onto a rack and let it cool for at least 15 minutes before cutting.

Oatmeal Bread

MAKES: *1 loaf, 16 slices*
COOKING TIME: *Rising time: 15 minutes; baking time: 15 to 18 minutes*

No cholesterol

1 cup rolled oats, plus 1 tablespoon for sprinkling on top
2 cups all-purpose flour
½ cup whole-wheat flour
2 packages rapid-rise yeast
2 tablespoons brown sugar
1½ teaspoons salt
2 tablespoons light olive or canola oil, plus 1 teaspoon to grease dish

Kids help

1. Place 1 cup rolled oats, the flours, yeast, sugar, and salt in the bowl of a food processor. Pulse on and off a few times to mix well.

2. Place 1 cup water in a 1-cup glass measure. Heat the water to 130°F in the microwave own, using the food sensor that comes with the oven, inserting the sensor end into the water. (If you have no food sensor, use very hot tap water).

3. With the processor running, pour the water and 2 tablespoons of oil into the bowl through the feed tube. Process until a soft dough forms and pulls away from the sides of the bowl. Add an additional 1 to 2 tablespoons warm water if necessary.

4. Scoop out the dough and knead it lightly, by placing it on a counter that has been sprinkled with 2 *tablespoons* flour. Push the dough down, fold it over, and turn it about 20 times, until it is shiny and elastic.

5. Form a loaf that is about 2 inches high, 3½ inches wide, and 7½ inches long. Grease an 8½ × 4½-inch glass or ceramic bread dish with 1 teaspoon olive oil. Place the formed dough into the dish. Sprinkle the remaining 1 tablespoon of oat flakes on top of the loaf.

6. Place the loaf dish and bread in a 2-quart rectangular glass dish holding 2 cups of boiling water. Cover both dishes with waxed paper. Microwave on WARM (10 percent power) for 3 minutes; let stand for 12 minutes, or until the dough has risen above the top of the dish. (Note: If your oven doesn't have a WARM power setting, place the bowl in the hot water and cover it with a cookie sheet for 30 minutes. In this case, a metal loaf pan may be substituted.)

7. Preheat the conventional oven to 450° F.

8. Gently remove the bread dish from the water bath and bake in the center of the oven for 15 to 18 minutes, or until the loaf sounds hollow when tapped on top. Turn the loaf out onto a rack and let it cool for at least 15 minutes before cutting.

Pizza

MAKES: *8 servings*
COOKING TIME: *Rising time: 12 minutes; baking time: 10 to 14 minutes*

Low-cholesterol variations

10.4 grams fat per serving

Kids help

We feel that this pizza combines the best characteristics of thin, crisp crust and juicy topping. We find that the rectangular shape is easier to deal with than the traditional round shape.

A black cookie sheet makes a crispier crust, but use what you have until you get around to purchasing a new one. We have given a black pan, along with this recipe, to several families as a gift—they love it!

2 cups all-purpose flour
1 package fast-rising yeast
½ teaspoon baking powder
½ teaspoon sugar
½ teaspoon salt
2 tablespoons olive oil
1 tablespoon cornmeal
1½ cups Tomato Pizza Sauce (recipe follows) or store-bought pizza sauce
8 ounces shredded part-skim mozzarella cheese

1. Place the flour, yeast, baking powder, sugar, and salt in the bowl of a food processor. Pulse on and off a few times to mix well.
2. Pour ¾ cup warm water into a 1-cup glass measure. Heat the water to 130° F in the microwave oven using the food sensor that comes with the oven, inserting the sensor end into the water. (If you have no food sensor, heat the water on HIGH for 1 to 1½ minutes, or use very hot tap water.)
3. With the processor running, pour the water and oil into the bowl through the feed tube. Process until a soft dough forms. Add an additional 1 to 2 tablespoons warm water if necessary.
4. Scoop out the dough and knead it lightly, by placing it on a counter that has been sprinkled with 2 *tablespoons* flour. Push the dough down, fold it over, and turn it about 20 times, until it is shiny and elastic.
5. Place the dough in a 1-quart microwave-safe bowl that has been greased with 1 teaspoon oil. Turn the dough to coat with the oil. Cover the bowl with a piece of waxed paper and set it in a 3-quart microwave-safe bowl holding 2 cups hot tap water. Microwave on WARM (10 percent power) for 2 minutes.
6. Let stand, covered, for 10 minutes, or until almost doubled. (Note: If your oven doesn't have a WARM power setting, place the bowl in the hot water and cover it with a cookie sheet for 30 minutes.)
7. Meanwhile, preheat the conventional oven to 500° F and position the oven rack on the bottom.
8. Prepare a 10½ × 15½ × 1-inch black cookie sheet or a round black pizza pan by greasing the bottom with 1 tablespoon olive oil and sprinkling it evenly with 1 tablespoon cornmeal.
9. With oiled hands, lightly and evenly push the

dough into the pan, making a ½-inch rim for a crust.
10. Spread the dough evenly with the tomato sauce. Sprinkle cheese on top.
11. Bake on the bottom shelf of the preheated oven for 10 to 14 minutes, until browned and crisped. Let stand 5 minutes. Cut with pizza wheel or kitchen shears, picking the pizza up slightly to prevent scratching the pan.

VARIATIONS   JALAPEÑO PIZZA (10.4 grams fat per serving): Thinly slice 4 jalapeño peppers and spread evenly over the tomato sauce and cheese (our favorite).

ITALIAN TURKEY SAUSAGE PIZZA (13.9 grams fat per serving): Cut ½ pound Italian turkey sausages (page 180) into ¼-inch pieces and cook in a skillet over medium heat on top of the conventional stove. Spread evenly over the tomato sauce and cheese.

MUSHROOM PIZZA (10.4 grams fat per serving): Thinly slice ¼ pound mushrooms and spread them evenly over the tomato sauce and cheese.

NO-CHOLESTEROL PIZZA (4.3 grams fat per serving): Eliminate the cheese.

SESAME-CRUST PIZZA (10.9 grams fat per serving): After assembling the pizza, sprinkle the edge of the crust with 1 tablespoon sesame seeds.

LOW-CHOLESTEROL VEGETABLE PIZZA (4.3 grams fat per serving): Top the pizza with the sauce. Eliminate the mozzarella cheese. Arrange 2 cups thinly sliced (⅛ inch thick) zucchini, thinly sliced mushrooms, thinly sliced red and green peppers, or a combination of all three on top. Brush lightly with olive oil and sprinkle with ¼ cup grated Parmesan.

Tomato Pizza Sauce

MAKES: *4 cups*
COOKING TIME: *5½ minutes*

No cholesterol

0.9 gram fat per ¼ cup

1 garlic clove, minced
1 tablespoon olive oil
1 can (28 ounces) crushed tomatoes
1 teaspoon dried basil leaves
¼ teaspoon freshly ground black pepper

1. Combine the garlic and oil in a 1-quart microwave-safe casserole. Microwave on HIGH for 30 seconds.
2. Stir in the remaining ingredients. Cover tightly with a lid or with plastic wrap turned back slightly. Microwave on HIGH for 5 minutes; stir well.

NOTE Only 1½ cups of the sauce are needed for the pizza. Freeze the remainder for another pizza, for a dipping sauce for Bread Sticks (page 54) or Calzones (page 255), or as a sauce for Vegetarian Quinoa Stuffed Peppers (page 122).

To defrost the frozen sauce, heat in a microwave storage container on HIGH for 5 minutes, stirring once or twice to break it up.

Individual Pizzas

MAKES: *4 servings*
COOKING TIME: *Rising time: 12 minutes; baking time: 10 to 12 minutes*

Low cholesterol

14.3 grams fat per serving

Kids help

Kids love to form and top their own pizzas. For variations, see those that follow the larger pizza recipe (page 46).

2 cups all-purpose flour
1 package fast-rising yeast
½ teaspoon baking powder
½ teaspoon sugar
½ teaspoon salt
2 tablespoons olive oil
1 tablespoon cornmeal
1 cup Tomato Pizza Sauce (page 48), or 1 can (8 ounces) purchased pizza sauce
4 ounces part-skim shredded mozzarella cheese

1. Place the flour, yeast, baking powder, sugar, and salt in the bowl of a food processor. Pulse on and off a few times to mix well.
2. Pour ¾ cup warm water into a 1-cup glass measure. Heat the water to 130° F in the microwave using the food sensor that comes with the oven, inserting the sensor end into the water. (If you have no food sensor, use very hot tap water.)
3. With the processor running, pour the water and oil into the bowl through the feed tube. Process until a soft dough forms. Add 1 to 2 tablespoons additional warm water if necessary.

4. Scoop out the dough and knead it lightly, by placing it on a counter that has been sprinkled with 2 *tablespoons* flour. Push the dough down, fold it over, and turn it about 20 times, until it is shiny and elastic. Form it into a ball.

5. Place the dough in a 1-quart microwave-safe bowl that has been greased with 1 teaspoon oil. Turn the dough to coat with the oil. Cover the bowl with a piece of waxed paper and set it in a 3-quart microwave-safe bowl holding 2 cups of hot tap water. Microwave on WARM (10 percent power) for 2 minutes.

6. Let stand, covered, for 10 minutes, or until almost doubled.

7. Meanwhile, preheat the conventional oven to 500° F and position the oven rack on the bottom.

8. Prepare two rectangular cookie sheets or one large round pizza pan (if using one cookie sheet you will only be able to cook two pizzas at a time) by greasing the bottom with 1 tablespoon olive oil and sprinkling it evenly with 1 tablespoon cornmeal.

9. Divide the pizza dough into four balls. Roll or stretch each ball into a 7-inch circle.

10. Place the dough on the pan; top each circle with ¼ cup pizza sauce and 1 ounce shredded cheese. Add toppings of choice, if desired.

11. Bake for 10 to 12 minutes, or until the crust is brown and the cheese is melted.

NOTE   If your oven doesn't have a WARM power setting, place the bowl in the hot water and cover it with a cookie sheet for 30 minutes.

Fast-Rising Focaccia (the fastest bread in town)

2 cups all-purpose flour
1 package fast-rising yeast
¼ teaspoon sugar
1 teaspoon salt
3 tablespoons olive oil
1 tablespoon cornmeal
½ teaspoon coarse salt
⅛ teaspoon freshly ground black pepper

1. Place flour, yeast, sugar, and salt in bowl of food processor. Pulse on and off a few times to mix well.

MAKES: *1 round loaf, 8 slices*
COOKING TIME: *Rising time:*
12 minutes
Baking time: 10 to 15 minutes

No cholesterol

5.7 grams fat per slice

SERVING SUGGESTIONS:
Serve focaccia with dinner or
with drinks, but most
important, serve it straight
from the oven!

This ancient Italian bread has
just recently gained popularity
in our country. Thelma's great
aunt in Germany used to
make a similar bread, which
she baked in her farmhouse
kitchen hearth. Though
delicious, it was a labor of
love, and I am sure she would
be shocked if she knew how
fast our version was.

Hers was called dinna,
which means "thin one." The
farmhands ate it with lunch,
spread with sour cream. We
give you some ideas for
toppings and invite you to be
creative.

2. Pour ¾ cup water into a 1-cup glass measure. Heat the water to 130° F in the microwave using the food sensor that comes with the oven, inserting the sensor end into the water. (If your oven has no food sensor, use very hot tap water.)
3. With the processor running, pour the water and oil into the bowl through the feed tube. Process until a soft dough forms. Scoop out the dough and knead it lightly by placing it on a counter that has been lightly sprinkled with 2 *tablespoons* flour. Push the dough down, fold it over, and turn it about 20 times, until it is shiny and elastic. Form the dough into a ball.
4. Place the dough in a 1-quart microwave-safe bowl that has been greased with 1 teaspoon oil. Turn the dough to coat with oil. Cover the bowl with a piece of waxed paper and set it in a 3-quart microwave-safe bowl holding 2 cups hot tap water. Microwave on WARM (10 percent power) for 2 minutes.
5. Let stand, covered, for 10 minutes, or until almost doubled. (Note: If your oven doesn't have a WARM power setting, place the bowl in the hot water and cover it with a cookie sheet for 30 minutes.)
6. Meanwhile, preheat the conventional oven to 500° F and position the oven rack on the bottom. Brush a 9-inch circular area on a round or black cookie sheet with 1 tablespoon olive oil and sprinkle with cornmeal.
7. Pat the dough into an 8- or 9-inch round and brush it with 1 tablespoon olive oil. Sprinkle with salt and pepper. Bake for 10 to 15 minutes, or until browned. Slice in wedges and serve immediately.

VARIATIONS   PESTO FOCACCIA (7.9 grams fat per slice): As soon as the focaccia comes out of the oven, spread the top with ¼ cup Pesto (page 335). Garnish with fresh basil leaves.

OLIVADA FOCACCIA (7 grams fat per slice): As soon as the foccacia comes out of the oven, spread the top with ¼ cup Olivada (page 314).

CHILI-PEPPER FOCACCIA (9 grams fat per slice): Right before baking, drizzle the top of the dough with 2 tablespoons hot-pepper oil and sprinkle on some hot-pepper flakes. For hot-food lovers!

ROSEMARY FOCACCIA (5.7 grams fat per slice): After the dough has risen, knead in 1 tablespoon chopped fresh rosemary before placing dough in the pan. Sprinkle with 1 tablespoon coarse salt before baking.

PRUNE FOCACCIA (5.7 grams fat per slice): Knead in ½ cup chopped prunes before the first rising. Sprinkle with 1 tablespoon kosher salt right before baking. Goes well with cocktails when sliced into thin strips.

Soft Pretzels

MAKES: *12 pretzels*
COOKING TIME: *Rising time: 12 minutes; baking time: 15 to 20 minutes*

No cholesterol

2.3 grams fat per pretzel

Kids help

SERVING SUGGESTIONS: Serve with mustard as a snack or as an addition to any meal.

When a recipe brings back memories it's an added bonus; this one certainly stirs up a lot of nostalgia! Marcia remembers being introduced to soft pretzels topped with mustard almost two decades ago in Philadelphia, where they are sold by street vendors all over the city. It seemed appropriate, then, that she should give her nieces, who live just outside of Philadelphia, this recipe, along with some measuring equipment and salt, for Christmas presents.

2½ cups all-purpose flour
1 envelope fast-rising yeast
1 tablespoon plus 2 teaspoons olive oil
2 tablespoons baking soda
2 teaspoons coarse salt

1. Place the flour and yeast in the bowl of a food processor. Pulse on and off a few times to mix well.
2. Pour ¾ cup water into a 1-cup glass measure. Heat the water to 130° F in the microwave oven using the food sensor that comes with the oven, inserting the sensor end into the water. (If you have no food sensor, use very hot tap water.)
3. With the processor running, pour the water and oil into the bowl through the feed tube. Process until a soft dough forms. Add an additional 1 to 2 tablespoons warm water if necessary. Form into a ball.
4. Scoop out the dough and knead it lightly, by placing it on a counter that has been sprinkled with 2 *tablespoons* flour. Push the dough down, fold it over, and turn it about 20 times, until it is shiny and elastic.
5. Place the dough in a 1-quart microwave-safe bowl that has been greased with 1 teaspoon oil. Turn the dough to coat with oil. Cover the bowl with a piece of waxed paper and set it in a 3-quart microwave-safe bowl holding 2 cups hot tap water. Microwave on WARM (10 percent power) for 2 minutes.
6. Let stand, covered, for 10 minutes, or until almost doubled. (Note: If your oven doesn't have a WARM power setting, place the bowl in the hot water and cover it with a cookie sheet for 30 minutes.)
7. Meanwhile, preheat the conventional oven to 400° F. Coat a cookie sheet with 1 teaspoon oil. Combine

For Thelma, pretzels were something she looked forward to when she visited her uncle and aunt in New Jersey. Her uncle would head out early on Saturday morning to buy authentic soft pretzels from a German bakery that made them only on that day; if he didn't get there before 8 A.M., there would be none left. They were wonderful with sweet butter and scrambled eggs for breakfast.

Later in the day they were eaten with lentil soup and cold cuts; the next day Thelma's aunt would sprinkle a little water on them and heat them in a toaster oven for another go-round. The German bakery no longer exists, but these pretzels go a long way toward bringing back those wonderful memories.

½ cup cold water with the baking soda; set aside.
8. Stretch the dough into a rectangle 12 inches long and 4 to 6 inches wide. With kitchen shears, cut the dough, crosswise, into 1-inch strips. Roll and stretch each piece into a 14-inch rope and twist it into a pretzel.
9. Stir the baking-soda solution again, just before dipping each pretzel. After dipping the pretzels, place them 1 inch apart on the oiled baking sheet. Sprinkle with coarse salt.
10. Bake in the preheated oven for 15 to 20 minutes, or until browned. Remove to cooling racks and cool for about 10 minutes.

Garlic Knots

MAKES: 12
COOKING TIME: *Rising time: 12 minutes*
Baking time: 10 to 15 minutes

No cholesterol

7.5 grams fat per garlic knot

Kids help

SERVING SUGGESTIONS:
Good with pasta or soup.

Although garlic knots aren't available in all parts of the country, they are quite

2 cups all-purpose flour
1 envelope fast-rising yeast
1 teaspoon salt
2 tablespoons plus 1 teaspoon olive oil

GARLIC OIL

1 large garlic clove
¼ cup olive oil

Pinch salt
Pinch garlic powder

1. Place the flour, yeast, and salt in the bowl of a food processor. Pulse on and off a few times to mix well.
2. Pour ¾ cup warm water into a 1-cup glass measure. Heat the water to 130° F in the microwave oven using the food sensor that comes with the oven, inserting the sensor end into the water. (If you have no food sensor, microwave water, or use very hot tap water.)

*common in many
northeastern Italian
restaurants and bakeries. Now
they can become common in
your kitchen, and if your kids
are like ours, they will love
them! They serve a dual
purpose: making them will
entertain the hungry clan and
leave you free to get the rest
of the dinner ready.*

3. With the processor running, pour the water and oil into the bowl through the feed tube. Process it until a soft dough forms. Add an additional 1 to 2 tablespoons warm water if necessary.

4. Scoop out the dough and knead it lightly, by placing it on a counter that has been sprinkled with 2 *tablespoons* flour. Push the dough down, fold it over, and turn it about 20 times, until it is shiny and elastic. Form into a ball.

5. Place the dough in a 1-quart microwave-safe bowl that has been greased with 1 teaspoon oil. Turn the dough to coat with the oil. Cover the bowl with a piece of waxed paper and set it in a 3-quart microwave-safe bowl holding 2 cups hot tap water. Microwave on WARM (10 percent power) for 2 minutes.

6. Let stand, covered, for 10 minutes, or until almost doubled. (Note: If your microwave oven doesn't have a WARM power setting, place the bowl in the hot water and cover it with a cookie sheet for 30 minutes.)

7. Meanwhile, preheat the conventional oven to 400° F and grease a baking sheet with 1 tablespoon oil.

8. Pat the dough into a 4 × 12-inch rectangle. With kitchen shears, cut the dough, crosswise, into 1-inch strips. Twist and cut each strip into a 10- to 12-inch piece. Form strips into loose knots.

9. Place the knots about 1 inch apart on the prepared cookie sheet. Bake for 10 to 15 minutes, or until lightly browned on top.

10. Meanwhile, make the garlic oil: In a food processor with the motor running, drop in garlic to mince finely. Pour the oil through the feed tube and process until creamy, stopping once or twice to scrape the sides of the bowl down with a spatula.

11. When the knots come out of the oven, remove them from the baking sheet and put them into a 1-quart bowl. Pour garlic oil over them and toss well. Sprinkle lightly with the salt and garlic powder.

VARIATION GARLIC-PARMESAN KNOTS (7.8 grams fat per knot): After baking knots and tossing them in garlic oil, sprinkle them lightly with 2 tablespoons Parmesan in addition to the salt and garlic powder.

Bread Sticks

MAKES: 12 bread sticks
COOKING TIME: Rising time:
12 minutes; baking time: 10
to 12 minutes

No cholesterol

1.5 grams fat per stick

Kids help

SERVING SUGGESTIONS:
Serve alongside pasta or dip
into Tomato Pizza Sauce (page
48) as a snack. They are
delicious with soups or stews,
in place of bread. Try them
with honey for breakfast or a
nutritious snack.

*With the help of a food
processor and microwave
oven, you can have these
bread sticks fresh on the table
in under an hour.*

2 cups all-purpose flour
1 envelope fast-rising yeast
1 teaspoon salt
1 tablespoon plus 2 teaspoons olive or canola oil
1 tablespoon cornmeal
2 tablespoons cold water
Toppings: 1 tablespoon caraway, poppy, or sesame
   seeds, or 2 teaspoons coarse salt, or 1 teaspoon
   coarsely ground black pepper

1. Place the flour, yeast, and salt in the bowl of a food processor. Pulse on and off a few times to mix well.
2. Pour ¾ cup water into a 1-cup glass measure. Heat the water to 130° F in the microwave oven using the food sensor that comes with the oven, inserting the sensor end into the water. (If you have no food sensor, use very hot tap water.)
3. With the processor running, pour the water and oil into the bowl through the feed tube. Process until a soft dough forms.
4. Scoop out the dough and knead it lightly, by placing it on a counter that has been sprinkled with 2 tablespoons flour. Push the dough down, fold it over, and turn it about 20 times, until the dough is shiny and elastic. Form into a ball.
5. Place the dough in a 1-quart microwave-safe bowl that has been greased with 1 teaspoon oil. Turn the dough to coat with oil. Cover the bowl with a piece of waxed paper and set it in a 3-quart microwave-safe bowl holding 2 cups hot tap water in it. Microwave on WARM (10 percent power) for 2 minutes.
6. Let stand, covered, for 10 minutes. (If your oven doesn't have a WARM setting, place the bowl in the hot water and cover with a cookie sheet for 30 minutes.)
7. Meanwhile, preheat the conventional oven to 450° F. Coat a cookie sheet with the remaining 1 teaspoon oil and sprinkle evenly with cornmeal.
8. Pat the dough into an 8 × 12-inch rectangle. With kitchen shears, cut the dough, crosswise, into 1-inch strips. Place on the prepared cookie sheet.
9. Brush each strip lightly with cold water and sprinkle with the topping of your choice. Bake in the preheated oven for 10 to 12 minutes, or until golden. Remove to a rack and let cool for at least 10 minutes before serving.

NOTE These may be made up to 3 days in advance and stored, tightly wrapped in plastic or foil. Crisp them in the toaster oven or conventional oven for 5 minutes at 400° F.

VARIATIONS PARMESAN BREAD STICKS (1.7 grams fat per stick): Add 2 tablespoons grated Parmesan with the flour.

SALT-AND-PEPPER BREAD STICKS (1.5 grams fat per stick): Sprinkle half of each stick with coarse salt, the other half with pepper.

GERMAN SALT-AND-CARAWAY STICKS (1.5 grams fat per stick): Sprinkle with coarse salt and caraway seeds.

Old-Fashioned Biscuits Made Light

MAKES: *12 biscuits*
COOKING TIME: *10 to 15 minutes*

Low cholesterol

5 grams fat per biscuit

Kids help

SERVING SUGGESTIONS: Great for breakfast or dinner. They make an excellent breakfast sandwich when paired with Turkey Sausages (page 180).

When our husbands developed cholesterol problems, we "lightened up" a traditional

2 cups all-purpose flour
2 teaspoons baking powder
1 teaspoon baking soda
½ teaspoon salt
¼ cup canola oil or light olive oil or vegetable oil
¾ cup buttermilk (see Note)

1. Preheat the conventional oven to 425° F.
2. Lightly oil a baking sheet, or use a Teflon sheet.
3. Place the flour, baking powder, baking soda, and salt in the bowl of a food processor and pulse twice to mix. Combine the oil and buttermilk. With the motor running, pour the liquid in all at once. Process until the dough forms a ball.
4. Pat or roll on a lightly floured surface to a ½-inch thickness. Cut with a 2- to 2½-inch round cookie cutter. Bake in the preheated oven for 10 to 15 minutes, or until golden and raised about 1½ inches.

NOTE If you don't happen to have any buttermilk on hand, combine 1 tablespoon lemon juice and ¾ cup skim milk; let stand 5 minutes.

biscuit with canola oil and found that the biscuits were more tender than the originals made with solid shortening!

These biscuits can be made very quickly using a food processor, and even mixing by hand takes very little time. For that reason, we usually don't start making them until the stew or soup is well on its way in the microwave oven. We find that our kids really like to pat, roll, and cut the dough.

Honey Bran Muffins

MAKES: *6 muffins*
COOKING TIME: *18 to 20 minutes (conventional oven); 30 seconds to 3 minutes (microwave oven)*

1 cup plus 2 tablespoons bran flakes
2 tablespoons vegetable oil
1 cup whole-wheat flour
2 tablespoons honey
1½ teaspoons baking powder
2 egg whites (see Note 1)
¼ cup raisins
¼ teaspoon ground nutmeg
½ teaspoon ground cinnamon

CONVENTIONAL OVEN

No cholesterol

5 grams fat per muffin

Kids help

1. Preheat the oven to 400° F.
2. Combine all the ingredients, except the 2 table-spoons bran flakes, in a large bowl. Stir until just mixed. *Do not overmix.*
3. Spoon into muffin tins lined with cupcake liners. Sprinkle the tops of the muffins with the remaining bran flakes. Bake for 18 to 20 minutes, or until a toothpick inserted in the center comes out clean.

MICROWAVE OVEN

SERVING SUGGESTIONS:
Serve for breakfast or with a hearty soup.

1. Combine all the ingredients, except the 2 table-spoons bran flakes, in a large bowl. Stir until just mixed. *Do not overmix.*
2. Place two cupcake liners in each of six 5- to 6-ounce custard cups or microwave-safe muffin tin cups. (Note: You can cook from one to six muffins at a time in the microwave.)
3. Spoon the batter into the cups, filling them only halfway. If using two or more custard cups, place them

This recipe can easily be doubled. You could even cook batches of six in your toaster oven.

We like them best hot from the conventional oven when they are to be served with a hearty soup. In the mornings, however, we often make one or two at a time in the microwave oven. The batter can be stored in the refrigerator in a tightly closed container for up to a week; stir before each usage.

at least 1 inch apart in the microwave. If using more than three, arrange them in a circle. Microwave as indicated below, or until muffins appear moist in places on the top but a toothpick inserted in the center comes out clean.

QUANTITY	POWER	TIME
1 muffin	HIGH	30 seconds
2 muffins	HIGH	1 minute
4 muffins	HIGH	1½ minutes; rearrange once (see Note 4)
6 muffins	HIGH	2½ to 3 minutes, rearrange once

NOTE 1   You may substitute 1 whole egg for the 2 egg whites, but you'll lose the low-cholesterol advantage.

NOTE 2   To reheat 1 frozen muffin, wrap in a paper towel and microwave on HIGH for 15 seconds.

NOTE 3   Overmixing of batter will toughen the dough and will produce a muffin that has a coarse grain and many tunnels.

NOTE 4   To rearrange, either switch the positions of the more-cooked and less-cooked muffins; or place muffin tins on a 10-inch round microwave-safe dish, and rotate one-quarter turn after 1 minute.

VARIATION   Substitute dried cranberries or dried cherries for raisins.

Blueberry Muffins

MAKES: 12 muffins
COOKING TIME: 20 to 25 minutes

No-cholesterol variation

¼ cup (½ stick) butter
2 cups cake flour or all-purpose flour
1 tablespoon baking powder
¼ cup sugar
½ teaspoon salt (optional)
1 cup milk
1 egg, beaten
1 teaspoon vanilla
1 cup fresh or frozen blueberries, broken up, mixed with 1 tablespoon flour

5.3 grams fat per muffin

Kids help

SERVING SUGGESTIONS:
Serve for breakfast, brunch,
and snacks or with salad or
soup meals.

*Depending on the texture
desired, you may use either
cake flour (for a lighter
muffin) or all-purpose flour
(for a regular muffin).*

VARIATIONS

*These muffins aren't made
in a microwave—we think the
lighter-colored batter turns
out looking better if baked in
a conventional oven.*

*If you prefer a sweeter
muffin, use ½ cup sugar and
eliminate the vanilla.*

1. Preheat the conventional oven to 400° F. Grease the
muffin tins or line them with muffin papers.
2. Place the butter in a 1-cup measure. Microwave on
MEDIUM for 1 to 2 minutes, until melted; set aside.
3. In a large bowl, combine the flour, baking powder,
sugar, and salt.
4. In a smaller bowl, combine the milk, egg, vanilla,
and melted butter. Gently fold the liquid mixture into
the dry mixture until just blended.
5. Fold the blueberries into the batter quickly and
gently. Spoon the batter into the prepared tins.
6. Bake for 15 to 20 minutes, or until muffins are
golden and a toothpick inserted comes out clean.

NO-CHOLESTEROL BLUEBERRY MUFFINS (4.9 grams fat
per muffin): Substitute ¼ cup canola or vegetable oil
for butter, skim milk for regular milk, and 2 beaten egg
whites for the egg. Use muffin papers instead of
greasing the pan.

LEMON-SCENTED BLUEBERRY MUFFINS: Add 1 teaspoon
grated lemon peel to batter.

Applesauce Muffins

MAKES: *12 muffins*
COOKING TIME: *8 minutes
microwave; 20 minutes
conventional*

3.7 grams fat per muffin

Kids help

1 cup applesauce or 2 baked apples, peeled, cored,
   and mashed (see Note)
⅓ cup cottage cheese
1 large egg
2 tablespoons canola or vegetable oil
¼ cup honey
1 cup whole-wheat flour
1 cup white flour
2 tablespoons toasted wheat germ
1 teapoon baking powder
2 teaspoons baking soda
½ teaspoon ground cinnamon
¾ cup raisins or currants

1. If baking conventionally, preheat the conventional
oven to 375° F.
2. In a large bowl, combine the applesauce, cottage
cheese, egg, oil, and honey.

A wholesome, not-too-sweet muffin that can be dressed up for breakfast with a fruit spread or served as a snack with peanut butter.

3. In a medium bowl, combine the flours, wheat germ, baking powder and soda, and cinnamon. Add the dry ingredients to the applesauce mixture, stirring just to moisten.

4. Stir in the raisins and divide the batter among 12 greased muffin cups.

5. Bake in the preheated oven for 20 minutes or until the muffins are golden and a toothpick inserted in the center comes out clean.

6. To microwave: Place 2 cupcake liners in each of six 5- or 6-ounce microwave-safe custard cups or muffin-tin cups. Fill the cups halfway with batter. Microwave on HIGH for 2½ to 4 minutes, or until the muffins appear moist in places on the top but a toothpick comes out clean when inserted in the center. Repeat the process as necessary.

NOTE Apples can be baked quickly in the microwave oven: Wash and slit the skins around the middle (to prevent bursting) and place in two custard cups or cereal bowls. Cover with waxed paper or plastic wrap and microwave on HIGH for 8 minutes, or until tender.

Maple-Nut Muffins

MAKES: *12 muffins*
COOKING TIME: *8 minutes microwave; 20 to 25 minutes conventional*

13 grams fat per muffin

Kids help

SERVING SUGGESTIONS:
Makes a great breakfast or dessert muffin for kids.

½ cup mashed ripe banana
½ cup chopped walnuts
½ cup yogurt or buttermilk
⅔ cup creamy peanut butter (natural preferred; see Note)
⅓ cup maple syrup
2 eggs
1 tablespoon walnut or vegetable oil
2 teaspoons vanilla
¾ cup whole-wheat flour
½ cup white flour
¼ cup toasted wheat germ
2 teaspoons baking powder
1 teaspoon ground cinnamon

1. If baking conventionally, preheat the oven to 375° F.
2. In a large bowl or food processor bowl, blend the banana, walnuts, yogurt, peanut butter, maple syrup, eggs, oil, and vanilla.
3. In medium bowl, combine remaining ingredients.
4. Combine the wet and dry ingredients and mix just

The flavor of the mashed
banana heightens that of the
maple syrup; it also adds a
good helping of potassium.

The slightly dark, dense
batter is good for microwave
baking.

enough to moisten the dry ingredients. Divide the
batter among 10 or 12 greased muffin cups.

5. Bake in the preheated oven for 20 to 25 minutes or
until the muffins are golden and a toothpick inserted in
the center comes out clean.

6. To microwave: Place 2 cupcake liners in each of six
5- or 6-ounce microwave-safe custard cups or a muffin-
tin cups. Fill the cups halfway with batter. Microwave
on HIGH for 2½ to 4 minutes, or until the muffins
appear moist in places on the top but a toothpick comes
out clean when inserted in the center. Repeat the
process as necessary.

NOTE If you buy your peanut butter in a glass jar and keep it
in the refrigerator, you can remove the lid and microwave one full jar on HIGH for 1 minute for easier
measuring.

Lemon-Scented Cranberry Bread

MAKES: 1 loaf, 16 slices
COOKING TIME: 45 minutes

No-cholesterol variation

5.6 grams fat per slice

SERVING SUGGESTIONS:
Serve a loaf with Turkey Soup
(page 104) and you've got a
great post-Thanksgiving
supper. When sliced thinly,
it's ideal for a turkey-salad
sandwich.

This is one of our favorite
combinations of flavors. We
serve this at Thanksgiving or
take it as a hostess gift.
We developed the
no-cholesterol version for our
husbands. After a comparative
taste test, most of our family

2 cups all-purpose flour
½ cup sugar
1 tablespoon baking powder
1½ to 2 teaspoons grated lemon rind
1 cup whole cranberries, fresh or frozen
½ cup coarsely chopped nuts (optional)
3 tablespoons butter
2 eggs, lightly beaten
⅔ cup milk

1. Preheat the conventional oven to 350° F.

2. Grease an 8½ × 4½ × 3-inch loaf pan.

3. Place the flour, sugar, baking powder, and lemon
rind in a large mixing bowl. Stir well to mix.

4. Add the cranberries and nuts to the flour and stir to
coat.

5. Place the butter in a 1-cup glass measure and
microwave on MEDIUM for 1 minute. (Melting on a
higher power may cause splattering.)

6. Add the butter, eggs, and milk all at once to the
flour mixture. Stir until just moistened, making sure
not to overmix.

7. Spread the batter evenly into the prepared pan.
Bake in the middle of the oven for 45 to 50 minutes, or
until a skewer inserted in the center of the loaf comes
out clean. Transfer the pan to a rack and let the bread

and friends voted both versions delicious, which means that from now on we'll probably serve the no-cholesterol version to all.

cool for 10 minutes. Remove from the pan and let it cool on the rack. Wrap and refrigerate for 1 to 2 days to improve the flavor, or freeze for up to 6 months.

VARIATION No-Cholesterol Lemon-Scented Cranberry Bread (2.5 grams fat per slice): Substitute skim milk for whole milk, 4 egg whites, beaten into soft peaks, for 2 whole eggs, and 3 tablespoons canola or light olive oil for butter. After beating the egg whites, fold in the milk and oil until well mixed but not overmixed. Add this mixture to the flour mixture in step 6.

Oven-Baked Corn Bread

MAKES *12 muffins or 12 squares or slices*
COOKING TIME: *20 to 25 minutes*

No-cholesterol variation

5.5 grams fat per serving

Kids help

SERVING SUGGESTIONS: Serve with Vegetarian Chili (page 111), with one of the clam chowders (pages 100–101), or with any fish meal.

¼ cup (½ stick) butter
1 cup cornmeal
1 cup all-purpose flour
¼ cup sugar
1 tablespoon baking powder
½ teaspoon salt (optional)
1 cup milk
1 egg, lightly beaten

1. Preheat the conventional oven to 400° F.
2. Grease an 8- or 9-inch square baking dish or muffin pan (or use muffin papers).
3. Place the butter in a 1-cup glass measure. Microwave on MEDIUM for 1 to 2 minutes, until melted.
4. In a large bowl, combine the cornmeal, flour, sugar, baking powder, and salt.
5. In a smaller bowl, combine the butter, milk, and egg. Stir into the dry ingredients until just moistened. Pour into the prepared pan or spoon into muffin cups.
6. Bake bread in the conventional oven for 20 to 25 minutes, or until it is golden and a toothpick inserted in the center comes out clean. Serve warm. Bake muffins for 15 to 20 minutes, or until they are golden and a toothpick inserted in the center comes out clean.

VARIATIONS

Don't be bashful about making the no-cholesterol version: our taste testers

No-Cholesterol Corn Muffins (5 grams fat per muffin): Line the muffin-tin cups with muffin papers instead of greasing them. Substitute canola oil for butter. Substitute skim milk for whole milk. Substitute 2 beaten egg whites for 1 whole egg.

voted it as delicious as the regular version, and it has become a staple in our house for kids, friends, and family alike.

JALAPEÑO CORN MUFFINS (5.5 grams fat per muffin): Add 1 tablespoon chopped jalapeño pepper to finished batter before baking.

BLUE CORNMEAL MUFFINS (5.5 grams fat per muffin): Substitute blue cornmeal for yellow.

REGULAR OR BLUE CORNMEAL AND BLUEBERRY MUFFINS (5.5 grams fat per muffin): Sprinkle 1 tablespoon flour over ¾ cup fresh or frozen blueberries in a bowl and toss together. Fold blueberries into the batter at the end until just mixed.

Microwave Corn Bread

MAKES: 16 2-inch-square pieces
COOKING TIME: 9 to 12 minutes

3.8 grams fat per serving

SERVING SUGGESTIONS: Serve with chili or clam chowder.

Make this in summer when you want to keep the kitchen cool. At other times of the year, we suggest that you make Oven-Baked Corn Bread

VARIATIONS

(page 61), leaving the microwave oven free to cook the main course.

1 cup all-purpose flour
1 cup cornmeal
¼ cup sugar
2 teaspoons baking powder
½ teaspoon salt
1 egg, beaten
¼ cup (½ stick) butter, melted
⅔ cup buttermilk

1. Combine all the ingredients in a large bowl, stirring until fairly smooth. Pour into an 8½-inch round microwave-safe cake dish and smooth the top of the batter.
2. Place the dish on top of an inverted microwave-safe cereal bowl. Microwave on MEDIUM for 8 minutes.
3. Microwave on HIGH for 1 to 4 minutes, or until a toothpick inserted in the center comes out clean, rotating one-quarter turn once or twice. (The top may appear damp but should not appear wet.) Let stand directly on the counter for 5 to 10 minutes before serving from the dish. Serve warm.

QUICK WHOLE-KERNEL CORN BREAD (3.8 grams fat per serving): Keep all ingredients the same, but add ½ cup cooked corn to the batter.

CRACKLIN' CORN BREAD (4 grams fat per serving): Keep all ingredients the same, but add 2 slices crisp bacon, broken into pieces, to the batter.

CALICO CORN BREAD (4 grams fat per serving): Add ¼ cup chopped green bell pepper and ½ cup chopped red bell pepper to the batter.

CAJUN CORN BREAD (4 grams fat per serving): Follow the Calico Corn Bread variation above but add 1 or 2 chopped jalapeño peppers to the batter. Nice and spicy!

Quick Beer Bread

MAKES: *1 loaf, 16 slices*
COOKING TIME: *45 minutes*

No cholesterol

2 grams fat per slice

3 cups self-rising flour
3 tablespoons sugar
12 ounces warm beer

1. Preheat the conventional oven to 375° F.
2. Grease a 9 × 5 × 3-inch loaf pan well.
3. Combine the flour and sugar in a large bowl and mix well. Add the beer and mix until all the flour is moistened.
4. Place the dough in the loaf pan and pat to make an even top.
5. Bake for 45 to 50 minutes, or until loaf is brown and a tester comes out clean. Remove from the pan and cool 5 to 10 minutes on a wire rack before slicing.

VARIATIONS

PARMESAN BEER BREAD (1.4 grams fat per slice): Add ¾ cup Parmesan to flour and sugar.

SEED BEER BREAD (1.3 grams fat per slice): Brush the top of the loaf with 1 tablespoon olive oil and sprinkle with 1 tablespoon poppy or sesame seeds before baking.

ONION BEER BREAD (1.1 grams fat per slice): Place 1 medium chopped onion and 1 tablespoon olive oil in a small microwave-safe dish. Microwave on HIGH for 2 minutes, or until tender but not brown. Add to the flour and sugar and stir to coat the onion well before adding the beer. (This will keep the onion from settling on the bottom of the loaf.)

ONION-CARAWAY BEER BREAD (1.1 grams fat per slice): Add 1 tablespoon caraway seeds, along with the onion, to Onion Beer Bread variation.

SERVING SUGGESTIONS: Wonderful with soups and stews on a brisk day. Put a soup or stew in the microwave oven and mix up your favorite variety of beer bread; pop it into the conventional oven. Sit back and relax for 40 minutes or so, and let the ''aroma therapy'' take over!!

There couldn't be an easier way to have homemade bread! This quick bread has a fine crumb and a moist texture. The beer adds a malty flavor and the sugar sweetens it slightly.

The bread may be supplemented with one of the many additions described here, and it is also delicious when toasted.

HERBED BEER BREAD: Add ¼ cup chopped fresh parsley, basil, chives, or dill, or a combination of two or more herbs, to the flour and sugar.

SHREDDED-WHEAT BEER BREAD (1.1 grams fat per slice): Substitute brown sugar for white sugar. Break 2 large shredded-wheat rectangles into the flour and sugar before adding the beer.

CHILI BEER BREAD (1.1. grams fat per slice): Stir 1 tablespoon chili powder, ½ teaspoon dried oregano leaves, and ½ teaspoon powdered cumin into the flour and sugar.

Soda Breads

When you have less than an hour to whip up a homemade bread, opt for one of these non-yeasted soda breads. You'll find that they are hearty breads with a firm crumb, particularly the brown variety, which makes them perfect alongside stews and wonderful for breakfast the next day. The ingredients change, but the procedure is the same for each recipe.

Basic Irish Soda Bread

MAKES: *1 loaf, 16 slices*
COOKING TIME: *35 to 40 minutes*

Low cholesterol

0.3 gram fat per slice

3 cups all-purpose flour
2 tablespoons sugar
1 teaspoon salt
1¼ teaspoons baking soda
Pinch cardamom
1 cup buttermilk
1 cup raisins or currants (optional)

1. Preheat the conventional oven to 375° F. Grease an 8½- or 9-inch round cake or pie pan.
2. Combine the dry ingredients in the bowl of a food processor. Pulse the processor on and off a few times to blend the ingredients. (Or blend in a large bowl with a spoon.)
3. Keeping the processor motor running, slowly pour the buttermilk into the mixture and process until a soft dough is formed. (Or pour the buttermilk into the dry ingredients in the bowl, stirring to make a soft dough.)
4. Remove the dough and work in the raisins, while kneading the dough six or seven times. Form the dough into a 6-inch round and place in the prepared pan. Cut

a large X about ½ inch deep on top of the loaf.

Bake for 35 to 40 minutes, or until the top is firm and lightly browned. Let stand for 3 to 4 minutes before removing the loaf from the pan. Let the loaf cool on a rack at least 5 minutes before serving.

Irish Brown Bread

MAKES: *1 loaf, 16 slices*
COOKING TIME: *35 to 40 minutes*

Low cholesterol

0.5 gram fat per slice

2 cups whole-wheat flour
1½ cups bran-flake cereal
2 tablespoons brown sugar
1 teaspoon salt
1 teaspoon baking soda
1 teaspoon baking powder
1 cup buttermilk
1 cup raisins or currants (optional)

1. Preheat the conventional oven to 375° F. Grease an 8½- or 9-inch round cake or pie pan.
2. Combine the dry ingredients in the bowl of a food processor. Pulse on and off a few times to blend the ingredients. (Or blend in a large bowl with a spoon.)
3. Keeping the processor motor running, slowly pour the buttermilk into the mixture and process until a soft dough is formed. (Or pour the buttermilk into the dry ingredients in the bowl, stirring to make a soft dough.)
4. Remove the dough and work in the raisins, while kneading the dough six or seven times. Form the dough into a 6-inch round and place in the prepared pan. Cut a large X about ½ inch deep on top of the loaf.
5. Bake for 35 to 40 minutes, or until the top is firm and lightly browned. Let stand for 3 to 4 minutes before removing the loaf from the pan. Let the loaf cool on a rack at least 5 minutes before serving.

Boston Brown Bread

MAKES: *2 loaves, 16 slices per loaf*

1 cup whole-wheat flour
½ cup cornmeal
½ teaspoon baking powder
½ teaspoon baking soda
½ cup molasses or honey
⅔ cup buttermilk
1 egg
½ cup raisins
¼ cup chopped walnuts (optional)

COOKING TIME: *6 to 8 minutes per loaf*

1.4 grams fat per slice

SERVING SUGGESTION:
Serve in the New England style with baked beans and codfish cakes for Friday night's dinner.

Thelma's mother used to buy brown bread in a can and heat it in a water bath for about half an hour. Made from scratch and cooked in a water bath, it took about 3 hours.
   We find that brown bread mixed from scratch and quickly steamed in a 2-cup measure in the microwave oven is more delicious and simpler than a canned loaf. It's excellent for dinner or breakfast—plain or spread with softened cream cheese.

1. Combine all the ingredients in a large bowl, stirring to mix well.
2. Cut two circles of waxed paper to fit the bottom inside of a 2-cup glass measure. Fit one of the circles into the measure. Spoon in half the batter; it will reach close to the 1⅓-cup mark. Cover with plastic wrap, vented on one side. Microwave on MEDIUM for 6 to 8 minutes, or until a toothpick inserted in the center comes out clean, rotating one-half turn halfway through cooking.
3. Let stand directly on counter for 5 to 10 minutes. With a knife, loosen the cooked loaf from the dish and turn out.
4. Repeat the same process with the second loaf.

Bruschetta

MAKES: *About 20 slices*
COOKING TIME: *2 minutes*

No cholesterol if made without cheese

8.3 grams fat per slice

SERVING SUGGESTION:
Serve with vegetable soups to round out the meal.

This bread from Tuscany and Umbria is traditionally heated over burning embers and served as a prelude to the meal. The most important

½ *cup olive oil*
3 *garlic cloves, minced*
8 *ounces low-fat mozzarella cheese, grated (optional)*
2 *tablespoons finely chopped fresh parsley*
1 *tablespoon fresh lemon juice*
¼ *teaspoon freshly ground black pepper*
1 *can (2 ounces) anchovies, drained and minced (optional)*
1 *loaf Italian bread, cut into ½-inch slices*

1. Preheat the broiler.
2. Combine the oil and garlic in a 1-cup glass measure. Microwave on HIGH for 1 minute. Set aside.
3. Combine the remaining ingredients, except the bread, in a bowl.
4. Place the bread on a cookie sheet and toast one side under the preheated broiler for about 30 seconds.
5. Brush both sides of the bread with garlic oil.
6. Place the toasted sides of the bread down on the

ingredient in bruschetta is the olive oil. Choose a virgin olive oil that is a deep-green-gold color for the fullest flavor.

cookie sheet and top each slice with 1 tablespoon of the cheese mixture.

7. Place under the broiler for about 30 seconds, or until the cheese is melted. *Watch closely to prevent burning.*

Cheese Croustades

MAKES: *8 croustades*
COOKING TIME: *3 minutes*

3.3 grams fat per croustade

SERVING SUGGESTIONS:
Serve with soups or salads.

8 ¼-inch slices semolina or other Italian bread (about 3½ x 2½ inches)
4 ounces cheese (such as Brie, feta, Montrachet, mozzarella, Muenster, or Havarti), cut into 8 ¼-inch slices (see Note)

1. Line a 2-quart rectangular microwave-safe dish with paper towels.
2. Arrange the bread slices around the outer edge of the dish, leaving the center open.
3. Microwave on HIGH for 2 minutes. If bread is not quite dry, microwave an additional 30 seconds, making sure not to burn.
4. Place one slice of cheese on each croustade.
5. Microwave on MEDIUM for 1 minute, or until the cheese is warmed and softened but not melted.

NOTE Choose low-fat mozzarella for a lower fat count (3 grams fat per croustade).

Warm Flour Tortillas

MAKES: *12 tortillas*
COOKING TIME: *6 to 8 minutes*

4.4 grams fat per tortilla

Kids help

SERVING SUGGESTIONS:
Use as wrappers for fajitas; serve with soups and stews in place of bread.

2 cups all-purpose flour
½ teaspoon salt
¼ cup solid vegetable shortening

1. Combine the flour and salt in the bowl of a food processor. Pulse on and off quickly to mix.
2. Add shortening. Pulse on and off five or six times, until the shortening is evenly mixed into the flour.
3. Pour ½ cup warm water into the feed tube and pulse on and off until the mixture just forms a ball.
4. Divide the dough into twelve balls by taking some of the dough in your hand, making a fist, and squeezing a ball out between your thumb and index finger.
5. Lightly grease your hands with shortening; roll each ball of dough between your hands to coat it lightly.
6. Place the balls on a counter or cookie sheet and

The whole family gets involved when we roll and cook these flat breads.

cover them with a clean tea towel. Let them rest for 15 to 30 minutes.

7. Lightly flour a board. With a rolling pin, roll each ball into a thin circle about 7 or 8 inches in diameter. Pull or gently stretch them if necessary.

8. Cook on a hot, ungreased 10-inch skillet, until brown speckles appear on the undersides. Air bubbles will form on top during frying; just press these down lightly with a metal spatula to flatten.

9. Flip the tortillas over and cook them on the other side for 30 seconds.

10. Place the cooked tortillas in a napkin-lined basket.

NOTE To store tortillas for more than 2 hours, place the cooked tortillas in a plastic bag in the refrigerator. Before heating, remove from the plastic bag and wrap six at a time in a lightly dampened paper towel. Microwave on HIGH for 1 minute.

HEATING PURCHASED FLOUR TORTILLAS Open a 10½-ounce bag of flour tortillas (2 grams fat per tortilla) and place the bag in the microwave. Heat on HIGH for 1 to 2 minutes. Serve in a napkin-lined basket.

SOUPS

Most of us grew up thinking soups could never stand alone and needed companionship—say a sandwich or four other dinner courses. We've now grown to love them as meals in themselves. That's the way we've designed the soups in this chapter; you'll have no reason to apologize for serving "just soup" for supper.

The fresh, true flavors of a homemade soup make it an appealing meal, especially when it has been cooked quickly in the microwave. (And shorter cooking times mean that fewer nutrients are lost.) The soups in this chapter deliciously meet the new nutritional standards: most of them have little meat or no meat at all.

We like to think of the following collection as an international potage because of the influences from Portugal, Germany, Japan, Italy, and various regions of the United States. These are recipes we make time and time again, because they satisfy at the table. Best of all, as the world becomes smaller, our choice of familiar soups grows larger.

Whenever you're in doubt about what to serve family or friends for dinner, think about a sturdy bowl of soup and a chunk of bread or bowl of rice. Chances are you'll be fixing just what they love most.

TO SERVE BREAD WITH A SOUP, STEW, OR OTHER MAIN DISH

- Mix the dough and raise it in the microwave oven.
- Bake the bread in the conventional oven while the soup or other dish cooks in the microwave.
- Or, make the bread earlier in the day and freeze it. To defrost 1 loaf of bread, wrap it in a paper towel and microwave on DEFROST for 1 minute.

TO PREPARE THE WHOLE MEAL

- Mix and raise bread (if necessary) in the microwave.
- Put the bread into the conventional oven to bake.
- Cook the soup in the microwave oven while the bread is baking.
- If you plan to serve a salad, prepare and toss it while the soup and bread are cooking.
- If adding pasta or rice to the soup, cook it on top of the range while the soup is simmering in the microwave.

Hearty Corn Chowder

MAKES: *4 servings*
COOKING TIME: *11 to 12 minutes*

No-cholesterol variation

5.4 grams fat per serving

SERVING SUGGESTIONS:
Serve with Blueberry Muffins (page 57) or Chili Beer Bread (page 63).

1 tablespoon butter or margarine
1 medium onion, chopped
½ cup cornmeal
2 cups chicken broth or clam broth
1 cup milk
2 cups fresh or frozen corn kernels (see Note)
¼ teaspoon freshly ground black pepper
⅛ teaspoon cayenne

GARNISHES

Chopped fresh cilantro, chopped tomato, Salsa Cruda (page 317), grated cheese, or yogurt

1. In a 3-quart microwave-safe casserole, combine the butter and onion. Microwave on HIGH for 1 to 2 minutes, or until the onion is tender.

This corn "stew" is thickened with cornmeal, which also sweetens it a bit. The recipe is based on Thelma's mother's "convenience soup." If she was in a hurry, it became a meatless main dish with the addition of cheese or yogurt.

2. Stir in the cornmeal.
3. Pour in the broth, milk, corn, pepper, and cayenne. Cover with a lid or with plastic wrap turned back slightly; microwave on HIGH for 6 to 8 minutes, or until soup is thickened and the corn is cooked, stirring after 3 minutes. Let stand for 3 minutes.
4. Serve with one of the garnishes.

NOTE

To defrost frozen corn, place corn in a nonmetallic box or bag in the microwave and cook on HIGH for 2 minutes.

VARIATIONS

HEARTY CORN CHOWDER WITH FISH (5.8 grams fat per serving): While the soup is standing (following step 3), place ½ pound scallops, shrimp, or firm fish, cut into ½-inch cubes, in a 1-quart casserole. Cover with a lid or with plastic wrap turned back slightly. Microwave on HIGH for 1½ to 2½ minutes, or until fish is cooked through, stirring after 1 minute. Add to the soup, along with the accumulated juices, and serve.

HEARTY CORN CHOWDER WITH CHICKEN (7.7 grams fat per serving): While the soup is standing (following step 3), place ½ pound cut-up, skinless, boneless chicken breasts on a small microwave-safe plate. Cover with plastic wrap turned back slightly. Microwave on HIGH for 2½ to 4 minutes, or until the juices run clear, stirring once halfway through.

NO-CHOLESTEROL CORN CHOWDER (5.4 grams fat per serving): Substitute canola or olive oil for butter and evaporated skim milk for regular milk.

Vegetarian Wild Mushroom and Barley Soup

1 package (.07 ounces) dried shiitake mushrooms
½ cup pearl barley
1 pound fresh mushrooms, trimmed
1 teaspoon olive oil
1 medium onion, chopped
1 garlic clove, minced
4 cups vegetable broth (made from cubes)
1 tablespoon fresh lemon juice
¼ cup chopped fresh parsley
2 tablespoons Madeira or dry sherry
1 can (12 ounces) evaporated skim milk

MAKES: *4 servings*
COOKING TIME: *37 to 40 minutes*

Low cholesterol

0.7 gram fat per serving

SERVING SUGGESTIONS:
For a lunch or light supper, serve with a salad and one of the shredded-wheat breads (pages 41, 42).

A deceptively rich-tasting soup that is actually low in fat, since it isn't loaded with butter and cream. The wild mushrooms impart a subtle woodsy flavor, while the barley adds a wonderful nutlike texture.

1. Place the dried shiitake mushrooms in a 4-cup glass measure and add 1 cup water. Microwave on HIGH for 3 minutes. Set aside.
2. Place the barley in a 2-quart microwave-safe casserole. Add 1 cup water. Cover tightly with a lid or with plastic wrap turned back slightly. Microwave on HIGH for 4 to 5 minutes, or until boiling; then cook on MEDIUM for 7 to 8 minutes, or until all of the water has been absorbed.
3. Meanwhile, in the food processor, chop the fresh mushrooms very fine.
4. Strain the dried mushrooms, reserving the soaking liquid. Cut them into ½-inch pieces.
5. In a 3-quart microwave-safe casserole, pour the oil over the onion and garlic. Microwave on HIGH for 1 minute.
6. Add the wild mushrooms and soaking liquid, cooked barley, chopped mushrooms, broth, lemon juice, parsley, and sherry to the casserole. Cover tightly, with a lid or with plastic wrap turned back slightly; microwave on HIGH for 20 minutes, stirring once.
7. Add the milk and microwave on HIGH for 2 minutes more. Let stand for 5 minutes before serving.

French Onion Soup

MAKES: *4 servings*
COOKING TIME: *30 minutes*

11.8 grams fat per serving

SERVING SUGGESTIONS:
Serve with a mixed green salad and Peach Melba (page 290) or Perfectly Poached Pears (page 238).

Our time-honored onion soup recipe started with ¼ pound of butter, but we find that

1 tablespoon olive oil
3 medium onions (1½ pounds, total), peeled and
   thinly sliced
¼ teaspoon sugar
1 tablespoon flour
4 cups beef broth
2 tablespoons Madeira or dry vermouth
1 teaspoon paprika
Freshly ground black pepper
4 ½-inch-thick slices French bread, toasted
4 ounces Gruyère or Swiss cheese, grated

1. Combine the oil, onion, and sugar in a 4-quart microwave-safe casserole; stir. Cover tightly with a lid or with plastic wrap turned back slightly. Microwave on HIGH for 12 to 14 minutes, or until the onion is tender, stirring after 5 minutes.
2. Sprinkle the flour over the onion and stir to blend.
3. Stir in the broth, Madeira, paprika, and pepper. Cover again and cook on HIGH for 10 to 12 minutes, or

*reducing the fat to 1
tablespoon of olive oil works
just as well and makes a
great-tasting soup.*

until bubbling, stirring once after 5 minutes.
4. Divide the soup between four soup bowls. Place a slice of toast on top of each bowl. Sprinkle with cheese and place the bowls in the microwave oven in a circular pattern. Cook, uncovered, on HIGH for 6 to 8 minutes, or until the cheese melts.

Winter Minestrone

MAKES: *4 servings*
COOKING TIME: *16 to 20 minutes*

Low cholesterol

4.9 grams fat per serving

SERVING SUGGESTIONS:
Stir in a tablespoon or two of Pesto (page 335) at the table. Serve with Parmesan Beer Bread (page 64), Herbed Beer Bread (page 64), or purchased crusty Italian or French bread.

Thelma's mother used to cook this soup, but it took her all day, because she had to soak the beans. We make ours with canned beans and tomatoes to speed up the process without sacrificing much flavor.

1 tablespoon olive oil
1 garlic clove, minced
1 medium onion, coarsely chopped
1 cup diced potato (1 large)
½ cup sliced carrot (1 medium)
½ cup thinly sliced celery (1 rib)
1 cup shredded cabbage
1 can (8 ounces) tomatoes, undrained, coarsely
   chopped
1 can (15½ ounces) kidney beans, undrained
1 cup vegetable, beef, or chicken stock, or water
¼ cup chopped fresh parsley
¼ cup chopped fresh basil, or 1 teaspoon dried
Freshly ground black pepper
½ cup small dry pasta
Freshly grated Parmesan
Pesto (page 335) (optional)

1. In a 2-quart microwave-safe casserole, combine the oil, garlic, and onion. Cover tightly with a lid or with plastic wrap turned back slightly. Microwave on HIGH for 1 minute.
2. Add the potato, carrot, celery, and cabbage. Drain the juice from the tomatoes into the casserole. Cover again and cook on HIGH for 6 to 8 minutes, or until the vegetables are tender.
3. Add the tomato, beans, broth, parsley, basil, and pepper. Cover again and cook on HIGH for 8 to 10 minutes, or until heated through.
4. Meanwhile, in a pot on top of the stove, heat 2 cups of water to boiling. Cook the pasta until al dente. Drain and stir into the soup at the end of the cooking time. To serve, sprinkle with Parmesan and stir in a dollop of pesto, if desired.

VARIATIONS SOUTHWESTERN MINESTRONE (4.9 grams fat per serving): Substitute canned black beans for kidney beans.

Add 1 box (10 ounces) frozen corn kernels, 1 small jalapeño pepper, chopped, and ½ teaspoon cumin powder with beans. Sprinkle with chopped fresh cilantro when serving.

SPRING AND SUMMER MINESTRONE (4.9 grams fat per serving): Substitute canned cannellini (white beans) for kidney beans. Add 1 cup sliced zucchini (1 medium) and ½ pound green beans, cut into ½-inch pieces, when adding beans. Serve with Mint Pesto (page 335).

Vegetarian Portales Peanut Soup

MAKES: *4 servings*
COOKING TIME: *12 to 14 minutes*

Low cholesterol

38 grams fat per serving

SERVING SUGGESTIONS: Serve with Oven-Baked Corn Bread (page 61) or Blue Cornmeal Bread (page 62).

This soup was initially inspired by a trip to Portales, New Mexico, where we tasted freshly harvested and toasted peanuts. The Forge restaurant, outside of Denver, gave us the idea of combining peppers and peanuts, as their specialty is a peanut butter–stuffed jalapeño pepper! If you are not a hot-pepper lover, you may eliminate the jalapeños and still have a very respectable soup.

¼ *cup shelled, skinned peanuts*
1 tablespoon peanut oil
1 medium onion, minced
1 tablespoon flour
2 cups chicken broth
1 cup creamy-style peanut butter
1 cup evaporated low-fat or skim milk
1 tablespoon fresh lemon juice
2 tablespoons finely chopped jalapeño pepper
¼ *teaspoon freshly ground black pepper*
¼ *teaspoon paprika*
Thin lemon slices
Crispy corn tortilla chips

1. Place the peanuts on a paper plate. Microwave on HIGH for 2 to 3 minutes, to toast. Set aside.
2. In a 3-quart microwave-safe casserole, combine the oil and onion. Microwave on HIGH for 1 to 2 minutes, or until onion is tender.
3. Stir in the flour, until smooth. Stir in the chicken broth and peanut butter, but don't be concerned with smoothness yet. Cover tightly, with a lid or with plastic wrap turned back slightly, and microwave on HIGH for 4 minutes; stir well to make a smooth soup.
4. Stir in the milk, lemon juice, jalapeño pepper, black pepper, and paprika. Cover again and cook on HIGH for 5 to 7 minutes, to heat through. To serve, sprinkle each bowl with some chopped peanuts and a slice of lemon. Serve with corn chips.

Vegetable Soup with Pistou

(Provençal Vegetable Soup with Garlic, Basil, and Herbs)

MAKES: *4 servings*
COOKING TIME: *18 to 20 minutes*

No cholesterol

2.7 grams fat per serving with 1 tablespoon Pistou

SERVING SUGGESTIONS:
Serve with Pleated Cheese Bread (page 38), Rosemary Focaccia (page 50), Bruschetta (page 66), or Large Garlic-Thyme Croutons (page 311).

Pistou differs slightly from cook to cook but is always made with fresh herbs, which give this soup its special flavor. Fresh basil is best, but if you don't have any, substitute dried basil with fresh parsley.

1 cup diced carrot (2 medium)
1 cup diced potato (1 medium) (thin-skinned potatoes need not be peeled)
1 cup coarsely chopped onion (1 large)
1 medium green bell pepper, cut into ½-inch dice
1 small zucchini (¼ pound), cut into ½-inch slices
1 can (10½ ounces) white or red kidney beans
Pistou (recipe follows)

1. In a 3-quart microwave-safe casserole, combine the carrot, potato, onion, and ½ cup water. Cover tightly, with a lid or with plastic wrap turned back slightly. Microwave on HIGH for 6 minutes, or until tender, stirring once.
2. Add the green pepper, zucchini, beans, and 2 cups water, stirring well. Cover again. Cook on HIGH for 6 to 8 minutes, or until all the vegetables are tender and the liquid is boiling.
3. Meanwhile, make the Pistou.
4. Stir in the Pistou. Cover again. Cook on HIGH for 4 to 6 minutes, or until heated through.
5. Spoon into serving bowls and serve with large chunks of crusty bread, or one of the other breads suggested.

Pistou

MAKES: *About ½ cup*

2 grams fat per tablespoon

2 garlic cloves, mashed into a paste with the side of a knife
2 tablespoons tomato paste
¼ cup chopped fresh basil, or 1 teaspoon dried basil and ¼ cup chopped fresh parsley
2 tablespoons grated Parmesan
1 tablespoon olive oil

In a small bowl, mix all the ingredients together.

Lentil Soup

MAKES: *4 servings*
COOKING TIME: *35 to 40 minutes*

No cholesterol

5 grams fat per serving

SERVING SUGGESTIONS:
Serve with purchased pumpernickel bread or Onion Beer Bread (page 64).

Lentils don't need any presoaking, and they cook in the microwave oven relatively quickly. While they make a complete protein when served with bread, some of our variations include a little meat or tofu to change the flavor and protein content.

5 cups vegetable broth (homemade or store-bought)
1 garlic clove
1 celery rib, cut into 2-inch chunks
1 large onion, quartered
1 medium carrot, cut into 2-inch chunks
1 tablespoon olive, canola, or vegetable oil
1 cup lentils, rinsed and picked over
½ teaspoon dried thyme leaves
¼ teaspoon salt
¼ teaspoon freshly ground black pepper
1 crushed bay leaf
Dash cayenne
1 tablespoon fresh lemon juice (optional)

1. Pour the broth into a 2-quart glass measure. Microwave on HIGH for 8 to 10 minutes, or until very hot.
2. Meanwhile, cut up the vegetables in the food processor: Drop the garlic into the feed tube while the processor is running. Add the celery, onion, and carrot and pulse on and off about four times. (If you don't have a food processor, mince the garlic and chop the vegetables coarsely by hand.)
3. In a 3-quart microwave-safe casserole, combine the chopped vegetables and oil. Cover tightly with a lid or with plastic wrap turned back slightly. Microwave on HIGH for 5 minutes, or until tender-crisp.
4. Stir in the remaining ingredients, except the lemon juice. Cover again and cook on HIGH for 30 to 35 minutes, or until the lentils are tender, stirring after 15 minutes. Stir in the lemon juice.

VARIATIONS

LENTIL SOUP WITH BACON (2.5 grams fat per serving):
Eliminate the oil. Cut a ⅛-pound slab of bacon into ½-inch cubes; place in a 3-quart microwave-safe casserole. Microwave, uncovered, on HIGH for 1 minute. Add the garlic and vegetables and proceed with the basic recipe, starting with Step 3. (*Note:* This variation is not a no-cholesterol soup.)

LENTIL SOUP WITH TOMATOES (5 grams fat per serving):
Add 1 can (8-ounces) tomatoes with juices, coarsely chopped, when adding lentils.

LENTIL SOUP WITH SAUSAGE (6 grams fat per serving):
Thinly slice 1 or 2 smoked sausages and add to the soup

during the last 10 minutes of cooking. (*Note:* This variation is not a no-cholesterol soup.)

LENTIL SOUP WITH TOFU (8 grams fat per serving): Cube 4 ounces tofu and add during the last 10 minutes of cooking.

Split Pea and Sweet Potato Soup

MAKES: *4 servings*
COOKING TIME: *35 to 40 minutes*

Low-cholesterol variation

4 grams fat per serving

SERVING SUGGESTIONS:
Top with a dollop of nonfat yogurt and a splash of Maggi (see Note) for added flavor. Serve with Onion-Caraway Beer Bread (page 64) or Irish Brown Bread (page 65).

Cubes of sweet potato add flavor, texture, and a pretty orange color to this soup.

5 cups chicken broth
4 ounces lean ham, chopped
1 medium onion, chopped
1 garlic clove, minced
1 celery rib, chopped
1 sweet potato (¾ pound), cut into ½-inch cubes
1 cup green split peas
¼ cup chopped fresh parsley
¼ teaspoon freshly ground black pepper
Pinch cayenne

1. Pour the broth into a 2-quart glass measure. Microwave on HIGH for 6 to 8 minutes. Meanwhile, prepare the vegetables.
2. In a 3-quart microwave-safe casserole, combine the ham, onion, garlic, and celery. Cover tightly with a lid or with plastic wrap turned back slightly. Microwave on HIGH for 2 minutes.
3. Add the warmed broth and the remaining ingredients. Cover again and cook on HIGH for 35 to 40 minutes, or until the peas are tender, stirring twice.
4. Let stand for 5 minutes.

● *Maggi is a Swiss vegetable-protein seasoning that is to Europe what soy sauce is to East Asia. It can be found in many grocery stores in the soup section, near the bouillon cubes. You'll also see Maggi in specialty food stores.*

VARIATION LOW-CHOLESTEROL SPLIT PEA AND SWEET POTATO SOUP (5.7 grams fat per serving): Eliminate the ham and substitute 1 tablespoon olive oil. Skim the fat from the chicken broth.

Vegetarian Black Bean Soup

MAKES: *4 servings*
COOKING TIME: *10 to 12 minutes*

No cholesterol

4.5 grams fat per serving

SERVING SUGGESTIONS:
This soup makes a dinner for four when served with rice. You may wish to add a salad and a loaf of crusty Portuguese, Cuban, or Italian bread for a heartier meal.

Thelma remembers this soup fondly from college vacations in San Juan. It was a new taste treat and an inexpensive meal for student wallets. With canned black beans she can bring back those memories in just minutes.

1 tablespoon olive oil
1 large onion, chopped
1 garlic clove, minced
1 jalapeño pepper, minced
2 cans (16 ounces each) black beans with juice
1 teaspoon ground cumin
½ teaspoon dried basil leaves
2 tablespoons Madeira or sherry
Basic Rice for Soup (page 94)
Garnishes: lemon slices, chopped onion, chopped fresh tomatoes, nonfat yogurt

1. In a 3-quart microwave-safe casserole, combine the oil, onion, garlic, and pepper. Microwave on HIGH for 1 minute.
2. Add the remaining ingredients except the garnishes. Cover tightly with a lid or with plastic wrap turned back slightly. Microwave on HIGH for 8 to 10 minutes, or until heated through.
3. Serve with Basic Rice and the garnishes listed above, or pass these condiments at the table.

Hearty Italian Sausage-and-Bean Soup

MAKES: *4 servings*
COOKING TIME: *14 to 18 minutes*

Low-cholesterol variation

9.6 grams fat per serving

½ pound Italian sausage (hot or sweet), casing removed, cut into 1-inch pieces
1 teaspoon olive oil
2 garlic cloves, minced
2 cups Savoy or other cabbage, thinly sliced
½ cup dry white wine, chicken broth, or water
1 can (19 ounces) cannellini (white kidney beans), undrained
¼ teaspoon freshly ground black pepper
¼ cup chopped fresh parsley

1. In a 10-inch skillet on top of the range, cook the sausage over medium heat for 6 to 8 minutes, until browned and cooked through.

A mixed green salad, a loaf of crusty Italian bread, and a glass of crisp white wine round out this soup meal nicely.

All the wonderful flavors in this soup make it very satisfying for a late fall or winter dinner, and the short cooking time makes it all the more enticing.

2. Meanwhile, combine the oil and garlic in a 3-quart microwave-safe casserole. Microwave on HIGH for 30 seconds to 1 minute, or until tender.
3. Add the cabbage and wine to the casserole. Cover tightly, with a lid or with plastic wrap turned back slightly on one side. Microwave on HIGH for 6 to 8 minutes, stirring after 4 minutes, or until the cabbage is tender-crisp.
4. While the cabbage is cooking, you may wish to turn up the heat on the sausage to brown. Watch it closely, turning it occasionally to keep it from burning. Tilt the skillet and move the sausage to the top part of the pan to drain the excess fat from the bottom of pan.
5. Add the drained sausage, beans, pepper, and parsley to the casserole; mix well. Cover again and microwave on HIGH for 5 to 7 minutes, or until heated through. Serve.

VARIATION HEARTY TURKEY SAUSAGE-AND-BEAN SOUP (8.6 grams fat per serving): Substitute ½ pound purchased chicken or turkey sausage, or make your own Turkey Sausages (page 180). Right before cooking, form sausage meat into 1-inch balls and heat in a skillet as described above. You will need to spray the pan with vegetable spray or watch the sausage a little more closely, as it contains only a small amount of fat and will tend to stick.

Pea Soup with Ham Bone

MAKES: *8 servings*
COOKING TIME: *50 to 60 minutes*

4 grams fat per serving

SERVING SUGGESTIONS:
This soup is best served with chunks of crusty bread and a bowl of crudités to be passed.

1 garlic clove, minced
¼ cup chopped fresh parsley, or 1 tablespoon dried
1 large onion, quartered
1 carrot, peeled and cut into 2-inch pieces
1 celery rib, cut into 2-inch pieces
1 pound dried split peas
1 ham bone with a small amount of meat
½ teaspoon salt
¼ teaspoon freshly ground black pepper
⅛ teaspoon cayenne (optional)

1. Pour 7 cups of water into a 4- or 5-quart microwave-safe casserole. Cover with a lid or with plastic wrap turned back slightly on one side. Microwave on HIGH for 8 to 10 minutes, while chopping and measuring the remaining ingredients. (Heating the water first will speed cooking later.)

*We traditionally serve this
soup on the Sunday after
Christmas, when everyone is
watching football and no one
wants to take the time to sit
down to a formal dinner.*

2. Chop the vegetables in the food processor; drop the garlic through the feed tube of the processor while it is running. Scrape down the sides. Place the parsley, onion, carrot, and celery in the bowl of the processor, along with the garlic, and pulse on and off four to five times, until coarsely chopped.

3. Add the vegetables to the hot water, along with the peas, ham bone, and remaining ingredients. Cover as before and cook on HIGH for 20 minutes, or until boiling; stir well.

4. Cover again and cook on MEDIUM for 35 to 40 minutes, or until the peas are tender. Let stand 5 to 10 minutes before serving.

Southwestern Bean Soup

MAKES: *4 servings*
COOKING TIME: *12 to 14 minutes*

Low cholesterol

5 grams fat per serving

GARNISHES

SERVING SUGGESTIONS:
Top soup with the optional garnishes listed below. By adding ½ cup of cooked rice to each bowl of soup, you'll form a complete protein. Prepare the rice first and let it stand while the soup is cooking.

Canned beans and broths are some of our all-time favorite convenience ingredients, and since we both live in places

1 cup chicken broth, defatted
1 tablespoon olive oil
1 garlic clove, minced
1 large onion, chopped
1 can (14½ ounces) Mexican-style stewed tomatoes with juice
2 cans (16 ounces each) black or pinto beans, with juice
1 jalapeño pepper, chopped, or more, depending on taste (the membrane holding the seeds is the hottest part)
½ teaspoon dried oregano
¼ teaspoon freshly ground black pepper

Chopped fresh cilantro, cooked rice, chopped onion, grated Monterey Jack cheese, cubed avocado (optional)

1. Pour the chicken broth into a 1-cup glass measure. Microwave on HIGH for 2½ minutes.

2. Meanwhile, in a 3-quart microwave-safe casserole, combine the oil, garlic, and onion. Microwave on HIGH for 2 to 3 minutes, or until tender.

3. Add the tomatoes and mash them slightly with a potato masher to break the pieces apart somewhat.

4. Add the remaining ingredients, including the warm broth. Cover tightly with a lid or with plastic wrap turned back slightly. Microwave on HIGH for 10 to 12

where we can be snowed in, they have also become our emergency staples.

VARIATION

minutes, or until heated through, stirring once. Serve with optional garnishes.

SOUTHWESTERN BEAN SOUP WITH SAUSAGE (13 grams fat per serving): Add ½ pound smoked chorizo, or other spicy smoked sausage, cut into ½-inch slices, when adding the remaining ingredients in step 4. (*Note:* This variation is not low in cholesterol.)

Bean Soup with a Kiss of Ham

MAKES: *4 servings*
COOKING TIME: *20 to 23 minutes*

12 grams fat per serving

SERVING SUGGESTIONS:
Top with cubed ripe tomatoes and grated Parmesan. Serve with Fast-Rising Focaccia (page 49) or crusty Italian bread.

We may have a ham on the bone or a pork butt only for holidays, so we like to stretch its flavor with this quick and economical soup. To speed preparation, we use the food processor for chopping.

VARIATION

For more color, you can use two different kinds of beans— red and white kidney beans or white kidney beans and black beans.

2 garlic cloves, peeled
1 medium carrot, peeled and cut into 2-inch pieces
1 celery rib, cut into 2-inch pieces
1 tablespoon olive oil
2 cans (16 ounces each) cannellini (white kidney beans) with juice
1 pork shoulder butt (½ pound), or meat from a ham bone, cut into ¼-inch pieces
2 tablespoons chopped fresh parsley
¼ teaspoon freshly ground black pepper
⅛ teaspoon dried hot-pepper flakes (optional)

1. Chop the first three ingredients in the food processor: Drop the garlic into the bowl while the motor is running; when chopped, scrape down the sides of the bowl. Drop the carrot and celery into the bowl; pulse on and off four to five times, until coarsely chopped.
2. Combine the chopped vegetables and oil in a 3-quart microwave-safe casserole. Cover tightly with a lid or with plastic wrap turned back slightly. Microwave on HIGH for 3 minutes, or until tender.
3. Add the beans, pork, parsley, peppers, and 1 cup water; stir well. Cover again and cook on HIGH for 18 to 20 minutes, or until heated through, stirring after 10 minutes.
4. Let stand for 5 minutes before serving.

PASTA-AND-BEAN SOUP WITH A KISS OF HAM (12 grams fat per serving): Cook 1 cup small macaroni (ditali, elbows, or tubetti) on top of the stove while the soup is cooking in the microwave oven. Drain the pasta and stir into the soup at the end of cooking.

Miso Soups

Miso soup, once foreign to most of us, is slowly working its way into the American home. Even in grocery stores in small midwestern towns, it's possible to find instant miso-soup mix or the soybean paste, itself called miso, from which the soup is made. The red miso is a blend of soybeans, rice mold, barley, and salt. For the protein it contains, it is a decent source of fiber, especially compared to meat, which has no fiber.

Marcia learned to make miso soup from her Japanese husband, who would eat it at every meal if she would prepare it. She prefers to make it from scratch, although many Japanese women do make it from a mix.

This soup is very simple to prepare, if you have the light fish broth or *dashi* already made, and even that can be made by adding hot water to instant granules. A recipe for *dashi* follows. Make the full 6 cups; use some now and refrigerate the rest for up to 4 or 5 days. If you still don't think you'll use that much, halve the recipe.

Dashi (Broth)

MAKES: *About 6 cups*
COOKING TIME: *10 to 12 minutes*

Low cholesterol

2 grams fat per serving

1 6-inch piece dried konbu, *wiped off (see Note)*
1 package (¾ ounce) dried bonito flakes

1. Combine 6 cups of water and *konbu* in a 2-quart microwave-safe casserole. Cover tightly with a lid or with plastic wrap turned back slightly. Microwave on HIGH for 7 to 10 minutes, until almost boiling.
2. Remove the *konbu* with chopsticks or a fork and stir in the bonito. (Leaving the *konbu* in longer will make the broth bitter.)
3. Cover the dish again and cook on HIGH for 3 to 5 minutes, or until the water comes to a boil. Let stand until the bonito flakes sink to the bottom of the casserole. (The longer the water and bonito sit, the fuller the flavor.) You can make a "light" *dashi* by letting the water sit for just 10 minutes. Or allow to stand until desired flavor has developed.
4. Strain and use for soup.

NOTE *Konbu*, or "kelp," is a large, brownish-green seaweed that is sold in dried form only. It can be found in Oriental grocery stores and health-food stores. *Konbu* is most commonly used to make a seafood broth. Do not wash off the powdery white substance on the surface; instead, wipe it off with a damp paper towel.

Miso Soup with Tofu

MAKES: *3 cups*
COOKING TIME: *6 to 10 minutes*

No cholesterol

3.5 grams fat per serving

SERVING SUGGESTIONS:
Serve with Basic Rice for Soup (page 94). Garnish soup with thinly sliced green onion.

Miso soup may be made with red aka *miso or white* shiro *miso. The red, the variety used in most Japanese restaurants in this country, is a little stronger. We prefer it in our homes as well. The white miso is lighter and has a slightly sweet flavor.*

3 *cups* dashi
3 *tablespoons* aka *or* shiro *miso*
¼ *cup dried* wakame, *broken up and soaked in water for 15 minutes (optional) (see Note)*
9 *ounces firm or soft tofu, drained and cut into small cubes*
2 *green onions, thinly sliced*

1. Pour *dashi* into a 4-cup glass measure. Microwave on HIGH for 3 to 5 minutes, or until hot.
2. Place the miso in a small bowl. Pour about ½ cup hot *dashi* into the miso and stir to dissolve. Pour back into the 4-cup glass measure. Microwave, uncovered, on HIGH for 1 to 2 minutes to heat through.
3. Drain *wakame* well and stir it into the soup.
4. Stir in tofu. Microwave, uncovered, on HIGH for 2 minutes more to heat through. Serve garnished with green onion.

It is easy to adjust the quantity of this recipe. Just figure ⅔ cup *dashi*, 1 tablespoon miso, and 3 ounces tofu per serving.

NOTE *Wakame* is a form of seaweed that is smaller than *konbu* (see page 82) and darker in color. Unlike *konbu*, which can have an overpowering flavor if boiled, *wakame* has a light flavor and a soft texture. It can be purchased fresh or dried, at Oriental grocery stores and health-food stores, and used in soups and salads. If purchased dried, it must be soaked for 10 minutes in water before using.

VARIATION MISO SOUP WITH POTATO AND SPINACH (1 gram fat per serving): Eliminate *wakame* and tofu. Peel two small boiling potatoes and place in a small microwave-safe casserole. Add 2 tablespoons water. Cover tightly with a lid or with plastic wrap turned back slightly. Microwave on HIGH for 4 to 5 minutes, or until tender. Let cool. Meanwhile, thoroughly wash 6 large spinach leaves with stems. After removing the potatoes, place undrained spinach in same casserole. Cover again. Cook on HIGH for 3 minutes, or until tender. Cut the potatoes into small cubes, and coarsely chop spinach. Add both to heated miso and *dashi*, as directed for *wakame* and tofu. Garnish with green onion, if desired.

Sweet Potato Soup

MAKES: *4 servings*
COOKING TIME: *14 to 18 minutes*

Low cholesterol

4.2 grams fat per serving

SERVING SUGGESTIONS:
This makes an impressive and delicious meal when served with Pleated Cheese Bread (page 38). If you are watching your cholesterol level, make the low-cholesterol version of the bread.

2 large sweet potatoes (about 1 pound, total)
3 cups chicken broth
¼ cup low-fat ricotta
¼ teaspoon salt
¼ teaspoon freshly ground black pepper
1 tablespoon fresh lemon juice
2 tablespoons brown sugar

1. Pierce the sweet potatoes with the tines of a fork on the top and bottom. Place them on a paper towel at least 1 inch apart in the microwave oven and cook on HIGH for 8 to 10 minutes, or until tender. Let stand 5 minutes.
2. Peel the potatoes and cut each potato into eight pieces. Place them in the bowl of the food processor and pulse on and off six to eight times, until pureed.
3. Combine pureed potato with remaining ingredients in a 2-quart microwave-safe casserole; stir until smooth. Microwave on HIGH for 6 to 8 minutes, or until heated through. Serve.

Butternut Squash Soup

MAKES: *4 servings*
COOKING TIME: *27 to 30 minutes*

Low cholesterol

4.5 grams fat per serving; 9 grams fat per serving with 1 tablespoon toasted squash seeds

SERVING SUGGESTION:
Serve with Bruschetta (page 66).

1 butternut squash (2 pounds)
1 tablespoon olive oil
1 garlic clove, minced
1 medium onion, chopped
1 celery rib, sliced
2 cups chicken broth
1 cup evaporated low-fat milk or ½ cup low-fat ricotta cheese
1 tablespoon brown sugar
¼ teaspoon ground nutmeg
¼ teaspoon ground ginger
Pinch cayenne
¼ teaspoon freshly ground black pepper
¼ cup Toasted Squash Seeds, Sunflower Seeds, or Walnuts (optional; recipe follows)

1. Pierce the squash with a fork on the top and bottom; place it on a microwave-safe plate. Microwave on HIGH for 6 minutes; turn the squash over and rotate the plate. Microwave on HIGH for 6 to 8 minutes more, or until the entire squash has turned a darker beige and is slightly blistered all over. Let stand for 5 minutes.
2. Meanwhile, in a 3-quart microwave-safe casserole,

combine the olive oil, garlic, onion, and celery. Cover tightly with a lid or with plastic wrap turned back slightly. Microwave on HIGH for 3 to 5 minutes, or until the vegetables are tender.

3. Cut the squash in half and remove the seeds and connective fiber with a spoon. (Remove the seeds from the fiber and set them aside for toasting, if desired.)

4. Pour the broth into a 4-cup glass measure and microwave on HIGH for 5 minutes.

5. Meanwhile, spoon the flesh from the squash and place it in a food processor along with the cooked vegetables. Process into a smooth puree. Add the milk, sugar, nutmeg, ginger, and peppers. Process quickly to blend.

6. Return to the casserole and stir in the warmed chicken broth. Cover again and cook on HIGH for 8 to 10 minutes, or until heated through. Let stand, covered, for 3 to 5 minutes. Serve with toasted seeds or nuts, if desired.

VARIATIONS CURRIED BUTTERNUT SQUASH SOUP: Eliminate the nutmeg and ground ginger. Substitute 1 tablespoon curry powder and ½ teaspoon ground cumin.

MAPLE-WALNUT BUTTERNUT SQUASH SOUP: Substitute 2 tablespoons maple syrup for brown sugar and garnish with toasted walnuts.

BUTTERNUT SQUASH AND CHICKEN (OR TURKEY) SOUP (8 grams fat per serving): Add 2 cups cooked and thinly sliced chicken (or turkey) when returning the vegetable puree to the casserole.

Toasted Squash Seeds

MAKES: *¼ cup*
COOKING TIME: *3 to 5 minutes*

4.6 grams fat per tablespoon

¼ cup acorn squash seeds, washed, drained, and patted dry
1 teaspoon olive oil (optional)
Salt (optional)

1. Line a pie plate with a double layer of paper towels.
2. Sprinkle the seeds evenly on top. Microwave on HIGH for 3 to 5 minutes, or until dried but still white, stirring once.

3. Stir the seeds into a bowl with olive oil and sprinkle with salt to taste.

VARIATION   TOASTED SUNFLOWER SEEDS OR WALNUTS: Substitute ¼ cup sunflower seeds or walnuts for squash seeds. Follow the instructions above, but microwave on HIGH for only 2 to 4 minutes.

Green Chili and Red Pepper Soup

MAKES: *4 servings*
COOKING TIME: *About 20 minutes*

Low cholesterol

7 grams fat per serving

SERVING SUGGESTION:
Serve with Video Nachos Grandes (page 260).

We developed this soup for the National Potato Board, and they liked it so much, they used it for a TV promotion. The unique red-and-green design is achieved by making two separate soups and pouring them simultaneously into each bowl.

2 tablespoons olive oil
2 garlic cloves
2 large baking potatoes, peeled and cut into 1-inch cubes
4 roasted mild Anaheim chilies, or 1 can (4 ounces) mild green chilies, drained
1 teaspoon salt
½ teaspoon freshly ground black pepper
¼ teaspoon dried thyme
2 cups evaporated skim milk
2 roasted and peeled red bellers peppers (recipe follows) or pimientos (½ cup)
⅛ teaspoon cayenne

1. To prepare the green chili soup: Place 1 tablespoon oil and 1 garlic clove in a 4-cup glass measure or microwave-safe casserole. Microwave on HIGH for 40 seconds.
2. Add half the potato cubes, leaving space in the center, and pour in ¼ cup water. Cover tightly with a lid or with plastic wrap turned back slightly; microwave on HIGH for 5 to 6 minutes, or until tender.
3. Pour the potato mixture into the bowl of a food processor. Add the chilies and process until smooth.
4. Pour the mixture back into the casserole. Add ½ teaspoon salt, ¼ teaspoon freshly ground black pepper, ¼ teaspoon thyme, and 1 cup milk; stir until smooth. Cover again and cook on HIGH for 2 to 6 minutes, or until heated through but not boiling. Set aside.
5. To prepare the red pepper soup: Follow the instructions above for the remaining ingredients, but add the red peppers instead of the green chilies and add the cayenne pepper in place of the thyme with the salt and pepper.
6. To serve: Ladle ½ cup of each soup into separate

cups and pour each simultaneously into a soup bowl from separate sides. The soup is thick and will meet in the center.

NOTE   Before serving, you may want to place both dishes of soup into the microwave oven to reheat. Microwave on HIGH for 2 to 6 minutes, or until heated through, but not boiling. Two 4-cup glass measures work well for this. (It's not a bad idea to have two anyway, for more efficient microwave cooking.)

"Roasted" Red Peppers

MAKES: *1 cup*
COOKING TIME: *16 to 18 minutes*

3.5 grams fat per ¼ cup

Here's an alternative way to roast peppers on those hot days when you just don't want to turn on the broiler, or when you don't want the charred appearance that the open flame gives.

1 pound (3 to 4) red bell peppers
1 tablespoon vegetable oil

1. Rub the peppers with the vegetable oil. Pierce both sides of each pepper with a sharp knife. Place the stem ends to the outside of a 10-inch glass pie plate or a 2-quart rectangular microwave-safe dish. Cover with a paper towel and microwave on HIGH for 8 minutes.
2. Turn the peppers over; cover again. Rotate the dish a half turn and cook on HIGH for 8 to 10 minutes more, or until the peppers are softened and slightly wrinkled, and the skins begin to separate from the peppers or blister slightly around the stems.
3. Roll the peppers in a kitchen towel to seal in the moisture. Let them stand for at least 10 minutes.
4. Cut the peppers in half and remove the stems and seeds. With a sharp knife, and under cool running water, pull off the skins.

VARIATION   "ROASTED" GREEN CHILIES: Substitute 1 pound of green chilies for the red peppers. Follow the directions above, cooking on HIGH for 4 minutes on the first side and 4 to 6 minutes on the second side.

Apple-Squash Soup

1 butternut squash (2 pounds)
1 onion, chopped
1 garlic clove, minced
1 celery rib, chopped
2 apples, peeled, cored, and cubed (Granny Smith, Northern Spy, or Macoun)
1 tablespoon olive oil

MAKES: *4 servings*
COOKING TIME: *About 30 minutes*

Low cholesterol

5.3 grams fat per serving

SERVING SUGGESTIONS:
Serve with pieces of cheese and bread, such as Oven-Baked Corn Bread (page 61) or Walnut Bread (page 43).

A slightly sweet soup that's great for fall.

2 cups chicken broth
½ cup low-fat ricotta cheese or skim evaporated milk
2 tablespoons brown sugar
¼ teaspoon ground cinnamon
¼ teaspoon ground ginger
Pinch cayenne
¼ cup Toasted Squash Seeds or Nuts (page 86) (optional)

1. Pierce the squash with a fork on the top and bottom. Place it on a microwave-safe plate. Microwave on HIGH for 6 minutes; turn the squash over and rotate the plate one-quarter turn.
2. Microwave on HIGH for 6 to 8 minutes more, or until the entire squash has turned a darker beige and is slightly blistered all over. Let stand for 5 minutes.
3. In a 3-quart microwave-safe casserole, combine the onion, garlic, celery, apple, and olive oil. Cover tightly with a lid or with plastic wrap turned back slightly; microwave on HIGH for 5 to 6 minutes, or until the apple and vegetables are tender.
4. Meanwhile, cut the squash in half and remove the seeds and connective fiber with a spoon. (Remove the seeds from the fiber and set them aside for toasting, if desired.)
5. Pour the broth into 4-cup glass measure and microwave on HIGH for 5 minutes.
6. Meanwhile, spoon the flesh from the squash and place it in a food processor, along with the cooked apple and vegetables. Process into a smooth puree.
7. Add the cheese, sugar, cinnamon, ginger, and pepper to the puree. Process quickly to blend.
8. Return to the casserole and stir in the warmed chicken broth. Cover again and cook on HIGH for 8 to 10 minutes, or until heated through. Let stand, covered, for 3 to 5 minutes. Serve with toasted seeds or nuts, if desired.

VARIATION APPLE-SQUASH SOUP WITH TURKEY OR CHICKEN (8 grams fat per serving): Add 2 cups cooked and thinly sliced turkey or chicken when returning the apple-vegetable puree to the casserole. Omit the cheese.

Meatball Soups

Marcia and her husband, Koji, were so fond of Oriental Meatball-Noodle Soup that we decided to try varying it a little and ended up expanding it into a quartet of soups, including Mexican, Italian, and German versions. The basic recipe is the same, with a few ingredient changes to obtain the desired flavors.

By using nonfat ground round and only the white of the egg, they all become low-cholesterol. If cholesterol count isn't something that concerns you, the meatballs may be made with a whole egg, except in the Oriental variation, where it is traditional to use only the white to produce a lighter meatball.

We like to grind our own beef by purchasing round steak and trimming all the fat, then cutting it into 2-inch cubes and processing the cubes in a food processor. We then add the remaining meatball ingredients and pulse two or three times. This method streamlines the whole meatball preparation.

Oriental Meatball-Noodle Soup

MAKES: *4 main-course servings, 8 first-course servings*
COOKING TIME: *18 to 20 minutes*

Low cholesterol

17 grams fat per main-course serving

SERVING SUGGESTIONS: Garnish with lemon slices and chopped fresh cilantro.

6 cups chicken or beef broth, fat skimmed

MEATBALLS

¾ pound lean ground beef
1 egg white
1 tablespoon low-sodium soy sauce
1 tablespoon chopped green onion
2 tablespoons cornstarch
2 tablespoons fine bread crumbs
1 tablespoon fresh cilantro
1 teaspoon freshly ground black pepper

10 ounces soba, ramen, or vermicelli (see Note)
1 teaspoon sesame oil
¼ cup chopped green onion
1 garlic clove, minced
1 package (10 ounces) frozen chopped spinach
1 teaspoon chopped fresh ginger
2 tablespoons low-sodium soy sauce

1. Pour the broth into a 2-quart microwave-safe measure or bowl. Microwave on HIGH for 6 to 8 minutes.
2. Meanwhile, combine all the meatball ingredients in the bowl of a food processor or mix in the 3-quart

microwave-safe casserole that will be used for cooking the soup. Form sixteen 1½-inch meatballs.

3. Place the meatballs around the outer rim of a 10-inch microwave-safe pie plate or a 2-quart rectangular microwave-safe dish. Cover with waxed paper. Remove the warm broth from the microwave oven. Microwave the meatballs on HIGH for 6 to 8 minutes, or until done, turning them over and rotating the dish one-quarter turn after 3 minutes.

4. While cooking the meatballs, bring a large pot of water to a boil on top of the range. Cook the noodles following package instructions. Drain.

5. When the meatballs are cooked, place the sesame oil, green onion, and garlic in the 3-quart microwave-safe casserole. Microwave on HIGH for 1 minute.

6. Add the frozen spinach and cover tightly with a lid or with plastic wrap turned back slightly. Microwave on HIGH for 4 minutes. With a spoon, break apart the spinach.

7. Add the ginger, soy sauce, meatballs, and warmed broth. Cover again and microwave on HIGH for 6 to 8 minutes, or until heated through.

8. To serve: Divide drained noodles between four large soup bowls. Arrange four meatballs in each bowl and spoon the spinach and broth into bowls.

NOTE   *Soba* noodles, the favorite noodles of Japan, are made of buckwheat flour, wheat flour, and water. *Ramen* are crinkly-style Chinese noodles. Both may be purchased in Oriental grocery stores, health-food stores, and some supermarkets.

VARIATION   ORIENTAL MEATBALL-NOODLE SOUP WITH BOK CHOY: Substitute 1 pound bok choy, washed and thinly sliced, for spinach.

Mexican Meatball-Noodle Soup

6 cups chicken or beef broth, fat skimmed

MEATBALLS

¾ pound lean ground beef
1 egg white
1 teaspoon ground cumin
1 tablespoon chopped green onion

MAKES: *4 main-course servings, 8 first-course servings*
COOKING TIME: *18 to 20 minutes*

Low cholesterol

17 grams fat per main-course serving

SERVING SUGGESTIONS: Garnish with chopped fresh cilantro. Serve with Warm Flour Tortillas (page 67) and Salsa Cruda (page 317), if desired.

2 tablespoons fine dry bread crumbs
1 tablespoon chopped fresh mint or 1 teaspoon dried
¼ teaspoon freshly ground black pepper

10 ounces vermicelli
1 teaspoon olive oil
¼ cup chopped green onion
1 garlic clove, minced
1 package (10 ounces) frozen chopped spinach
1 teaspoon chopped jalapeño pepper

1. Pour the broth into a 2-quart glass measure or microwave-safe bowl. Microwave on HIGH for 6 to 8 minutes.
2. Meanwhile, combine all the meatball ingredients in the bowl of a food processor or in the 3-quart microwave-safe casserole that will be used for cooking the soup. Form sixteen 1½-inch meatballs.
3. Place the meatballs around the outer rim of a 10-inch microwave-safe pie plate or 2-quart rectangular microwave-safe dish. Cover with waxed paper. Remove the warm broth from the microwave oven. Microwave the meatballs on HIGH for 6 to 8 minutes, turning them over and rotating the dish one-quarter turn after 3 minutes.
4. While cooking the meatballs, bring a large pot of water to a boil on top of the range. Cook the noodles following the package instructions. Drain.
5. When the meatballs are cooked, place the oil, green onion, and garlic in the 3-quart microwave-safe casserole. Microwave on HIGH for 1 minute.
6. Add the frozen spinach; cover tightly with a lid or with plastic wrap turned back slightly. Cook on HIGH for 4 minutes. With a spoon, break apart the spinach.
7. Add the green pepper, meatballs, and warmed broth. Cover again and microwave on HIGH for 6 to 8 minutes, or until heated through.
8. To serve: Divide the drained noodles between four large soup bowls. Arrange four meatballs in each bowl and spoon the spinach and broth into the bowls.

Italian Meatball-Noodle Soup

MAKES: *4 main-course servings, 8 first-course servings*
COOKING TIME: *18 to 20 minutes*

Low cholesterol

17 grams fat per main-course serving

SERVING SUGGESTIONS:
Garnish with extra Parmesan and serve with Focaccia (page 49) or a crusty purchased Italian bread.

6 cups chicken or beef broth, fat skimmed
1 can (8 ounces) tomato sauce

MEATBALLS

¾ pound lean ground beef
1 egg white
1 tablespoon grated Parmesan
1 tablespoon chopped green onion
2 tablespoons fine dry bread crumbs
1 tablespoon chopped fresh parsley or 2 teaspoons dried
¼ teaspoon freshly ground black pepper

10 ounces vermicelli
1 teaspoon olive oil
¼ cup chopped green onion
2 garlic cloves, minced
1 package (10 ounces) frozen chopped spinach

1. Pour the broth and tomato sauce into a 2-quart microwave-safe measure or bowl. Microwave on HIGH for 6 to 8 minutes.
2. Meanwhile, combine all the meatball ingredients in the bowl of a food processor or the 3-quart microwave-safe casserole in which you will cook the soup. Form sixteen 1½-inch meatballs.
3. Place the meatballs around the outer rim of a 10-inch microwave-safe pie plate or 2-quart microwave-safe rectangular dish. Cover with waxed paper. Remove the warm broth mixture from the microwave oven. Microwave the meatballs on HIGH for 6 to 8 minutes, turning them over and rotating the dish one-quarter turn after 3 minutes.
4. Meanwhile, bring a large pot of water to boil on top of the range. Cook the noodles following the package instructions. Drain.
5. When the meatballs are cooked, place the oil, green onion, and garlic in the 3-quart microwave-safe casserole. Microwave on HIGH for 1 minute.
6. Add the frozen spinach. Cover tightly with a lid or with plastic wrap turned back slightly. Microwave on HIGH for 4 minutes. With a spoon, break apart the spinach.
7. Add the meatballs and warm broth. Cover and microwave on HIGH for 6 to 8 minutes until heated through.

8. To serve: Divide the drained noodles between four large soup bowls. Arrange four meatballs in each bowl and spoon the spinach and broth into the bowls.

German Meatball- Noodle Soup

MAKES: *4 main-course servings, or 8 first-course servings*
COOKING TIME: *18 to 20 minutes*

Low cholesterol

17 grams fat per main-course serving

SERVING SUGGESTIONS: Serve garnished with lemon slices and chunks of Onion-Caraway Beer Bread (page 63) or purchased pumpernickel bread.

6 cups chicken or beef broth, fat skimmed

MEATBALLS

¾ pound lean ground beef
1 egg white
¼ teaspoon ground nutmeg
1 tablespoon chopped green onion
2 tablespoons fine dry bread crumbs
2 tablespoons chopped fresh parsley or 2 teaspoons dried
¼ teaspoon freshly ground black pepper

1 ounce vermicelli or Spätzle (page 113)
1 teaspoon olive or vegetable oil
1 medium onion, chopped
1 garlic clove, minced
1 package (10 ounces) frozen spinach
¼ cup chopped fresh parsley
2 tablespoons dry sherry
¼ teaspoon ground nutmeg

1. Pour the broth into a 2-quart glass measure or microwave-safe bowl. Microwave on HIGH for 6 to 8 minutes.
2. Meanwhile, combine all the meatball ingredients in the bowl of a food processor or the 3-quart microwave-safe casserole that will be used for cooking the soup. Form sixteen 1½-inch meatballs.
3. Place the meatballs around the outer rim of a 10-inch pie plate or 2-quart rectangular microwave-safe dish. Cover with waxed paper. Remove the warm broth from the microwave oven. Microwave the meatballs on HIGH for 6 to 8 minutes, turning them over and rotating the dish one-quarter turn after 3 minutes.
4. Meanwhile, bring a large pot of water to boil on top of the range. Cook the noodles following package instructions. Drain.
5. When the meatballs are cooked, place the oil, onion, and garlic in the 3-quart microwave-safe casserole.

Microwave on HIGH for 1 minute.

6. Add the frozen spinach. Cover tightly with a lid or with plastic wrap turned back slightly. Microwave on HIGH for 4 minutes. With a spoon, break apart the spinach.

7. Add the parsley, sherry, nutmeg, meatballs, and warmed broth. Cover again and microwave on HIGH for 6 to 8 minutes, or until heated through.

8. To serve: Divide the drained noodles between four large soup bowls. Arrange four meatballs in each bowl and spoon the spinach and broth into the bowls.

Italian Broccoli Soup

MAKES: *4 servings*
COOKING TIME: *20 minutes*

Low cholesterol

6 grams fat per serving

SERVING SUGGESTION:
Serve with Bruschetta (page 66).

This earthy soup is redolent with garlic and hot-pepper flakes.

3 cups vegetable broth or low-sodium chicken broth
1 head broccoli (1½ pounds), tough ends trimmed, stalks and florets cut into 3-inch pieces
3 garlic cloves, minced
1 tablespoon olive oil
¼ cup chopped fresh parsley
½ teaspoon salt
¼ teaspoon red-pepper flakes

1. Pour the broth into a 4-cup glass measure. Microwave on HIGH for 5 minutes. Meanwhile, prepare the broccoli and garlic.

2. In a 3-quart microwave-safe casserole, combine the garlic, broccoli, and olive oil, placing the stalk pieces around the outer rim of the casserole. Cover tightly with a lid or with plastic wrap turned back slightly. Microwave on HIGH for 8 to 10 minutes, or until the broccoli is tender.

3. Spoon the mixture into the bowl of a food processor and pulse on and off until chopped very fine.

4. Return to the casserole. Add the parsley, salt, and pepper flakes. Cover again and heat on HIGH for 5 to 8 minutes, or until heated through.

Basic Rice for Soup

¾ cup long-grain rice

1. Combine rice and 1¼ cups water in a 2-quart microwave-safe casserole. Cover tightly with a lid or with plastic wrap turned back slightly. Microwave on HIGH for 3 to 5 minutes, or until boiling; microwave on

MEDIUM for 7 to 10 minutes, or until most of the water is absorbed.
2. Remove from oven. Stir and let stand for 3 minutes.

Use this recipe when you need to prepare a small amount of cooked rice.

MAKES: *4 cups*
COOKING TIME: *10 to 15 minutes*

Low cholesterol

0.2 gram fat per ½ cup

Mexican Chicken, Avocado, and Rice Soup

MAKES: *4 servings*
COOKING TIME: *17 minutes for soup; 15 minutes for rice*

Low cholesterol

15 grams fat per serving

SERVING SUGGESTIONS:
Serve with warm Flour Tortillas (page 67) or purchased crisp corn tortillas and Salsa Cruda (page 317).

The number of jalapeño peppers added will depend on your "heat" tolerance. Remember—the white membranes holding the seeds are the hottest part.

1 recipe Basic Rice for Soup (page 94)
1 teaspoon olive oil
1 medium onion, chopped
1 garlic clove, minced
1 pound skinless, boneless chicken breast, cut into
    ½-inch cubes
6 cups chicken broth, fat skimmed
2 tablespoons sherry
1 or 2 thinly sliced jalapeño peppers
1 ripe avocado, cut into ½-inch cubes
8 red radishes, thinly sliced
¼ cup chopped fresh cilantro (optional)
Thin lime slices (optional)

1. Cook the rice while cutting and chopping the ingredients for the soup.
2. In a 3-quart microwave-safe casserole, combine the oil, onion, and garlic. Microwave on HIGH for 1 minute.
3. Place the chicken cubes in a single layer on the bottom of the casserole. Cover tightly with a lid or with plastic wrap turned back slightly. Microwave on HIGH for 6 to 8 minutes, until cooked through; stir after 3 minutes to move the lesser-cooked cubes to the outside.
4. Add the broth, sherry, and pepper. Cover and cook on HIGH for 8 to 10 minutes, or until heated through.
5. To serve: Divide the cooked rice between four large bowls. Divide chicken with broth, avocado, and radishes between the bowls. Garnish with cilantro and lime slices, if desired.

VARIATIONS

MEXICAN CHICKEN, CORN, AND RICE SOUP (8 grams fat per serving): Add 1 package (10 ounces) frozen corn to soup when adding stock. Eliminate the avocado.

MEXICAN TURKEY, AVOCADO, AND RICE SOUP (15 grams fat per serving): Substitute boneless turkey breasts for chicken breasts.

Oriental Chicken, Rice, and Bok Choy Soup

MAKES: *4 servings*
COOKING TIME: *17 minutes for soup; 15 minutes for rice*

Low cholesterol

6.2 grams fat per serving

SERVING SUGGESTION:
When time is of the essence, you may wish to cook the rice on top of the range while the soup is simmering in the microwave oven.

When we don't have bok choy, we substitute frozen chopped spinach.

1 recipe Basic Rice for Soup (page 94)
1 teaspoon sesame oil
¼ cup thinly sliced green onion
1 garlic clove, minced
1 teaspoon chopped fresh ginger
2 whole chicken breasts, cut into ¼-inch slices
1 pound bok choy, thinly sliced
6 cups chicken broth, fat skimmed
2 tablespoons low-sodium soy sauce
2 tablespoons sherry

1. Cook the rice in the microwave oven while cutting up the ingredients for the soup.
2. In a 3-quart microwave-safe casserole, combine the oil, green onion, garlic, and ginger. Microwave on HIGH for 45 seconds.
3. Add the chicken slices in a single layer and cover tightly with a lid or with plastic wrap turned back slightly. Microwave on HIGH for 6 to 8 minutes, or until cooked through, stirring after 3 minutes and moving the lesser-cooked pieces to the outside.
4. Add the bok choy. Cover again and cook on HIGH for 3 minutes.
5. Add the remaining ingredients. Cover again and cook on HIGH for 8 to 10 minutes, or until heated through. To serve: Divide the rice between the serving bowls and spoon the soup over it.

Seafood and Smoked-Sausage Gumbo

MAKES: *8 main-course servings*
COOKING TIME: *55 minutes*

Low-cholesterol variation

14 grams fat per serving

1 recipe Basic Rice for Soup (page 94)
3 tablespoons vegetable oil or olive oil
¼ cup flour
1 large onion, finely chopped
2 celery ribs, chopped
2 green bell peppers, chopped
½ teaspoon garlic powder
1 teaspoon freshly ground black pepper
1 teaspoon cayenne
½ teaspoon dried thyme leaves
1 package (10 ounces) sliced frozen okra or 2 cups fresh okra, cut into ¼-inch slices
1 can (14½ ounces) stewed tomatoes with juice
3 cups clam juice
1 bay leaf

Serve with Oven-Baked Corn Bread (page 61) or Chili Beer Bread (page 64).

Gumbo is a flavorful and spicy Cajun soup. It is thickened with okra or a roux or both. It seems that every cook has his or her own special favorite ingredients and cooking methods.

This is our microwave version, made with a roux but trimmed of half the fat. You'll make it in half the time with half the pots, too. When we make this thick and luscious dish, we like to prepare enough for two meals. We either serve it again a few evenings later (it keeps, refrigerated, for 1 week), or freeze it to defrost on a busy day.

¾ pound smoked sausage (andouille or kielbasa), cut into ¼-inch slices
¾ pound small- to medium-size shrimp, peeled

1. Cook the rice while you chop the vegetables for the gumbo. (The rice will stay warm for 1 hour.)
2. Pour the oil into the corner of a 3-quart microwave-safe casserole. Holding the casserole at an angle, whisk the flour into the oil until smooth. Microwave, uncovered, on HIGH for 6 to 8 minutes, stirring every 2 minutes, until bubbling and slightly brown.
3. Add the onion, celery, green pepper, garlic powder, black pepper, cayenne, and thyme. Cover tightly with a lid or with plastic wrap turned back slightly. Microwave on HIGH for 3 to 4 minutes, or until the vegetables are softened; stir well.
4. Add the okra. Cover again and cook on HIGH for 3 to 5 minutes, or until you can break up the frozen okra pieces.
5. Add the tomatoes, clam juice, and bay leaf. Cover again and cook on HIGH for 10 minutes, or until boiling.
6. Stir in the sausage and shrimp. Cover again and cook on HIGH for 10 to 14 minutes, or until the shrimp are opaque and the gumbo is heated through, stirring after 5 minutes.
7. To serve: Place ¾ cup rice in the center of a large soup plate and spoon the gumbo around the rice. Repeat with remaining servings.

VARIATIONS LOW-CHOLESTEROL SEAFOOD AND SAUSAGE GUMBO (12 grams fat per serving): Substitute Turkey Sausage (page 180) that has been cut into ½-inch pieces for smoked sausage. Substitute scallops, or any thick fish fillet (cod, bass, tuna) that has been cut into 1-inch cubes, for shrimp.

CHICKEN AND SMOKED-SAUSAGE GUMBO (13 grams fat per serving): Substitute ¾ pound boneless chicken breast, cut into 1-inch cubes, or 1½ cups leftover cooked, cubed chicken or turkey for fish.

Portuguese Bean-and-Sausage Soup

MAKES: *4 servings*
COOKING TIME: *18 to 20 minutes*

12 grams fat per serving

SERVING SUGGESTIONS:
Serve with crusty Portuguese or Italian bread.

This colorful red, white, and green soup was a favorite of many Portuguese fishermen when they wanted a break from eating fish. It's chock-full of beans, potatoes, smoked sausage, and leafy kale.

1 tablespoon olive oil
1 garlic clove, minced
1 medium onion, coarsely chopped
½ pound thin-skinned potatoes, scrubbed but not peeled, cut into ½-inch cubes
½ pound smoked linguiça, chorizo, or kielbasa, cut into ¼-inch slices
1 bunch kale (1 pound; leaves only), washed and cut into ½-inch strips
1 can (16 ounces) red kidney beans, with juice
2 tablespoons red-wine vinegar
¼ teaspoon freshly ground black pepper

1. In a 3-quart microwave-safe casserole, combine the oil, garlic, and onion. Microwave on HIGH for 1 to 2 minutes, or until tender.
2. Add the potato, sausage, and 1 cup water. Cover tightly with a lid or with plastic wrap turned back slightly: microwave on HIGH for 6 to 8 minutes, or until the potatoes are almost tender.
3. Add the kale. Cover again and cook on HIGH for 3 minutes, or until slightly cooked down.
4. Add the remaining ingredients, stirring well to mix. Cover again and cook on HIGH for 8 to 10 minutes, or until heated thoroughly, stirring after 4 minutes.

Wonton Soup

MAKES: *4 servings*
COOKING TIME: *16 minutes*

Low cholesterol

15 grams fat per serving with turkey filling; 11.5 with turkey-and-cabbage filling

Kids help

At a very early age Marcia's children were good wonton stuffers and folders. Her daughter, at three years, had her own unique way of

TURKEY FILLING

¾ pound ground turkey
1 tablespoon low-sodium soy sauce
1 tablespoon sherry or sake
1 green onion, thinly sliced
1 egg white
½ teaspoon cornstarch

or

TURKEY-AND-CABBAGE FILLING

½ pound ground turkey
½ cup finely chopped cabbage
1 tablespoon low-sodium soy sauce
1 tablespoon sherry or sake
1 green onion, thinly sliced
½ teaspoon cornstarch
½ teaspoon minced fresh ginger

folding the square wontons or round gyozas and took pride in identifying her finished product. When her daughter and husband took over the task of filling and folding the wontons, Marcia's hands were free to finish the broth and make the other parts of the meal.

A large bowl with eight wontons makes a wonderful lunch or dinner. Finish with some fruit for dessert. As our personal tastes lean toward hot spices, we place a container of nanami togarashi (assorted Japanese chili peppers) or Chili Oil (page 305) on the table and add just a few drops to each bowl.

1 package (about ½ pound) 3- to 4½-inch wonton or gyoza skins (about 32)
4 cups chicken broth, fat skimmed
1 tablespoon low-sodium soy sauce
1 teaspoon sesame oil
1 green onion, thinly sliced

1. Combine either the turkey or turkey-and-cabbage filling ingredients in a medium mixing bowl.
2. Place a rounded teaspoon of filling in the center of a wonton square or *gyoza*. Fold the wontons in half and bring the corners together to form a triangle. Wet the outer edges with your fingers and overlap the corners; press and seal. Arrange in concentric circles on a large plate.
3. Meanwhile, make the broth: In a 3-quart microwave-safe casserole, combine the chicken broth, soy sauce, sesame oil, and green onion. Cover tightly with a lid or with plastic wrap turned back slightly. Microwave on HIGH for 8 to 12 minutes, until boiling. (It is important that the broth comes to a boil.)
4. Add the wontons to the hot broth. Cover again and cook on HIGH for 7 to 10 minutes, or until the wontons are cooked through, stirring once. Spoon into large soup bowls and enjoy.

VARIATION WONTON SOUP WITH SPINACH (11.5 grams fat per serving): Prepare filling and wontons as indicated. Place half of a 7-ounce package of frozen spinach in the 3-quart microwave-safe casserole that will be used to heat the broth. Cover with a lid or with plastic wrap turned back slightly on one side. Microwave on HIGH for 2 to 4 minutes; break up the spinach. Add the broth and remaining ingredients. Heat the broth as indicated in the main recipe and add wontons to cook.

Clam Chowders

Which is best—red (Manhattan) or white (New England) clam chowder? There seems to be no end to the discussion among Northeasterners. Those who answer "white" like the buttery, tongue-coating creaminess of a white chowder made with quahog clams. Those who say "red" think that the sweet, acidic tomatoes and extra vegetables are a wonderful foil for the clams and potatoes.

We'll let you be the judge, for here we provide both versions. Traditionally, both tend to be somewhat high in fat. We have eliminated the salt pork or cream (depending on the version) so that you can enjoy these chowders more often!

New England Clam Chowder

MAKES: *4 main-course servings*
COOKING TIME: *24 to 30 minutes*

Low cholesterol

4 grams fat per serving

SERVING SUGGESTIONS:
Serve this soup for supper with Oven-Baked Corn Bread (page 61) or soda or oyster crackers and a salad.

Evaporated skim milk gives this chowder its creamy consistency and flavor, without the fat. If you wish to enrich it at the end, swirl in a tablespoon or two of butter.

2 dozen medium-size cherrystone clams
1½ cups bottled clam juice (optional)
1 tablespoon vegetable oil
1 large onion, chopped
1 garlic clove, minced
2 tablespoons flour
1 large potato, peeled, or two smaller, thin-skinned potatoes, peels left on, cut into ½-inch cubes
1 can (12 ounces) evaporated skim or low-fat milk
½ teaspoon freshly ground black pepper
½ cup chopped fresh parsley (optional)

1. Scrub the clams well and arrange one dozen at a time around the outer rim of a 3-quart flat-bottomed microwave-safe casserole (with a 10-inch or larger base) or a 10-inch pie plate. Add ¼ cup water. Cover tightly with another pie plate or with plastic wrap turned back slightly. Microwave on HIGH for 6 to 8 minutes, or until the clams are opened, rotating the dish after 3 minutes. Discard any unopened clams.
2. If the clams don't all fit around the outer rim, place a few in the center; after 3 or 4 minutes, take any opened clams out of the dish and move the center clams to the outside. Reserve the cooking juices.
3. Repeat process with remaining clams. Remove the clams and let them stand until cool enough to handle. Strain the cooking liquid through a fine mesh strainer after each cooking; there should be about 1½ cups all together; if not, add water or bottled clam juice to make that amount.
4. In a *deep* 3-quart microwave-safe casserole, combine the oil, onion, and garlic. Cook on HIGH for 3 minutes, or until tender.
5. Stir in the flour until smooth. Add the potato and the reserved clam broth; stir until smooth. Cover tightly with a lid or with plastic wrap turned back slightly. Microwave on HIGH for 7 to 9 minutes, or

until the potato is tender and the liquid has thickened, stirring after 4 minutes.

6. Meanwhile, remove the clams from their shells. Place them in the food processor and chop coarsely.

7. Add the chopped clams, milk, and pepper to the casserole; stir well. Cover again and cook on HIGH for 5 to 6 minutes, or until heated through, stirring once. Do not boil. Serve in bowls, sprinkled with parsley, if desired.

VARIATION   NEW ENGLAND CLAM-AND-CORN CHOWDER (4.4 grams fat per serving): Add 1 package (10 ounces) frozen corn when adding clams. Microwave on HIGH for 6 to 8 minutes.

Manhattan Clam Chowder

MAKES: *6 to 8 servings*
COOKING TIME: *40 minutes*

Low-cholesterol variation

1.2 grams fat per serving for 6; 0.9 gram fat per serving for 8

SERVING SUGGESTIONS:
Great with warm Herbed Beer Bread (page 64) or Oven-Baked Corn Bread (page 61). If serving for company, make the chowder in advance and offer crudités and cheese while it is reheating. Serve an ice-cream pie (pages 283–86) for dessert.

This soup benefits from being made early in the morning or the night before we plan to serve it.

12 quahog or chowder clams, washed well, or 2½ cups canned minced clams
2 slices bacon
2 cups potatoes, scrubbed but not peeled, cut into ½-inch cubes
1 cup carrots, thinly sliced
1 cup celery, chopped
1 medium onion, chopped
1 small green bell pepper, chopped
1 garlic clove, minced
1 can (16 ounces) crushed tomatoes
1 bay leaf
2 teaspoons fresh thyme leaves or ½ teaspoon dried
¼ teaspoon freshly ground black pepper

1. Pour 2 cups water into a medium-size pot and add the clams. Cover and bring to a boil on top of the range. Reduce heat and simmer until all the shells are open, about 15 minutes. Discard any unopened clams.

2. Meanwhile, cut the bacon into ½-inch pieces and place in a 4-quart microwave-safe casserole with a lid. Cover and microwave on HIGH for 1½ minutes.

3. Add the potato, carrot, celery, onion, green pepper, and garlic. Cover tightly with a lid or with plastic wrap turned back slightly. Microwave on HIGH for 10 minutes, or until the vegetables are tender, stirring after 5 minutes.

4. When the clams have opened, strain them and

Thelma has been making
this clam chowder for
twenty-seven years with
freshly dug clams. It used to
take her several hours to
make, but now, with
microwave oven and food
processor humming away, this
displaced New Englander
makes a New York version of
clam chowder in about an
hour.

reserve the broth. You should have 5 cups; if not, add water to make that amount.

5. Add the broth to the vegetables, along with the tomatoes, bay leaf, thyme, and black pepper. Cover again and cook on HIGH for 10 minutes.

6. Meanwhile, remove the clams from their shells, place them in the food processor, and chop coarsely. Add them to the soup and cook on HIGH for 10 minutes more, or until heated through. Let stand 5 minutes before serving.

VARIATION

LOW-CHOLESTEROL MANHATTAN CLAM CHOWDER (2.2 grams fat per serving for 6; 1.7 grams fat per serving for 8): Eliminate the bacon and cook the vegetables with 1 tablespoon olive or canola oil.

Fisherman's Catch

MAKES: 4 servings
COOKING TIME: 15 to 20 minutes

Low cholesterol

6.3 grams fat per serving

SERVING SUGGESTIONS:
Serve with lots of crusty bread, or make Herbed Beer Bread (page 64) for dunking into the delicious broth. Round out the meal with a green salad. If you have any left over, serve it the next day, with a dollop of Olivada (page 314) in each bowl . . . it's delicious!

2 tablespoons olive oil
1 garlic clove, minced
1 small onion, chopped
1 medium carrot, peeled and cut into ¼-inch slices
½ pound red-skinned potatoes, scrubbed and cut into
    ½-inch cubes
1 can (14½ ounces) stewed tomatoes with juice
1 bottle (8 ounces) clam juice or 1 cup water
Juice from 1 lemon
2 tablespoons chopped fresh basil or 1 teaspoon dried
½ teaspoon dried thyme leaves
2 tablespoons chopped fresh parsley
⅛ teaspoon red-pepper flakes (optional)
1 pound thick fish fillets (sea trout, tile fish), with
    skin on, cut into 1½-inch chunks

1. In a 3-quart microwave-safe casserole, combine the oil, garlic, onion, carrot, and potato. Cover tightly with a lid or with plastic wrap turned back slightly. Microwave on HIGH for 6 to 8 minutes, or until the vegetables are tender, stirring once.

2. With kitchen shears, cut the tomatoes into quarters and add to the casserole.

3. Add the remaining ingredients, except the fish. Cover again and cook on HIGH for 5 to 7 minutes, or until boiling.

4. Add the fish pieces. Cover again and cook on HIGH

The flavors of this stew are so wonderful, your guests will think you slaved over a hot stove for hours. The red-pepper flakes give a nice kick, but if you don't care for spicy food, you can eliminate them.

for 3 to 5 minutes, or until the fish has cooked through. Divide between four bowls.

To Double the Recipe: Double all the ingredients except the oil. Choose 1 pound thick fish fillets and ½ pound *each* scallops and peeled shrimp. In a 4-quart microwave-safe casserole, combine 1 tablespoon oil, the garlic, onion, carrot, and potato. Cover and microwave on HIGH for 10 to 12 minutes or until tender. Add the remaining ingredients, except the fish; cover and microwave on HIGH for 10 to 12 minutes, or until boiling. Add the fish and microwave on HIGH for 5 to 7 minutes, or until boiling. Divide between eight bowls. Serve each bowl with two Large Garlic-Thyme Croutons (page 311).

Bourride (French Fish Soup)

MAKES: *4 servings*
COOKING TIME: *18 minutes, including Aïoli*

Low cholesterol

11.5 grams fat per serving without aïoli; 25 grams fat with aïoli

SERVING SUGGESTIONS:
Serve with a green salad and crusty French bread. A glass of Côtes du Rhône would complement this meal nicely.

When we make this soup, we try to include two or three varieties of fish, although it is traditionally made with a larger assortment. The

1 cup Aïoli (recipe follows)
3 cups White Fish Stock (page 105) or 2 cups bottled clam juice plus 1 cup dry white wine
1 tablespoon fresh lemon juice
⅛ teaspoon dried thyme
⅛ teaspoon fennel seeds, crushed
1 pound assorted lean firm-fleshed fish (choose two or three varieties), such as cod, monkfish, haddock, halibut, or sea bass
8 ½-inch-thick slices French bread, toasted
¼ cup chopped fresh parsley

1. Begin preparing the Aïoli by cooking the potato in the microwave oven.
2. Meanwhile, combine all the remaining ingredients, except the fish and bread, in a 3-quart microwave-safe casserole. Cover tightly with a lid or with plastic wrap turned back slightly on one side. Microwave on HIGH for 6 to 10 minutes, or until boiling.
3. Slide the fish into the hot broth and cook on HIGH for 6 to 10 minutes, or until the fish flakes. (Be careful not to overcook the fish.)
4. While the fish is cooking, finish preparing the Aïoli.
5. Place two slices of toasted French bread into each of four large soup bowls. With a slotted spoon, remove the fish from the broth and divide the pieces between the bowls, placing them on top of the toast.

important thing is to serve Bourride with aïoli so that the soup takes on its characteristic creaminess and garlic flavor.

6. Whisk the Aïoli into the broth and divide the broth between the soup bowls. Sprinkle with parsley.

Aïoli

MAKES: *1 cup*
COOKING TIME: *3 to 4 minutes*

Low cholesterol

13.6 grams fat per tablespoon

Aïoli is a luscious, creamy, yellow substance stirred into fish and vegetable soups to thicken and enrich them. In southern France it is made with uncooked eggs, garlic, lemon, and oil. We have developed this version without the raw eggs (since everyone is afraid of serving them nowadays) and with potato. Although it won't be as smooth as the traditional version, we think you'll find it more than acceptable.

1 medium baking potato
3 garlic cloves, peeled
1 tablespoon fresh lemon juice
¼ teaspoon salt
¾ cup olive oil

1. Pierce the potato with fork once on the top and once on the bottom. Place on a paper towel in the microwave oven. Microwave on HIGH for 3 to 4 minutes, or until tender. Let stand for 5 minutes. Peel.
2. Meanwhile, with the motor of your food processor running, add 1 garlic clove at a time through the feeding tube. Scrape down any garlic that has stuck to the sides of the bowl with a rubber spatula.
3. Cut the peeled potato in quarters and place in the processor; puree until smooth, but do not overprocess or the potato will get gummy.
4. Add the lemon juice and salt; process to blend. Add the oil very slowly while the processor is running and process just until a medium-thick puree forms.

Turkey Soup

MAKES: *8 servings*
COOKING TIME: *60 to 80 minutes*

1.3 grams fat per serving

Low cholesterol

1 cooked turkey carcass from a 12-pound bird, broken up
Turkey innards, except the liver, if not used in gravy
Refrigerated cooking juices, fat removed
1 large onion, sliced (about 1 cup)
2 garlic cloves, smashed
1 cup celery tops with leaves, thinly sliced
1 large or 2 medium carrots, cut into ¼-inch slices (about ½ cup)
¼ cup chopped fresh parsley with stems
½ teaspoon dried thyme
½ teaspoon freshly ground black pepper

Serve with Refrigerated
Shredded-Wheat Bread (page
41) or Shredded-Wheat Beer
Bread (page 42).

*Turkey Soup is the kind of
recipe that rarely appears in
cookbooks because it is such a
"home" type of dish—the
kind you usually learned to
make from watching Mom or
Grandma and the kind that is
never written down.*

*Well, now we've committed
ours to writing.*

1 teaspoon salt
1 bay leaf, crushed

1. Place all the ingredients in a 4-quart microwave-safe
casserole. Cover tightly with a lid or with plastic wrap
turned back slightly. Microwave on HIGH for 20 minutes; then microwave on MEDIUM for 40 to 60 minutes,
until meat falls off the turkey and a flavorful broth has
developed.
2. With a slotted spoon, remove the turkey bones and
meat from the cooking dish. When cool enough to
handle, remove the meat from the bones. Cut into
bite-sized pieces and return to soup.

NOTE You'll probably end up with leftovers. Freeze half, if
desired, or use 2 cups of strained broth for Deep-Dish
Turkey Pot Pie (page 178).

VARIATION TURKEY-VEGETABLE SOUP (1.6 grams fat per serving):
For every 4 cups of soup, add 1 package (10 ounces)
frozen corn, peas, carrots, or mixed vegetables or 2 cups
fresh-cooked vegetables and 8 ounces cooked noodles or
rice.

White Fish Stock

MAKES: *3 cups*
COOKING TIME: *25 minutes*

0.5 gram fat per cup

SERVING SUGGESTIONS:
Use in Bourride (page 103) or
Fisherman's Catch (page 102)
in place of clam juice.

*We have limited our stock
recipes to this simple fish
stock and the turkey stock
because they are two of the*

1 pound fish bones and trimmings (no gills), from
    any white fish (such as flounder, sole, or whiting),
    chopped up
1 large onion, coarsely chopped
6 sprigs fresh parsley
2 tablespoons fresh lemon juice
½ teaspoon salt
¼ teaspoon freshly ground black pepper
1 cup dry white wine

1. In a 3-quart microwave-safe casserole, combine the
fish bones, onion, parsley, lemon juice, salt, and pepper.
Cover tightly with a lid or with plastic wrap turned
back slightly. Microwave on HIGH for 5 minutes.
2. Add 2 cups of water and the wine. Cover again and
cook on HIGH for 20 minutes. Let stand for 5 minutes.
Strain through a fine mesh strainer.

NOTE: This stock freezes well. To defrost: Remove cover;

more difficult stocks to find ready-made. If you're going to make beef or chicken stock, simmer them in large quantities on the stovetop.

microwave on HIGH for 3 minutes. Transfer to a 2-quart microwave-safe dish. Microwave on HIGH for 10 to 15 minutes, until defrosted, stirring a few times.

Turkey Stock and Poached Turkey Breast

MAKES: *6 cups stock, plus 3 additional turkey meals*
COOKING TIME: *1 hour*

1.3 grams fat per cup stock

SERVING SUGGESTIONS:
Slice off the turkey for lunch sandwiches, turkey salads (pages 178, 179), Turkey-Bean Burritos (page 182), and Turkey-Noodle Soup (page 106).

This recipe requires little effort, produces a tasty broth, and leaves you with several meal options later in the week.

1 tablespoon olive oil
1 garlic clove, crushed
1 large onion, chopped
1 medium leek, coarsely chopped
2 celery ribs, with greens, sliced
2 carrots, sliced
½ cup chopped fresh parsley with stems
1 turkey breast (6 pounds)
2 bay leaves
1 teaspoon dried thyme
1 teaspoon salt
½ teaspoon freshly ground black pepper
2 whole cloves

1. Combine the oil, garlic, onion, leek, celery, carrot, and parsley in a 4-quart microwave-safe casserole. Cover tightly with a lid or with plastic wrap turned back slightly. Microwave on HIGH for 5 minutes.
2. Place the turkey breast, skin side down, in the casserole.
3. Add 5 cups water and the remaining ingredients. Cover again and microwave on HIGH for 55 minutes, turning the turkey breast over after 30 minutes.
4. Let stand 10 minutes. Strain the stock and refrigerate (see Note) or freeze for later use. Wrap the cooked breast and use in other recipes during the week.

NOTE When you refrigerate the stock, the fat will rise to the top and can be easily removed.

Turkey-Noodle Soup

10 ounces vermicelli
6 cups Turkey Stock (page 104), fat skimmed
2 cups cubed turkey breast
¼ cup thinly sliced green onion
2 tablespoons chopped fresh parsley
¼ teaspoon grated nutmeg

Salt and pepper to taste
Lemon slices

1. Bring 4 quarts of water to a boil on top of the stove and cook the noodles until just tender.
2. Meanwhile, put the remaining ingredients into a 3-quart microwave-safe casserole. Cover tightly with a lid or with plastic wrap turned back on one side to vent the steam. Microwave on HIGH for 10 to 12 minutes, or until heated through.
3. Taste and season with the salt and pepper, if desired. Divide the drained noodles between four large soup bowls and spoon the soup on top. Garnish with lemon slices.

VARIATION   TURKEY-RICE SOUP (4 grams fat per serving): Eliminate the noodles and cook 1 recipe Basic Rice for Soup (page 94) before preparing the soup.

Tomato-Beef Soup

MAKES: *4 servings (with meat left over for another meal)*
COOKING TIME: *50 to 60 minutes*

14.5 grams fat per serving

SERVING SUGGESTIONS:
This meal can be put together in a variety of ways. Our favorite is to serve the soup with slices of meat and a boiled potato in the broth. Later in the week we use the remainder of the cooked meat for a family favorite, Tamales in the Round (page 158).

4 whole cloves
1 bottom round steak (2 pounds), trimmed
1 can (14½ ounces) stewed tomatoes with juice
1 onion, chopped
1 garlic clove, minced
2 carrots, washed and cut into ¼-inch slices
1 celery rib, thinly sliced
¼ teaspoon freshly ground black pepper
¼ cup chopped fresh parsley
¼ teaspoon dried thyme
4 medium boiling potatoes, washed but not peeled
Horseradish

1. Stick the cloves into the meat.
2. Combine the meat, 2 cups water, and tomatoes in a 3-quart microwave-safe casserole. Cover tightly, with a lid or with plastic wrap turned back slightly on one side. Microwave on HIGH for 10 to 12 minutes.
3. Add the onion, garlic, carrot, and celery to the meat along with the pepper, parsley, and thyme. Microwave on HIGH for 10 to 12 minutes, or until boiling.
4. Turn the meat over. Cover again and microwave on MEDIUM for 25 to 40 minutes, or until the meat is tender. Let stand, covered, for 5 to 10 minutes.

5. Meanwhile, combine the potatoes with ¼ cup water in a 1-quart microwave-safe casserole. Cover tightly with a lid or with plastic wrap turned back slightly. Microwave on HIGH for 8 to 12 minutes, or until tender.

6. While potatoes are cooking, remove the beef from the casserole. Thinly slice half of the beef across the grain. Place one-quarter of the sliced beef in each soup bowl, along with a potato.

7. Spoon the vegetable broth over the meat and potatoes. If there is any extra broth, spoon it into the soup bowls later in the meal. (If there is any broth remaining at the end of the meal, pour it into a smaller bowl, along with the reserved beef, and refrigerate for later in the week.) Serve with horseradish on the side.

Because of the quantity of beef called for, this soup takes slightly longer to cook than most of our other soups, but since it requires little attention, you can make it on an evening when you want to relax a little before serving dinner.

If cholesterol is not a problem, you may wish to substitute a piece of brisket, which will be moister and fattier, for the leaner bottom round.

GRAINS
AND BEANS

Grains and beans are treasures often overlooked in the American diet. They should, however, be given serious consideration since they have no cholesterol and insignificant amounts of fat (except for soybeans and soybean products such as miso and tofu, which are quite high in fat), and beans actually contain cholesterol-lowering substances. They're inexpensive, too.

The exciting thing about cooking with beans and grains is that they not only burst with flavors and textures but are further enhanced when cooked with exotic spices and herbs. If you don't believe us, just try our North African Couscous, Indian Dal, or Vegetarian Chili.

The two problems with serving beans and grains are that they usually take more time to cook than meat, fish, or poultry—especially when the beans have to be soaked—and many people don't know how to combine grains and beans to form a complete protein. Here are some solutions to both problems:

When there is no time for soaking and precooking,

canned beans are a good choice. The taste and appearance will be comparable to those of cooked dry beans, and there will only be a slight difference in texture (cooked dry beans are firmer). Canned beans will also have a higher sodium content. Be sure to drain the beans and rinse them in cool water before using them if you're watching your sodium intake.

Making a Complete Protein: Proteins consist of amino acids that link in different combinations. The body requires twenty-two protein combinations for health maintenance; nine of these are considered "essential" because the body can't manufacture them, and they must be found in the diet.

Animal sources of protein (meat, fish, poultry, eggs, and dairy products) contain all of these nine essential proteins, but no plant source alone except quinoa (see page 122) does unless it is combined with another, *complementary,* plant or dairy source.

The four categories of proteins we'll discuss are:

GRAINS: Rice, bulghur, wheat, corn, oats, etc.

LEGUMES: Chick-peas, soybeans (and soy-bean derivatives, such as tofu and miso), and other dried beans, dried peas, lentils, peanuts, etc.

MILK: Cheese, yogurt, milk, etc.

SEEDS: Sesame seeds, sunflower seeds, etc.

The following pairs will complement each other, making the complete proteins that your body needs.

GRAINS + LEGUMES (Rice and red beans, tortillas and refried beans, rice and tofu, peanut-butter sandwich, vegetarian chili, whole-grain bread and lentil soup)

GRAINS + MILK (Grilled cheese sandwich, macaroni and cheese, risotto, cereal and milk)

GRAINS + SEEDS (Breads made with seeds, bread with a sesame-seed spread)

LEGUMES + MILK (Grated cheese on refried beans)

LEGUMES + SEEDS (Hummus: a mixture of chick-peas and sesame-seed paste)

Even if you don't want to serve strictly vegetarian

meals, it's a good idea to start making grains or legumes the focal point and meat the side dish. Or use a little meat to flavor the grains or legumes.

To Prepare the Whole Meal

- Combine the beans and grains in a single dish, such as Vegetarian Chili (page 111), where the beans are cooked with bulghur.
- If you plan to serve beans and grains together but they must be cooked separately, cook the grains on top of the stove while the beans cook in the microwave. On the other hand, if the beans are canned (and thus require little cooking time), the grains can be first cooked in the microwave and allowed to stand while the beans are then heated in the microwave. Rice, bulghur, and barley are good served in bean soups.
- Look in the Bread and Soup chapters to make your own vegetarian combinations, or cook some of the grains in this chapter and stir them into the bean soups.

Vegetarian Chili

MAKES: *8 servings*
COOKING TIME: *40 to 50 minutes*

No cholesterol

3 grams fat per serving

SERVING SUGGESTIONS:
Serve with Oven-Baked Corn Bread (page 61) or Quick Beer Bread (page 63). This makes a great party dish. Leftovers can be used in Deep-Dish Vegetarian Enchiladas (recipe follows).

1 tablespoon olive oil
3 garlic cloves, minced
2 large onions, coarsely chopped
3 green bell peppers, coarsely chopped, or 1 red, 1 green, and 1 yellow bell pepper, coarsely chopped
3 celery ribs, coarsely chopped
1 jalapeño pepper, finely chopped
3 cans (16 ounces each) stewed tomatoes
1 can (16 ounces) black beans, undrained
1 can (16 ounces) garbanzo beans, undrained
1 cup bulghur
3 tablespoons chili powder
1 tablespoon dried oregano
1 teaspoon ground cumin
½ teaspoon dried thyme leaves
½ teaspoon salt
¼ teaspoon freshly ground black pepper

1. In a 4-quart microwave-safe casserole, combine the oil, garlic, onion, green pepper, celery, and jalapeño pepper. Cover tightly with a lid or with plastic wrap turned back slightly. Microwave on HIGH for 6 to 8

This vegetarian chili is so easy and delicious that you may never make chili with meat again. Indeed, this fresh-tasting, inexpensive, and healthy dish has become one of our most asked-for recipes.

NOTE

Make it as colorful as possible by using red, yellow, and green peppers and a combination of beans.

minutes, or until the vegetables are tender-crisp, stirring once.

2. Stir in the remaining ingredients. Cover again and cook on HIGH for 10 to 15 minutes, or until boiling; stir. Cover again and cook on MEDIUM for 25 to 30 minutes, or until the bulghur is tender and the flavors are blended.

To reheat, add a little tomato juice or water to refrigerated chili. Cover with a lid or with plastic wrap turned back slightly on one side, and microwave on HIGH for 10 minutes; stir. Cover again and cook on HIGH for 5 to 10 minutes more.

To reheat a single serving, place it in a bowl and cover with waxed paper. Microwave on HIGH for 3 to 5 minutes, stirring once. If too dry, add a little water.

Deep-Dish Vegetarian Chili Enchiladas

MAKES: *4 servings*
COOKING TIME: *10 to 15 minutes*

22.4 grams fat per serving

4 cups Vegetarian Chili (page 111)
8 flour tortillas
1 can (10 ounces) mild, medium, or hot enchilada
    sauce
4 ounces cheddar, grated

1. Place the chili in a 2-quart microwave-safe casserole. Cover with a lid or with plastic wrap turned back slightly on one side. Microwave on HIGH for 5 to 8 minutes, stirring once, until heated through.

2. Spoon ½ cup warm chili into a tortilla and roll, jelly-roll style. Arrange, seam down, in a 2-quart rectangular microwave-safe dish. Follow the same procedure with the remaining tortillas.

3. Pour the enchilada sauce over the rolls and sprinkle with cheese. Cover with waxed paper and microwave on MEDIUM for 5 to 8 minutes, or until the cheese is melted.

Lentil Stew (Dal)

1 tablespoon olive or vegetable oil
1 tablespoon chopped fresh ginger
1 garlic clove, minced
1 cup dried lentils (no presoaking required)
3½ cups vegetable bouillon (made with vegetable
    bouillon cubes)

MAKES: *4 servings*
COOKING TIME: *42 to 50 minutes*

No cholesterol

4.2 grams fat per serving

SERVING SUGGESTIONS: Cook rice or Spätzle (pages 113, 118) on the conventional range while the lentils are cooking in the microwave oven. Marcia likes to serve this with Mint Raita (page 319), a cucumber-yogurt sauce, on the side, while Thelma prefers plain yogurt.

VARIATION

When Thelma was growing up, her family ate two or three meatless meals a week. One consisted of lentil puree and Spätzle—a Schwabian noodle dish—a combination that makes a complete protein. When Marcia was in India she became very fond of dal—a flavorful lentil puree—served with rice and a variety of Indian breads.

2 tablespoons tomato paste
¼ teaspoon ground turmeric
⅛ teaspoon cayenne
1 tablespoon fresh lemon juice
Cooked rice
Pita or other Indian breads

1. Combine the oil, ginger, and garlic in a 3-quart microwave-safe casserole. Microwave on HIGH for 1½ minutes.
2. Stir in the remaining ingredients, except for the lemon juice, rice, and breads. Cover with a lid or with plastic wrap turned back slightly; microwave on HIGH for 10 minutes. Cover again and cook on MEDIUM for 30 to 40 minutes, or until the liquid is absorbed and lentils are tender.
3. Stir in the lemon juice. Serve with rice and pita or other Indian breads.

LINSENPUREE (GERMAN LENTIL PUREE): Substitute 1 medium onion, chopped, and 1 celery rib, thinly sliced, for the garlic and ginger. Eliminate the turmeric; follow the recipe, but mash the lentil mixture after cooking it (but before adding the lemon juice).

Spätzle

MAKES: *4 servings*
COOKING TIME: *About 15 minutes*

3.7 grams fat per serving

Kids help

1 cup flour
½ teaspoon salt
⅛ teaspoon freshly grated nutmeg
1 egg
½ cup milk
1 teaspoon vegetable oil

1. Pour 8 cups of water into a 3- or 4-quart saucepan and bring to a boil on top of the stove.
2. Meanwhile, combine the flour, salt, and nutmeg in

This makes a meal for four when served with Lentil Puree (page 119) or added to German Meatball-Noodle Soup (page 93) in place of other noodles.

the bowl of a food processor. Pulse twice to mix the dry ingredients.

3. Add egg and milk and process until a soft dough forms.

4. Oil the inside of a colander. Using a rubber spatula, scrape the dough into it. Holding the colander over the boiling water, push the dough through the holes with a wooden spoon. Cook until the water comes to a boil again and the Spätzle rise to the surface, about 1 minute.

5. Remove with a slotted spoon and serve.

NOTE If the Spätzle are cooked before the rest of the meal is finished, place them in a bowl of warm water (to prevent them from sticking together) and drain before serving.

Mexican Refried Beans

MAKES: 2 main-dish servings or 4 side-dish servings
COOKING TIME: 5 to 6 minutes

7 grams fat per serving

SERVING SUGGESTIONS:
When served with rice, Polenta (page 120), or any other grain, this becomes a main dish.

Refried beans complement tamales, burritos, or tacos beautifully, but we were unhappy to discover how

1 tablespoon olive oil
2 garlic cloves, minced
1 can (15½ ounces) pinto beans
⅛ teaspoon freshly ground black pepper
2 ounces grated Monterey Jack cheese (use low-fat variety if you are watching cholesterol)

1. Place the oil and garlic in a 9-inch microwave-safe pie plate. Microwave on HIGH for 45 seconds.

2. Meanwhile, drain the beans, reserving ⅓ cup of the juices.

3. Add the beans and reserved juices to the pie plate. Mash the beans with a potato masher until they are all broken up. Add the pepper and mix well with the beans and garlic. Cover with waxed paper.

4. Microwave on HIGH for 3 minutes; stir well and smooth out the top to make it even.

5. Sprinkle with grated cheese. Microwave, uncovered, on MEDIUM for 2 to 3 minutes, or until the cheese is melted. Cut into four wedges and serve.

VARIATIONS REFRIED BLACK BEANS (7 grams fat per serving): Substitute black beans for pinto beans.

REFRIED BEAN BURRITO (9 grams fat per serving): To serve four people, double the ingredients and cook for

much lard they contained. We have cut out the lard but not the flavor.

twice as long. Spoon 2 tablespoons of the beans into a crisp taco shell or soft taco and top with some Salsa Cruda (page 317), sour cream or plain yogurt, chopped lettuce, and tomato. Repeat with remaining tacos.

Mexicali Beans

MAKES: *4 servings*
COOKING TIME: *7 to 9 minutes*

18 grams fat per serving

SERVING SUGGESTION:
To make a complete meal, serve with rice or grits.

The earthy flavors of the Southwest are featured in this tasty dish.

1 teaspoon olive oil
1 garlic clove, minced
1 small yellow onion, chopped
½ jalapeño pepper, seeded and finely chopped
1 can (14½ ounces) stewed tomatoes, drained
1 can (16 ounces) pinto, black, or red kidney beans
½ teaspoon dried oregano leaves
2 tablespoons chopped fresh cilantro
Freshly ground black pepper to taste
1 cup grated low-fat Monterey Jack cheese
1 small Spanish onion, chopped

1. In a ½-quart microwave-safe casserole, combine the oil, garlic, and yellow onion. Microwave on HIGH for 1 to 2 minutes, or until slightly softened.
2. Add the jalapeño pepper and drained tomatoes. Cover with waxed paper and microwave on HIGH for 3 minutes.
3. Stir in the beans, oregano, cilantro, and black pepper. Cover again and microwave on HIGH for 3 to 4 minutes, or until heated through, stirring once.
4. To serve, pass the grated cheese and chopped Spanish onion to be used as toppings.

Red Beans and Rice

MAKES: *4 servings*
COOKING TIME: *8 to 10 minutes*

No cholesterol

6 grams fat per serving

1 tablespoon olive or vegetable oil
1 celery rib, finely chopped
1 small onion, chopped
½ teaspoon Tabasco
½ teaspoon dried thyme
¼ teaspoon garlic powder
½ teaspoon freshly ground black pepper
2 cans (16 ounces each) red kidney beans or small red beans
1 recipe Basic Long-Grain Rice (page 118) or Grits (page 120)
Creole Sauce (page 323) (optional)

When cooked with ham and sausage, this is a traditional New Orleans dish. We've left out the meat to make a vegetarian meal and added spices to keep the fat to a minimum.

1. In a 2-quart microwave-safe casserole, combine the oil, celery, and onion. Microwave on HIGH for 2 to 3 minutes, until tender-crisp.
2. Add the remaining ingredients except the rice and sauce; stir well. Cover with waxed paper. Microwave on HIGH for 5 to 8 minutes, or until heated through. Serve with rice or grits and Creole Sauce.

Rice Pilaf

MAKES: *4 to 6 side-dish servings*
COOKING TIME: *13 to 19 minutes*

Low cholesterol

2.8 grams fat per serving for 6; 4.2 grams fat per serving for 4

1 tablespoon canola or olive oil
1 medium onion, finely chopped
1 cup long-grain, converted, or basmati rice
1¾ cups chicken broth, fat skimmed
1 tablespoon chopped fresh parsley, or 1 teaspoon
   dried

1. Combine the oil and onion in a 3-quart microwave-safe casserole. Microwave on HIGH for 2 to 3 minutes, or until the onion is tender.
2. Stir in the rice, coating every grain. Stir in the broth. Cover tightly with a lid or with plastic wrap turned back slightly on one side. Microwave on HIGH for 4 to 6 minutes, or until the liquid is boiling.
3. Turn down the power and cook on MEDIUM for 7 to 10 minutes, or until most of the liquid has been absorbed and the rice is tender. Stir in the parsley. Cover again and let stand for 5 minutes.

Barley Pilaf

MAKES: *4 servings*
COOKING TIME: *14 to 20 minutes*

Low cholesterol

4.5 grams fat per serving

SERVING SUGGESTIONS:
Serve this in place of rice with grilled fish, chili, or stews.

1 tablespoon olive oil
1 onion, chopped
1 cup pearl barley
1¾ cups chicken broth, fat skimmed
1 tablespoon fresh lemon juice
¼ teaspoon freshly ground black pepper

1. Combine the oil and onion in a 3-quart microwave-safe casserole. Microwave, uncovered, on HIGH for 3 to 4 minutes, or until the onion is tender.
2. Stir in the barley, coating every grain. Add the broth, lemon juice, and pepper. Cover tightly with lid or with plastic wrap turned back slightly. Microwave on HIGH for 4 to 6 minutes, or until the liquid is

boiling; then microwave on MEDIUM for 7 to 10 minutes, or until most of the liquid has been absorbed and the barley is tender.

Cover again and let stand for 5 minutes.

VARIATION MUSHROOM-BARLEY PILAF: Combine ¼ pound sliced mushrooms with the oil and onion. Microwave, uncovered, on HIGH for 5 to 6 minutes or until the onion is tender. Proceed with the basic recipe.

CHOOSE THE RIGHT-SIZE DISH. When cooking foods that must come to a boil, use a dish twice the height of the ingredients to prevent the liquid from frothing over the top.

Millet

MAKES: *2 cups*
COOKING TIME: *20 to 22 minutes*

5.5 grams fat per ½ cup

SERVING SUGGESTIONS: Serve millet in mounds or packed into small custard dishes and unmolded into timbales.

Millet is an ancient grain that, unfortunately, is nowadays sold most often as birdseed. Millet for human beings has the hull removed

VARIATION

to make it digestible. It is higher in protein than rice and a good grain substitute for those who can't tolerate wheat.

1¾ *cups chicken broth (fat skimmed), clam juice diluted with water (1 8-ounce bottle plus ¾ cup water), or plain water*
2 *tablespoons olive oil*
4 *green onions, white parts only, finely chopped*
¾ *cup millet*

1. Pour the broth into a 2-cup glass measure. Microwave on HIGH for 3 minutes.
2. Combine the oil, green onion, and millet in a 3-quart microwave-safe casserole; microwave on HIGH for 3 minutes.
3. Stir in the broth. Cover tightly with a lid or with plastic wrap turned back slightly on one side. Microwave on HIGH for 8 minutes.
4. Turn down the power to MEDIUM and cook for 8 to 10 minutes, or until the liquid is absorbed and the millet is cracked and fluffy.
5. Uncover and stir well to let the excess steam escape.

MILLET WITH RADISHES AND GREEN ONIONS (5.5 grams fat per cup): Cook millet as directed above. Let cool. Before serving, toss cooked millet with 1 tablespoon lemon juice, chopped greens from 4 green onions, 1 cup thinly sliced radishes, ¼ cup chopped fresh parsley, and ¼ teaspoon freshly ground black pepper.

Bulghur Pilaf

MAKES: 4 to 6 servings
COOKING TIME: 13 to 19 minutes

Low cholesterol

4.3 grams fat per serving for 4; 2.8 grams fat per serving for 6

Bulghur is one of the main ingredients in our Vegetarian Chili (page 111), but it can also stand on its own as a side dish. It is very high in B vitamins, and we find it a delicious, high-fiber alternative to rice.

1 tablespoon canola or olive oil
1 medium onion, finely chopped
1 cup bulghur
1¾ cups chicken broth, fat skimmed
1 tablespoon chopped fresh parsley or 1 teaspoon dried

1. Combine oil and onion in 3-quart microwave-safe casserole. Microwave on HIGH for 2 to 3 minutes.
2. Stir in the bulghur, coating every grain. Stir in the broth. Cover tightly with a lid or with plastic wrap turned back slightly on one side. Microwave on HIGH for 4 to 6 minutes, or until the liquid is boiling.
3. Turn down the power and cook on MEDIUM for 7 to 10 minutes, or until most of the liquid has been absorbed and the bulghur is tender.
4. Stir in the parsley. Cover again and let stand for 5 minutes.

Basic Long-Grain Rice

MAKES: 3 cups
COOKING TIME: 14 to 17 minutes

Low cholesterol

0.2 gram fat per ½ cup

½ teaspoon salt (optional)
1 cup raw long-grain or converted rice

1. Combine 1¾ cups water and the salt in a 3-quart microwave-safe casserole. Stir in the rice. Cover tightly with a lid or with plastic wrap turned back slightly. Microwave on HIGH for 4 to 7 minutes, or until the liquid begins to boil.
2. Reduce the power to MEDIUM; cook for 10 minutes, or until most of the liquid is absorbed and the rice is tender. Let stand, covered, for 5 minutes.

TO DOUBLE THE RECIPE: Double all the ingredients and use a 4-quart microwave-safe casserole. Cover tightly and microwave on HIGH for 7 to 10 minutes, or until boiling. Reduce power to MEDIUM and microwave for 12 to 14 minutes, or until the liquid is absorbed.

Brown Rice

½ teaspoon salt (optional)
1 cup brown rice

1. Combine 2⅓ cups water and the salt in a 3-quart microwave-safe casserole. Stir in the rice. Cover tightly

MAKES: *3 cups*
COOKING TIME: *31 to 40 minutes*

0.6 gram fat per ½ cup

with a lid or with plastic wrap turned back slightly. Microwave on HIGH for 6 to 10 minutes, or until the water begins to boil.
2. Reduce the power to MEDIUM and microwave for 25 to 30 minutes, or until most of the liquid is absorbed. Let stand, covered, for 5 minutes.

Basic Risotto

MAKES: *About 2½ cups*
COOKING TIME: *15 minutes*

4.9 grams fat per ½ cup

Low cholesterol

SERVING SUGGESTIONS:
Serve with Grilled Turkey (page 175) or Lemon-Mustard Grilled Chicken (page 212).

1¾ cups hot chicken broth (almost boiling), fat skimmed
1 tablespoon olive oil
1 medium-size onion, finely chopped
1 cup Arborio or short-grain rice, or converted long-grain rice
⅓ cup grated Parmesan

1. In a 4-cup glass measure, microwave the broth on HIGH for 6 to 8 minutes, until almost boiling.
2. Combine the oil and onion in a 3-quart microwave-safe casserole. Microwave on HIGH for 1½ to 2 minutes, or until the onion is tender.
3. Add the rice and stir well to coat. Stir in the broth. Cover with a lid or with plastic wrap turned back slightly. Microwave on HIGH for 4 to 6 minutes, or until the broth boils; stir.
4. Cover again and microwave on MEDIUM for 6 to 8 minutes, or until the rice swells, absorbing almost all the liquid yet remaining firm to the bite. Do not stir during cooking.
5. Stir in the cheese. Cover. Let stand for 5 minutes.

Shellfish Risotto with Leeks

2 tablespoons olive oil
1 leek (½ pound), white part only, thinly sliced
1 garlic clove, minced
1 cup Arborio or long-grain rice
1½ cups clam juice or chicken broth
¼ cup dry white wine
¼ teaspoon freshly ground black pepper
¾ pound medium shrimp
1 dozen mussels or littleneck clams, scrubbed
3 tablespoons grated Parmesan
¼ cup chopped fresh parsley

1. In a 3-quart microwave-safe casserole, combine the oil, leek, and garlic. Microwave on HIGH for 3 minutes, stirring once.
2. Stir in the rice, broth, wine, and pepper. Cover tightly with a lid or with plastic wrap turned back slightly. Microwave on HIGH for 6 to 8 minutes, or until the broth boils.
3. Stir in the shrimp. Cover again and cook on MEDIUM for 5 minutes; stir.
4. Place the mussels on top of the rice. Cover again and cook on HIGH for 5 to 9 minutes, or until the mussels have all opened, discarding any that are unopened. Sprinkle cheese and parsley on top. Let stand, covered, for 5 minutes.

VARIATION SAFFRON SHELLFISH RISOTTO WITH LEEKS: Add ¼ teaspoon saffron threads with rice.

● *Arborio rice is grown in the Po River Valley in northern Italy. It is a short-grain rice with a white spot in the center and can be found in specialty or Italian grocery stores. In some areas you will find "pearl rice," which is quite similar to Arborio. If you can't find that, substitute long-grain rice. It won't have the same texture but will cook in the same amount of time.*

Grits or Polenta

VARIATIONS

1 cup white or yellow cornmeal
½ teaspoon salt (optional)

1. Combine cornmeal, salt, and 3½ cups water in a 3-quart microwave-safe casserole. Cover tightly with a lid or with plastic wrap turned back slightly. Microwave on HIGH for 5 minutes; stir.
2. Cover again and cook on HIGH for 4 to 7 minutes, or until all of the water has been absorbed; stir once more.

GRILLED GRITS OR POLENTA: Prepare the basic recipe and spoon evenly into a 2-quart rectangular dish. (This is easiest with a spoon that has been dipped into water.) Cover the grits or polenta and refrigerate for 2 hours or overnight.

Cut into 8 pieces, about 3½ × 3 inches each. Brush with olive oil. Grill or broil for about 1 minute on each

Southern menus, served with maple syrup or with eggs for breakfast, or as a side dish with meat and gravy.

Polenta is the Italian version of grits, made with coarse yellow cornmeal. Making it conventionally is time-consuming because constant stirring is required. Some people purchase a pricey polenta maker. The microwave is the perfect alternative to either method.

One way to serve polenta is warm from the oven, with tomato sauce, but we also use it as a pie topping and as an edible wrapping for tamales.

side, or until lightly browned. Serve with barbecued meats, fish, and vegetables. Delicious!

SAUTÉED GRITS OR POLENTA: Follow Grilled Grits or Polenta variation, but instead of grilling, heat a 12-inch skillet over high heat for 2 to 3 minutes. Add 1 tablespoon olive or canola oil and heat for 30 seconds. Add the chilled and cut grits or polenta to the hot oil and brown about 1 minute on each side. Serve with any stew, especially Chicken Cacciatore (pages 184, 185), or any fish or chicken cutlets with a sauce. Serve for breakfast with Quick Piperade (page 320), stewed fruits, compote, and Frizzled Ham or Canadian Bacon (page 27).

"Cassoulet"

MAKES: 4 servings
COOKING TIME: 15 to 20 minutes

13.6 grams fat per serving

SERVING SUGGESTION:
Serve with a mixed green salad.

True cassoulet is a thick stew from southwestern France, made with beans, pork sausage, and sometimes with pieces of goose or duck conserve. Ours is similar, but we keep it light with our own turkey sausages and no goose!

6 Turkey Sausages (page 180)
1 tablespoon olive oil
2 garlic cloves, minced
2 cans (16 ounces each) cannellini (white kidney beans), drained
2 large ripe tomatoes, cut into ½-inch cubes
½ teaspoon dried thyme leaves
¼ teaspoon freshly ground black pepper

TOPPING

¼ cup dry bread crumbs
¼ cup chopped fresh parsley
1 tablespoon Dijon mustard
1 teaspoon olive oil

1. On top of the stove, heat a well-seasoned cast-iron skillet or nonstick frying pan and cook the turkey-sausage patties as directed on page 180, breaking them up into smaller pieces after they have browned.
2. Meanwhile, combine the oil and garlic in a 2-quart microwave-safe casserole. Microwave on HIGH for 30 seconds.
3. Add the beans, tomato, thyme, pepper, and sausage; stir. Cover with waxed paper and microwave on HIGH

for 5 to 6 minutes, or until heated through, stirring once.

4. Meanwhile, in a small bowl, combine the topping ingredients. Sprinkle over the casserole. Cover again and heat on HIGH for 2 to 3 minutes more. Serve.

Vegetarian Quinoa-Stuffed Peppers

MAKES: *4 servings*
COOKING TIME: *28 to 30 minutes*

No cholesterol (does not apply to Variations)

6.5 grams fat per serving

SERVING SUGGESTIONS:
Serve with a mixed vegetable salad and one of the shredded-wheat breads (pages 41, 42).

1 ounce dried porcini
¾ cup quinoa (see Note)
1 recipe Basic Tomato Sauce (page 145)
4 medium green bell peppers

1. Place the porcini and ½ cup water in a 2-cup glass measure. Cover with plastic wrap turned back slightly on one side. Microwave on HIGH for 2 minutes. Set aside.

2. Rinse the quinoa in a small strainer. Combine the quinoa and 1¾ cups water in a 2-quart microwave-safe casserole or glass measure. Cover with plastic wrap turned back slightly. Microwave on HIGH for 10 to 14 minutes, or until the water is absorbed and the grains appear translucent.

3. Prepare the tomato sauce.

4. Meanwhile, cut ½ inch from the stem ends of the peppers and refrigerate for another use. Remove the ribs and seeds from the peppers. Place the peppers, cut side down, in an 8-inch round or square microwave-safe cake dish or flat-bottomed casserole. Cover with plastic wrap turned back slightly. Set aside.

5. Cut the porcini into ¼-inch pieces; stir them, plus their cooking liquid, into the cooked quinoa.

6. Mix half of the tomato sauce with the cooked quinoa and mushrooms.

7. Turn the cooked peppers over and spoon the quinoa mixture into the cavities. Spoon the remaining sauce over the filled peppers. Cover with waxed paper and microwave on MEDIUM for 4 to 5 minutes.

- *QUINOA (pronounced keena-wa) is a grain that comes from the Andes Mountains. It was one of the three staple foods, along with corn and potatoes, of the Inca civilization. When cooked, quinoa becomes a complete protein with an essential-amino-acid balance similar to milk. It is now grown in the United States and may be purchased in the grains section of health-food stores and some grocery stores.*

VARIATIONS   CHEESE-TOPPED QUINOA-STUFFED PEPPERS (11.5 grams fat per serving): Sprinkle the tops of the sauced peppers with 4 ounces grated low-fat or part–skim milk mozzarella cheese; do not cover when heating.

MEXICAN QUINOA-STUFFED PEPPERS (11.5 grams fat per serving): Eliminate the dried porcini. Substitute Mexican Tomato Sauce (page 319) for the Basic Tomato Sauce and top with 4 ounces of low-fat or part–skim milk grated Monterey Jack cheese.

Couscous

Couscous is a form of semolina wheat (the type of wheat typically used to make pasta) that is the base for many North African dishes. But *couscous* also describes the total dish, which includes couscous (the grain) in a flavorful meat, chicken, and vegetable mélange.

The traditional method of cooking couscous involves soaking the dry grain in cold water for 10 minutes. It is then drained and steamed in a *couscoussiere*, or fine-mesh colander, set over a pot of steaming water. The meat or vegetables are steamed above the grain so that the juices drip in and flavor the grain. The effect is marvelous but the method is very time-consuming.

We find that the microwave method, in which the couscous is cooked separately from the other ingredients, yields just as delicious a couscous—and one that's less greasy than many restaurant versions. On top of that, it takes only 30 minutes or less to prepare any of our three versions.

We included two versions of the spicy harissa sauce that is added at the table. Don't forget this sauce, as it really makes the dish for "hot" food lovers.

You'll find that packaged uncooked or precooked couscous is available in health-food and specialty groceries, and in many supermarkets.

To reheat any of the couscous dishes after they have been refrigerated, add about 2 tablespoons water, tomato juice, or broth per serving before reheating. Microwave on HIGH, covered with a lid or vented plastic wrap, for 3 to 6 minutes per serving, stirring after 2 minutes.

Couscous

MAKES: *About 2½ cups*
COOKING TIME: *3 to 4 minutes*

No cholesterol

2.7 grams fat per ½ cup

1 cup couscous
1 tablespoon olive oil
¼ teaspoon freshly ground black pepper (optional)
¼ teaspoon ground allspice (optional)

1. Combine the couscous and oil in a 2-quart microwave-safe casserole, stirring until all the grains are coated well. (This keeps them from sticking.) Stir in the pepper and allspice. Microwave, uncovered, on HIGH for 1 minute; stir well.
2. Pour in 1½ cups water and stir. Microwave, uncovered, on HIGH for 2 to 3 minutes, or until the liquid has been absorbed. Fluff and stir with two forks to separate grains and let some steam escape.

Harissa #1

MAKES: *About 2 tablespoons*

No cholesterol

2.2 grams fat per teaspoon

This may appear to make a small amount, but it's all you need—it is very hot! Please try this at least once; couscous really isn't couscous without it.

2 garlic cloves
2 jalapeño peppers
1 teaspoon crushed hot-pepper flakes
1 teaspoon ground cumin
½ teaspoon freshly ground black pepper
2 tablespoons olive oil

Blend the ingredients in a blender or food processor. If using a food processor, start the machine and add the garlic, one clove at a time, to mince. Then add the remaining ingredients. Using a rubber spatula, scrape the ingredients down from the sides of the processor to blend. If chopping by hand, mince the garlic and peppers and stir in the remaining ingredients.

Harissa #2

1.5 grams fat per ½ teaspoon

This is a simplified version of harissa, but it's just as delicious! The blend becomes hotter with age and keeps a long time in a cool, dry place.

2 tablespoons hot-pepper flakes
¼ cup peanut oil

Combine ingredients in a glass jar.

Algerian Couscous with Chicken Legs and Vegetables

MAKES: *4 servings*
COOKING TIME: *23 to 26 minutes*

Low-cholesterol variation

19 grams fat per serving

SERVING SUGGESTIONS:
The couscous is made during the stew's standing time; the harissa (hot sauce) is made while the stew is cooking.

1 teaspoon olive oil
1 medium onion, coarsely chopped
1 garlic clove, minced
1 medium carrot, peeled and cut into ½-inch chunks
1 can (16 ounces) stewed tomatoes, drained
¼ teaspoon ground ginger
¼ teaspoon ground cinnamon
¼ teaspoon freshly ground black pepper
½ teaspoon salt
4 chicken legs (about 1½ pounds)
1 can (10½ ounces) chick-peas, drained
1 small zucchini (¼ pound), cut into ½-inch slices
1 recipe Couscous (page 124)
Harissa (page 124) (optional)
Chopped fresh parsley or mint (optional)
Fresh lemon juice (optional)

1. In a 3-quart microwave-safe casserole, combine the oil, onion, garlic, and carrot. Cover tightly with a lid or with plastic wrap turned back slightly on one side. Microwave on HIGH for 3 to 5 minutes, or until the vegetables are tender-crisp.
2. Stir in the tomatoes, ginger, cinnamon, pepper, and salt.
3. Place the chicken legs, with thicker sections positioned toward the outside of the dish, over the vegetable mixture. Cover again and cook on HIGH for 10 minutes.
4. Move the chicken pieces to one side and stir the chick-peas and zucchini into the vegetable mixture. Turn the chicken pieces over, keeping the thicker sections positioned toward the outside of the dish.
5. Cover again and cook on HIGH for 10 to 14 minutes, or until the chicken is tender. Set aside and let stand, covered, while cooking couscous.
6. To serve: Divide the couscous between four dinner plates, forming a mound on each plate. Place a chicken leg on each plate and divide the vegetable mixture between the plates, spooning the vegetables and juices around the couscous. Serve with harissa, chopped fresh parsley or mint, and lemon juice, if desired.

VARIATION LOW-CHOLESTEROL ALGERIAN COUSCOUS WITH CHICKEN LEGS AND VEGETABLES (11 grams fat per serving): Remove the skin from the chicken before cooking.

Meatball Couscous

MAKES: *4 servings*
COOKING TIME: *23 to 26 minutes*

Low cholesterol

16.5 grams fat per serving

In this couscous, the chicken and other, more traditional, cuts of meat are replaced by easy-to-make meatballs.

MEATBALLS

¾ pound lean ground round
2 tablespoons finely chopped onion
2 tablespoons dry bread crumbs
1 egg white
2 tablespoons chopped fresh parsley
⅛ teaspoon ground turmeric
⅛ teaspoon ground ginger
⅛ teaspoon ground nutmeg

COUSCOUS AND VEGETABLES

1 teaspoon olive oil
1 medium onion, coarsely chopped
1 garlic clove, minced
1 medium carrot, peeled and cut into ½-inch chunks
1 can (16 ounces) stewed tomatoes, drained
¼ teaspoon ground ginger
¼ teaspoon ground cinnamon
¼ teaspoon freshly ground black pepper
½ teaspoon salt
1 can (10½ ounces) chick-peas, drained
1 small zucchini (¼ pound), cut into ½-inch slices
1 recipe Couscous (page 124)
Harissa (page 124) (optional)
Chopped fresh parsley or mint (optional)
Fresh lemon juice (optional)

1. Combine all the ingredients for the meatballs in a bowl and form into twelve 2-inch balls.
2. Meanwhile, in a 3-quart microwave-safe casserole, combine the oil, onion, garlic, and carrot. Cover tightly with a lid or with plastic wrap turned back slightly. Microwave on HIGH for 3 to 5 minutes, or until the vegetables are tender-crisp. Stir in the tomatoes, ginger, cinnamon, pepper, and salt.
3. Place the meatballs around the outer rim of the dish, over the vegetable mixture. Cover again and cook on HIGH for 10 minutes.
4. Move the meatballs to one side and stir the chick-peas and zucchini into the vegetable mixture. Turn the meatballs over and reposition them toward the outside of the dish. Cover again and cook on HIGH for 10 to 14 minutes, or until the vegetables are tender. Set aside and let stand, covered, while cooking couscous.

5. To serve: Divide the couscous between four dinner plates, forming a mound on each plate. Place two to three meatballs on each plate and divide the vegetable mixture between the plates, spooning the vegetables and juices around the couscous. Serve with harissa, chopped fresh parsley or mint, and lemon juice, if desired.

Moroccan Vegetable Couscous

MAKES: *4 to 6 servings*
COOKING TIME: *13 to 16 minutes*

No cholesterol

19.4 grams fat per serving

SERVING SUGGESTION: Serve with nonfat yogurt and/or feta cheese to make a complete protein. This will add some cholesterol.

1 tablespoon olive oil
1 large onion, coarsely chopped
1 garlic clove, minced
2 medium carrots, peeled and cut into ½-inch chunks
1 can (16 ounces) stewed tomatoes
1 can (16 ounces) chick-peas, undrained
2 medium zucchini, cut into ½-inch cubes (about 2½ cups)
1 green bell pepper, seeded and cut into ½-inch squares
1 cup blanched almonds
1 teaspoon ground cumin or 1 tablespoon cumin seeds
¼ teaspoon ground ginger
¼ teaspoon ground cinnamon
½ teaspoon ground turmeric
½ teaspoon salt (optional)
¼ teaspoon freshly ground black pepper
1 fresh or pickled jalapeño pepper, chopped (optional)
1 recipe Couscous (page 124)
Juice of 1 lemon
¼ cup chopped fresh parsley
Harissa (page 124) (optional)

1. In a 3-quart microwave-safe casserole, combine the oil, onion, garlic, and carrot. Cover tightly with a lid or with plastic wrap turned back slightly. Microwave on HIGH for 4 to 6 minutes, or until the vegetables are tender-crisp.
2. Add the remaining ingredients, except the couscous, lemon juice, parsley, and harissa; stir well. Cover again and cook on HIGH for 8 to 10 minutes, stirring once.
3. Serve over couscous; sprinkle with lemon juice, chopped parsley, and harissa, as desired.

PASTA

THESE ARE the meals that we rely on when we run into the house, short of breath, and are met with the desperate query of "When are we eating?" "Very soon" is always a good response, but it must be followed by one of our speedy pasta meals to restore calm and well-being.

To make this happen, we serve a conventionally boiled pasta, tossed with a savory sauce that was simmered in the microwave. All of this can be accomplished in 12 to 20 minutes—a short investment considering the long-lasting peace and satisfaction it brings.

Pot stickers and other dumplings are also family favorites. Though they take a bit of time to prepare, the process brings together many hands in a common goal—a delicious dinner in which everyone takes part.

In short, this chapter will give you the peace of mind of knowing that you can always pull together a marvelous meal in less than half an hour.

To Prepare the Whole Meal

- Heat the water for the pasta on top of the stove; for pot stickers, warm the pan.
- Prepare and cook the sauce in the microwave oven; meanwhile cook the pasta conventionally.
- While the pasta and sauce are cooking, toss a salad.

Pot Stickers and Other Dumplings

Pot stickers is the term we use in this country for meat dumplings that are sautéed on one side and then steamed. While it is a term usually associated with Chinese and Korean cooking, we found enough similarities in other countries' dumplings to attempt to streamline the assembly and cooking method of one to fit them all. You'll find that once you've made one of the recipes, you'll be able to follow the others very easily.

In Marcia's home, making *gyozas* (the Japanese term for pot stickers) is a family affair. Marcia whirs the meat filling in the food processor and then passes the prepared filling over to her husband and daughters, who fill and pleat the dumplings at the kitchen table. It's a time to talk and unwind from the day, and it occupies little fingers that might be getting into mischief right before dinner.

Either square wonton skins, found in most grocery stores, or the more traditional round *gyoza* skins, found in Asian grocery stores, may be used in these recipes. Most are dusted with cornstarch, and when that is dabbed with a little water on the edges, the filled and pinched dumplings stay closed during cooking.

Gyozas (Japanese Pot Stickers)

FILLING

¾ pound ground turkey, beef, or pork
¼ medium cabbage, finely chopped (about ½ cup)
1 tablespoon low-sodium soy sauce
1 tablespoon sherry, sake, or mirin (sweet rice cooking wine)
1 green onion, thinly sliced
½ teaspoon cornstarch
½ tablespoon minced fresh ginger

MAKES: *About 36 (6 servings)*
COOKING TIME: *About 7 minutes*

Low cholesterol (when using turkey)

Kids help

12.8 grams fat per 6 dumplings; 14.6 grams fat with ¼ cup sauce

These meat-filled dumplings are browned on one side and then steamed in the same pan. If you want to increase the amount of filling, add more chopped cabbage and adjust the seasonings to taste.

½ teaspoon cornstarch (optional if skins have a powdery surface)
1 package (10 to 14 ounces) gyoza or wonton skins
2 tablespoons vegetable, canola, or light olive oil

SAUCE

Asian Vegetable Sauce for Pasta (page 146), Tomato-Ginger Sauce (page 146), Southeast Asian Sauce for Pasta (page 147), or a mixture of 3 parts rice vinegar and 1 part soy sauce with a dash of sesame seed oil

1. If using the Asian Vegetable or Tomato-Ginger Sauce, prepare it first.
2. Combine all the filling ingredients in a medium bowl. To prepare in the food processor, cut the ¼ cabbage into three pieces (instead of chopping it) and place in the bowl of the food processor. Add the remaining ingredients and pulse four or five times.
3. In a small bowl, combine ½ teaspoon cornstarch with about 1 tablespoon water to dissolve.
4. Place a rounded teaspoon of filling in the center of each *gyoza* or wonton skin. With your finger, rub the edges with the cornstarch mixture and fold in half.
5. Heat a 12-inch or larger skillet over high heat on the stovetop. (A nonstick skillet is best.) Pour in 2 tablespoons oil (3 tablespoons if using a larger skillet). Test the oil by sticking the end of a *gyoza* in—it should sputter.
6. Turn the heat down to medium-high. In concentric circles starting from the outside, place the *gyozas*, pleated side up (if using wontons, pinched side up), close together in one layer in the pan. (If the dumplings are folded in half, just lay them on their sides.) You may have to cook them in two batches.
7. Gently brown the bottoms of the dumplings for about 2 minutes, checking the bottoms and rearranging them if necessary. Turn the heat down to medium.
8. Carefully pour in ¾ cup water and cover the pan. Steam for 5 to 6 minutes, or until most of the liquid is absorbed. Uncover the pan and let the rest of the liquid cook off. (This should take only a minute or two.)
9. Transfer the *gyozas* to a serving platter, angling them so that the browned sides are up.
10. Pour the Asian Vegetable Sauce or Tomato-Ginger

Sauce over the platter of *gyozas* and serve. If using the Southeast Asian Sauce or the rice vinegar–soy sauce, pour sauce into one or two bowls for dipping. Let each person serve him- or herself to dumplings with chopsticks and dip them into the sauce.

- *To freeze uncooked pot stickers, place them on a floured tray, making sure they're not touching, and place the tray in the freezer. When frozen, remove the tray and tap it on the counter to loosen the pot stickers. Place them in sealed bags or containers and freeze for 2 to 3 weeks. No need to defrost before cooking, but steaming may take a few more minutes.*

VARIATION While we prefer the above method of sautéeing the pot stickers, they may also be cooked in a broth and served as a hearty soup, just like Wonton Soup (page 98).

Potato Virtiniai

MAKES: *36 dumplings (6 servings)*
COOKING TIME: *About 20 minutes*

No-cholesterol variation

5.6 grams fat per 6 dumplings

Kids help

SERVING SUGGESTIONS: Although these dumplings are traditionally served with sour cream, we have substituted low-fat yogurt. Serve with Pink Applesauce (page 239), Spring Rhubarb Sauce (page 242), or Spiced Plums (page 238) for dessert, or with Olivada (page 314) as a side dish.

FILLING

1½ pounds potatoes, peeled and cut into eighths
2 tablespoons butter
½ cup cold milk
Salt and pepper to taste
2 green onions, thinly sliced

½ teaspoon cornstarch (optional if skins have a powdery surface)
1 package (about 14 ounces) gyoza or wonton skins (30 to 34)
Low-fat yogurt

1. To make the filling, combine the potatoes and ½ cup water in a 2-quart microwave-safe casserole. Cover tightly with a lid or with plastic wrap turned back slightly. Microwave on HIGH for 12 to 14 minutes, or until potatoes are very tender, stirring once halfway through cooking.
2. Leaving the water in the dish, mash the potatoes well with a potato masher to remove all the lumps.
3. Stir in the butter to melt. Pour in the milk and whip until fluffy; add 1 or 2 tablespoons more milk if necessary. Add salt and pepper to taste. Stir in the green onion.

Thelma's Lithuanian friends Albina and Vinnie Alekna introduced us to this tasty version of "filled dumplings," as they call them; they make a delicious meatless dinner.

4. Fill, fold, and cook the dumplings according to the directions on page 130. Serve with yogurt and one of the other suggested sauces.

VARIATIONS

No-Cholesterol Potato Virtiniai (3.7 grams fat per 6 dumplings): Substitute skim milk for whole milk and 1 tablespoon olive oil for the butter. Serve with nonfat yogurt.

Potato and Cheese Virtiniai (11.3 grams fat per 6 dumplings): Peel and cut up ¾ pound potatoes. Combine with ¼ cup water in a 1-quart microwave-safe casserole. Cover; microwave on HIGH for 6 to 7 minutes, or until very tender, stirring once halfway through cooking. Mash; stir in 1 tablespoon butter and ¼ cup cold milk before whipping. Add salt and pepper to taste and 1 thinly sliced green onion. Stir in 1 cup low-fat ricotta or cottage cheese. (We prefer ricotta because it is drier; if using cottage cheese, drain in a colander to let excess moisture drip out.) This version is particularly good served with yogurt and poached fruit.

Schwäbische Maultaschen (German Dumplings)

MAKES: *36 dumplings (6 servings)*
COOKING TIME: *About 10 minutes*

Low-cholesterol variation

11 grams fat per dumpling

FILLING

½ cup chopped cooked spinach, well drained (see Note)
½ pound ground turkey, low-fat beef, or pork
2 tablespoons dried bread crumbs
1 green onion, thinly sliced
1 egg, lightly beaten
½ teaspoon salt
¼ teaspoon freshly ground black pepper
¼ teaspoon ground nutmeg
2 tablespoons chopped fresh parsley or 2 teaspoons dried parsley

½ teaspoon cornstarch (optional if skins have a powdery surface)
1 package (about 14 ounces) wonton or gyoza skins (30 to 34)
1 large onion, thinly sliced
2 tablespoons butter

Kids help

Thelma's mother grew up in Schwenningen, a town in the Black Forest of southwestern Germany. She would make Maultaschen (literally, "mouth pockets") for a special treat.

The procedure was

NOTE

time-consuming. First she made the dough, then let it sit while she cooked and chopped the fresh spinach or other greens. After that the dough

VARIATION

was rolled, cut, and filled. Prepackaged wonton skins have now simplified the task of making "mouth pockets."

1. Combine all the filling ingredients in a medium bowl or food processor.
2. Fill, fold, and cook the dumplings according to the directions on page 130.
3. Just before serving, combine the onion and butter in a small microwave-safe dish. Microwave on HIGH for 2 to 4 minutes, or until onion is tender. Spoon over the dumplings and serve.

TO COOK ½ BOX SPINACH: Cover half of the box with aluminum foil. Microwave on HIGH for 2 minutes. Cut the box in half; put the section that was under aluminum foil (and hence still frozen) back in the freezer for later use. Microwave remaining half on HIGH for 2 to 3 minutes; squeeze out the excess liquid.

LOW-CHOLESTEROL SCHWÄBISCHE MAULTASCHEN (8 grams fat per serving): Use turkey or extra-lean beef and substitute 2 egg whites for 1 whole egg. Cook the onion in 1 tablespoon olive or canola oil instead of butter.

Italian Ricotta-Filled Dumplings

MAKES: 36 dumplings (6 servings)
COOKING TIME: About 7 minutes

Low-cholesterol variation

11.3 grams fat per dumpling

SERVING SUGGESTIONS:
Serve with Basic Tomato Sauce (page 145), Tomato and Cream Sauce (page 147), Tomato and Cream Sauce with

FILLING

12 ounces ricotta or cottage cheese, well drained
1 egg
½ teaspoon salt
¼ teaspoon freshly ground black pepper
¼ cup grated Parmesan

½ teaspoon cornstarch (optional if skins have a powdery surface)
1 package (about 14 ounces) gyoza or wonton skins (30 to 34)

1. Prepare one of the sauces first (see Serving Suggestions), and keep it warm.
2. Combine the filling ingredients in a medium bowl.
3. Fill, fold, and cook the dumplings according to the directions on page 130.
4. Spoon the sauce over the dumplings and serve.

Olives (page 147), or Tomato
and Cream Sauce with
Broccoli (page 147).

LOW-CHOLESTEROL ITALIAN RICOTTA-FILLED DUMP-
LINGS (8.3 grams fat per dumpling): Substitute low-fat
ricotta cheese or low-fat cottage cheese for regular and
2 egg whites for 1 whole egg.

Southwestern Bean Dumplings

MAKES: *36 dumplings (6 servings)*
COOKING TIME: *About 7 minutes*

10 grams fat per serving

1 recipe Southwestern Tomato Sauce (page 146)
1 recipe Refried Black Beans (page 114)
½ teaspoon cornstarch (optional if skins have a powdery surface)
1 package (about 14 ounces) gyoza or wonton skins (30 to 34)

1. Prepare the tomato sauce and keep it warm.
2. Prepare the beans for the filling. Fill, fold, and cook the dumplings according to the directions on page 130.
3. Spoon tomato sauce on top; serve.

Squash and Ricotta–Filled Dumplings

MAKES: *36 dumplings (6 servings)*
COOKING TIME: *7 minutes*

Low-cholesterol variation

Kids help

5 grams fat per serving

FILLING

1 cup Butternut Squash Puree (page 226) or canned pumpkin puree (see Note)
½ cup ricotta cheese
1 egg, lightly beaten
¼ teaspoon freshly grated nutmeg
⅛ teaspoon freshly ground black pepper

½ teaspoon cornstarch (optional if skins have a powdery surface)
1 package (about 14 ounces) 3- to 4½-inch gyoza or wonton skins
1 recipe Tomato and Cream Sauce (page 147), Basic Tomato Sauce (page 145), or Southeast Asian Sauce (page 147).

1. Prepare the sauce of your choice.
2. Combine the filling ingredients in a medium bowl or the bowl of a food processor. Freeze filling 10 to 20 minutes, or until chilled. (This will make it easier to work with; see Note.)

3. Fill, fold, and cook the dumplings according to the directions on page 130.

4. Spoon sauce on top; serve.

NOTE   If possible, make the filling the night before and refrigerate it until needed.

VARIATION   Low-Cholesterol Squash and Ricotta–Filled Dumplings (3.3 grams fat per serving): Use low-fat ricotta cheese and substitute 2 egg whites for the whole egg.

Scallop and Mushroom Dumplings

MAKES: *36 dumplings*
COOKING TIME: *About 7 minutes*

3.9 grams fat per dumpling, with sauce

FILLING

1 tablespoon butter or canola oil
1 green onion, thinly sliced
1 tablespoon all-purpose flour
½ pound scallops
½ pound mushrooms
¼ teaspoon salt
⅛ teaspoon freshly ground black pepper

½ teaspoon cornstarch (optional if skins have a powdery surface)
1 package (14 ounces) gyoza *or wonton skins (30 to 34)*

SAUCE

Tomato and Cream Sauce (page 147)
        or
½ cup (1 stick) butter
¼ cup chopped fresh basil or parsley
1 tablespoon pine nuts

1. If serving with the Tomato Cream Sauce, prepare sauce first and keep warm.

2. For the filling: Combine 1 tablespoon butter and green onion in a 1-quart microwave-safe casserole. Microwave on HIGH for 1 minute. Stir in the flour to form a paste.

3. Place the scallops and mushrooms in the bowl of a food processor; pulse on and off six to eight times, or until finely chopped.

4. Stir the scallop-mushroom mixture, salt, and pepper

into the butter-flour mixture. Microwave, uncovered, on HIGH for 4 minutes, stirring twice, to form a smooth paste.

5. Fill, fold, and cook the dumplings according to the directions on page 130.

6. Spoon Tomato Cream Sauce over dumplings and serve. To make butter sauce: Place the butter in a 1-cup glass measure. Microwave on HIGH for 2 minutes to melt. Stir in the basil and pine nuts. Serve over dumplings.

Macaroni with Tomato and Cheese Sauce

MAKES: *4 servings*
COOKING TIME: *15 minutes*

Low-cholesterol variation

14 grams fat per serving

Kids help

This is a delicious "pantry shelf" meal that can be whipped up when dinner has gone unplanned and there is no time to run to the grocery store. Unlike the traditional "mac'n cheese," this is made in the Italian style with a creamy tomato-cheese sauce.

1 tablespoon olive or vegetable oil
1 medium onion, chopped fine
3 tablespoons flour
1½ cups milk
¼ teaspoon freshly ground black pepper
¾ cup grated Parmesan
1 can (14½ ounces) stewed tomatoes, drained and
    coarsely chopped
½ pound rigatoni, elbow, or other macaroni, cooked
    and drained (about 4 cups)

1. In a 2-quart microwave-safe casserole, combine the oil and onion. Microwave on HIGH for 1 to 2½ minutes, or until the onion is tender.

2. Stir in the flour to coat the onion pieces. Pour in the milk, stirring constantly to blend. Microwave, uncovered, on HIGH for 5 to 7 minutes, or until the sauce comes to a boil and thickens, stirring three times.

3. Stir in the pepper, ½ cup of cheese, and the tomatoes. Fold in the macaroni.

4. Sprinkle the remaining ¼ cup cheese evenly on the top. Cover with waxed paper. Microwave on MEDIUM for 12 to 14 minutes, or until the macaroni is heated through, rotating one-quarter turn halfway through cooking.

VARIATIONS BAKED MACARONI WITH HAM (14.4 grams fat per serving): Add ¾ cup chopped cooked ham (about 3 ounces) with the macaroni.

LOW-CHOLESTEROL BAKED MACARONI WITH TURKEY (13 grams fat per serving): Substitute skim milk for whole.

Add ¾ cup chopped smoked turkey (about 3 ounces) with the macaroni.

DINOSAUR MACARONI: Substitute dinosaur-shaped noodles for macaroni. A "kid-pleaser."

Pasta Primavera

MAKES: *4 to 6 servings*
COOKING TIME: *17 minutes*

15 grams fat per serving for 4; 10.5 grams fat per serving for 6

1 pound spaghetti
2 tablespoons olive oil
2 garlic cloves, minced
½ pound ripe tomatoes (preferably plum), peeled, seeded, and chopped, or 1 cup undrained canned tomatoes, chopped
1 tablespoon tomato paste
1½ teaspoons finely chopped fresh basil or ½ teaspoon crushed dried
½ cup grated Parmesan
½ cup half-and-half
2 cups broccoli florets (about 1 bunch), cut into bite-size pieces
2 small zucchini, cut into ¼-inch slices
2 cups thinly sliced mushrooms (about ¼ pound)
½ teaspoon salt (optional)
¼ teaspoon freshly ground black pepper
¼ teaspoon red-pepper flakes (optional)

1. Bring 4 quarts of water to a boil on top of the conventional stove and cook the spaghetti until it is al dente, or still firm to the bite.
2. Meanwhile, combine the oil and garlic in a 3-quart microwave-safe casserole. Microwave on HIGH for 1½ minutes, or until the garlic is tender but not brown.
3. Add the tomato, tomato paste, and basil. Microwave on HIGH for 5 minutes, stirring once.
4. Stir in the cheese and half-and-half. Add the broccoli and stir. Cover with a lid or with plastic wrap turned back slightly. Microwave on HIGH for 3 to 5 minutes, or until the broccoli is partially cooked, stirring once.
5. Add the remaining ingredients; stir well. Cover again and microwave on HIGH for 4 to 6 minutes, or until heated through but not boiling, stirring once.
6. Drain the spaghetti and place it in a serving bowl. Pour the sauce over the spaghetti and toss well. Serve immediately with additional Parmesan.

The Other Pasta Primavera

MAKES: *4 to 6 servings*
COOKING TIME: *13 to 18 minutes*

Low cholesterol

5.3 grams fat per serving for 4; 5.3 grams fat per serving for 6

This is a recipe for those who love pasta with fresh spring vegetables but want to avoid the cream sauce. We've added a little more fresh basil for flavor and substituted skim milk for cream, bringing each serving in at about 280 calories.

1 pound spaghetti
2 teaspoons olive oil
2 garlic cloves, minced
1 pound ripe tomatoes (preferably plum), peeled, seeded and chopped, or 1 cup undrained canned tomatoes, chopped
1 cup chopped pimiento, drained
2 tablespoons tomato paste
¼ cup chopped fresh basil, or 1 teaspoon crushed dried
½ cup grated Parmesan
½ cup skim milk
1 pound asparagus tips, cut into 2-inch-long pieces (2 cups)
2 small zucchini, cut into ¼-inch slices
¼ pound mushrooms, thinly sliced (2 cups)
¼ teaspoon red-pepper flakes (optional)
Freshly ground black pepper

1. Bring 4 quarts of water to a boil on top of the conventional stove and cook the spaghetti until it is al dente, or still firm to the bite.
2. Meanwhile, in a 3-quart microwave-safe casserole with a lid, combine the oil and garlic. Microwave on HIGH for 1½ minutes, or until the garlic is tender but not brown.
3. Stir in the tomato, pimiento, tomato paste, and basil. Cook on HIGH for 5 minutes, stirring once.
4. Stir in the cheese, milk, and asparagus tips. Cover with a lid or with plastic wrap turned back on one side. Microwave on HIGH for 3 to 5 minutes, or until the asparagus is almost tender, stirring once.
5. Add the zucchini, mushrooms, and red and black peppers to taste; stir well. Cover again and cook on HIGH for 4 to 6 minutes, or until heated through but not boiling, stirring once.
6. Drain the spaghetti and place it in a serving bowl. Pour the sauce over the spaghetti and toss well. Serve immediately with additional Parmesan.

Linguine with White Clam Sauce

MAKES: *4 servings*
COOKING TIME: *8 to 10 minutes*

Low cholesterol

12 grams fat per serving

This is one of those meals that can be whipped up on the run and yet gives all the satisfaction of a meal that has cooked all day. The secret is to use fresh herbs.

We prefer this low-fat version to the one we remember making in our carefree butter-and-cream days. (We used to make this with a cup of heavy cream and half a cup of butter—it doesn't even sound appealing anymore!)

1 pound linguine
2 tablespoons olive oil
3 garlic cloves, minced
2 tablespoons flour
1½ cups skim milk
¼ cup chopped fresh parsley
¼ cup chopped fresh basil, or 1 teaspoon dried
1 teaspoon chopped fresh thyme, or ½ teaspoon dried
Freshly ground black pepper to taste
¼ cup grated Parmesan
2 cans clams (5 ounces each), drained and rinsed to remove excess salt

1. Bring 4 quarts of water to a boil on top of the stove and cook linguine until al dente, or still firm to the bite.
2. Meanwhile, combine the oil and garlic in a 1-quart microwave-safe casserole. Microwave on HIGH for 1 minute.
3. Stir in the flour until smooth. Stir in the milk. Cook, uncovered, on HIGH for 3 minutes; stir well to dissolve any lumps. Cook on HIGH for 2 to 3 minutes more, or until the mixture has boiled and thickened.
4. Stir in parsley, basil, thyme, pepper, Parmesan, and clams. Cook on HIGH for 2 to 3 minutes, or until heated through.
5. Serve over cooked and drained linguine. Pass extra Parmesan at the table along with fresh black peppercorns to grind.

Gnocchi

MAKES: *4 servings*
COOKING TIME: *15 minutes*

1.8 grams fat per serving

Kids help

SERVING SUGGESTIONS:
Serve with Basic Tomato Sauce (page 145), which can be started after the potatoes

4 medium potatoes (about 1½ pounds), unpeeled
¾ cup all-purpose flour
1 egg yolk
Freshly grated Parmesan, for sprinkling, if desired

1. Prick each potato with a fork once on the top and bottom.
2. Place a piece of paper towel in the microwave oven and place the potatoes in a circle on top, allowing about an inch space between them. Cook on HIGH for 10 to 14 minutes, or until the potatoes give slightly when squeezed between the fingers, turning over once. Let them stand for 5 minutes.

are first cooked in the microwave, or with a fresh basil Pesto (page 335). A simple topping of melted butter and a handful of freshly grated Parmesan is also delicious.

Gnocchi are easier to prepare than you might think. Kids enjoy pushing the potatoes through a sieve or ricer and then watching the boiling dumplings bob to the surface. For the young just starting on table food, these dumplings are good plain. Those a little

NOTE

older will prefer them with Parmesan that they can sprinkle on themselves.

3. Meanwhile, bring about 5 quarts of salted water to a boil on top of the stove.
4. Peel the potatoes. (Be careful, as they will still be hot!) Push them through a ricer or food mill into a medium bowl. (Or mash them thoroughly, removing all lumps.)
5. Add the flour and egg yolk. Blend with your hands to make a smooth dough that is still slightly sticky. If more flour is needed, add it 1 tablespoon at a time. Spoon out rounded teaspoonfuls, with a regular table teaspoon, and divide each in half. Roll each half into a cylinder.
6. Boil for 10 seconds, or until the dumplings bob to the surface. With a slotted spoon, lift the dumplings, a few at a time, from the water and transfer to a shallow platter.

When making gnocchi with kids, we usually boil a few at a time, while the kids are making more. If you want to make the whole batch first and then boil them, lay them out on a platter and cover them with a damp towel.

Squid in Ginger Sauce with Soba

MAKES: *4 servings*
COOKING TIME: *About 15 minutes*

8.8 grams fat per serving

Soba noodles are made with buckwheat flour. If you are unable to find them in an

1 tablespoon finely chopped, peeled fresh ginger
1 medium onion, thinly sliced
2 garlic cloves, minced
2 teaspoons sesame oil
1 teaspoon hot chili oil
1 pound soba
3 tablespoons soy sauce
1 tablespoon mirin (sweet Oriental cooking wine)
1 tablespoon white vinegar
1 tablespoon cornstarch
1 pound squid, cleaned (see Note 1)
4 green onions, thinly sliced

1. In a 2-quart microwave-safe casserole, combine the ginger, onion, garlic, and oils. Microwave on HIGH for 2 to 3 minutes, or until the onion is tender.
2. Bring 4 quarts of water to a boil on top of the conventional stove and cook the soba until al dente, or still firm to the bite.
3. Meanwhile, in a small bowl, combine the soy sauce,

Oriental store or your supermarket, look for a good-quality whole-wheat spaghetti.

mirin, vinegar, and cornstarch. Stir until smooth. Add to the onion mixture.

4. Cut the squid crosswise into ¼-inch circles; cut the tentacles in half lengthwise. Add the squid to the onion mixture and stir to coat. Cover tightly with a lid or with plastic wrap turned back slightly on one side. Microwave on HIGH for 10 to 12 minutes, or until the squid is tender and opaque, stirring after 4 minutes. Let stand, covered, for 5 minutes.

5. Drain the soba. Divide between six serving bowls. Spoon the squid and sauce over the noodles and sprinkle with green onions.

NOTE 1 Ask to have the squid dressed at your market, or prepare it yourself by first removing the two layers of skin—an outer, speckled skin and a transparent skin underneath it. Remove the beak, eyes, the digestive tract, and what appears to be a plastic cartilage or backbone. Rinse well and dry.

NOTE 2 If you have made the squid and sauce in advance, reheat, covered, on HIGH for 5 to 6 minutes, stirring once.

Linguine with Red-Pepper Sauce

MAKES: *4 servings*
COOKING TIME: *8 to 10 minutes*

Low cholesterol

15.9 grams fat per serving

1 pound linguine or other pasta
¼ cup olive oil
2 garlic cloves, minced
1 cup "roasted" red peppers, cut into ¼-inch strips (see page 87)
2 tablespoons chopped fresh basil
1 tablespoon chopped fresh parsley
¼ teaspoon freshly ground black pepper
Grated Parmesan

1. In a large pot of lightly salted boiling water, cook the linguine. Drain.

2. Combine the oil and garlic in a 1-quart microwave-safe casserole. Microwave on HIGH for 45 seconds.

3. Stir in the red pepper, basil, parsley, and black pepper. Cover with waxed paper and microwave on HIGH for 3 minutes. To serve, toss the pasta and sauce and sprinkle with Parmesan.

Pasta e Fagioli

MAKES: *4 servings*
COOKING TIME: *10 to 14 minutes*

Low cholesterol

6.2 grams fat per serving

Fresh basil adds such a wonderful flavor that we use much more than the dried equivalent when it's available.

1 tablespoon olive oil
2 garlic cloves, minced
1 can (28 ounces) whole tomatoes with puree, coarsely chopped
¼ cup fresh basil leaves, chopped, or ½ teaspoon dried basil
½ teaspoon salt
¼ teaspoon freshly ground black pepper
1 can (15½ ounces) cannellini (white kidney beans), great northern beans, or navy beans
2 tablespoons grated Parmesan
¼ pound ditalini, cooked

1. Combine the oil and garlic in a 2½-quart microwave-safe casserole. Microwave on HIGH for 35 to 40 seconds.
2. Stir in the tomatoes, basil, salt, and pepper. Cover with a lid or with plastic wrap turned back slightly on one side. Cook on HIGH for 4 minutes.
3. Stir in the beans, cheese, and ditalini. Cover and cook for 2 to 4 minutes more, or until heated through.

Individual Lasagna Packages

MAKES: *4 servings*
COOKING TIME: *20 minutes*

Low cholesterol

17.5 grams fat per serving

SERVING SUGGESTIONS:
Serve with a crispy salad and plenty of crusty Italian bread to mop up any extra sauce. Perfectly Poached Pears (page 238) or plain fresh pears make a nice dessert.

4 lasagne noodles
1 recipe Basic Tomato Sauce (page 145)
8 ounces part-skim ricotta cheese
4 ounces grated part-skim mozzarella cheese
2 tablespoons grated Parmesan

1. Bring a large pot of water (about 8 cups) to a boil on top of the stove. Cook the lasagne noodles for about 8 to 10 minutes, or until al dente, or still firm to the bite; drain.
2. Meanwhile, prepare and cook the tomato sauce.
3. In a small bowl, combine the ricotta, 2 ounces of the mozzarella, and the Parmesan.
4. Spread one-quarter of the cheese mixture evenly over each cooked lasagne noodle. Taking one end of a noodle, fold one-third over the center (about 3½ inches). Fold the other side over the piece that was just folded, making a three-fold package. Repeat with remaining noodles.
5. Place the folded noodles in an 8-inch round or square microwave-safe dish. Spoon the sauce into the dish. (It will seem like a lot of sauce.) Sprinkle the

remaining mozzarella cheese evenly over each package. Cover with waxed paper. Microwave on HIGH for 8 to 10 minutes, until packages are heated through and the cheese is melted.

6. Place each noodle package on an individual serving plate and spoon the sauce around it, dividing it evenly.

Types and Shapes of Pasta

Even though the basic dough for making any type of pasta is the same, the shape it takes determines the texture of the cooked pasta and how you choose to sauce it.

We find that family and friends alike enjoy getting involved in choosing the types and shapes of pastas to be served.

Here are some of the more popular shapes available and suggestions for saucing them. We hope you will be encouraged to add new varieties and sauces to your repertoire.

SPAGHETTI: The best known of all pastas. The name comes from the Italian word for "strings," which this pasta resembles when cooked. Spaghetti may be purchased in varying degrees of thickness. It goes well with all tomato sauces. The thinnest is called *angel hair pasta* and is ideal for Pasta Primavera (page 137) or in broth. *Spaghettini* is a little thicker and goes well with Basic Tomato Sauce (page 145), and Red Clam Sauce (page 145).

MACARONI: A family of hollow noodles of varying sizes and thicknesses. *Penne*, meaning "pen nibs," are about ¼ inch in diameter and are cut on the diagonal into 2-inch lengths. Goes well with Arrabbiata Sauce (page 145) or Wild Mushroom Sauce (page 148). *Rigatoni*, meaning "lines" or "ridges," are the largest of these noodles. They are about ¾ inch in diameter and are cut into 2-inch lengths. Serve with Tomato and Meatball Sauce (page 146).

SHELLS: Called *conchiglie* in Italian, these are shaped like conch shells and vary in size. Try serving the ½-inch size with Tuna Tomato Sauce (page 146).

FARFALLE: Bow tie–shaped pasta. It would give a special touch to Tomato and Cream Sauce (page 147).

FETTUCCINE: Long, thin, flat noodles (literally "ribbons"), usually about ⅛ inch wide. The flat surface works well in picking up a creamy cheese sauce such as Gorgonzola Sauce (page 148).

FUSILLI: Spiral-shaped curls that come in varying lengths and widths. We like the way that Tomato and Cream Sauce (page 147) clings to their twists.

LINGUINE: Flatter than spaghetti. It goes well with seafood sauces such as Red Clam Sauce (page 145) and Tuna Tomato Sauce (page 146).

• *To Cook 1 Pound Dry Pasta*

1. In a large pot on top of the range, bring 4 quarts of water to a boil.
2. When the water boils, add the pasta. Stir immediately so that all of the pasta is covered with water and the strands remain separate. Stir occasionally to keep pasta from sticking.
3. To determine doneness, bite into a piece of the pasta. If you see a lighter-colored line or dot in the center, it is still too undercooked to serve. When the raw spot disappears, the pasta is ready.
4. Pour the pasta into a colander and shake to allow excess water to drain. Toss immediately with the desired sauce to keep the pasta from sticking together. To prevent unsauced pasta from clumping together, toss with 1 or 2 teaspoons of olive oil.

• *Peeling Tomatoes*

The easiest way to peel tomatoes is to drop them into boiling water. Although this takes as long in the microwave oven as it does on top of the range, we use the time to chop and assemble the remaining ingredients for the sauce.

It is most efficient to peel no more than 2 pounds of tomatoes at a time and then quickly reheat the water for the second batch.

2 pounds tomatoes

1. Pour 5 cups of water into an 8-cup glass measure or a 2-quart microwave-safe bowl. Cover with plastic

wrap turned back slightly. Microwave on HIGH for 10 to 12 minutes, or until boiling.

2. Plunge tomatoes into water and let sit for 1 minute.

3. To peel: spear with a fork and remove core with a sharp knife. Gently pull off peel.

4. To peel the second batch, re-cover water and microwave on HIGH for 3 to 4 minutes, or until almost boiling. Proceed as above.

NOTE To seed tomatoes, gently squeeze cross-cut halves; most of the seeds will slide out.

Basic Tomato Sauce

MAKES: *About 2 cups*
COOKING TIME: *10 to 14 minutes*

Low cholesterol

5 grams fat per ½ cup

SERVING SUGGESTION:
Serve over pasta.

1 tablespoon olive oil
2 garlic cloves, minced
1 can (28 ounces) whole tomatoes with puree, coarsely chopped (see Note)
½ cup fresh basil leaves, chopped (much preferable to dried), or ½ teaspoon dried
½ teaspoon salt
¼ teaspoon freshly ground black pepper
2 tablespoons grated Parmesan

1. Combine the oil and garlic in a 2½-quart microwave-safe casserole. Microwave on HIGH for 35 to 40 seconds.

2. Stir in the tomato, basil, salt, and pepper. Cover with a lid or with plastic wrap turned back slightly on one side. Microwave on HIGH for 5 minutes, stirring after 3 minutes.

3. Stir in the cheese and cook, uncovered, on HIGH for 2 to 4 minutes, or until the sauce is heated through.

NOTE If you are unable to find tomatoes with puree, stir in 2 tablespoons of tomato paste when adding the tomato and seasonings.

VARIATIONS ARRABBIATA SAUCE (5 grams fat per ½ cup): Add ½ teaspoon red pepper flakes when adding cheese. Serve over penne, tubeti, ditalini, or other tubular macaroni.

RED CLAM SAUCE (5.8 grams fat per ½ cup): Add 2 cans (6½ ounces each) drained chopped clams and ¼ cup chopped fresh parsley when adding cheese. Microwave on MEDIUM for 4 to 5 minutes, or until heated through.

TOMATO-GINGER SAUCE (4.9 grams fat per ½ cup): Add 1 tablespoon chopped fresh ginger to the garlic when sautéeing. Cook as directed. Substitute chopped cilantro for chopped basil. Eliminate Parmesan. Serve over Gyozas (page 129) or soba.

SOUTHWESTERN TOMATO SAUCE (4.5 grams fat per ½ cup): Add 1 chopped medium onion to garlic and microwave on HIGH for 2 minutes. Add 1 chopped jalapeño pepper, or more to taste. Substitute 1 teaspoon dried oregano for basil. Eliminate grated Parmesan. Serve over Southwestern Bean Dumplings (page 134) or purchased chili pasta.

TUNA TOMATO SAUCE (6 grams fat per ½ cup): Add 1 can (7½ ounces) drained tuna and ¼ cup chopped fresh parsley when adding the cheese. Microwave on MEDIUM for 2 to 3 minutes, or until heated through.

TOMATO AND MEATBALL SAUCE (17 grams fat per ½ cup): Add 1 recipe Basic Meatballs (page 158) to sauce when adding cheese.

Asian Vegetable Sauce for Pasta

MAKES: *About 2 cups*
COOKING TIME: *8 to 10 minutes*

No cholesterol

3.4 grams fat per ½ cup

SERVING SUGGESTIONS: Delicious when served over Gyozas (page 129), soba, or angel-hair pasta.

1 tablespoon sesame oil or Chili Oil (page 305)
2 garlic cloves, minced
1 tablespoon grated fresh ginger
1 teaspoon cornstarch
¼ cup soy sauce
2 tablespoons orange juice
1 tablespoon rice vinegar or white vinegar
1 tablespoon sherry, sake, or mirin (sweet cooking rice wine) (optional)
¼ pound snow pea pods, ends removed
¼ pound mushrooms, sliced
2 carrots, peeled and thinly sliced

1. In a 2-quart microwave-safe casserole, combine the oil, garlic, and ginger. Microwave, uncovered, on HIGH for 45 seconds.
2. In a small bowl, combine the cornstarch with the soy sauce until smooth.
3. Add soy-sauce mixture to the garlic-ginger, along with the orange juice, vinegar, and sherry. Mix well. Microwave, uncovered, on HIGH for 2 to 3 minutes,

until boiling and slightly thickened, stirring after 1 minute and then at the end, to make a smooth sauce. 4. Add the vegetables. Cover tightly with a lid or with plastic wrap turned back slightly on one side. Microwave on HIGH for 3 to 4 minutes, stirring once, until tender-crisp. Serve over pasta or dumplings.

VARIATION SOUTHEAST ASIAN SAUCE FOR PASTA: Prepare in a 1-quart microwave-safe bowl. Eliminate snow peas, mushrooms, and carrots. Use purchased hot chili oil or the Chili Oil on page 305. Reduce soy sauce to 1 tablespoon and add 3 tablespoons water with it. Cook as directed, eliminating the vegetable cooking time.

Tomato and Cream Sauce

MAKES: *About 2 cups*
COOKING TIME: *10 to 14 minutes*

17.2 grams fat per ½ cup

1 tablespoon olive oil
2 garlic cloves, minced
1 can (28 ounces) whole tomatoes with puree, coarsely chopped
½ cup fresh basil leaves, chopped, or ½ teaspoon dried
½ teaspoon salt
¼ teaspoon freshly ground black pepper
2 tablespoons grated Parmesan
½ cup half-and-half
¼ cup chopped fresh parsley

1. Combine the oil and garlic in a 2½-quart microwave-safe casserole. Microwave on HIGH for 35 to 40 seconds.
2. Stir in the tomato, basil, salt, and pepper. Cover with a lid or with plastic wrap turned back slightly on one side. Cook on HIGH for 5 minutes, stirring after 3 minutes.
3. Stir in the cheese, half-and-half, and parsley. Microwave, uncovered, on HIGH for 2 to 4 minutes, or until the sauce is heated through.

VARIATIONS TOMATO AND CREAM SAUCE WITH OLIVES (19.6 grams fat per ½ cup): Add ½ cup pitted and coarsely chopped Gaeta olives with cream.

TOMATO AND CREAM SAUCE WITH BROCCOLI (17.2 grams fat per ½ cup): Add one recipe Steamed Broccoli (page 232) and ¼ teaspoon hot-pepper flakes with the cheese and cream. Cover and microwave on HIGH for 2 to 3 minutes, or until heated through.

Wild Mushroom Sauce

MAKES: *4 servings*
COOKING TIME: *6 to 8 minutes*

10.3 grams fat per serving

1 ounce dried porcini
1 tablespoon butter
1 tablespoon flour
12 ounces domestic mushrooms, thinly sliced
½ cup half-and-half
¼ cup chopped fresh parsley
2 tablespoons grated Parmesan
Salt and freshly ground black pepper to taste

1. Soak the porcini in 1 cup of hot water for 30 minutes. Place the butter in a 2½-quart microwave-safe casserole. Microwave on HIGH for 35 seconds to 1 minute to melt.
2. Stir in the flour until smooth.
3. Drain the porcini and reserve the soaking liquid. Chop the mushrooms coarsely. Add all mushrooms to the casserole and stir well. Microwave, uncovered, on HIGH for 3 minutes; stir.
4. Stir in the remaining ingredients and ½ cup of reserved liquid. Microwave on HIGH for 3 to 5 minutes, stirring once, until the sauce is heated through.

Gorgonzola Sauce

MAKES: *4 servings*
COOKING TIME: *5 to 9 minutes*

21.5 grams fat per serving

4 ounces Gorgonzola or other blue cheese
⅓ cup milk
3 tablespoons butter
¼ cup half-and-half
⅓ cup grated Parmesan

1. Place the cheese in a 1-quart microwave-safe casserole. Mash with a fork; stir in the milk and butter. Microwave on MEDIUM for 3 to 5 minutes, or until creamy, stirring twice. Set aside.
2. Stir in the half-and-half and the Parmesan. Microwave on MEDIUM for 2 to 4 minutes, or until the sauce is heated through.

MEAT

Although less meat is being eaten than in the past, it still plays an integral part in most American diets. In fact, because red meat is an extremely efficient source of iron, women of reproductive age who cut out red meat (or drastically reduce the amount they eat) are at risk of developing anemia. You'd have to eat about 1 pound of fish to obtain the iron found in one 3-ounce serving of beef!

And what most people don't realize is that certain cuts of meat have no more fat than an equal serving of poultry. The key is to choose the right cuts: those that are lean, with very little fat marbled through the grain. Round, chuck, flank, and sirloin are good choices, and all have between 156 and 171 calories per 3-ounce serving.

Lean ground beef (90 percent lean) has slightly less cholesterol than ground turkey, so even a good old-fashioned meat loaf needn't tip the cholesterol scale too much. And by the way, cooking that lean meat loaf in the microwave oven will yield a moister meat loaf than would the conventional oven, and in only 20 minutes!

Meat Loaves

When it comes to preparing meat loaves in the microwave oven, a rectangular meat loaf formed in a traditional loaf dish just doesn't produce great results. It comes out steamed in flavor and appearance, and the juices run out all over the oven floor. Through trial and error our round microwave meat loaf was born. It is formed on a dinner plate, pie plate, or some other platter. As a result, the surface of the loaf takes on a more browned, less steamed appearance. The round shape also cooks more evenly in the microwave.

DEFROSTING GROUND MEAT

1. Before freezing, form ground meat into a thick ring with a hole in the middle for better defrosting.
2. Uncover the frozen meat and remove all liners before defrosting, or as soon as possible during defrosting, to prevent any buildup of heat under the packaging, which might begin to cook the meat.
3. Place the frozen meat on a microwave roasting rack in a rectangular microwave-safe dish to raise it above the liquid that will come out in the defrosting process. If you don't have a rack, substitute a small microwave-safe dish and invert it in the rectangular dish.
4. Frozen packages of ground meat with thin edges need to be watched closely and broken in half partway through defrosting to rearrange the thicker inside portions to the outside.
5. Turn ground beef over halfway through defrosting.
6. After defrosting, meat should still have some ice crystals, which will disappear during the 5-minute standing time.

1 pound ground meat	Microwave on DEFROST for 4 to 7 minutes
1½ pounds ground meat	Microwave on DEFROST for 7 to 10 minutes

Basic Meat Loaf

1½ pounds lean (90 percent lean) ground round (see Note)
1 medium onion, finely chopped
½ cup fine dry bread crumbs or rolled oats
1 egg, beaten
2 tablespoons chopped fresh parsley or 2 teaspoons dried
½ teaspoon salt

*19.6 grams fat per serving for
6; 14.5 grams fat per serving
for 8*

SERVING SUGGESTIONS:
Serve to company with Basic
Tomato and Pepper Sauce
(page 336) or Mushroom
Sauce (recipe follows).

*Leftover (or "planned over"
meat loaf, in this case) is
much better for you than
bologna or salami and more
economical. If you plan to
serve this cold, add a minced*

NOTE

*garlic clove and 1 teaspoon
dried thyme leaves for
additional flavor. Serve it with
a good mustard and
horseradish.*

*This meat loaf was voted a
moister and more flavorful
loaf than its conventional
counterpart by a panel of
cooking experts. Our secret?
It's made with low-fat beef
but still stays moist in the
microwave, unlike the
dried-out loaf that results
from conventional cooking.*

VARIATIONS

*¼ teaspoon freshly ground black pepper
1 can (8 ounces) tomato sauce or ½ cup catsup*

1. Place the meat on a 10-inch or larger microwave-safe dinner or pie plate, or a larger round platter or oval platter (see Note), and make a well in the center.
2. Place the remaining ingredients, except half the tomato sauce, in the center of the meat. Combine all the ingredients well with your hands. Form a firm 6½-inch round loaf (or a 4 × 6½-inch oval for the oval platter), and place it in the middle of the dish.
3. Spread the remaining tomato sauce on top of the meat loaf. (You can arrange it decoratively down the center if you like.) Microwave on HIGH for 16 to 20 minutes, or until done, rotating after 7 minutes. (Meat loaf is done if a thermometer inserted in the center registers 145 to 155° F and the top is firm, except for the center, which will finish cooking during standing time.) Let stand for 5 minutes.

Any meat loaf not made with lean ground beef should be cooked in a dish with sides, such as a 2-quart rectangular microwave-safe dish, because of the fat that will cook out. Drain the fat before serving.

TO MAKE 2 SERVINGS: On a microwave-safe dinner plate, combine ½ pound ground beef, ¼ cup bread crumbs, 1 small onion, chopped, 1 egg white or whole egg, 1 tablespoon chopped fresh parsley or 1 teaspoon dried, ¼ teaspoon salt, ⅛ teaspoon freshly ground black pepper, and 2 tablespoons catsup. Form a 3-inch-diameter loaf and spoon 2 tablespoons catsup over the top. Microwave on HIGH for 6 to 8 minutes.

TO MAKE 6 TO 8 SERVINGS: On a large microwave-safe dinner plate or 11-inch platter, combine 2 pounds ground beef, 1 cup bread crumbs, 1 large onion, chopped, 1 egg, ¼ cup chopped fresh parsley or 2 tablespoons dried, ¾ teaspoon salt, ½ teaspoon freshly ground black pepper, and 1 can (8 ounces) tomato sauce. Form a 7-inch round loaf. Pour 1 can (8 ounces) tomato sauce on top. Microwave on HIGH for 20 to 24 minutes.

SWEET-AND-SOUR GLAZED MEAT LOAF (19.6 grams fat per serving for 5; 14.5 grams fat per serving for 8): Use

¼ cup catsup in the meat-loaf mixture. For the glaze, combine ¼ cup apricot or pineapple preserves and 1 tablespoon each brown sugar and Dijon-style mustard in a small bowl. Spread over the meat before cooking. This version browns beautifully because of the additional sugar!

THREE-MEAT MEAT LOAF (17.9 grams fat per serving for 6; 12.8 grams fat per serving for 8): Substitute 1 pound ground beef and ¼ pound each ground veal and pork for the 1½ pounds ground round. Proceed as directed, but cook in a dish with sides to catch extra fat.

TURKEY MEAT LOAF (15.3 grams fat per serving for 6; 11.4 grams fat per serving for 8): Substitute fresh ground turkey for beef.

VEAL MEAT LOAF (13.7 grams fat per serving for 6; 10.3 grams fat per serving for 8): Substitute ground veal for beef. Add ¼ teaspoon freshly grated nutmeg and 1 teaspoon dried thyme leaves. This is delicious served cold!

DIJON MUSTARD MEAT LOAF (19.6 grams fat per serving for 6; 14.5 grams fat per serving for 8): Use ¼ cup catsup in the meat-loaf mixture and add 2 tablespoons Dijon mustard. Eliminate the sauce on top before cooking.

Mushroom Sauce

MAKES: *1 cup*
COOKING TIME: *8 to 10 minutes*

No cholesterol

0.9 gram fat per tablespoon

SERVING SUGGESTION:
Serve with Basic Meat Loaf (page 150).

1 tablespoon olive oil
2 teaspoons flour
1 cup beef broth
1 teaspoon fresh lemon juice
Freshly ground black pepper
¼ teaspoon dried thyme or 1 sprig fresh thyme
¼ pound fresh mushrooms, sliced

1. In a 2-cup glass measure, combine the oil and flour to make a smooth paste. Stir in the broth and lemon juice. Microwave on HIGH for 4 to 5 minutes, or until slightly thickened, stirring once.
2. Stir in the black pepper, thyme, and mushrooms. Microwave on HIGH for 4 to 5 minutes, or until the mushrooms are heated through.

We remember this type of sauce being served at church socials and potluck suppers, but it was usually made with butter, canned mushrooms, and canned soup. We have updated it to be lighter and fresher-tasting. This sauce also works with butter.

MARSALA MUSHROOM SAUCE (.9 gram fat per tablespoon): Add 2 tablespoons Marsala with the broth. This will sweeten the sauce just a touch.

HERBED MUSHROOM SAUCE (.9 gram fat per tablespoon): Add ¼ cup chopped fresh parsley or chives at the end of cooking.

ROSY MUSHROOM SAUCE (.9 gram fat per tablespoon): Add 1 tablespoon tomato paste with the broth.

Low-Cholesterol, Low-Sodium Meat Loaf

MAKES: 6 to 8 servings
COOKING TIME: 16 to 20 minutes

18.6 grams fat per serving for 6; 14 grams fat per serving for 8

Don't forgo meat loaf made with beef just because of the fat: this loaf has only 67 milligrams of cholesterol per serving. Its turkey counterpart boasts 76 milligrams! Substituting egg whites for whole eggs and using lean ground beef make the difference.

1½ pounds lean (90 percent lean) ground round
1 medium onion, finely chopped
1 garlic clove, minced
½ cup rolled oats
2 egg whites
¼ cup chopped fresh parsley or 2 teaspoons dried
1 cup whole fresh parsley, washed and drained (optional)
1 teaspoon chopped fresh thyme or ½ teaspoon dried
½ teaspoon freshly ground black pepper
⅛ teaspoon ground cayenne
1 can (8 ounces) low-sodium tomato sauce

Follow the directions for Basic Meat Loaf (page 150), saving the whole parsley for garnish around the meat loaf after it has cooked.

Southwestern Meat Loaf

MAKES: *6 to 8 servings*
COOKING TIME: *16 to 20 minutes*

22.4 grams fat per serving for 6; 16.8 grams fat per serving for 8

SERVING SUGGESTION:
Serve with Mexican Tomato Sauce (page 319).

1½ pounds lean (90 percent lean) ground round
1 medium onion, finely chopped
½ cup fine dry bread crumbs
1 egg, beaten
1 can (4 ounces) mild green chilies, drained and chopped
1 fresh jalapeño or Refrigerator Pickled Jalapeño Pepper (page 314)
1 tablespoon chili powder
1 teaspoon ground cumin
1 teaspoon dried oregano leaves
½ teaspoon salt
¼ teaspoon freshly ground black pepper
1 can (8 ounces) tomato sauce
4 ounces grated Monterey Jack cheese
¼ cup chopped fresh cilantro (optional)

1. Follow the directions for Basic Meat Loaf (page 150), reserving the grated cheese and cilantro for addition later.
2. After the cooking is completed but before the standing time, sprinkle the loaf with grated cheese. Microwave on MEDIUM for 3 to 4 minutes, or until the cheese just melts.
3. Sprinkle with cilantro and allow to stand for 5 minutes.

Veal and Spinach Loaf

MAKES: *6 to 8 servings*
COOKING TIME: *20 to 27 minutes*

Low-cholesterol variation

14.7 grams fat per serving for 6; 11 grams fat per serving for 8

SERVING SUGGESTIONS:
We prefer this chilled, thinly sliced, and spread with a good

1 package (10 ounces) frozen chopped spinach
1½ pounds ground veal
1 medium onion, finely chopped
½ cup dry bread crumbs
2 eggs, beaten
2 tablespoons chopped fresh parsley
1 teaspoon dried thyme
½ teaspoon salt
¼ teaspoon grated nutmeg
¼ teaspoon freshly ground black pepper

1. Place the spinach in 1-quart microwave-safe casserole. Cover tightly with a lid or with plastic wrap turned back slightly. Microwave on HIGH for 2 minutes; stir. Cover again and cook on HIGH for 2 to 5 minutes, or until no ice crystals remain. Drain well.
2. Meanwhile, combine the remaining ingredients in a

grainy mustard. Tuck the slices into whole-wheat pita halves along with sprouts and tomato and mushroom slices; or line a plate with fresh spinach leaves; top with ripe tomato slices, then with veal slices spread with mustard.

VARIATION

We like to chill this light meat loaf and use it in place of less nutritious cold cuts.

large bowl. Add the spinach and mix well. Form the mixture into a firm 4 × 6½-inch loaf, rounding the corners.

3. Place in a 2-quart rectangular microwave-safe baking dish, making sure that the loaf doesn't touch the sides of the dish. Microwave on HIGH for 16 to 20 minutes, or until cooked through. Chill.

LOW-CHOLESTEROL TURKEY AND SPINACH LOAF (12 grams fat per serving for 6; 9.6 grams fat per serving for 8): Substitute ground turkey for ground veal.

Intense Chili

MAKES: *8 servings*
COOKING TIME: *50 minutes*

18.5 grams fat per serving

SERVING SUGGESTION:
Leftovers can become Deep-Dish Burritos (recipe follows) later in the week.

This was voted "favorite chili" by friends and family alike. The secret ingredient is the chocolate. Your chili may still be delicious without it, but it will lack the depth and intensity of flavor. We hope that you agree.

This chili has been the main component of many great parties and wonderful family meals. Cooking it on a lower power setting allows the flavors to blend; it also allows you to put up your feet, since you only need to stir once after 20 minutes.

1 tablespoon vegetable oil
2 garlic cloves, minced
2 large onions, coarsely chopped
3 to 6 tablespoons chili powder
1 tablespoon whole cumin seed or 1 teaspoon powdered cumin
1 teaspoon dried oregano
1 teaspoon ground cinnamon
1 teaspoon salt
½ teaspoon freshly ground black pepper
½ teaspoon cayenne
2 pounds ground round
2 cans (16 ounces each) stewed tomatoes
2 cans (16 ounces each) black or pinto beans (or one of each), undrained
2 green bell peppers, coarsely chopped
1 can (6 ounces) tomato paste
1 ounce unsweetened chocolate, coarsely chopped (optional)

GARNISHES

Sour cream, plain yogurt, grated Monterey Jack cheese, Salsa Cruda (page 317), and tortilla chips (optional)

1. In a 4-quart microwave-safe casserole, combine the oil, garlic, onion, chili powder, cumin, oregano, cinnamon, salt, black pepper, and cayenne. Cover tightly with a lid or with plastic wrap turned back slightly on

one side. Microwave on HIGH for 4 to 6 minutes, or until the onions are tender-crisp.

2. Spread the ground beef evenly over the mixture. Cover again and microwave on HIGH for 8 to 10 minutes, until most of the pink color is gone, stirring after 5 minutes to move the less-cooked sections to the outside of the dish.

3. Stir in the remaining ingredients. Cover again and cook on HIGH for 10 minutes; stir.

4. Cover again and cook on MEDIUM for 30 to 35 minutes, or until the flavors are blended, stirring once or twice.

5. Let stand for 5 to 10 minutes before serving.

6. Serve with optional garnishes, if desired.

Deep-Dish Burritos

MAKES: *4 servings*
COOKING TIME: *9 to 14 minutes*

25.5 grams fat per serving

This is a favorite leftover meal for us, although we have been known to whip up a pot of chili just so that we could savor this soul-satisfying dish. Using the MEDIUM power setting ensures even heating without overcooking the cheese.

2 cups Intense Chili (page 156) or other chili
4 flour tortillas
4 ounces grated low-fat Monterey Jack or cheddar cheese
Salsa Cruda (page 317) (optional)

1. Spoon the chili into a 1-quart microwave-safe casserole. Cover tightly with a lid or with plastic wrap turned back slightly on one side. Microwave on HIGH for 6 to 8 minutes, or until heated through, stirring twice.

2. Wrap two of the tortillas in a piece of paper towel. Microwave on HIGH for 30 seconds to soften.

3. Place the heated tortillas in a 2-quart rectangular microwave-safe dish. Spoon ½ cup of the heated chili onto the center of each.

4. Fold the bottom third of one tortilla up over the filling. Fold the right and left sides toward the center, overlapping them. Fold the top third down, making a rectangular package. Place the burrito seam side down in the dish. Repeat with the second tortilla.

5. Repeat the heating and folding process with the two remaining tortillas.

6. Sprinkle the burritos evenly with cheese. Cover with waxed paper. Cook on MEDIUM for 3 to 6 minutes, or until the cheese is melted. Serve with Salsa Cruda, if desired.

Beef-Filled Tacos or Tostadas

MAKES: *6 servings (12 tacos or 6 tostadas)*
COOKING TIME: *10 to 12 minutes*

Low-cholesterol variation

18.6 grams fat per 2 tacos

1 teaspoon vegetable oil
1 garlic clove, minced
1 medium onion, chopped
1 pound lean ground beef
1 can (8 ounces) California- or Spanish-style tomato sauce
2 tablespoons chili powder
1 teaspoon ground cumin
½ teaspoon salt
¼ teaspoon freshly ground black pepper
12 precooked taco shells or 6 precooked tostada shells

TOPPINGS

2 cups shredded lettuce
2 large tomatoes, chopped
1 onion, chopped (optional)
4 ounces grated Monterey Jack or cheddar cheese
1 cup sour cream
Salsa Cruda (page 317)

1. In a 2-quart microwave-safe casserole, combine the oil, garlic, and onion. Microwave on HIGH for 1 to 3 minutes, or until tender.
2. Spread the beef evenly over the onion in the bottom of the dish. Cover with waxed paper and microwave on HIGH for 5 to 8 minutes, or until just a bit of pink color remains, stirring once. Drain the excess fat. With a pancake turner, chop the beef into small pieces.
3. Add the tomato sauce, chili powder, cumin, salt, and pepper. Cover again with waxed paper and cook on HIGH for 3 to 5 minutes, stirring after 2 minutes.
4. Microwave the precooked shells on HIGH for 1 to 3 minutes, following instructions on the package.
5. Divide the filling between the shells and top with suggested toppings.

VARIATION LOW-CHOLESTEROL TURKEY TACOS OR TOSTADAS (13.7 grams fat per 2 tacos): Substitute ground turkey for ground beef and drain well. Eliminate cheese toppings and substitute nonfat yogurt for sour cream.

Basic
Meatballs

MAKES: *4 servings*
COOKING TIME: *5 to 8 minutes*

Low-cholesterol variation

16.3 grams fat per serving

Kids help

SERVING SUGGESTIONS:
Add to Basic Tomato Sauce
(page 145) and serve over
pasta or on hero rolls.

1 pound lean (90 percent lean) ground round or
  turkey
1 egg, beaten
1 medium onion, finely chopped
2 tablespoons chopped fresh parsley or 2 teaspoons
  dried
½ teaspoon dried oregano
¼ cup fine dry bread crumbs
⅛ teaspoon freshly ground black pepper
3 tablespoons grated Parmesan

1. Combine all ingredients in the bowl of a food
processor or in a large bowl.
2. Form into 1½-inch meatballs.
3. Place around the outer rim of a 10-inch microwave-
safe pie plate. Cover with waxed paper.
4. Microwave on HIGH for 6 to 8 minutes, turning the
meatballs over and rotating the dish one-quarter turn
after 4 minutes.
5. Drain and add to recipes.

VARIATION LOW-CHOLESTEROL MEATBALLS (14.8 grams fat per
serving): Substitute 1 egg white for whole egg.

Meatball
Hoagies

MAKES: *4 servings*

22 grams fat per serving

1 recipe Tomato and Meatball Sauce (page 146)
4 hero rolls, split lengthwise and toasted
Grated Parmesan

Spoon meatballs and sauce onto toasted rolls and
sprinkle with Parmesan.

Tamales
in the Round

MAKES: *6 servings*
COOKING TIME: *15 to 20*
minutes

1 cup yellow cornmeal
½ teaspoon salt
1 tablespoon olive oil
¼ tablespoon cayenne
1 pound round steak or Tamale Meat Filling (page
  160)
⅔ cup Mexican Tomato Sauce (page 319) or 1 can (5
  ounces) purchased red chili sauce (enchilada sauce)

10.4 grams fat per serving

SERVING SUGGESTION:
A great follow-up to Tomato
Beef Soup (page 107).

*Tamales traditionally consist
of corn dough (masa) mixed
with lard, which is then
spread on corn husks and
hand-wrapped around a
shredded meat filling. They
are labor-intensive and are
considered party or festival
fare in Mexico. We decided to
streamline the wrapping
process, make them in a
casserole dish, and substitute
for the lard a minimal
amount of olive oil to mix
with the cornmeal and low-fat
beef for the filling.*

1. In a 3-quart microwave-safe casserole, combine the cornmeal, salt, olive oil, 3½ cups water, and cayenne. Cover tightly with a lid or with plastic wrap turned back slightly on one side. Microwave on HIGH for 5 minutes; stir well to separate the grains.
2. Cover again and continue to cook on HIGH for 4 to 7 minutes, or until the liquid is absorbed. Stir well.
3. Meanwhile, cut the meat into 2-inch chunks. Process in the food processor to shred coarsely, or cut into ½-inch or smaller cubes by hand. Mix in a bowl with half the tomato sauce.
4. Spread half of the cooked cornmeal on the bottom of a 10-inch glass pie plate. Smooth by dipping a rubber spatula into water and spreading evenly.
5. Spoon the meat mixture evenly over the spread cornmeal, pushing it into the cornmeal slightly.
6. Spoon the remaining cornmeal over the meat, smoothing with a rubber spatula that has been dipped into water.
7. Pour the remaining tomato sauce over the pie and spread evenly.
8. Cover with waxed paper and microwave on MEDIUM for 8 to 10 minutes to heat through. Let stand 5 minutes before serving. Cut into wedges and serve.

NOTE

Extra pieces may be refrigerated and served later in the week, or to late dinner arrivals, by heating for 3 minutes on MEDIUM.

To freeze any remaining tamale wedges, let them cool and put them in individual freezer bags; place them in the freezer. To heat, take one out of the bag and place on a microwave-safe plate. Cover with waxed paper and heat on HIGH for 6 to 8 minutes, until heated through.

VARIATION

TAMALES IN THE ROUND WITH CHEESE (15.4 grams fat per serving): After the tamale has been heated through, sprinkle the top with 4 ounces grated Monterey Jack cheese. Heat on MEDIUM for 2 to 4 minutes more, or until the cheese is melted. (*Note:* Variation is not low-cholesterol.)

Tamale Meat Filling

MAKES: *12 servings*
COOKING TIME:

7.4 grams fat

SERVING SUGGESTIONS:
Use for filling in Tamales in the Round (page 158). This makes enough for two recipes. Freeze half the amount for a later meal.

1 bottom round steak (2 pounds), trimmed
1 medium onion, chopped
1 garlic clove, minced
¼ teaspoon freshly ground black pepper
½ teaspoon ground cumin
1 can (14½ ounces) stewed tomatoes with juice

1. Place the meat in a 3-quart microwave-safe casserole; add the remaining ingredients. Cover tightly, with a lid or with plastic wrap turned back slightly on one side. Microwave on HIGH for 8 to 12 minutes, until the tomato liquid is boiling.
2. Turn the meat over. Cover again and microwave on MEDIUM for 20 to 30 minutes, until the meat is tender. Let stand, covered, for 10 minutes.
3. Remove meat and cut in half. Follow step 3 on page 159 to make tamale filling, using the sauce in the casserole.

NOTE Cut the remaining meat into 2-inch chunks and freeze for later use in a sealable freezer bag. To defrost: Unseal bag halfway. Microwave on DEFROST for 7 to 8 minutes. Let stand 5 minutes.

DEFROSTING
WHOLE PIECES
OF MEAT

1. Unwrap frozen meat (beef, pork, or veal) and place on a microwave roasting rack in a rectangular microwave-safe dish. The rack is used to raise the meat above the liquids that collect during defrosting. You can substitute a small microwave-safe dish— invert it in the rectangular dish and place the meat on top. If you cannot unwrap the meat when first removed from the freezer, microwave with wrapping for 3 minutes on MEDIUM, then try again.
2. Microwave on MEDIUM for 5 to 6 minutes per pound, then on DEFROST for 5 to 6 minutes per pound, turning roast over twice.
3. Cover areas that appear to be cooking with a layer of foil, which will reflect microwaves.
4. Let roast stand (10 to 15 minutes for a medium-size roast and 30 minutes for a large one) to complete the defrosting process. Any remaining ice crystals will disappear during this time.

- Choose a uniformly shaped roast for even cooking.
- Begin cooking the roast with the fat side (or skin side) down; turn once during cooking.
- Shield areas that appear to be overcooking with a smooth layer of aluminum foil.
- To best judge doneness, insert a microwave thermometer into the meatiest part of the roast, avoiding contact with bone. Consult the Roasting Guide below to determine the correct internal temperature.
- The roast may look underdone when removed from the microwave oven but will finish cooking during the standing time. The meat needs to stand for at least 10 to 15 minutes, covered loosely with an aluminum foil "tent"—place the shiny side down to reflect heat into the roast.

ROASTING GUIDE

TYPE OF ROAST	START ON HIGH POWER	FINISH ON MEDIUM POWER	REMOVE AT INTERNAL TEMPERATURE	SPECIAL INSTRUCTIONS
Beef (rolled rump, eye of round, rib roast)	5 min. for roast 5 in. or less in diameter 10 min. for roast over 5 in. in diameter	Rare: 7 to 9 min./lb. Medium: 9 to 12 min./lb. Well: 12 to 14 min./lb.	Rare: 115° to 120°F Medium: 130°F Well: 145°F	Cook uncovered; don't add liquid
Pork Loin	5 min.	11 to 12 min./lb.	165°F	Cook covered; add ½ cup liquid
Veal (boneless breast or loin)	15 min.	50 to 60 min.	160°F, or until tender	Cook covered; add ¼ to ¾ cup liquid

Beef Roast au Jus

MAKES: *8 servings*
COOKING TIME: *About 30 minutes*

1 boneless beef roast (3 pounds) (rolled rib, eye round, or sirloin tip)
1 cup beef broth
Salt and pepper

1. Place the roast, fat-side down, on a microwave-safe roasting rack (or inverted saucer) in a 2-quart rectangular microwave-safe dish.

24 grams fat per serving

SERVING SUGGESTIONS:
Cook this large roast, even if
you have a small family, and
incorporate the remainders
into leftovers such as Tamales
in the Round (page 158)
and Beef Heros (recipe
follows).

*To calculate the cooking time
for a beef roast, you must
consider the diameter as well
as the weight of the meat. See
the Roasting Guide (page 161)
for details.*

2. If roast is more than 5 inches in diameter, microwave on HIGH for 10 minutes; if less than 5 inches in
diameter, microwave on HIGH for 5 minutes. Then
follow the guidelines below for the desired degree of
doneness, turning the roast over halfway through the
total cooking time:

- RARE (115 to 120°F)—cook on MEDIUM for 7 to 9
  minutes per pound
- MEDIUM (130°F)—cook on MEDIUM for 9 to 12 minutes
  per pound
- WELL DONE (145°F)—cook on MEDIUM for 12 to 14
  minutes per pound

3. Transfer roast to a serving platter. Let stand, tented
with aluminum foil, for 10 to 15 minutes.
4. Remove the rack from the dish. Remove any excess
fat from the meat juices. Stir 1 cup of beef broth into
the meat juices. Microwave, uncovered, on HIGH for 4
to 6 minutes, or until boiling, stirring once. Salt and
pepper to taste.

Beef Heros

4 servings

28 grams fat per serving

*¾ pound thinly sliced roast beef
4 4- to 6-inch hero rolls, split and toasted*

TOPPINGS

*Refrigerator Pickled Jalapeño Peppers (page 314)
Tomato slices
Shredded lettuce
Thinly sliced onions*

Divide the roast beef between the hero rolls. Add
toppings as desired.

Ham
on the Bone

MAKES: *18 to 20 servings*
COOKING TIME: *1 to 1½ hours*

*1 fully cooked ham on the bone (6 to 8 pounds)
Mustard Glaze or Fruit Glaze (recipes follow)
   (optional)*

1. Place the ham in an 8 × 12-inch (or 5-quart)
rectangular microwave-safe casserole. Cover the bone
with foil. Add ¼ cup water.

11 grams fat in 3 ounces of
fat and lean; 4 grams of fat in
3 ounces of lean only

SERVING SUGGESTIONS:
Serve with Creamy Mashed
Sweet Potatoes (page 228) or
Sweet Potato Pie with

NOTE

Mandarin Oranges and Pecans
(page 229) and Oven-Baked
Corn Bread (page 61).
Cranberry, Plum, or Tomato
Chutney (pages 330, 333) adds
great flavor contrast to the
meal.

*You'll probably have quite a
lot of ham left over. The day
after you serve it, divide it
up: leave some for sandwiches
and some for later use in ham
salad, macaroni and cheese,
pea soup, and omelets.*

2. Cover with a lid or with plastic wrap turned back
slightly on one side. Microwave on HIGH for 5 minutes;
then cook on MEDIUM for 10 to 12 minutes per pound,
or until the ham reaches 125°F, turning it over halfway
through the total cooking time.
3. Glaze, if desired, during the last 5 minutes, leaving
the ham uncovered. Let stand for 10 minutes.

If you want to free your microwave for other cooking
(e.g., vegetable and side dishes), follow these conventional cooking recommendations from the National
Pork Board: Preheat the oven to 325° F. Cook the ham
for 20 to 25 minutes per pound, or until the internal
temperature reaches 160° F.

Mustard Glaze

MAKES: *1 cup*

0.5 gram fat per tablespoon

*Slightly spicy and slightly
sweet at the same time!*

*½ cup prepared mustard (preferably Dijon)
2 tablespoons vinegar
2 tablespoons brown sugar
2 tablespoons honey
2 tablespoons catsup
½ teaspoon red-pepper flakes (optional)*

Combine all the ingredients in a small bowl and mix
well.

Fruit Glaze

MAKES: *¾ cup*

0.2 gram fat per tablespoon

*½ cup apricot preserves, orange marmalade, or
    pineapple preserves
2 tablespoons Dijon mustard
2 tablespoons brown sugar or honey*

Combine all the ingredients in a small bowl and mix
well.

Ham Salad
from
Holiday Ham

MAKES: *1¼ cups*

6.7 grams fat per ¼ cup

SERVING SUGGESTIONS:
Great as a sandwich spread or
a topping for crackers or
croustades.

1 cup cooked ham, cut into 2-inch chunks
⅓ cup sweet relish
1 teaspoon lemon juice
2 tablespoons low-cholesterol mayonnaise
2 tablespoons nonfat yogurt

1. Place the ham in the bowl of a food processor; pulse
on and off three or four times, or until coarsely
chopped.
2. In a small bowl, combine the ham with the remaining ingredients.

Leg of Lamb

MAKES: *8 servings (or two
meals for 4)*
COOKING TIME: *30 minutes for
medium; 35 to 40 minutes for
well done*

*16.1 grams fat per 3 ounces
fat and lean; 6 grams fat per
3 ounces lean only*

SERVING SUGGESTIONS:
Serve with cooking juices or
Lamb Gravy (recipe follows)
and Mint Sauce (page 318) for
the first meal. A colorful
presentation can be made by
surrounding the sliced lamb
with Herb-Topped Tomatoes
(page 221) and Dilled Small
Potatoes (page 232). Use the
remaining meat to whip up a
Shepherd's Pie (page 165) or
Mideastern Pita Pockets (page
166).

1 leg of lamb (3 to 4 pounds)
1 tablespoon olive oil
1 garlic clove, minced
½ teaspoon freshly ground black pepper
½ teaspoon dried thyme leaves

1. Trim most of the fell (the white sheet that resembles
parchment) and fat from the lamb. Rub with oil and
garlic and sprinkle with pepper and thyme.
2. Place the lamb on a roasting rack in a 3-quart
microwave-safe dish. Microwave on HIGH for 5 minutes. Turn the meat over and cook on HIGH for 5 more
minutes. Reduce power to MEDIUM and cook for 20
minutes for medium-rare (145°F on a meat thermometer), or until the juices run rosy, not red when pricked
deeply, and 30 minutes for well done (160°F on a meat
thermometer), or until the juices run clear. Let stand
for 10 minutes before carving.
3. To serve: Thinly slice half the meat and place on
serving plates. Tip the cooking dish and spoon the
cooking juices over the meat. Reserve the remaining
meat for "planned overs."

Lamb is succulent when cooked in the microwave oven. For optimum flavor, we prefer it cooked medium-rare.

Lamb Gravy

MAKES: ½ cup
COOKING TIME: 2 to 3 minutes

0.6 gram fat per tablespoon

½ cup beef broth
1 tablespoon flour
Pan juices from lamb, defatted

1. After cooking and standing time, transfer the lamb to a platter and remove the rack.
2. In a small microwave-safe bowl, combine 2 tablespoons of the beef broth with the flour; stir to form a paste.
3. Add the pan juices from the lamb, the remaining beef broth, and 1 tablespoon water. Microwave on HIGH for 2 to 3 minutes.

Shepherd's Pie

MAKES: 4 servings
COOKING TIME: 35 minutes

18.6 grams fat per serving

This is a tasty way to turn leftover leg of lamb into a triumphant second-day meal.

About 2 cups cooked lamb, in 2-inch cubes
1 medium onion, chopped
1 tablespoon olive oil
2 tablespoons flour
1 cup beef broth
1 package (10 ounces) frozen peas
¼ teaspoon dried thyme
1 recipe Old-Fashioned Mashed Potatoes (page 223) (about 3 cups)
2 tablespoons grated Parmesan (optional)
½ teaspoon paprika

1. Place the cooked lamb cubes in the bowl of a food processor and pulse until coarsely ground.
2. Combine the onion and oil in a 10-inch microwave-safe pie plate. Microwave on HIGH for 1 to 2 minutes, or until tender.
3. Sprinkle the flour over the onion and stir until evenly absorbed.
4. Add the broth and cook on HIGH for 3 to 4 minutes, or until boiling and thickened, stirring once.
5. Add the peas and cook on HIGH for 2 to 3 minutes, or until peas are thawed.

6. Stir in the thyme and lamb. Cover tightly with a lid or with plastic wrap turned back on one side. Microwave on HIGH for 8 to 10 minutes, or until heated through, stirring once.

7. Smooth the meat out in the same pie plate, making an even layer, and spoon the mashed potatoes around the outer rim. Spread the potatoes with a rubber spatula.

8. Sprinkle the top with cheese and paprika; cover with waxed paper. Microwave on MEDIUM for 10 to 12 minutes, or until heated through.

NOTE   If you don't have any leftover mashed potatoes and plan to cook potatoes in the microwave oven, it is best to do so before cooking the meat filling. They can then be standing while the meat filling is simmering and be ready to mash for the pie topping.

Mideastern Pita Pockets

MAKES: *4 servings*
COOKING TIME: *5 minutes*

Low-cholesterol variations

8.3 grams fat per serving

4 large pita pockets, cut in half crosswise
About 2 cups thinly sliced cooked lamb (12 ounces)
1 large tomato, thinly sliced
½ head lettuce, shredded
1 small onion, thinly sliced (optional)
Yogurt Sauce (page 318)

1. Toast the pita bread.
2. For each sandwich: Split the toasted pita in half and divide 3 ounces of meat between the halves.
3. Add the tomato, lettuce, and onion slices. Spoon 1 or 2 tablespoons sauce into each half. Assemble the remaining pitas.

VARIATIONS   Low-Cholesterol Turkey Pita Pockets (6.6 grams fat per serving): Substitute cooked turkey for lamb, removing any skin.

SERVING SUGGESTION:
Sprouts and thinly sliced cucumbers make interesting additions to these pockets.

A quick lunch or light evening meal.

Low-Cholesterol Chicken Pita Pockets (5.5 grams fat per serving): Substitute Poached Boneless Chicken Breasts (page 185), sliced (either warm or chilled), for lamb.

Basic Stew

MAKES: *8 servings*
COOKING TIME: *60 to 70 minutes*

7.9 grams fat per serving for beef; 9.8 grams fat per serving for lamb; 5.9 grams fat per serving for veal; 6.7 grams fat per serving for pork

SERVING SUGGESTIONS:
All of our stews are designed to make two meals. For the first meal, divide half of the stew between four soup bowls. Serve with chunks of Fast-Rise Whole-Wheat Shredded-Wheat Bread (page 42) or over noodles or rice, which can be cooked conventionally while the stew is simmering in the microwave oven. For a follow-up meal, the remaining stew can be turned into a tasty filling for Modern Pot Pies (pages 169–72).

The microwave oven cuts the cooking time in half. And stirring is kept to a minimum. Once it starts to simmer, you can relax for 30 minutes.

1 pound pearl onions, peeled (see Note), or 1 large onion, chopped
1 garlic clove, minced
1 tablespoon olive oil
1 pound carrots, cut into ½-inch pieces
1½ pounds veal shoulder, beef round, lamb, or lean pork, cut into 1-inch pieces and trimmed of fat.
1 can (16 ounces) sliced stewed tomatoes with juice, undrained
1 cup red wine and 1 cup beef broth, or 2 cups beef broth
2 tablespoons tomato paste
1 teaspoon dried thyme leaves
½ cup chopped fresh parsley
¼ teaspoon freshly ground black pepper

1. In a 4-quart microwave-safe casserole, combine the peeled onions, garlic, olive oil, and carrots. Cover tightly with a lid or with plastic wrap turned back slightly on one side. Microwave on HIGH for 5 minutes.
2. Place the meat cubes over the vegetables in a single layer. Cover again and cook on HIGH for 10 minutes, stirring after 5 minutes, moving the lesser-cooked pieces of meat to the outside.
3. Stir in the remaining ingredients and cook on HIGH for 15 to 17 minutes, or until boiling; stir well. Cover again and cook on MEDIUM for 35 to 40 minutes, or until the meat is tender. Let stand for 5 to 10 minutes before serving.

NOTE
Blanch the pearl onions for peeling by placing them in a 1-quart microwave-safe casserole with ¼ cup water. Cover tightly with a lid or with plastic wrap turned back slightly on one side. Microwave on HIGH for 3 to 4 minutes, or until the onions start to hiss, stirring after 2 minutes. Rinse with cold water immediately to make handling easier. Peel.

VARIATIONS
BASIC STEW WITH PARSNIPS AND CARROTS: Substitute ½ pound of parsnips for ½ pound of the carrots.

BASIC STEW WITH POTATOES AND CARROTS: Substitute ½ pound of potatoes, peeled and cut into ½-inch cubes, for ½ pound of the carrots.

Green Chili, Pork, and Butternut Squash Stew

MAKES: *6 servings*
COOKING TIME: *55 minutes*

6.5 grams fat per serving

SERVING SUGGESTIONS:
Serve with Warm Flour Tortillas (page 67) or Chili Beer Bread (page 64) to sop up the thin gravy. Try serving in a blue bowl for a striking color contrast.

Ever since we visited the Southwest, this dish has appeared in some form on our tables—at breakfast, lunch, or dinner. Butternut squash lends a New England touch to this tasty version; if it's not available, substitute sweet potatoes.

3 cups chicken broth
1 tablespoon olive oil
2 garlic cloves, minced
1 onion, chopped
1½ pounds boneless pork, trimmed of fat, cut into ½-inch pieces
2 tablespoons flour
1 butternut squash (1½ pounds) peeled, seeded, and cut into 1-inch cubes
2 cans (4 ounces each) chopped mild green chilies
1 jalapeño pepper, chopped (more if you like)
1 teaspoon dried oregano
½ teaspoon salt
Chopped fresh cilantro (optional)

1. Pour the broth into a 4-cup glass measure. Microwave on HIGH for 6 to 8 minutes (this step speeds heating later).
2. In a 3-quart microwave-safe casserole, combine the oil, garlic, and onion. Microwave on HIGH for 2 minutes.
3. Add the pork and sprinkle it with flour to coat. Cover with a lid or with plastic wrap turned back slightly on one side. Microwave on HIGH for 6 minutes, stirring after 3 minutes to move the less-cooked pieces to the outside.
4. Stir in the heated broth and remaining ingredients. Cover again and cook on HIGH for 6 to 8 minutes, or until boiling; stir. Cover again and cook on MEDIUM for 40 minutes, or until meat and squash are tender. Let stand for 5 minutes before serving.

Pork, Cabbage, and Red Potato Stew

MAKES: *4 servings*
COOKING TIME: *30 minutes*

18.5 grams fat per serving

1 pork shoulder butt (about 1½ pounds)
1 tablespoon olive, canola, or vegetable oil
1 medium onion, chopped
1 garlic clove, minced
1 pound small red potatoes, scrubbed and quartered
1 pound cabbage, cut into ¼-inch strips (4 cups)
1 cup red wine or water
½ teaspoon dried thyme leaves
1 cup beef broth
¼ teaspoon freshly ground black pepper
Dash cayenne

Serve with Onion-Caraway
Beer Bread (page 63), which
can be mixed and put in the
conventional oven before the
stew is started, or purchased
rye bread.

Prepare this stew once and
you'll have two meals. Serve
them in the same week, or
freeze the piece of pork that is
cut off for a second meal later
in the month.

*Thelma remembers her
German mother making this
delicious cold-weather
soup/stew. The ham, cabbage,
and potatoes had to be cooked
separately. For convenience
and optimum flavor, we have
combined everything in one
"cook-and-serve" dish.*

1. Cut a ¾-pound chunk (i.e., about half the meat) from the pork butt. Wrap and refrigerate (for up to 1 week) or freeze (for up to 1 month).
2. In a 3-quart microwave-safe casserole, combine the oil, onion, and garlic. Microwave on HIGH for 1 minute. Add the pork and the remaining ingredients. Cover tightly with a lid or with plastic wrap turned back on one side. Cook on HIGH for 10 minutes; stir well.
3. Cover again and cook on HIGH for 18 to 20 minutes more, or until the potatoes and cabbage are tender, stirring twice. Let stand for 5 minutes before serving.

Modern Pot Pies

Pot pies were some of our favorite childhood meals. We remember that they took a long time to prepare: the filling had to be cooked, then the crusts prepared and rolled out for the final baking. Then along came frozen pot pies, which became convenient "baby-sitter meals" when our parents went out for an evening alone.

We feel that our pot pies are a good compromise between the two: they are still quick, but loving care and lots of fun go into the preparation of the various toppings. They still make great kids' meals, too, and children love to help make the pie toppings.

We have made the top crusts lower in fat and have also eliminated the bottom crusts to save time. The "topper" may be baked in a toaster oven or conventional oven, while the filling simmers in the microwave. All the toppers that follow are adequate for a four-serving stew.

You may wish to add one 10-ounce package of frozen vegetables to leftover stews when using them for pie fillings. (We like frozen peas or corn.) If you do so, cook the fillings an additional 2 to 3 minutes on HIGH.

Biscuit Pot Pies

MAKES: *4 individual pies*
COOKING TIME: *15 minutes*

*5 grams fat per serving
(biscuit topping)*

SERVING SUGGESTIONS:
We like these best with
Fisherman's Catch (page 102),
Deep-Dish Turkey Pot Pie
(page 178), and Basic Stew
with Potatoes and Carrots
(page 167).

4 servings stew (pages 167–68)
1 recipe Old-Fashioned Biscuits Made Light (page 55)

1. Preheat a toaster oven or conventional oven to 450°F.
2. Lightly rub a cookie sheet or the toaster-oven pan with olive, canola, or vegetable oil.
3. Place the stew in a 3-quart microwave-safe casserole. Cover with a lid or with plastic wrap turned back slightly on one side. Microwave on HIGH for 10 to 15 minutes, or until hot, stirring once.
4. Meanwhile, combine the biscuit mixture following steps 3 and 4 on page 55.
5. Place the dough on a lightly floured surface. Roll or pat out into a 7½ × 11½-inch rectangle about ½ inch thick. Cut into eight 2-inch squares (or use cookie cutters for other shapes).
6. Place on prepared baking sheet; bake for 8 to 10 minutes, or until lightly browned.
7. Divide the warm stew between four large soup bowls, and top each one with two biscuits.

Polenta Pot Pies

MAKES: *4 individual pies*
COOKING TIME: *5 to 8 minutes*

*1.2 grams fat per serving
(polenta topping)*

SERVING SUGGESTIONS:
Cook the polenta the night
before or earlier in the day, to
allow time for chilling and
setting. This is particularly
good when made with Chicken
Cacciatore (page 184 or 185),
Basic Stew (page 167) made
with veal, or Green Chili,
Pork, and Butternut Squash
Stew (page 168).

4 servings stew (pages 167–68)
½ cup coarse cornmeal
1 teaspoon olive oil

1. The night before, combine all the ingredients with 1¾ cups water in a 2-quart microwave-safe casserole. Cover tightly with a lid or with plastic wrap turned back slightly on one side. Microwave on HIGH for 3 minutes; stir. Cover again and cook on HIGH for 2 to 5 minutes more, or until all the water is absorbed; stir once again.
2. Pour into a 9-inch round or 8-inch square flat-bottomed dish and spread out evenly. Cover and refrigerate until cooled and set or until you're ready to use it.
3. Preheat broiler (or preheat toaster oven to "broil" setting).
4. Lightly rub a cookie sheet or the toaster-oven pan with olive, canola, or vegetable oil.
5. Place the stew in a 3-quart microwave-safe casserole. Cover with a lid or with plastic wrap turned back slightly on one side. Microwave on HIGH for 10 to 15

Polenta (cooked cornmeal) makes a quick and delicious topper—if you have never tried it, you are in for a treat.

minutes, or until hot, stirring once.

6. Cut the polenta into 2-inch diamond shapes or use a cookie cutter for other shapes. Place on the cookie sheet and run under the broiler to brown, watching closely to prevent burning.

7. Divide the stew between four large soup bowls. Top with two or three polenta cutouts.

VARIATIONS

CHEESE POLENTA (2.2 grams fat per serving): Stir 3 tablespoons grated Parmesan into the polenta at the end of cooking.

SAGE POLENTA: Stir ¼ teaspoon dried sage leaves into the polenta at the end of cooking.

Mashed-Potato Pot Pies

MAKES: *4 individual pies*
COOKING TIME: *22 to 25 minutes*

5.4 grams fat per serving with mashed potato topping; 2.4 grams fat with low-cholesterol mashed potatoes

1 recipe Old-Fashioned Mashed Potatoes (page 223)
4 servings stew (pages 167–68)
Paprika (optional)

1. Cook the potatoes for mashed potatoes before reheating the stew.

2. Place the stew in a 3-quart microwave-safe casserole and cover with a lid or with plastic wrap turned back slightly on one side. Microwave on HIGH for 10 to 15 minutes, or until hot, stirring once.

3. Mash the potatoes.

4. Divide the stew between four large soup bowls. Spoon the potatoes over the stew; sprinkle with paprika, if desired.

Traditional Pastry Pot Pies

MAKES: *4 individual pies*
COOKING TIME: *15 minutes*

4 servings stew (pages 167–68)
1 recipe Basic Pastry (recipe follows) or 1 package (15 ounces) refrigerated 9-inch flat pie crust (see Note)

1. Preheat the toaster oven or conventional oven to 400° F.

2. Place the stew in a 3-quart microwave-safe casserole and cover with a lid or with plastic wrap turned back slightly on one side. Microwave on HIGH for 10 to 15 minutes, or until hot, stirring once.

10 grams fat per serving (pastry topping)

A standard pie crust transforms any stew into a delicious pot pie.

3. Roll the Basic Pastry into a 12-inch circle. (If using packaged pastry, just unwrap and lay out.) Using a 2-inch cookie cutter, cut out twelve shapes.
4. Place on an ungreased cookie sheet and bake for 8 to 10 minutes, or until lightly browned, dry, and opaque.
5. Spoon the warm stew into four large soup bowls and top each with three pastry cutouts.

NOTE   Refrigerate remaining crust for future use.

Basic Pastry

MAKES: *1 bottom or top crust for a 9-inch pie or 12 cutouts for Traditional Pastry Pot Pies (page 289).*

9.4 grams fat per serving for 8 (pastry topping)

1 cup all-purpose flour
½ teaspoon salt
3 tablespoons cold butter, cut into 6 pieces
3 tablespoons solid vegetable shortening, cut into 6 pieces
2 to 3 tablespoons ice water

1. Place the flour and salt in the bowl of a food processor; pulse on and off twice to blend.
2. Add butter and shortening and pulse on and off six to eight times, until fat particles are pea-size.
3. Add water, 1 tablespoon at a time, pulsing on and off until particles can be gathered lightly into a ball.
4. Flatten the dough into a pancake approximately 4½ inches in diameter. Cover with plastic wrap; freeze for 30 minutes, if in a hurry, or refrigerate for at least 1 hour or up to 3 days. (The dough may be frozen at this point for up to 1 month; see Note.)

NOTE   To freeze pie dough for longer than 30 minutes, wrap tightly in plastic wrap.
   To defrost frozen pie dough, unwrap and place on plastic wrap in the microwave oven. Microwave on DEFROST for 1 to 2 minutes to soften.

POULTRY

Turkeys are not just for holidays anymore. We find them a wise choice for menu planning and cook one about once a month, usually when they are on sale at our local market. A whole turkey will feed our family for days with salads, club sandwiches, fajitas, and pot pies.

We show you how to prepare a whole turkey using a combination method—microwave and conventional oven. And if grilled turkey is your preference, we have a variation for that too. We also provide a recipe for cooking a smaller turkey breast in the microwave oven only. Our primary goal is to give you the succulent meat but not the crispy skin. To this end, the microwave oven works just as well as any conventional means and, of course, is much faster.

Chicken is also much more versatile today because it is so easy to buy just the parts that you want—legs, thighs, breasts, or wings. Skinless, boneless chicken breasts (sometimes called chicken cutlets) are so quick to prepare that we recommend them as a freezer staple.

By keeping a pound of chicken cutlets frozen at all times, you'll have the makings for a freezer-to-table meal that takes less than 30 minutes. Some examples are Chicken Cutlets Parmigiana, Deep-Dish Chicken Enchiladas, and Warm Chicken Salad with Papaya and Sake-Lime Dressing. If you do nothing more than make Poached Boneless Chicken Breasts and then splash them with a Cranberry-Pepper Vinaigrette, or Garlic, Rosemary, and Thyme Vinaigrette from your home pantry, you'll have a meal to remember.

SPEED DEFROSTING WHOLE TURKEY AND TURKEY BREAST

1. Unwrap frozen turkey or turkey breasts and place on a microwave roasting rack in a rectangular microwave-safe dish. The rack is used to raise the meat above the liquids that collect during defrosting. You can substitute a small microwave-safe dish—invert it in the rectangular dish and place the meat on top.
2. Microwave on HIGH for 1 minute per pound, then on MEDIUM for 2 minutes per pound, then on DEFROST or LOW for 1 minute per pound. Begin with the turkey skin-side down; turn over halfway through the cooking process, discarding the defrosted liquids.
3. If wing or leg areas appear to be cooking, cover them smoothly with foil, which will reflect microwaves.
4. When removed from the oven, whole birds should have ice crystals inside and between legs and wings and body.
5. Place the oven-defrosted bird in a cold-water bath to melt any remaining ice crystals. Remove the giblets as soon as possible during this time. If you're in a hurry, run hot water into the cavity to remove the ice and giblets quickly.
6. After the ice crystals have melted, let the bird stand until completely defrosted: 30 minutes to 1 hour.

Oven-Browned Turkey

1 turkey (12 to 16 pounds)

1. Truss the turkey by tying the legs together and the wings to the body. *Do not use metal skewers.*
2. Place it breast side down in a 3-quart rectangular microwave-safe baking dish. Microwave, uncovered, on MEDIUM-HIGH for 9 minutes per pound, turning

Low cholesterol (as long as you don't eat the skin!)

4.2 grams fat per 3-ounce serving of light and dark meat; 3.2 grams fat per 3-ounce serving of light meat only

SERVING SUGGESTIONS:
Serve with Cranberry Sauce (page 322) and Mixed

NOTE

Vegetable Platter with Lemon Sauce (page 227), which can be cooked during the turkey's

VARIATION

standing time. For a more festive meal, add Sweet Potato Pie with Mandarin Oranges and Pecans (page 229), prepared earlier and reheated right before serving. To finish off the remains, make Deep-Dish Turkey Pot Pie (page 178) and then a soup.

Herbed Bread Stuffing

MAKES: *Stuffing for a 14- to 16-pound turkey*
COOKING TIME: *10 minutes*

Low-cholesterol variation

over halfway through cooking. Drain any fat with a bulb baster. (If your oven has no MEDIUM-HIGH setting, cook on HIGH for 10 minutes and then on MEDIUM for 10 to 12 minutes per pound. Check the wing and leg areas when approximately 20 minutes of cooking time remains to see if they are done; if so, cover them with foil to prevent overcooking.)

3. During the last 15 minutes of microwave cooking, preheat the conventional oven to 500° F.

4. Transfer the microwave-cooked turkey to the preheated oven for 5 to 10 minutes to crisp and brown. Let the turkey stand, covered, for 20 minutes or so before slicing.

Reserve all cooking juices (you should have about 2 to 3 cups) and refrigerate them overnight. Remove the fat from the top and add to soup or use as broth for pot pies.

GRILLED TURKEY: Follow basic cooking instructions above, but preheat grill instead of conventional oven. Spray the grill *well* with a nonstick spray. Place the turkey on the grill and cook for 10 to 15 minutes, or until brown, turning the turkey over after about 5 minutes of cooking, or when the first side is browned. Cook the second side for 5 to 8 minutes, or until browned and crisped. (To turn over, spear the inner cavity with a large fork and grab one of the legs with an oven mitt.) Let stand, covered, for 20 minutes.

½ cup (1 stick) butter or margarine
1 cup finely chopped onion
2 cups thinly sliced celery
8 cups dry bread cubes (see Note 1)
½ cup chopped fresh parsley, or 1 tablespoon dried
1 tablespoon chopped fresh sage, or 1 teaspoon crumbled dried
½ teaspoon salt
½ teaspoon freshly ground black pepper
1 teaspoon dried thyme
2 cups chicken broth or water

1. In a 3-quart microwave-safe casserole, combine the butter, onion, and celery. Cover tightly with a lid or

10 grams fat per serving for 12 servings

with plastic wrap turned back slightly on one side. Microwave on HIGH for 5 to 6 minutes, or until the vegetables are tender. Add in the bread cubes and seasonings; stir well.

2. Pour the broth or water into a 4-cup glass measure. Microwave on HIGH for 5 to 6 minutes, or until boiling. Pour into the stuffing mixture and stir well to moisten.

NOTE 1   To DRY THE BREAD CUBES, place 4 cups of bread cubes in a rectangular microwave-safe dish. Microwave on HIGH for 6 to 7 minutes, stirring once. Repeat the process.

NOTE 2   This stuffing may be prepared a day in advance and refrigerated. However, *do not* stuff the bird until just before cooking.

NOTE 3   To CUT RECIPE IN HALF, halve the ingredients and cooking times.

VARIATIONS   MUSHROOM STUFFING (10 grams fat per serving for 8): Add 2 cups coarsely chopped mushrooms with onions and celery.

LOW-CHOLESTEROL BREAD STUFFING (1 gram fat per serving for 8): Substitute ¼ cup water for butter or margarine when cooking the onion and celery.

WHOLE-WHEAT BREAD STUFFING (10 grams fat per serving for 8): Substitute whole-wheat bread for white bread.

Giblet Gravy

MAKES: *3 to 3½ cups*
COOKING TIME: *9 to 11 minutes*

0.4 gram fat per tablespoon

SERVING SUGGESTION:
It is best to make the giblet stock the day before you serve the turkey, or earlier in the day, and make the gravy while the turkey is standing.

2 to 2½ cups Turkey Giblet Stock (recipe follows)
3 tablespoons all-purpose flour (see Note)
Juices from turkey cooking dish, fat removed (about 1 cup)
Salt and pepper to taste

1. Pour all but ¼ cup of the stock into a 2-quart microwave-safe casserole.
2. In a small bowl combine the flour and ¼ cup stock; blend to make a smooth paste. Add back in to the remaining stock; beat with a wire whisk until smooth.
3. Add the turkey juices to the stock; stir. Microwave on HIGH for 9 to 11 minutes, or until boiling and slightly thickened. Salt and pepper to taste.

NOTE For a thicker gravy, add an extra 1 tablespoon of flour.

VARIATION MADEIRA GIBLET GRAVY: Add ¼ cup Madeira to giblet stock.

Turkey Giblet Stock

MAKES: *2 to 2½ cups*
COOKING TIME: *8 to 10 minutes*

2.1 grams fat per cup

Giblets from 1 turkey (excluding liver)
3 cups chicken broth
1 onion, halved
1 carrot, cut into large chunks
1 celery rib, cut into large chunks
3 sprigs parsley or 1 teaspoon dried
1 bay leaf, broken in half
1 sprig fresh thyme or ¼ teaspoon dried

Combine all the ingredients in a 3-quart microwave-safe casserole. Cover with a lid or with plastic wrap turned back slightly on one side. Microwave on HIGH for 8 to 10 minutes. Strain.

Glazed Turkey Breast

MAKES: *8 servings*
COOKING TIME: *45 minutes*

Low cholesterol (as long as you don't eat the skin!)

7 grams fat per 3 ounce serving with skin; 3.2 grams fat per 3-ounce serving without skin

½ cup apricot preserves
2 tablespoons fresh lemon juice
1 turkey breast (5 pounds)

1. Mix the preserves and lemon juice in a 2-cup glass measure. Microwave on HIGH for 1 to 2 minutes, until melted.
2. Place the turkey breast, skin side down, in a 2-quart rectangular microwave-safe dish. Brush the breast with half of the glaze. Microwave on MEDIUM-HIGH (70 percent power) for 23 minutes.
3. Turn the breast skin side up. Brush with the remaining glaze. Continue to cook on MEDIUM-HIGH for 22 to 25 minutes, or until the juices run clear from the meatiest area of the breast (see Note). Let stand, tented with aluminum foil, for 10 minutes before slicing.

NOTE A turkey breast needs to cook for about 9 minutes per pound on MEDIUM-HIGH (70 percent power) or 7 minutes per pound on HIGH, then 8 minutes per pound on MEDIUM. The temperature in the meatiest area should reach 170° F before standing time.

SERVING SUGGESTIONS:
Follow suggestions for Oven-Browned Turkey (page 174) or use for sandwiches and salads.

Warm Turkey and Orange Salad

MAKES: *4 servings*
COOKING TIME: *3 to 5 minutes*

Low cholesterol

14.4 grams fat per serving

SERVING SUGGESTIONS:
For a complete meal,
serve with Refrigerated
Shredded-Wheat Bread (page
41), purchased whole-wheat
bread, Bulghur Pilaf (page
118), or Barley Pilaf (page
116).

2 large oranges
½ cup orange juice
4 teaspoons low-sodium soy sauce
2 teaspoons grated fresh ginger
1½ teaspoons cornstarch
¾ pound cooked turkey, skin removed, meat cut into
   ½-inch cubes
6 cups mixed salad greens (romaine, radicchio, curly
   endive, leaf lettuce, or watercress)
2 green onions, thinly sliced
¼ cup coarsely chopped walnuts

1. Cut long, thin slivers of orange peel for garnish.
2. Peel and segment the oranges and set aside.
3. Pour the orange juice into a 4-cup glass measure. Add the soy sauce, ginger, and cornstarch; stir to blend. Microwave, uncovered, on HIGH for 1½ to 2 minutes, or until the mixture boils.
4. Add the turkey and toss to coat with mixture. Cover with waxed paper and microwave on HIGH for 1½ to 2 minutes, or until the turkey is heated through.
5. Line four plates with salad greens. Spoon the turkey and sauce on top of the greens. Arrange the orange segments around the turkey and sprinkle with green onion and walnuts. Garnish with orange peel if desired.

Deep-Dish Turkey Pot Pie

MAKES: *4 servings*
COOKING TIME: *15 to 18 minutes*

Kids help

Low cholesterol

10.3 grams fat per serving with 1 biscuit

1 tablespoon olive or canola oil
1 medium onion, coarsely chopped
1 clove garlic, minced
1 large potato, cut into ½-inch cubes (1 cup)
2 tablespoons flour
1 package (10 ounces) frozen peas and carrots (see
   Note)
2 cups cubed cooked turkey
2 cups chicken broth
½ cup dry white wine, vermouth, or water
¼ pound mushrooms, thinly sliced (optional)
¼ teaspoon dried thyme
⅛ teaspoon cayenne
½ recipe Old-Fashioned Biscuits Made Light (page
   55)

1. Preheat the toaster oven or conventional oven to 450° F.

You can cover this with any of the pot-pie toppings (pages 169–72), but we prefer a biscuit topping (see page 55). When kids help with the toppings, use large chicken- or turkey-shaped cookie cutters or other favorite shapes.

2. In a 2-quart microwave-safe casserole, combine the oil, onion, garlic, and potato. Cover tightly with a lid or with plastic wrap turned back slightly on one side. Microwave on HIGH for 5 to 7 minutes, or until the potato is tender.

3. Sprinkle with flour and stir until absorbed. Stir in the frozen vegetables and cover again. Cook on HIGH for 2 minutes.

4. Add the remaining ingredients, except the biscuit mix; stir well. Cover again and cook on HIGH for 8 to 10 minutes, stirring once, until heated through and bubbling.

5. Meanwhile, combine the biscuit mixture following steps 3 and 4 on page 55. Place the dough on a lightly floured surface. Roll or pat out into a 7½ x 11-inch rectangle about ½ inch thick. Cut into eight 2-inch rectangles (or use cookie cutters for other shapes).

6. To serve: Divide the stew between four large soup bowls and top each with two biscuits.

NOTE You may substitute 1 cup fresh peas and 1 cup fresh carrots for frozen. Add carrots to recipe in step 2 with potatoes and cook for 7 to 9 minutes instead of 5 to 7 minutes. Add peas in step 3 and cook for 4 minutes instead of 2 minutes.

Turkey Salad for Sandwiches

MAKES: *4 cups (8 servings)*

VARIATION

Low-cholesterol variation

7.4 grams fat per serving

SERVING SUGGESTIONS:
Spoon onto toasted bread and

2 cups cooked turkey, cut into bite-size chunks
1 cup thinly sliced celery
¼ cup thinly sliced green onion tops or chives
¼ cup mayonnaise
¼ cup plain yogurt
1 tablespoon fresh lemon juice

Toss all the ingredients together in a bowl. Refrigerate until ready to serve.

LOW-CHOLESTEROL TURKEY SALAD (4.1 grams fat per serving): Substitute low-cholesterol mayonnaise for regular mayonnaise and nonfat yogurt for regular yogurt.

top with lettuce and tomato.
For a sandwich with a
different twist, try serving on
Lemon-Scented Cranberry
Bread (page 60) or toasted
Refrigerated Shredded-Wheat
Bread (page 41). Spoon
Cranberry Chutney (page 330)
on top or alongside.

Turkey Sausages

MAKES: *16 patties*

Low cholesterol

7 grams fat per pattie

Kids help

SERVING SUGGESTIONS:
Keep on hand in the freezer
for weekend breakfasts or
additions to pasta sauces and
"Cassoulet" (page 121).

*Thelma remembers the
natural, appealing sausage
made in her Connecticut
hometown by local farmers.
She started making her own
pork sausages many years
ago.*

NOTE

*Pork gave way to turkey
after friends Rudy and Pat
Masaryk introduced her to
homemade turkey sausages.
At that time we had to go to
a local turkey farm for freshly
ground turkey.*

2 pounds ground turkey
1 teaspoon salt
½ teaspoon freshly ground black pepper
¼ teaspoon dried basil
¼ teaspoon freshly grated nutmeg
¼ teaspoon paprika
¼ teaspoon dried sage
¼ teaspoon dried thyme

1. Blend the ground turkey and seasonings in the bowl
of a food processor or a mixing bowl. If you use a
mixing bowl, mix with a spoon or your hands. (Dip
your hands into cold water first to prevent sticking.)
Refrigerate the mixture, covered, for at least 12 hours,
to let the flavors develop.
2. To form the patties: Cut two 12-inch squares of
waxed paper. Using a ¼-cup measure that has been
dipped into cold water (to prevent sticking), spoon out
sixteen ¼-cup portions.
3. With wet hands, pat into 3-inch patties; place eight
patties on each square of waxed paper. Fold the edges of
the paper over the patties. Repeat the process until all
the sausages are made. Refrigerate for up to 3 days.

These sausages can be frozen in moistureproof freezer
bags for up to 3 months.

TO DEFROST A PACKAGE OF EIGHT: Heat on DEFROST
for 3 to 5 minutes.
TO COOK: Heat a seasoned cast-iron pan or nonstick
skillet until very hot. Brown each side of the patties
quickly, then turn the heat down and let the patties
cook through slowly.

If using in a pasta sauce or "Cassoulet," break each pattie into six or eight pieces after cooking.

VARIATIONS   ITALIAN-STYLE TURKEY SAUSAGES (7 grams fat per pattie): Add 1 tablespoon fennel seed.

HOT ITALIAN-STYLE TURKEY SAUSAGES (7 grams fat per pattie): Add 1 tablespoon fennel seed and 1 to 2 teaspoons crushed red-pepper flakes. (This is our favorite!)

SOUTHWESTERN TURKEY SAUSAGES (7 grams fat per pattie): Add 1 teaspoon cumin seed.

Turkey Sausage and Peppers

MAKES: *6 servings*
COOKING TIME: *16 to 19 minutes*

Low cholesterol

11.2 grams fat per serving

SERVING SUGGESTIONS: Serve on toasted hero rolls or over pasta.

A freezer meal that comes to the rescue on a busy day.

2 cups frozen Basic Tomato and Pepper Sauce (page 336)
8 Turkey Sausages, frozen
1 tablespoon canola or olive oil

1. Unseal the freezer bag containing the Tomato and Pepper Sauce halfway. Microwave on HIGH for 3 minutes to defrost partially.
2. Unseal the freezer bag containing the frozen sausage halfway. Microwave on DEFROST for 3 to 6 minutes to defrost partially.
3. Squeeze the sauce into a 2-quart microwave-safe casserole. Cover with waxed paper. Microwave on HIGH for 8 to 10 minutes, or until heated through, stirring after 4 minutes.
4. Meanwhile, pour the oil into a large skillet. On a conventional stove top, heat the oil over medium-high flame for 1 minute. Add the sausage patties; brown each side quickly, then turn the heat down to medium-low. Cover pan and allow to cook through slowly, 5 to 6 minutes. Break each pattie into eight pieces.
5. Add sausage to sauce; re-cover with waxed paper. Microwave on HIGH for 3 to 5 minutes, or until heated through.

Turkey-Bean Burritos

MAKES: *4 servings*
COOKING TIME: *4 to 5 minutes*

7 grams fat per serving with corn tortilla; 11.5 with cheese added; 8.8 grams fat per serving with flour tortilla; 13.3 with cheese added

SERVING SUGGESTIONS:
A follow-up meal to Oven-Browned Turkey (page 174), Glazed Turkey Breast (page 177), or Poached Turkey Breast (page 104).

Vary this recipe by using different types of beans.

¾ *pound cooked turkey*
1 teaspoon olive oil
1 small onion, chopped
1 can (15 to 16 ounces) pinto, kidney, or black beans, with ½ cup liquid
2 teaspoons chili powder
½ *teaspoon ground cumin*
8 soft flour or corn tortillas
2 cups chopped lettuce (romaine preferred)
2 tomatoes, chopped
¼ *cup grated lowfat Monterey Jack cheese (optional)*
Tabasco or other hot sauce (optional)

1. Cut the turkey into 2-inch chunks and coarsely shred in a food processor or blender by pulsing on and off three or four times, or chop with a knife.
2. Combine the oil and onion in a 2-quart microwave-safe casserole. Microwave on HIGH for 1 minute, or until the onion is tender. Add the shredded turkey, beans with juice, chili powder, and cumin; stir to blend. Cover tightly with a lid or with plastic wrap turned back slightly on one side. Microwave on HIGH for 3 to 4 minutes, or until heated through.
3. Remove the bag of soft tortillas from the bag and place them in the microwave oven. Heat on HIGH for 1½ to 2 minutes. Divide the turkey mixture between the warm tortillas and top with the lettuce, tomato, and cheese.

NOTE   To heat one tortilla at a time, wrap it loosely in paper towel and microwave on HIGH for 15 seconds.

Crisp Rosemary Roast Chicken

MAKES: *6 servings*
COOKING TIME: *25 to 30 minutes*

13.6 grams fat per serving of light and dark meat with skin;

1 chicken (3 pounds)
1 lemon, quartered
2 sprigs fresh rosemary or 1 teaspoon dried
Salt
Freshly ground black pepper

1. Rub the chicken with the lemon quarters. Place the lemon quarters in the cavity, along with the 2 sprigs of rosemary or ½ teaspoon of the dried rosemary. Sprinkle the remaining dried rosemary on the chicken; lightly salt and pepper.

6.7 grams fat without skin;
9.1 for light meat with skin;
4.5 for light meat without
skin

SERVING SUGGESTIONS:
Serve with a flavorful grain
pilaf and a fruit chutney.

*This succulent bird with a
crisp brown skin is table-ready
in a jiffy because it's cooked
by both microwave and
conventional oven.*

2. Truss the bird by tying its legs together, and the wings to the body, with kitchen twine.
3. Place the chicken, breast side down, in a 2-quart oval or rectangular microwave- and oven-safe dish. Microwave on HIGH for 10 minutes. Turn the bird over. Preheat the conventional oven to 500° F. Return the chicken to the microwave oven and continue cooking on HIGH for 8 to 10 minutes, or until the juices run clear when the chicken is pierced in the thickest part of the leg and body.
4. Transfer the dish to the preheated oven and cook for 5 to 8 minutes to crisp—be sure to check after 5 minutes to prevent burning. Let stand for 5 to 10 minutes before serving.

Quick
Fried Chicken

MAKES: *4 to 6 servings*
COOKING TIME: *20 to 25 minutes*

1.6 grams fat per serving of light and dark meat; 1.2 grams fat per serving of light meat only

SERVING SUGGESTION:
While the chicken is microwaving, peel the potatoes for Old-Fashioned Mashed Potatoes (page 223); cook them in the microwave oven and mash them while the chicken is frying.

This combination method calls for very little added fat, but yields a moist chicken with a crispy golden skin.

1 chicken (2½ to 3 pounds), cut into 8 serving pieces
¼ cup vegetable oil
½ cup all-purpose flour
½ teaspoon salt
¼ teaspoon freshly ground black pepper

1. Wash and dry the chicken well. Place it, skin side up, in a 2-quart rectangular microwave-safe dish, with the thicker sections toward the outside. Cover with a paper towel. Microwave on HIGH for 15 to 18 minutes, or until the juices run clear when meat is pierced in the thickest section, rearranging the chicken pieces after 8 minutes so that the uncooked portions are to the outside.
2. Heat the oil in a 12-inch skillet on top of the conventional range.
3. Meanwhile, in a small paper bag (*not* plastic), combine the flour, salt, and pepper.
4. Drop the warm chicken pieces, one at a time, into the bag. Shake to coat each piece. Place the pieces on a platter until the oil is hot enough for frying (see Note).
5. Add the chicken to the pan and cook for 5 to 10 minutes, or until golden, turning twice. (The amount of fat absorbed increases with the length of cooking time.) Remove the chicken pieces from the pan and drain on paper towels. Serve warm or cold.

NOTE To see if the fat is hot enough, place a cube of bread in the fat—it should brown in about 1 minute.

Chicken Cacciatore #1

MAKES: *6 servings*
COOKING TIME: *25 minutes*

Low-cholesterol variation

15.6 grams fat per serving of light and dark meat with skin; 8.7 grams fat without skin; 6 grams fat per serving of light meat without skin

SERVING SUGGESTIONS:
Serve with pasta or polenta, which can be cooked on the conventional range while the chicken simmers in the microwave oven.

This dish is a cool-weather favorite.

1 teaspoon olive oil
1 medium onion, coarsely chopped
1 garlic clove, minced
1 green bell pepper, stem and seeds removed, cut into ¼-inch strips
¼ cup tomato paste
1 carrot, coarsely chopped
1 can (16 ounces) stewed tomatoes, undrained (see Note)
¼ cup dry white wine (optional)
1 tablespoon chopped fresh basil or 1 teaspoon crushed dried
¼ teaspoon salt
⅛ teaspoon freshly ground black pepper
1½ pounds boneless chicken breasts

1. In a 3-quart microwave-safe casserole, combine the oil, onion, garlic, and green pepper. Cover tightly with a lid or with plastic wrap turned back slightly. Microwave on HIGH for 2 to 3 minutes, or until the vegetables are tender-crisp.
2. Stir in the tomato paste. Add the remaining ingredients except the chicken; stir.
3. Place the chicken pieces, skin side down, in the casserole, with the thicker pieces to the outside. Cover again and cook on HIGH for 10 minutes. Turn the chicken over and reposition the pieces to allow the thicker portions to cook more evenly.
4. Cover again and continue to cook on HIGH for 10 to 12 minutes, or until the chicken is tender. Let stand 5 minutes before serving.

NOTE For a smoother sauce, pour the canned tomatoes into the bowl of a food processor and pulse on and off a few times to chop coarsely.

VARIATION LOW-CHOLESTEROL CHICKEN CACCIATORE #1 (4.7 grams fat per serving): Remove the skin from the chicken before cooking.

Chicken Cacciatore #2

2 cups frozen Basic Tomato and Pepper Sauce (page 336)
3 to 3½ pounds chicken parts

MAKES: *6 servings*
COOKING TIME: *About 30 minutes*

Low-cholesterol variation

Grams fat same as for Chicken Cacciatore #1

SERVING SUGGESTIONS:
Serve with pasta or rice, which can be cooked on top of the range while the chicken is cooking in the microwave oven.

VARIATION

This quick version relies on a freezer-ready sauce.

1. Unseal the freezer bag containing the sauce halfway. Microwave on HIGH for 3 minutes. Pour sauce into a 3-quart microwave-safe casserole. Microwave on HIGH for 3 to 4 minutes, stirring and breaking the sauce up.
2. Add the chicken pieces to the tomato sauce, placing the thicker portions toward the outside of the dish. Cover with waxed paper. Microwave on HIGH for 22 to 28 minutes, or until the chicken is tender and juices run clear when pricked with a fork, turning over and repositioning the less-cooked portions to the outside halfway through cooking. Let stand, covered, for 10 minutes.

LOW-CHOLESTEROL CHICKEN CACCIATORE #2: Substitute 2 pounds skinless, boneless chicken breasts, cut into 2-inch cubes, for cut-up chicken pieces. Shorten cooking time in step 2 to 12 to 15 minutes.

Poached Boneless Chicken Breasts

MAKES: *4 servings*
COOKING TIME: *6 to 8 minutes*

Low cholesterol

2.9 grams fat per serving

SERVING SUGGESTIONS:
Serve with Corn Salsa (page 317), Olivada (page 314), or any of the chutneys (pages 330–33). Slice or chop for

VARIATIONS

main-course sandwiches, salads, or fillings. The broth that remains after cooking can

2 whole skinless, boneless chicken breasts (1 to 1½ pounds), split
1 tablespoon fresh lemon juice, white wine, or dry vermouth

1. Place the chicken breasts between two pieces of waxed paper. Flatten with a meat pounder to about ½-inch thickness.
2. Arrange the chicken on a 10-inch microwave-safe pie or dinner plate with the thicker portions toward the outside, leaving the center open. Sprinkle with lemon juice.
3. Cover with waxed paper. Microwave on HIGH for 6 to 8 minutes, or until the juices run clear when chicken is pierced in the center, turning over after 4 minutes. Let stand 2 to 3 minutes before serving or slicing.

SINGLE SERVING: Place half a chicken breast in an individual microwave-safe serving dish or ramekin. Sprinkle with 1 teaspoon lemon juice. Cover with waxed paper and microwave on HIGH for 2 to 3 minutes, or until the juices run clear from the center parts, turning over after 1 minute.

be added to enrich the sauces served alongside.

Skinless, boneless chicken breasts are a boon to the busy cook. They cook up succulently in the microwave oven and can be tempered with many different cooking sauces.

CHICKEN BREASTS SIMMERED IN MEXICAN TOMATO SAUCE (4.5 grams fat per serving): Cook 1 recipe Mexican Tomato Sauce (page 319) in a 2- to 2½-quart flat-bottomed microwave-safe casserole. Add the chicken breasts to the sauce. Eliminate the lemon juice. Cover with waxed paper and cook according to the basic recipe.

CHICKEN BREASTS SIMMERED IN TOMATO SAUCE (7.9 grams fat per serving): Cook 1 recipe Basic Tomato Sauce (page 145) in a 2- to 2½-quart flat-bottomed casserole. Add the chicken cutlets to the sauce. Eliminate the lemon juice. Cover with waxed paper and cook according to the basic recipe. Serve with pasta, cooked on top of the stove while the chicken is cooking.

CHICKEN BREASTS SIMMERED IN HONEY-SHERRY ONION MARMALADE (7 grams fat per serving): Cook 1 recipe Honey-Sherry Onion Marmalade (page 321) in a 2-quart flat-bottomed microwave-safe casserole. Add the chicken breasts to the marmalade. Eliminate the lemon juice. Cover with waxed paper and cook according to the basic recipe. Serve with Old-Fashioned Mashed Potatoes (page 223) that have been cooked before the chicken.

CHICKEN BREASTS SIMMERED IN PLUM SAUCE (3.3 grams fat per serving): Prepare 1 recipe Plum Sauce (page 332) in a 2-quart flat-bottomed microwave-safe casserole. Add the chicken breasts to the sauce. Eliminate the lemon juice. Cover with waxed paper and cook according to the basic recipe. Serve with rice, which can be cooked on top of the stove while the chicken is cooking.

LOW-CALORIE CHICKEN AND PEAR SALAD WITH CRANBERRY-PEPPER VINEGAR (3 grams fat per serving): Thinly slice the poached chicken. Wash and thinly slice one pear, apple, or peeled papaya. Arrange chicken and fruit on plates and splash with Cranberry-Pepper Vinegar (page 306).

LOW-CALORIE CHICKEN AND ZUCCHINI SALAD WITH CUMIN–HOT PEPPER VINEGAR (3 grams fat per serving): Thinly slice the poached chicken. Wash and cut 2 medium zucchini (½ pound each) into matchsticks. Place in a 2-quart microwave-safe casserole. Cover tightly with a lid or with plastic wrap turned back slightly. Microwave on HIGH for 3 to 7 minutes, or until tender, stirring once. Arrange the chicken and zucchini on plates and splash with Cumin–Hot Pepper Vinegar (page 306).

LOW-CALORIE CHICKEN AND PEPPER SALAD WITH GARLIC, ROSEMARY, AND THYME VINEGAR (2.9 grams fat per serving): Thinly slice the poached chicken. Wash and thinly slice 1 red and 1 green bell pepper. Arrange the chicken and pepper strips on plates and splash with Garlic, Rosemary, and Thyme Vinegar (page 305).

TO PREPARE THE WHOLE MEAL

- WITH RICE: Cook the rice in the microwave oven while preparing the chicken, or cook the rice on top of the stove while the chicken is cooking.
- WITH NOODLES: Cook the noodles on top of the stove while the chicken is cooking.
- WITH BAKED POTATOES: Cook the potatoes in the microwave oven first. Place them in a preheated (450° F) conventional oven or toaster oven, while the chicken is cooking, to crisp them.
- WITH MASHED POTATOES: Cook the potatoes in the microwave oven; mash them while the chicken is cooking. Reheat the potatoes on HIGH for 1 to 3 minutes before serving, if necessary.
- WITH A SALAD: Toss a salad while the chicken is cooking.
- WITH A VEGETABLE: Cook the vegetable in the microwave oven while slicing and saucing the chicken.
- WITH A SALSA, CHUTNEY, OR VINEGAR: Use one that's on hand in the freezer, refrigerator, or pantry; or prepare one while the chicken is cooking and cook it while the chicken is standing.

DEFROSTING SKINLESS, BONELESS CHICKEN BREASTS

1. Unwrap the chicken breasts and place them on a microwave roasting rack (or an inverted microwave-safe dish in a shallow microwave-safe dish), so that the juices will drain, placing the thicker portions of the chicken to the outside of the dish.
2. Microwave on DEFROST for 6 to 7 minutes per pound. Halfway through the cooking time, break the pieces apart and turn them over, placing the icier sections toward the outside of the dish.

3. After defrosting, the poultry pieces should still be cold to the touch on the meatier portions, with some ice crystals present in the center. The ice crystals will disappear during the standing time.
4. Remove from the microwave and rinse the chicken pieces in cold water. Let them stand for 5 minutes.

Chicken Fajitas

MAKES: *4 servings*
COOKING TIME: *15 minutes*

Low cholesterol

10 grams fat per serving

SERVING SUGGESTION:
Cook the Sizzled Peppers and Onions while slicing the chicken and mixing the salsa.

1 recipe Poached Boneless Chicken Breasts (page 185)
12 flour tortillas, purchased
1 recipe Sizzled Peppers and Onions (page 209)
1 recipe Salsa Cruda (page 317) or purchased salsa

1. Slice the chicken thinly crosswise.
2. Wrap the tortillas in a dampened paper towel. Microwave on HIGH for 1 to 1½ minutes, or until warm to the touch.
3. Place a few pieces of chicken in the middle of a tortilla; top with some Sizzled Peppers and Onions and Salsa Cruda. Roll; repeat with remaining tortillas.

VARIATION   TURKEY FAJITAS (10.3 grams fat per serving): Substitute ¾ pound cooked and sliced turkey breast for chicken.

Chicken Tacos

MAKES: *12 tacos (4 servings)*
COOKING TIME: *10 to 12 minutes*

Low cholesterol (if nonfat yogurt is used for topping)

7.4 grams fat per serving

Kids help

1 recipe Poached Boneless Chicken Breasts (page 185)
1 teaspoon canola, olive, or vegetable oil
1 garlic clove, minced
1 small onion, chopped, or 2 green onions, thinly sliced
¼ teaspoon salt
¼ teaspoon freshly ground black pepper
¼ teaspoon ground cumin
12 prepared corn taco shells

TOPPINGS

Salsa Cruda (page 317) or purchased salsa
Sliced tomatoes

Shredded lettuce
Sour cream or nonfat yogurt

1. Place the cooked chicken in the bowl of a food processor and chop; or coarsely chop with a knife.
2. In a 2-quart microwave-safe casserole, combine the oil, garlic, and onion. Microwave on HIGH for 2 minutes. Add the chicken, salt, pepper, and cumin; mix well.
3. Cover with waxed paper and microwave on HIGH for 3 to 6 minutes, or until heated through, stirring after 2 minutes. Let stand 1 to 2 minutes.
4. Place tacos on a paper towel–lined plate. Microwave on HIGH for 1 to 3 minutes, or until warm to the touch.
5. Spoon filling into warmed taco shells. Add toppings of your choice.

Lightly Breaded Chicken Cutlets Milan Style

MAKES: *4 servings*
COOKING TIME: *5 to 6 minutes*

Low-cholesterol variation

11.6 grams fat per serving

SERVING SUGGESTIONS:
To round out the meal, start cooking Rice, Bulghur, or Barley Pilaf (pages 116, 118, and 116) in the microwave oven before breading and cooking the cutlets on top of the range. Mix a salad while both are cooking.

These are more affordable than veal cutlets. To keep the calorie count down, we have cut down on the breading

¾ to 1 pound skinless, boneless chicken breasts
1 egg
½ cup fine, dry, unflavored bread crumbs
2 to 3 tablespoons canola or light olive oil
Salt and pepper
Lemon wedges

1. Place each breast between two pieces of waxed paper and pound to ½- to ¼-inch thickness.
2. Break the egg into a soup plate and beat lightly with a fork. Sprinkle the crumbs on a dinner plate.
3. Dip both sides of each cutlet in the egg and then in the bread crumbs.
4. Heat the oil in a 10-inch skillet on top of the conventional range (if you use a 12-inch skillet, you will need 3 tablespoons of oil) over medium-high heat until the oil sizzles when you dip the end of a cutlet into it. Place the cutlets in the pan in one layer and brown them quickly (30 seconds to 1 minute).
5. Turn the cutlets over and brown the other side for the same amount of time. Turn down the heat to low. Cover the pan and cook for 3 to 4 minutes more, or until cutlets are cooked through. (This method requires relatively little fat.)
6. Place the cutlets on paper towels to absorb any excess oil. Lightly salt and pepper, if desired. Serve with lemon wedges.

and sautéed the cutlets conventionally in just 2 tablespoons of oil for a short period of time.

LOW-CHOLESTEROL CHICKEN CUTLETS, MILAN STYLE (10.2 grams fat per serving): Substitute 2 egg whites

Chicken Cutlets Parmigiana

MAKES: *4 servings*
COOKING TIME: *15 to 20 minutes*

21 grams fat per serving

These lightly breaded cutlets, served with tomato sauce and melted mozzarella cheese, are sure to be a family favorite.

1 recipe Basic Tomato Sauce (page 145), or 2 cups purchased tomato sauce (see Note 1)
1 recipe Lightly Breaded Chicken Cutlets, Milan Style (page 189)
4 ounces part–skim milk mozzarella cheese, thinly sliced

1. Prepare and cook the tomato sauce in the microwave oven.
2. Meanwhile, prepare and cook the chicken cutlets on top of the conventional range.
3. Place the cooked cutlets around the outer rim of a 9- or 10-inch microwave-safe pie dish, leaving the center open.
4. Spoon ½ cup sauce over each cutlet and top with 1 ounce of cheese. Cover with waxed paper and microwave on MEDIUM for 4 to 8 minutes, or until the sauce is heated and the cheese is melted (see Note 2). Let stand for 3 minutes before serving.

NOTE

1. If using purchased sauce, or if sauce has been made earlier and refrigerated, microwave on HIGH for 2 to 4 minutes, or until heated through, before spooning over the cutlets.

2. When cheese is added as a topping to a recipe that is to be heated in the microwave oven, the MEDIUM setting is used to prevent the cheese from becoming rubbery. Waxed paper allows the cheese to heat evenly without adding excess moisture.

Deep-Dish Chicken Enchiladas

MAKES: *4 servings*
COOKING TIME: *12 to 15 minutes*

19.6 grams fat per serving without avocado; 27 grams fat per serving with avocado

SERVING SUGGESTIONS:
You may wish to add a little "heat" by serving these with Salsa Cruda (page 317) or a purchased hot sauce of your choice.

We were introduced to this dish in the early sixties in Scottsdale, Arizona. We have cut out the long simmering and preparation time by using skinless, boneless chicken breasts.

1 pound skinless, boneless chicken breasts
1 tablespoon fresh lemon juice, white wine, or dry vermouth
1 can (10 ounces) enchilada sauce
2 green onions, thinly sliced
8 6-inch soft corn tortillas
6 ounces Monterey Jack or cheddar cheese, grated
1 avocado, cut into ½-inch cubes (optional)
2 cups shredded lettuce
Sour cream or low-fat yogurt

1. Place the chicken breasts between two pieces of waxed paper. Flatten with a meat pounder to about a ½-inch thickness.
2. Arrange the chicken on a 10-inch microwave-safe pie or dinner plate, with the thicker portions toward the outside, leaving the center open. Sprinkle with lemon juice.
3. Cover with waxed paper. Microwave on HIGH for 6 to 8 minutes, or until the juices run clear when the chicken is pierced in the center, turning over after 4 minutes.
4. Cut the cooked chicken breasts into quarters. Place the chicken in the bowl of food processor, along with the cooking juices (you'll have about ⅓ cup). Pulse on and off six to eight times to shred coarsely. Scrape into a small bowl and stir in half of the enchilada sauce and the green onion.
5. Soften one tortilla at a time by placing it in the microwave oven and cooking on HIGH for 12 seconds. Spoon 2 tablespoons of the chopped chicken mixture into the center of the enchilada; top with 2 tablespoons of cheese. Fold one side over the center and roll the tortilla up. Repeat with the remaining tortillas. Place them seam side down in a 2-quart rectangular 11½ × 7½-inch microwave-safe dish.
6. Spoon the remaining sauce over the enchiladas and sprinkle with remaining cheese. Cover with waxed paper and microwave on HIGH for 6 to 8 minutes. Let stand 3 minutes.
7. Serve with avocado cubes, shredded lettuce, and sour cream.

Warm Chicken and Walnut Salad

MAKES: *4 servings*
COOKING TIME: *7 to 9 minutes*

20 grams fat per serving

SERVING SUGGESTIONS:
Serve with Herbed Beer Bread (page 64) or a good-quality purchased bread.

A delicious salad meal that cooks up in minutes.

1 recipe Poached Boneless Chicken Breasts (page 145)
1 bunch watercress, washed and dried
1 bunch red-leaf or other leaf lettuce (such as oak leaf or romaine), washed and torn into bite-size pieces
2 green onions, thinly sliced
¼ cup coarsely chopped walnuts
¼ cup Walnut-Flavored Oil (page 304) or olive oil
3 tablespoons balsamic or red-wine vinegar
½ teaspoon salt
¼ teaspoon freshly ground black pepper

1. While the chicken breasts are cooking, wash and dry the greens and line four plates with them. Sprinkle evenly with green onion.
2. Slice the chicken, lengthwise, into thin strips and arrange on the lettuce.
3. Place the remaining ingredients in a 4-cup glass measure. Microwave on HIGH for 1 to 2 minutes, or until warm but not boiling. Mix well with a fork and spoon evenly over the chicken.

VARIATIONS

WARM CHICKEN AND WALNUT SALAD WITH MELON (20 grams fat per serving): Remove the rind and seeds from a ripe cantaloupe and slice thinly. Arrange the melon slices on the lettuce. Place the chicken slices on top of the melon and pour on dressing.

WARM CHICKEN AND PINE NUT SALAD WITH PAPAYA (20 grams fat per serving): Remove the peel and seeds from a ripe papaya and slice thinly. Arrange the slices on the lettuce. Substitute Cumin–Hot Pepper Vinegar (page 306) for balsamic vinegar and olive oil for Walnut Oil. Substitute pine nuts for walnuts.

Curried Chicken Salad with Grapes

1 recipe Poached Boneless Chicken Breasts (page 145)
2 cups seedless grapes
2 green onions, thinly sliced
¼ cup mayonnaise
¼ cup plain yogurt
1 teaspoon curry powder

MAKES: *4 servings*
COOKING TIME: *8 minutes, plus 1 hour to chill*

Low-cholesterol variation

14.6 grams fat per serving

VARIATION

SERVING SUGGESTIONS:
Serve on lettuce leaves with Irish Brown Bread (page 65) or purchased whole-grain bread, and Peach Chutney (page 331).

1. Chill chicken in the refrigerator for at least 1 hour or overnight.
2. Cut the chilled chicken into ½-inch cubes.
3. In a medium bowl, combine the chicken with remaining ingredients. Serve.

LOW-CHOLESTEROL CURRIED CHICKEN SALAD WITH GRAPES (7 grams fat per serving): Substitute low-cholesterol mayonnaise for regular mayonnaise and nonfat yogurt for regular yogurt.

Warm Chicken Salad with Papaya and Sake-Lime Dressing

MAKES: *4 servings*
COOKING TIME: *About 10 minutes*

14 grams fat per serving

SERVING SUGGESTIONS:
Serve with Oven-Baked Corn Bread (page 61) or a good-quality purchased bread to make a complete meal.

2 whole chicken breasts (about 1½ pounds, total), split in half
1 tablespoon fresh lime juice
2 cups julienned jícama (about 1 pound)
1 bunch arugula, washed, with stems removed
1 head Boston lettuce (½ pound), washed and dried
1 papaya, seeded, peeled, and cut lengthwise in ¼-inch-thick strips
1 recipe Sake-Lime Dressing (page 308)
4 lime slices

1. Place chicken in a 9-inch microwave-safe pie plate with the thicker sections to the outside. Sprinkle with the lime juice. Cover with waxed paper.
2. Microwave on HIGH for 4 minutes. Turn pieces over, placing the lesser-cooked sections to the outside. Cover again and cook on HIGH for 3 to 5 minutes, or until chicken is cooked through and tender. Let stand, covered, for 10 minutes.
3. While the chicken is standing, place the jícama in a 1-quart microwave-safe casserole. Cover tightly with a lid or with plastic wrap turned back slightly on one side. Microwave on HIGH for 2 minutes; set aside.
4. Line four large dinner plates with arugula and Boston lettuce. Divide papaya strips and arrange them on one side of each plate. Place one-quarter of the jícama in the center of each plate.

5. Slice the chicken breasts lengthwise into ¼-inch strips (see Note). Arrange next to the Jícama.
6. Spoon dressing over salads. Garnish with lime slices and serve.

NOTE   The chicken will slice more easily if allowed to stand for a short time after cooking.

Oriental Chicken, Orange, and Vegetable Salad

MAKES: *4 servings*
COOKING TIME: *10 minutes, plus 1 hour to chill*

Low cholesterol

6.3 grams fat per serving

1 recipe Poached Boneless Chicken Breasts (page 145)
1 red bell pepper, thinly sliced lengthwise
2 cups peeled and julienned jícama
¼ pound pea pods, cut into 1-inch strips
2 medium oranges, peeled and segmented
1 recipe Oriental Dressing (page 308)

1. Chill chicken in refrigerator for at least 1 hour or overnight.
2. Combine the chicken in a medium bowl with pepper, jícama, pea pods, and orange.
3. Toss salad with dressing. Serve.

Gingered Chicken, Peas, and Pepper

MAKES: *4 servings*
COOKING TIME: *8 to 10 minutes*

Low cholesterol

4 grams fat per serving

1 teaspoon sesame, canola, or vegetable oil
2 garlic cloves, minced
1 tablespoon minced fresh ginger
¾ to 1 pound skinless, boneless chicken breasts, sliced into ¼-inch strips
1 tablespoon rice wine or dry sherry
1 tablespoon soy sauce
1 tablespoon dark brown sugar
1½ teaspoons cornstarch
½ pound snow peas, trimmed
1 red or green bell pepper, cut into ¼-inch strips
3 green onions, cut into 2-inch pieces

1. In a 10-inch microwave-safe pie plate, combine the oil, garlic, and ginger. Microwave on HIGH for 1 minute. Stir in the chicken pieces.

SERVING SUGGESTION:
Serve with Basic Long-Grain
Rice (page 118), which can be
cooked in the microwave oven
while the chicken and
vegetables are being cut up.
(Rice will stay warm, if
covered, for up to 1 hour.)

*Because this dish is cooked in
the microwave, it requires
virtually no added fat.*

2. In a 1-cup glass measure or small bowl, combine the wine, soy sauce, sugar, and cornstarch, stirring well to blend. Pour evenly over the chicken; stir.
3. Push the chicken strips to the outer rim of the dish, making a ring about 2 inches wide. Place the peas and pepper in the center of the dish. Cover with waxed paper and microwave on HIGH for 4 minutes.
4. Add the green onion; stir well to mix the chicken and vegetables together. Cover again and microwave on HIGH for 2 to 4 minutes, or until the chicken is cooked through.

Skewered Chicken Cubes with Honey-Mustard Sauce

MAKES: *6 small skewers (snack for 2 or dinner for 1 child)*
COOKING TIME: *2 minutes*

Low cholesterol

2.9 grams fat per dinner; 1.5 grams fat per snack

Kids help

SERVING SUGGESTIONS:
Serve with carrot sticks or other raw vegetable sticks and frozen fruit pieces for a kid's meal.

Serve this quick and easy meal to your kids before an "adults-only" dinner.

12 wooden toothpicks
1 skinless, boneless chicken breast (4 ounces), cut
    into 1-inch cubes
2 tablespoons mustard
2 teaspoons honey

1. Insert each toothpick into two pieces of chicken.
2. Arrange chicken around the outer rim of a paper plate.
3. Microwave on HIGH for 2 minutes; let stand for 2 minutes.
4. Meanwhile, combine the mustard and honey in a small paper cup.
5. Dip chicken into mustard sauce and eat.

FISH

AMERICANS ARE BEING urged to cut their fat intake by 20 to 25 percent and are therefore turning to leaner sources of protein. Because fish is generally much lower in fat than meat and poultry, increasing the amount of fish you consume can lower the percentage of your overall fat intake.

Fillets are among the easiest and quickest forms of fish to cook and can be accompanied by so many different chutneys or sauces that they never cease to delight the palate. When the catch is fresh, there is nothing to compare with a steamed fillet, a simmered fish stew, or a grilled fish steak.

If you live "in the interior," fish is not quite as abundant as it is on the coasts and is often quite expensive as a result. Dried cod, which can be soaked and made into codfish cakes, may be a more reasonable alternative. Also, supermarkets will often freeze scallops in generous 1-pound portions and sell them for much less than the market price. By following the defrosting guides and one of the scallop recipes, you'll discover luscious ways to prepare them.

To Prepare the Whole Meal

Fish cooks in no time in the microwave, so everything else to be cooked in the microwave should be cooked before it. Otherwise, foods should be started ahead if cooked on top of the stove. Here are some suggestions for how to accomplish this:

- WITH RICE: Cook the rice in the microwave while preparing the fish, or cook the rice on top of the stove while the fish is cooking.
- WITH POTATOES: Cook Parslied Small Potatoes (page 232) first and let them stand while the fish is cooking.
- WITH NOODLES: Cook the noodles on top of the stove. (Begin to bring the water to a boil on top of the range about 8 minutes before cooking the fish.)
- WITH VEGETABLES: In general, cook the vegetables first and let them stand during the short cooking time of the fish. Herb-Topped Tomatoes (page 221) should be cooked in the microwave after the fish is cooked; Lightly Creamed Spinach (page 230) should be cooked before the fish is placed in the microwave and then reheated on HIGH for 1 minute. Both go well with any of the fish dishes. (The spinach provides the needed iron that fish lacks.)

Another approach is to make an entire meal in a single soup or stew dish.

DEFROSTING FISH FILLETS AND SCALLOPS

1. Unwrap the fish or scallops. Place on a microwave roasting rack, or inverted microwave-safe saucer, in a microwave-safe dish. (This lifts the fish above its juices.)
2. Microwave on DEFROST for 6 minutes per pound. Turn the fish over halfway through.
3. When finished, the fish should still have ice crystals and will be frozen in the middle.
4. Place the fish in cold water for 5 minutes. (The ice crystals will dissolve.) Pat the fish dry before cooking.

Basic Fish Fillets

MAKES: *4 servings*
COOKING TIME: *3 to 5 minutes*

Low cholesterol

1.3 grams fat per serving

SERVING SUGGESTIONS:
Sauces and serving suggestions follow in the variations.

NOTE

There is no better way to prepare fish fillets than in the microwave; they taste so fresh and succulent! With this basic method you'll have many options to sauce them or serve them in a warm salad.

3/4 to 1 pound fish fillets, each 1/4 inch thick (see Note)
1 tablespoon fresh lemon juice

1. If the fillets are wider than 2 to 3 inches, cut them in half lengthwise. Fold the thinner ends of each fillet under the thicker center in two-fold letter fashion.
2. Place the folded fillets, seam-side down, around the outside rim of a 9- to 12-inch round microwave-safe serving plate, leaving the center open.
3. Sprinkle with lemon juice. Lightly cover with a paper towel. Microwave, on HIGH for 2½ to 5 minutes, or until the fish flakes when pressed with a fork.

NOTE   To cook thick fish fillets or steaks (more than ¼ inch thick) in the microwave oven: Place fillets or steaks in a 10- or 12-inch round microwave-safe dish, with the thicker sections toward the outside, and sprinkle with 1 tablespoon lemon juice. Cover with a lid or with plastic wrap turned back slightly. Microwave on MEDIUM for 9 to 11 minutes per pound, or until the fish flakes when pressed with a fork, turning the fish over after 5 minutes.

NOTE   The fish and sauces listed below are all low in cholesterol.

VARIATIONS   FISH FILLETS WITH BALSAMIC PEPPERCORN SAUCE (1.3 grams fat per serving): Make Balsamic Peppercorn Sauce (page 317) and spoon over cooked fillets. Serve with rice and a salad.

FISH FILLETS WITH SALSA CRUDA (1.3 grams fat per serving): Make Salsa Cruda (page 317) and serve alongside cooked fillets. Serve with Polenta (page 120), rice, or tortilla chips, and a salad.

FISH FILLETS WITH SOUTHWESTERN VINEGAR (1.3 grams fat per serving): Make Cumin–Hot Pepper Vinegar (page 306) and splash on top of cooked fillets. Serve with rice and zucchini or tomatoes.

FISH FILLETS WITH GINGER SAUCE (1.3 grams fat per serving): Make Ginger Sauce (page 321) and spoon over cooked fish. Serve with rice.

FISH FILLETS WITH BASIC TOMATO SAUCE (6 grams fat per serving): In a 2-quart flat-bottomed microwave-safe casserole, prepare Basic Tomato Sauce (page 145). Place the folded, uncooked fish in the sauce around the outer rim of the casserole. Eliminate lemon juice. Cover with waxed paper and microwave on HIGH for 3 to 5 minutes. (Thicker fillets or fish steaks may be cooked on MEDIUM for 10 to 12 minutes.) Serve with pasta, which can be cooked on top of the stove while the sauce and fish are cooking in the microwave oven.

FISH FILLETS WITH QUICK PIPERADE (4.7 grams fat per serving): In a 2-quart flat-bottomed microwave-safe casserole, prepare Quick Piperade (page 320). Place the folded, uncooked fish on top of the piperade around the outer rim of the casserole. Cover with waxed paper and microwave for 3 to 5 minutes. (Thick fillets or steaks may be cooked on MEDIUM for 10 to 12 minutes.) Serve with rice or Parslied Small Potatoes (page 232), which can be cooked first and reheated if necessary.

FISH FILLETS WITH CREOLE SAUCE (5 grams fat per serving): In a 2-quart flat-bottomed microwave-safe casserole, prepare Creole Sauce (page 323). Place the folded, uncooked fish in the sauce, around the outer rim of the casserole. Cover with waxed paper and microwave on HIGH for 3 to 5 minutes. (Thick fillets or steaks may be cooked on MEDIUM for 10 to 12 minutes.) Serve with grits, polenta, or rice, which can be cooked first, then reheated.

SAUCES AND TOPPERS THAT GO WELL WITH FISH NOT INCLUDED IN A RECIPE OR VARIATION

All of the following sauces are low in cholesterol or have a low-cholesterol variation included in their recipe:

MUSTARD HORSERADISH SAUCE (PAGE 324)
Aïoli (page 104)

TOMATO VINAIGRETTE (PAGE 309)
Mint Pesto (page 335)

TOMATO CHUTNEY (PAGE 333)
Cranberry Chutney (page 330)

PLUM CHUTNEY (PAGE 333)

Fragrant Fish and Apple Salad

MAKES: *4 servings*
COOKING TIME: *9 to 11 minutes*

Low-cholesterol variation

18.5 grams fat per serving

SERVING SUGGESTIONS: Serve with Herbed Beer Bread (page 64) or a crusty purchased bread.

1 thick fish fillet (¾ pound) (bluefish, tuna, mullet, or salmon)
1 tablespoon fresh lemon juice
1 cup cubed tart apple (Granny Smith works well)
¼ cup thinly sliced celery
¼ cup chopped fresh parsley
2 green onions, thinly sliced
¼ cup plain yogurt
¼ cup mayonnaise
1 tablespoon balsamic vinegar
4 cups mixed greens (romaine, endive, radicchio, Boston lettuce)
Lemon slices

1. Place the fillet in 9-inch microwave-safe pie plate and sprinkle with lemon juice. Cover tightly with plastic wrap turned back slightly. Microwave on MEDIUM for 9 to 11 minutes, turning over once. Chill in refrigerator for 1 hour or "speed-chill" for 15 minutes in freezer.
2. Remove any skin from cooled fish; drain. Place fish in a medium mixing bowl and flake with a fork. Add apple, celery, parsley, and green onion.
3. In a small bowl, combine yogurt, mayonnaise, and vinegar. Toss with the fish mixture to moisten.
4. Line a plate or bowl with the greens and spoon in the salad. Garnish with lemon slices.

VARIATION   LOW-CHOLESTEROL FRAGRANT FISH AND APPLE SALAD (7.8 grams fat per serving): Substitute low-cholesterol mayonnaise for regular mayonnaise and nonfat yogurt for regular yogurt.

Choucroute with Salmon, Halibut, or Swordfish

1 teaspoon olive oil
1 carrot, julienned
1 medium onion, sliced
1½ pounds sauerkraut, rinsed well
1 cup dry white wine
2 tablespoons chopped fresh parsley
¼ teaspoon freshly ground black pepper

MAKES: *4 servings*
COOKING TIME: *30 minutes*

Low cholesterol

13 grams fat per serving

SERVING SUGGESTIONS:
We like to serve this with
either Garlic Mashed Potatoes
(page 223), which we cook
first in the microwave oven
and then heat for a minute
before serving, or simple
boiled potatoes cooked on top
of the stove while the
choucroute is in the
microwave oven.

Choucroute garnie *is a hearty
dish of sauerkraut, salt pork,
ham, and sausages served
with potatoes. This is a
low-cholesterol version of that
beloved traditional dish.*
    *Instead of a caraway or
juniper-berry seasoning, we
use basil in a garlic-crumb
topping.*

TOPPING

¼ cup dry bread crumbs
1 garlic clove, minced
1 tablespoon olive oil
1 tablespoon finely chopped fresh parsley
1 tablespoon minced fresh basil or 1 teaspoon dried

*1 thick fish fillet (1 pound) (salmon, halibut, or
    swordfish), cut into four serving pieces*

1. Combine the oil, carrot, and onion in a 3-quart
microwave-safe casserole. Cover tightly with a lid or
with plastic wrap turned back slightly. Microwave on
HIGH for 2 minutes.
2. Add the sauerkraut, wine, parsley, and pepper; stir
well. Cover again and cook on HIGH for 20 minutes,
stirring once.
3. Meanwhile, combine the topping ingredients in a
small bowl.
4. Stir sauerkraut mixture well; divide it into four
mounds, leaving center open. Place a piece of fish on
top of each mound. Sprinkle with topping. Cover with
waxed paper and microwave on HIGH for 10 minutes, or
until fish flakes when pressed with fork.
5. To serve, place a mound of sauerkraut with fish on
top on each plate.

Scallops with Bread-Crumb Topping

MAKES: *4 servings*
COOKING TIME: *5 to 8 minutes*

Low cholesterol

7.6 grams fat per serving

SERVING SUGGESTIONS:
Serve with a grain pilaf (pages

1 tablespoon olive oil
2 garlic cloves, minced
¼ cup dry bread crumbs
¼ teaspoon salt
⅛ teaspoon freshly ground black pepper
1 pound scallops
2 tablespoons chopped fresh parsley
Lemon wedges

1. In a small microwave-safe bowl, combine the oil and
garlic. Microwave on HIGH for 35 to 40 seconds, or
until the garlic is tender but not brown. Stir in the
bread crumbs, salt, and pepper.
2. In a 9-inch round microwave-safe dish, spread the
scallops in a single layer, leaving the center open.
Sprinkle with bread-crumb mixture and parsley. Cover

116–18), which can be cooked in the microwave oven before the scallops, and a crisp salad.

with a piece of paper towel. Microwave on MEDIUM for 5 to 7 minutes, or until the scallops are opaque (see Note). Serve with lemon wedges.

NOTE

Cooking the scallops on MEDIUM will help prevent popping and splitting.

VARIATION

SCALLOPS WITH NUT OR SEED TOPPING (11.2 grams fat per serving): Combine 2 tablespoons pine nuts, sesame seeds, or chopped walnuts with bread crumbs.

Choose a nice-looking 9-inch cooking dish that can be brought to the table, and cleanup will be a breeze.

Sautéed Scallops In Mashed-Potato Nests

MAKES: *4 servings*
COOKING TIME: *15 to 20 minutes*

Low-cholesterol variation

15.7 grams fat per serving

SERVING SUGGESTIONS:
Serve with a salad or crudités, which can be prepared while the potatoes are cooking.

Delicious, attractive, and easy to prepare.

1½ pounds potatoes, peeled and cut into eighths
2 to 4 tablespoons butter
1 cup milk
Ground nutmeg to taste
2 tablespoons canola or olive oil
1 pound scallops
¼ teaspoon paprika
2 tablespoons dry bread crumbs
2 tablespoons chopped fresh parsley
Lemon wedges
Salt and pepper to taste

1. In a 2-quart microwave-safe casserole, combine the potatoes with ½ cup water. Cover tightly with a lid or plastic wrap turned back slightly. Microwave on HIGH for 12 to 14 minutes, or until very tender, stirring once halfway through cooking.
2. Leaving the water in the dish, mash the potatoes with a potato masher to remove all the lumps.
3. Meanwhile, place the butter and milk in a 1-cup glass measure. Microwave on HIGH for 45 seconds to warm. Add the warm milk-butter mixture to the potatoes and whip until light and fluffy; add 1 or 2 tablespoons additional milk if necessary. Add nutmeg to taste. Set aside.
4. Place oil in a 10-inch frying pan (a larger pan will require more oil) and heat on top of the stove. The oil should sputter when a little water is flicked into it.
5. Meanwhile, place the scallops on a dinner plate. In a small bowl, combine the bread crumbs and paprika.

Sprinkle over the scallops, turning to coat. Add to the hot frying pan. Cook for 1 minute on one side; turn over and cook for 30 seconds to 1 minute on the second side, or until opaque, making sure not to overcook.

6. Form four nests out of the mashed potatoes (about 5½ inches long and 3½ inches wide). Spoon the scallops into the nests, including any crumbs in the pan. Sprinkle with chopped parsley. Serve with lemon wedges and salt and pepper to taste.

VARIATION   Low-Cholesterol Sautéed Scallops in Mashed-Potato Nests (14.3 grams fat per serving): Substitute 1 tablespoon olive oil for butter when mashing potatoes; substitute skim milk for regular.

Codfish Cakes

MAKES: *6 servings*
COOKING TIME: *About 20 minutes, plus 12 hours to soak cod*

Low-cholesterol variation

5.4 grams fat per serving

SERVING SUGGESTIONS:
Barbecued Baked Beans (page 218) and a tossed salad or Coleslaw (page 237).

In New England, codfish cakes are a traditional favorite for Friday evening meals, served with baked beans and coleslaw. Dried cod, available in Italian and Greek groceries, must be soaked, so we make up a few batches of cod cakes and freeze them. Fresh cod or scrod can be substituted—the result will be a little different in flavor but equally good.

½ pound dried cod
2 pounds potatoes (about 8 medium), peeled and quartered
2 eggs, lightly beaten
Salt and freshly ground pepper to taste
1 tablespoon vegetable oil

1. Place the cod in a 3-quart microwave-safe dish and cover with cold water. Refrigerate and soak for 12 hours, changing the water a few times.
2. Drain the water and put the cod back in the same dish. Add ½ cup fresh water. Cover tightly with a lid or with plastic wrap turned back slightly. Microwave on HIGH for 4 to 6 minutes, or until the fish flakes when pressed with a fork. Drain well and flake into small pieces.
3. Combine potatoes with ½ cup water in a 3-quart microwave-safe casserole. Cover tightly with a lid or with plastic wrap turned back slightly. Microwave on HIGH for 10 to 12 minutes, or until the potatoes are tender, stirring once after 5 minutes. Mash, along with the cooking water, with a potato masher or hand mixer until smooth.
4. Combine cod, mashed potatoes, eggs, salt, and pepper in a large bowl. Line a cookie sheet with waxed paper and form twelve round patties (3 inches in diameter and ½ inch thick) with wet hands.
5. Place the vegetable oil in a 10- to 12-inch skillet and

heat over a medium-high flame for about 1 minute, or until hot but not smoking. Fry patties for about 2 minutes on each side, until nicely browned and heated through. You may lower the heat and cook slightly longer if desired.

NOTE To freeze codfish cakes:

Refrigerate uncooked codfish cakes for a few hours. Place four cakes, side by side, in a flat plastic freezer bag. Place the bag (or bags) flat on a cookie sheet and freeze. Once the cakes are frozen, remove the cookie sheet and stack the bags.

To defrost codfish cakes:

Open the bags. Microwave one bag on defrost for 3 to 5 minutes, until slightly softened, with some ice crystals remaining. Cook as in recipe above.

VARIATION Low-Cholesterol Codfish Cakes (3.5 grams fat per serving): Substitute 4 egg whites for the whole eggs.

Fresh Codfish Cakes (2.5 grams fat per serving): Substitute 1 pound fresh cod for ½ pound soaked dry cod, and eliminate the soaking. Place fresh cod in a single layer on a microwave-safe plate. Cover with waxed paper. Microwave on high for 4 to 6 minutes, or until the fish flakes when pressed with a fork. Drain well and flake into small pieces.

Warm Peppered Shrimp on Romaine with Basil-Lemon Vinaigrette

¾ pound large shrimp, peeled, with tails attached
4 tablespoons fresh lemon juice
¾ teaspoon coarsely ground black pepper
⅛ teaspoon cayenne pepper
2 small heads romaine lettuce (1 pound), leaves separated, washed and dried
¼ cup olive oil
2 tablespoons chopped fresh basil leaves
½ teaspoon salt

MAKES: *4 servings*
COOKING TIME: *2 to 3 minutes*

15.5 grams fat per serving

SERVING SUGGESTIONS:
Serve with Quick Beer Bread
(page 63) or a crusty
purchased bread.

1. Place shrimp in two rows around the outer edge of a 10-inch microwave-safe pie plate, leaving the center open. Sprinkle evenly with 1 tablespoon lemon juice, black pepper, and cayenne. Cover with paper towel. Microwave on HIGH for 2 to 3 minutes, or until pink. Let stand 2 minutes.
2. Meanwhile, fan out romaine leaves on four dinner plates. Arrange shrimp on lettuce.
3. In a small bowl, mix together remaining lemon juice, olive oil, basil, and salt. Drizzle over shrimp and greens.

Spinach Salad with Warm Fish Fillets and Tomato Vinaigrette

*1 pound fresh spinach, washed and torn into
  bite-size pieces*
1 recipe Basic Fish Fillets (page 198)
Tomato Vinaigrette (page 309)

1. Line four dinner plates with washed spinach.
2. Place a warm fillet in the center of each plate and spoon Tomato Vinaigrette over each arranged salad, dividing evenly.

MAKES: *4 servings*
COOKING TIME: *3 to 5 minutes*

Low cholesterol

19.3 grams fat per serving

SERVING SUGGESTIONS:
Serve with a crusty bread or
Large Garlic-Thyme Croutons
(page 311).

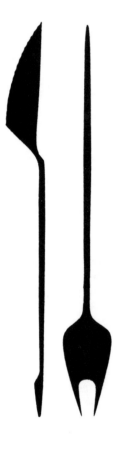

GRILLING

Taking a post at the grill year-round used to be only for fair-weather folk or diehards who couldn't go another day without a taste of barbecue. But with gas grills and their ability to shorten cooking time and pinpoint it, too, the grill may be as much of an "appliance" as the mixer or food processor.

It's often best to start grilled foods in the microwave oven first. This will keep them moist and ensure an exact grilling time. Turkey, chicken, fish, and briskets are among the meats that work well using this method. We provide cooking instructions and sauce suggestions for all of them, and for other meats as well, in this chapter.

We also find that the longer-cooking vegetables, with a low moisture content, benefit from being cooked in the microwave before they are grilled. This not only speeds up the cooking process and produces more succulent veggies, but again allows you to predict with accuracy when they'll be done.

To Prepare the Whole Meal

- If using a homemade barbecue sauce, prepare and cook first.
- Place the meat, poultry, or whole fish in the microwave to preheat.
- Light the grill. (If you are not using a gas or electric grill, prepare and start the charcoal grill *before* meat is precooked in the microwave. It will take about ½ hour for it to heat to the desired temperature for grilling.)
- Place vegetables to be precooked in the microwave after meat has been precooked.
- Cook nongrilled vegetables and rice in the microwave while the meat, poultry, or fish is grilling. If you plan to serve salad, it would also be prepared at this time.

GUIDELINES FOR GRILLED-MEAT TEMPERATURES AND DONENESS

Cuts need to be 1 inch thick before a meat thermometer can take an accurate reading. Insert the thermometer into the center of the cut.

Pork, fresh	160° F (medium)
	170° F (well done)
Beef	140° F (rare)
	150° F (medium)
	160–170° F (well done)

Touching the surface of the cooked meat with a fingertip will also give an indication of doneness. Rare meat depresses somewhat, medium has just a little give, and well done won't give at all.

Piercing the meat with a fork will reveal the color of the juice in the center of the meat. It should be red for rare, pink for medium, and have no trace of pink for well done.

Marinated London Broil

MAKES: *10 servings*
COOKING TIME: *12 to 18 minutes*

¾ cup red wine, or ¾ cup beef broth plus 2 tablespoons vinegar
2 tablespoons fresh lemon juice
2 tablespoons brown sugar
3 tablespoons low-sodium soy sauce
2 tablespoons olive or vegetable oil
2 green onions, thinly sliced
1 garlic clove, minced
3 pounds top round steak (London broil), 1½ inches thick

19 grams fat per serving

SERVING SUGGESTIONS:
Serve with baked potatoes (or
over toasted buns) and a large
vegetable salad the first day.
Save half of the meat for a
fajita dinner (page 208) a few
nights later.

*Because this cut is lean, it
satisfies our craving for red
meat without raising
cholesterol counts too much,
especially if serving sizes are
kept small.*

*By heating the marinade
and then quickly warming a
thin piece of meat in it, the
marinating process takes only
about 30 minutes.*

VARIATION

1. In a 2- or 3-quart rectangular microwave-safe dish,
combine all the ingredients except the meat. Microwave
on HIGH for 4 to 5 minutes, or until hot but not boiling,
stirring once.
2. Meanwhile, pierce the meat with a fork every inch
or so. Place the meat in the warm marinade. Microwave, uncovered, on HIGH for 1½ minutes. Turn the
meat over. Microwave on HIGH for 1½ minutes more.
3. Light grill (see page 207).
4. Cover the meat and let it stand for 30 minutes,
turning it over after 15 minutes. Place the meat on the
heated grill, reserving the marinade.
5. Grill the meat to the desired doneness (about 2 to 5
minutes per side for medium-rare).
6. Slice the meat into ½-inch pieces diagonally across
the grain.
7. Meanwhile, pour the reserved marinade into a
4-cup glass measure. Microwave on HIGH for 3 to 5
minutes. Serve as a sauce with the steak.

MARINATED GINGERED LONDON BROIL: Add 1 tablespoon grated fresh ginger to marinade.

Beef Fajitas

MAKES: *4 servings*
COOKING TIME: *8 to 10
minutes*

14.6 grams fat per serving

SERVING SUGGESTION:
To put these tasty rolls
together, cook the Sizzled
Peppers and Onions while
slicing the beef and mixing up
the Salsa Cruda.

*This is a good way to serve
leftover grilled Marinated
London Broil (page 207). You
can grill an extra steak to
make "planned overs" later in
the week.*

¾ pound grilled London broil, thinly sliced
12 flour tortillas, heated, purchased
1 recipe Sizzled Peppers and Onions (recipe follows)
1 recipe Salsa Cruda (page 317) or purchased salsa

1. Arrange the meat slices in a single layer on a
microwave-safe platter. Cover with waxed paper. Microwave on HIGH for 1 to 2 minutes, until just warm,
watching closely to make sure that the meat doesn't
overcook.
2. Wrap the flour tortillas in a dampened paper towel.
Microwave on HIGH for 1 to 1½ minutes, until warm to
the touch.
3. Place a piece of meat in the middle of a tortilla; top
with some Sizzled Peppers and Onions and Salsa
Cruda. Roll and enjoy.

Sizzled Peppers and Onions

MAKES: *6 servings*
COOKING TIME: *5 to 8 minutes*

Low cholesterol

0.7 gram fat per serving

SERVING SUGGESTIONS:
Serve on Beef Fajitas (page 208) or Turkey Fajitas (page 188) or with grilled meats.

1 teaspoon olive or vegetable oil
2 large Spanish onions, peeled and thinly sliced
2 bell peppers, sliced into ¼-inch strips

In a 2-quart microwave-safe casserole, combine all the ingredients. Cover with waxed paper. Microwave on HIGH for 5 to 8 minutes, until tender-crisp, stirring once.

Barbecued Brisket with Hot Sweet-and-Sour Sauce

MAKES: *10 servings*
COOKING TIME: *1 hour*

20 grams fat per serving

SERVING SUGGESTIONS:
Serve on good-quality burger-type rolls. Add pitchers of iced tea and sides of Coleslaw (page 237), pickles (page 312–14), and chips of choice.

This brisket is great for casual entertaining, Southern-style, or a family meal and will yield leftovers to serve later in the week.

1 lean beef brisket (3 pounds)
1 recipe Hot Sweet-and-Sour Sauce (page 216)
Good-quality soft rolls

1. Place the brisket, fat side down, in a 2- to 3-quart rectangular microwave-safe dish.
2. In a small bowl, combine ¼ cup sauce with ¼ cup water; stir until blended. Spoon half the mixture over the beef. Cover tightly with a lid or with plastic wrap turned back slightly on one side. Microwave on HIGH for 5 minutes; turn over. Microwave on MEDIUM for 10 minutes per pound, turning and basting the top with the remaining mixture halfway through cooking time.
3. Preheat the grill while the meat is cooking in the microwave oven.
4. Transfer the meat to the grill, reserving the drippings. Grill the beef for 5 minutes on each side, or to desired doneness, basting with the sauce two to three times. Let stand 10 minutes before slicing.
5. Add ½ cup of the reserved drippings to the remaining sauce. Microwave on HIGH for 3 minutes, stirring once.
6. Slice the meat thinly, on the diagonal. Toast the rolls on the grill. Serve meat on toasted rolls, topped with heated sauce.

Barbecued Hawaiian Pork Loin

MAKES: *8 servings*
COOKING TIME: *60 minutes*

20 grams fat per serving

SERVING SUGGESTIONS:
Grilled Sweet Potatoes (pages 216–17) go well with this. They can be cooked in the microwave oven after the roast is placed on the grill and can finish cooking on the grill along with the pork. Add a green salad or crudités.

1 recipe Hawaiian Barbecue Sauce (page 215)
1 pork loin (3 pounds)

1. When preparing barbecue sauce, do not add the pineapple chunks until after half of the sauce has been added to the pork.
2. Place pork, fat-side down, in a 3-quart microwave-safe casserole. Pour half of the sauce over the pork. Cover tightly with a lid or with plastic wrap turned back slightly.
3. Microwave on HIGH for 5 minutes, then on MEDIUM for 30 minutes, turning the pork over halfway through cooking time.
4. Preheat the grill while the meat is cooking in the microwave oven.
5. Transfer the meat to the grill, reserving the cooking juices. Grill for 15 minutes per side or until meat reaches 170° F, turning and brushing with sauce five or six times.
6. Add pineapple chunks to the reserved sauce. Slice pork and serve with sauce.

Barbecued Pork Butt

MAKES: *8 servings*
COOKING TIME: *45 to 50 minutes*

23.9 grams fat per serving

SERVING SUGGESTIONS:
Serve on toasted buns with Coleslaw (page 237), Barbecued Baked Beans (page 218), Bread-and-Butter Pickle Chips (pages 313, 314), and Refrigerator Pickled Jalapeño Peppers (page 314). Have pitchers of lemonade, iced tea, or beer on hand.

1 fresh pork butt (2 pounds)
1 recipe All-Purpose Barbecue Sauce (page 214)
Good-quality soft rolls

1. Remove the netting from the pork. Place the pork in a 3-quart microwave-safe casserole. Pour half the sauce over the pork. Cover tightly with a lid or with plastic wrap turned back slightly.
2. Microwave on HIGH for 5 minutes, then on MEDIUM for 20 minutes, turning the pork over halfway through cooking time.
3. Preheat the grill while the meat is cooking in the microwave.
4. Transfer the meat to the grill, reserving the drippings. Grill for 20 to 25 minutes, until the internal temperature reaches 170° F, turning and basting four or five times with reserved drippings.
5. Slice the meat thinly. Toast the rolls on the grill. Serve meat on toasted rolls, topped with extra barbecue sauce.

Barbecued Pork Ribs

MAKES: *8 servings*
COOKING TIME: *55 minutes*

29.6 grams fat per serving

SERVING SUGGESTIONS:
Serve with New Potato Salad (page 235) made earlier in the day and Grilled Corn (pages 216–17), which can be microwaved after the meat has been removed and added to the grill as the meat is finishing. For heartier appetites you may wish to add Barbecued Baked Beans (page 218).

3 pounds pork spareribs
1 recipe All-Purpose Barbecue Sauce (page 214)

1. Cut the pork between the rib bones into serving-size portions. Place ribs, meaty-sides down, in a 3-quart rectangular microwave-safe dish, with thicker sections to the outside, overlapping if necessary. Cover with waxed paper.
2. Microwave on HIGH for 5 minutes, then on MEDIUM for 15 minutes.
3. Drain any excess fat from the ribs. Turn the ribs over and rearrange them, placing the less-cooked sections toward the outside of the dish. Brush with ½ cup of barbecue sauce. Cover again and microwave on MEDIUM for 15 minutes, or until tender.
4. While the meat is cooking in the microwave oven, heat the grill.
5. Transfer the meat to the grill. Cook about 5 minutes on each side, basting with barbecue sauce four or five times. Serve with remaining sauce.

BARBECUING PORK

Here are some simple guidelines for barbecuing pork in combination with the microwave.

PORK ROASTS AND FRESH HAM
Pour ½ cup broth, juice, or sauce over roast or ham in a 3- to 4-quart microwave-safe casserole. Cover tightly with a lid or plastic wrap turned back slightly. Microwave on HIGH for 5 minutes, then on MEDIUM for 10 minutes per pound, turning over once while cooking. Transfer the meat to the grill for 20 to 25 minutes; turn four or five times and baste with a barbecue sauce.

PORK SPARERIBS
Place the ribs, fat side down, in a rectangular microwave-safe dish. Cover with waxed paper; microwave on HIGH for 5 minutes, then on MEDIUM for 10 minutes per pound, turning over and rearranging once while cooking. Transfer to a preheated grill for 10 minutes; turn once and baste with sauce.

Quick Barbecued Chicken

MAKES: *4 servings*
COOKING TIME: *20 minutes*

13.6 grams fat per serving of light and dark meat; 9 grams fat per serving of light meat only

1 chicken (3 pounds), cut into 8 pieces
1 recipe All-Purpose Barbecue Sauce (page 214)

1. Preheat the grill.
2. Place the chicken pieces, skin side down, in a 2-quart microwave-safe dish, arranging the thicker portions to the outside. Cover tightly with plastic wrap turned back slightly. Microwave on HIGH for 15 minutes, turning the chicken over once halfway through cooking.
3. Place the chicken on the preheated grill and baste with sauce. Grill 4 to 5 minutes per side, basting frequently with more sauce, until the chicken reaches a desired crispness. Pass the remaining barbecue sauce at the table.

VARIATION

QUICK BARBECUED CHICKEN WITH RASPBERRY-MINT SAUCE: Substitute Raspberry-Mint Sauce (page 325) for All-Purpose Barbecue Sauce.

SERVING SUGGESTIONS:
Serve with Grilled Vegetables (pages 216–17) of your choice, Barbecued Baked Beans (page 218), and/or Coleslaw (page 237).

NOTE

To double recipe: Cook chicken in two batches as directed in basic recipe. Grill according to instructions in step 3.

Lemon-Mustard Grilled Chicken

MAKES: *4 servings*
COOKING TIME: *20 to 25 minutes*

13.6 grams fat per serving of light and dark meat; 9 grams fat per serving of light meat only

1 chicken (3 pounds), cut into 8 serving pieces
2 tablespoons fresh lemon juice
2 tablespoons Dijon mustard
2 tablespoons chopped fresh herbs (parsley, chives, dill, tarragon)
¼ teaspoon salt
⅛ teaspoon freshly ground black pepper

1. Preheat the grill.
2. Place the chicken pieces, skin side up, in a 2-quart microwave-safe dish, arranging the thicker portions to the outside.
3. In a small bowl, mix together the remaining ingredients. Brush onto the chicken.
4. Cover the dish with waxed paper. Microwave on

Serve with Dilled Small Potatoes (page 232) and Wilted Greens Salad (page 236). Prepare both while the chicken is grilling.

This savory grilled chicken marinates quickly while it cooks in the microwave oven. Giving the chicken a quick turn on a preheated grill adds the desired flavor and crispness while sealing in tenderness.

HIGH for 15 minutes, turning the chicken over and basting with sauce after 8 minutes.

5. Place the chicken on the preheated grill and baste with cooking juices. Grill for 3 to 5 minutes per side, basting frequently, or until the chicken reaches desired crispness.

Honey-Mustard Glazed Turkey Drumsticks

MAKES: *4 servings*
COOKING TIME: *55 minutes*

9.8 grams fat per serving

SERVING SUGGESTIONS:
Serve with Rhubarb or Cranberry Chutney (pages 330, 332) from the pantry and Grilled Sweet Potatoes (pages 216–217), which can be cooked in the microwave oven after the meat is placed on the grill and finished on the grill with the meat. Oven-Baked Corn Bread (page 61) is a nice addition.

2 to 3 pounds turkey drumsticks
1 recipe Honey-Mustard Barbecue Sauce (page 215)

1. Arrange drumsticks in a 2-quart rectangular microwave-safe dish, with thicker portions toward the outside of dish; cover with waxed paper.
2. Microwave on HIGH for 6 minutes, then on MEDIUM for 35 minutes, turning once.
3. Transfer drumsticks to grill. Cook for 5 minutes on each side, basting with ½ cup sauce three or four times, until meat is tender and skin is slightly crisp. Serve with remaining sauce.

- According to a "Kitchen Report" from *Cook's* magazine's test kitchen, a turkey that is first microwaved and then browned and crisped on a grill or in a conventional oven is moister than one that is completely cooked by the conventional methods!
- Follow the "Grilled Turkey" variation of Oven-Browned Turkey (page 175) for a wonderful meal for guests or family.

Grilling Fish

Not all fish need pre-microwaving—only whole fish, because it is so thick.

1. Grease the grill well to prevent the fish from sticking.
2. Preheat the grill for at least 10 minutes.
3. Brush the fish well with olive oil.
4. If steaks are ½ inch or more thick, grill about 3 minutes on each side. If they are less than ½ inch thick, grill 1 to 2 minutes per side.
5. To grill a whole fish: Cook fish first in the microwave oven to ensure that the center will be cooked through when grilling:

    Place the whole fish in a 2- or 3-quart microwave-safe dish. Add 2 tablespoons lemon juice. Cover tightly with a lid or plastic wrap turned back on one side. Microwave on MEDIUM for 7 minutes per pound. Brush the grill and fish well with oil, or place fish in a special grilling basket. Grill 5 minutes on each side on preheated grill, or until the flesh of the fish can be pressed with a finger without leaving a dent.
6. Serve grilled fish with Mustard-Horseradish Sauce (page 324), Mint Pesto (page 335), Tomato Vinaigrette (page 309), or Herb Butter (page 315).

All-Purpose Barbecue Sauce

MAKES: *About 2 cups*
COOKING TIME: *7 to 10 minutes*

No cholesterol

0.9 gram fat per tablespoon

SERVING SUGGESTIONS:
Use to baste foods while grilling; serve extra sauce at the table. Good on ribs, steaks, chops, chicken, and

2 tablespoons olive or vegetable oil
1 garlic clove, minced
1 medium onion, chopped
¼ cup brown sugar
1 cup catsup
3 tablespoons cider vinegar
2 tablespoons Dijon mustard
2 tablespoons low-sodium soy sauce
2 tablespoons fresh lemon juice
1 tablespoon Worcestershire sauce
2 to 3 drops hot-pepper sauce

In a 4-cup glass measure, combine the oil, garlic, and onion. Microwave, uncovered, on HIGH for 2 to 3 minutes, or until tender. Stir in the remaining ingredients and ½ cup water. Microwave on HIGH for 5 to 7 minutes, or until boiling, stirring after 2 minutes.

ALL-PURPOSE BARBECUE SAUCE WITH CHILI POWDER: Add 1 tablespoon chili powder with remaining ingredients.

even on grilled vegetables. Try it with grilled eggplant slices—you'll think you are eating steak!

We make a double portion of this sauce and keep it in a tightly covered jar in the refrigerator. (It will keep, refrigerated, for 1 month.)

Honey-Mustard Barbecue Sauce

MAKES: *1 cup (enough to baste and be served with 3 to 4 pounds of meat)*
COOKING TIME: *2 to 3 minutes*

No cholesterol

0.2 gram fat per tablespoon

SERVING SUGGESTIONS:
This is tasty with chicken or pork. Cook the chicken following the instructions for Quick Barbecued Chicken (page 212). For pork, follow the instructions for Pork Roasts and Fresh Ham (page 210) or Barbecued Pork Ribs (page 211).

½ cup honey
¼ cup country-style Dijon mustard
1 tablespoon low-sodium soy sauce
1 teaspoon chopped fresh ginger or ¼ teaspoon ground

1. Combine all the ingredients in a 4-cup glass measure. Microwave on HIGH for 2 to 3 minutes, or until heated through, stirring once.
2. Baste the chicken or pork with a small amount of sauce while grilling. Serve remaining sauce with chicken or pork.

Hawaiian Barbecue Sauce

½ cup pineapple juice
1 tablespoon fresh lemon juice
¼ cup brown sugar
2 tablespoons catsup
1 tablespoon country-style Dijon mustard
2 cups fresh or canned unsweetened pineapple chunks (see Note)

MAKES: ¾ cup
COOKING TIME: *5 minutes*

No cholesterol

0.1 gram fat per tablespoon

SERVING SUGGESTIONS:
A perfect sauce for barbecued pork or chicken

1. In a 4-cup glass measure, combine all the ingredients, except the pineapple chunks. Microwave, uncovered, on HIGH for 4 to 5 minutes, stirring once.
2. Use half the sauce, without the pineapple chunks, for basting.
3. Add the pineapple chunks to the remaining sauce and serve as a condiment at the table.

NOTE If using canned pineapple chunks, reserve the juice and use it in the recipe.

Hot Sweet-and-Sour Sauce

MAKES: *1½ cups*
COOKING TIME: *4 to 6 minutes*

No cholesterol

0.6 gram fat per tablespoon

SERVING SUGGESTIONS:
This sauce is delicious when basted on brisket, ribs, turkey drumsticks, or chicken pieces.

1 tablespoon oil
1 medium onion, chopped
1 tablespoon chili powder
1 teaspoon dry mustard
½ cup catsup
½ cup apricot preserves
¼ cup brown sugar
2 tablespoons low-sodium soy sauce
2 tablespoons Worcestershire sauce
⅛ teaspoon hot pepper sauce

1. In a 4-cup glass measure, combine the oil, onion, and chili powder. Microwave on HIGH for 1 to 2 minutes, or until the onion is tender.
2. Stir in the remaining ingredients. Microwave on HIGH for 3 to 5 minutes, stirring once, until heated through and well blended.

GRILLING VEGETABLES Cooking vegetables in the microwave before grilling them speeds up the cooking process, produces more succulent veggies, and allows you to predict the serving time accurately.

After following the microwave instructions below, the vegetables can be grilled for 2 to 8 minutes, depending on the heat of the fire and the desired amount of charring.

Please note that fat grams are determined by the sauce used and the amount of fat brushed onto the vegetable; the vegetables have negligible amounts of fat on their own.

WHITE OR SWEET POTATOES: Scrub potatoes and pierce with a fork; place on a piece of paper towel in the microwave oven. Turn over once during cooking.

Serve with Herb Butter (page 315), Mint Pesto (page 335), or Yogurt Sauce (page 318).

4 potatoes	HIGH for 10 minutes
6 potatoes	HIGH for 12 minutes

CORN: Pull back husks of 4 to 6 ears of corn and remove silk; replace husks. Place directly in microwave oven (or place husked ears on a microwave-safe platter with ¼ cup water and a cover of plastic wrap turned back slightly). Rearrange once during cooking.

4 ears	HIGH for 10 minutes
6 ears	HIGH for 12 minutes

Serve with Herb Butter (page 315). For low-cholesterol corn, brush with low-sodium soy sauce.

ONIONS: Peel 4 large onions (about 3 inches in diameter) and halve them crosswise. Place in a 2-quart rectangular microwave-safe dish. Cover tightly with plastic wrap turned back slightly. Microwave on HIGH for 5 minutes. Brush with olive oil and put on the grill.

Serve plain or topped with Mint Pesto (page 335) or Herb Butter (page 315).

EGGPLANT: Place 1 medium eggplant, cut into 8 crosswise slices, in a 2-quart rectangular microwave-safe dish, or substitute 4 miniature eggplants, sliced lengthwise up to but not through the stem end, fanned out in a 10-inch microwave-safe pie plate. Cover tightly with plastic wrap turned back slightly. Microwave on HIGH for 3 minutes, or until slightly softened. Brush with olive or sesame oil before placing on grill.

Serve plain or with All-Purpose Barbecue Sauce (page 214), Basic Tomato and Pepper Sauce (page 336), or Yogurt Sauce (page 318).

VARIATION   MARINATED EGGPLANT: Pour ⅓ cup of a vinaigrette (pages 310–11) over eggplant before cooking in the microwave oven. Baste with marinade while grilling.

Barbecued Baked Beans

MAKES: *8 servings*
COOKING TIME: *12 to 15 minutes*

No-cholesterol variation

5.3 grams fat per serving

VARIATIONS

SERVING SUGGESTIONS:
Serve these with any of the barbecued meats, such as Barbecued Brisket (page 209), Barbecued Pork Ribs (page 211), Barbecued Pork Butt (page 210), or Quick Barbecued Chicken (page 212). Cook in the microwave oven while the meat is grilling.

The taste of this dish will vary, depending on the barbecue sauce you use. If you really want to add a smoky barbecue flavor to the beans, transfer them to an old pot (one that you don't care about very much); cover it and keep the beans warm on the back or top rack of your grill.

2 slices bacon, cut into ½-inch pieces
1 onion, finely chopped
2 cans (16 ounces each) baked beans
¼ cup brown sugar
¼ cup of barbecue sauce that you are using on meat, or ¼ cup catsup plus 1 tablespoon Dijon mustard

1. Combine the bacon and onion in a 2-quart microwave-safe casserole. Microwave on HIGH for 3 to 5 minutes, or until the onion is tender and the bacon partially cooked.
2. Stir in the remaining ingredients. Cover with waxed paper; microwave on MEDIUM for 8 to 10 minutes, or until heated through, stirring after 4 minutes.

NO-CHOLESTEROL BARBECUED BAKED BEANS (3.5 grams fat per serving): Substitute 1 teaspoon olive oil for bacon. Cook the oil and onion for 1 minute. Substitute vegetarian baked beans for regular beans (i.e., beans with bacon in them).

BARBECUED BLACK BEANS: Substitute canned black beans for baked beans. This version is not as sweet as the original.

FRUITS AND VEGETABLES

AFTER JUST one day in the refrigerator, cooked fruits and vegetables have only about three-fourths as much vitamin C as they had when freshly cooked. Each day thereafter, more vitamin C is lost. That's why it makes real sense to cook only the quantity of fruits and vegetables you'll need for each meal—and of course that can be done speedily in the microwave.

Mashed potatoes are an exception to this rule. We often do have some leftovers (or wish we did), which we savor in the delicious fish, meat and vegetable cakes we learned to love growing up. Fortunately, in the initial cooking of the potatoes, more of the vitamin C is retained with microwave cooking than with any other means of cooking because less water and cooking time are needed.

Some of the most streamlined recipes in this chapter are our favorites. When in season and served right on the platter on which they are cooked, tender-crisp green beans, asparagus, or broccoli with a hot garlic oil or chilled tomato vinaigrette, rival even the most elaborate vegetable presentations.

Making Vegetables and Fruits Part of the Whole Meal

- Most vegetables are cooked during the standing time of the microwave main dish or while the main dish is being grilled or cooked conventionally.
- Two vegetables that should be cooked in the microwave *before* the main dish are winter squash and potatoes.
- Marinated vegetables for salads are also cooked before the main dish so that the flavors may develop during refrigeration.
- Cook longer-cooking vegetable casseroles in the microwave oven for maximum vitamin retention. To make meal preparation more time-efficient, serve them with a main course that is cooked on the grill or stove top, or even with a takeout dish.

TO COOK 2 CUPS OF VEGETABLES

- For raw corn kernels or cubed carrots, add 2 tablespoons of liquid (water, broth, or orange juice, as appropriate) and place in a small microwave-safe casserole. Cover tightly with a lid or plastic wrap turned back slightly on one side. Microwave on HIGH for 4 to 8 minutes, stirring once.
- For green beans, peas, trimmed asparagus spears, broccoli or cauliflower florets, or shredded cabbage, add ¼ cup liquid and place in a 1-quart microwave-safe casserole. Cover (as directed above) and microwave on HIGH for 4 to 8 minutes.
- For spinach, chard, or beet greens (2 pounds), wash but do not dry. Place in a 3-quart microwave-safe casserole and cover tightly (as directed above); cook on HIGH for 7 to 10 minutes, or until tender, stirring once.
- For sliced or chopped tomatoes, eggplant, peppers, or zucchini, place in a small casserole, with no liquid, and cover (as directed above). Microwave on HIGH for 3 to 6 minutes, or until tender, stirring once.
- For sliced mushrooms, place in a small casserole. Microwave, uncovered, on HIGH for 2 to 5 minutes, or until tender, stirring once.

Zucchini
in a Flash

MAKES: *4 servings*
COOKING TIME: *3 to 5 minutes*

No cholesterol

3.5 grams fat per serving

VARIATION

This is a quick and always appreciated side dish; it goes well with most meals.

4 small or 2 medium zucchini (1 pound), washed, ends removed, but not peeled.
1 tablespoon olive oil
2 garlic cloves, minced

1. Cut the zucchini into thin matchsticks or coarsely grate.
2. In a 1-quart microwave-safe casserole, combine the oil and garlic. Microwave on HIGH for 35 seconds. Stir in the zucchini and coat well. Microwave on HIGH for 2½ to 4 minutes, or until tender-crisp, stirring once. Serve.

CARROTS AND ZUCCHINI IN A FLASH: Eliminate half the zucchini and substitute 1 large carrot, cut into matchsticks or coarsely grated.

Herb-Topped
Tomatoes

MAKES: *4 servings*
COOKING TIME: *2½ to 3½ minutes*

No cholesterol

3.7 grams fat per serving

SERVING SUGGESTIONS:
Prepare while grilling a piece of meat or fish.

When our gardens are in full bloom, we love to gather all the ingredients for this recipe. You can also pick up fresh ingredients at a local farm stand. The microwave oven helps preserve garden-fresh flavor.

4 firm ripe tomatoes (about 3 inches in diameter) or 8 plum tomatoes
Salt
Freshly ground black pepper
1 slice fresh bread with crust
1 tablespoon olive oil
1 garlic clove, minced
1 green onion, thinly sliced (about 2 tablespoons)
1 tablespoon finely chopped fresh parsley
1 tablespoon minced fresh basil or 1 teaspoon dried

1. Remove the tomato stems and cut the tomatoes in half crosswise (if using plum tomatoes, cut lengthwise). Place the tomato halves, cut sides up, in a 9-inch round microwave-safe dish. Season with salt and pepper. Set aside.
2. In the bowl of a food processor, combine the remaining ingredients. Pulse (or combine in a small bowl and chop). Spoon evenly over the tomato halves.
3. Cover loosely with waxed paper. Microwave on HIGH for 2½ to 3½ minutes, or until heated through.

Harvest Red Cabbage

MAKES: *4 servings*
COOKING TIME: *17 to 18 minutes*

No cholesterol

3.4 grams fat per serving

SERVING SUGGESTIONS:
A tasty side dish for fish and poultry. Our favorite way to serve this is with smoked meat. (By adding 1 pound of smoked meat at the end of cabbage cooking time, you'll have a one-dish meal in only 10 extra minutes.) To make this part of a quick company meal, cut a Perfectly Poached

VARIATION

Pear (page 238) in half and spoon Cranberry Chutney (page 330) into the cavities. Serve with Onion-Caraway Beer Bread (page 63) or purchased crusty pumpernickel bread.

1 tablespoon olive oil
1 garlic clove, minced
1 large onion, thinly sliced
4 cups grated red cabbage (1 pound)
⅛ teaspoon dried thyme leaves
⅛ teaspoon powdered allspice
1 large tart apple (Granny Smith), washed and grated coarsely
¼ cup dry red wine
2 tablespoons red-wine vinegar
2 tablespoons brown sugar
2 tablespoons raisins or dried cranberries

1. In a 3-quart microwave-safe casserole, combine the oil, garlic, and onion.
2. Microwave, uncovered, on HIGH for 2 to 3 minutes, or until tender. Stir in remaining ingredients.
3. Cover tightly with a lid or plastic wrap turned back slightly. Microwave on HIGH for 10 to 12 minutes; stir well.
4. Cover again and microwave on HIGH for 5 to 8 minutes, or until tender. Let stand for 5 minutes before serving.

NOTE To double either the basic recipe or the variations, double all the ingredients and use a 4-quart casserole. Double the cooking times.

HARVEST RED CABBAGE WITH SMOKED MEATS (23 grams fat per serving): After the cabbage has finished cooking, but before standing time, push half of the cabbage to one side and smooth out the other half in the bottom of the casserole dish. Place ¾ pound of smoked sausage or smoked pork chops on top of bottom layer of cabbage. Cover with remaining cabbage.

Cover tightly and microwave on MEDIUM for 10 minutes, or until the meat is heated through. Let stand for 5 minutes before serving.

LOW-CHOLESTEROL HARVEST RED CABBAGE WITH SMOKED TURKEY (6.6 grams fat per serving): Follow recipe for Harvest Red Cabbage with Smoked Meat, substituting ¾ pound smoked turkey, cut into 4 serving pieces, for sausages or pork chops.

Old-Fashioned Mashed Potatoes

MAKES: *6 servings*
COOKING TIME: *12 to 14 minutes*

No-cholesterol variation

5.4 grams fat per serving

SERVING SUGGESTIONS:
Good with any of the meat loaves (pages 150–54), Quick Fried Chicken (page 183), or Oven-Browned Turkey (page 174).

NOTE

You can prepare these potatoes in about one-third the time that it would take conventionally.

Thelma's husband, a real mashed-potato connoisseur, just wouldn't go for the microwaved variety— until Thelma discovered a way to give them the right consistency. The secret? Adding more water (which adds 1 or 2 extra minutes of

VARIATIONS

cooking time) and then mashing the cooking water right into the potatoes before adding the milk, butter, and seasonings.

1½ pounds potatoes, peeled and cut into eighths
2 to 4 tablespoons butter
1 cup milk
Salt and pepper to taste
Ground nutmeg (optional)

1. In a 2-quart microwave-safe casserole, combine the potatoes and ½ cup water. Cover tightly with a lid or plastic wrap turned back slightly. Microwave on HIGH for 12 to 14 minutes, or until very tender, stirring once halfway through cooking.
2. Leaving the water in the dish, mash the potatoes well with a potato masher to remove all the lumps.
3. Meanwhile, place the butter and milk in a 1-cup glass measure. Microwave on HIGH for 45 seconds to warm.
4. Add the warm milk to the potatoes and whip until light and fluffy; add 1 or 2 more tablespoons of milk if necessary. Salt and pepper to taste. Add nutmeg if desired.

TO FREEZE MASHED POTATOES: Spoon 1-, 2-, or 3-cup servings into sealable freezer bags or freezer containers; flatten and freeze. See preserving chapter for more details.

TO DEFROST MASHED POTATOES: Place opened container or freezer bag with mashed potatoes in microwave oven and heat on MEDIUM for 2 minutes (for 1-cup portion) or 3 to 5 minutes (for 2- to 3-cup portions).

Transfer the potatoes to a larger bowl or glass measure to allow for stirring. Cover with waxed paper and microwave on HIGH for 3 to 6 minutes, or until heated through, stirring every 2 minutes to equalize heat. Serve as is or use for one of the leftover mashed-potato recipes.

NO-CHOLESTEROL MASHED POTATOES (2.4 grams fat per serving): Substitute 1 tablespoon olive oil for butter. Substitute skim milk for whole milk.

GARLIC MASHED POTATOES: Add 2 to 4 peeled garlic cloves, depending on the size and amount of garlic flavor desired. Cook and mash with potatoes; make either regular or no-cholesterol variation.

SCALLION MASHED POTATOES: After mashing the potatoes, fold in ¼ cup thinly sliced scallions (green onions).

OLIVE MASHED POTATOES (3.4 grams fat per serving): Add 2 tablespoons chopped, pitted black or purple olives to the mashed potatoes.

LEFTOVER MASHED-POTATO RECIPES

Mashed potatoes, when combined with other leftovers such as vegetables, fish, poultry, or meats, make delicious little patties that can be served as a main course or in smaller portions as tasty appetizers. They can be paired with chutneys or sauces, and yogurt for a complete and simple lunch. Mashed potatoes also make the perfect base for soups, served warm in winter or chilled in summer.

Fish or Meat Cakes Made with Mashed Potatoes

MAKES: *2 main-course servings, or 4 first-course or appetizer servings*
COOKING TIME: *4 to 5 minutes*

No-cholesterol variation

8.7 grams fat per main-course serving

SERVING SUGGESTIONS:
Serve with a mixed green salad and chutney or fruit.

½ cup flaked cooked fish or finely chopped chicken, ham, or meat
1 cup mashed potatoes (any variety) (pages 223–24)
1 egg yolk, lightly beaten
Freshly ground black pepper to taste
1 tablespoon vegetable or olive oil

1. Combine all ingredients except the oil in a medium bowl.
2. Form into four round patties, 3 inches in diameter and ½ inch thick. (Wetting your hands makes this job easier.)
3. Place the oil in a large skillet and heat until the pan is hot but not quite smoking.
4. Fry the patties for about 2 minutes on each side, or until nicely browned and heated through. You may lower heat and cook slightly longer if you wish.

TO SERVE AS AN APPETIZER: Form into patties 1½ inches in diameter and ½ inch thick; fry as indicated above. Serve topped with chutney or 1 cup plain yogurt or sour cream that has been mixed with ¼ cup chopped chives.

VARIATION NO-CHOLESTEROL FISH OR MEAT CAKES: Use No-

Cholesterol Mashed Potatoes (page 223); substitute 1 egg white for yolk and combine with fish, turkey, or chicken.

Vegetable Patties

MAKES: *4 side-dish or appetizer servings, or 2 vegetarian main-course servings*
COOKING TIME: *4 to 5 minutes*

No-cholesterol variation

2.4 grams fat per main-course serving

SERVING SUGGESTIONS: Serve with Mint Raita (page 319).

1 cup mashed potatoes (pages 223–24)
1 cup uncooked carrots (2 medium), zucchini, or parsnips, grated
1 egg yolk, lightly beaten
⅛ teaspoon freshly ground black pepper
⅛ teaspoon grated nutmeg
1 tablespoon vegetable or olive oil

1. Combine all the ingredients except the oil in a medium bowl.
2. Form into four round patties, 3 inches in diameter and ½ inch thick. Wetting your hands makes this job easier.
3. Place oil in a large skillet and heat until the pan is hot but not quite smoking.
4. Fry patties for about 2 minutes on each side, or until nicely browned and heated through. You may lower heat and cook slightly longer if you wish.

TO SERVE AS AN APPETIZER: Form into patties 1½ inches in diameter and ½ inch thick; fry as indicated above. Serve topped with any chutney (pages 330–33) or Mint Raita.

VARIATION   NO-CHOLESTEROL VEGETABLE PATTIES (1.2 grams fat per main-course serving): Use No-Cholesterol Mashed Potatoes (page 223); substitute 1 egg white for yolk.

Carrot and Mashed-Potato Soup

1 teaspoon olive or vegetable oil, or butter
1 small onion, finely chopped
1 cup grated carrots (2 medium)
1 cup mashed potatoes (pages 223–24)
¾ cup vegetable or chicken broth, milk, or water
⅛ teaspoon thyme leaves
⅛ teaspoon grated nutmeg (optional)

1. Combine oil, onion, and carrot in a 4-cup glass measure or microwave-safe casserole. Cover with

MAKES: *4 light lunch servings
or first-course dinner servings*
COOKING TIME: *6 to 8 minutes*

No-cholesterol variation

4 grams fat per serving

NOTE

SERVING SUGGESTION:
If serving for lunch, add some
whole-grain bread.

waxed paper; microwave on HIGH for 3 to 4 minutes, or
until carrot is tender.
2. Stir in remaining ingredients. Cover again with
waxed paper; microwave on HIGH for 3 to 5 minutes, or
until heated through.

TO MAKE 2 SERVINGS: Cut ingredients and cooking
times in half.

VARIATIONS

ZUCCHINI AND MASHED-POTATO SOUP (4 grams fat per
serving): Substitute 1 cup grated zucchini for carrot.
Reduce microwaving time in step 1 to 2 minutes.

ONION AND MASHED-POTATO SOUP (4 grams fat per
serving): Substitute 1 large onion, chopped (1 cup), for
grated carrot. Microwave for 4 to 5 minutes, or until
tender, in step 1.

NO-CHOLESTEROL VEGETABLE AND MASHED-POTATO
SOUP (2.3 grams fat per serving): In any of the
versions, use No-Cholesterol Mashed Potatoes (page
223); substitute olive oil for butter and skim milk,
broth, or water for the liquid.

Butternut
Squash Puree

MAKES: *4 servings*
COOKING TIME: *10 to 12
minutes*

No cholesterol

0.2 gram fat per serving

SERVING SUGGESTIONS:
A great stuffed-pasta filling
and also an excellent side dish,
by itself or in combination
with another vegetable.

*1 butternut squash (2 pounds)
¼ cup plain nonfat yogurt
⅛ teaspoon freshly ground nutmeg*

1. Pierce the squash with the tines of a fork on the top
and bottom.
2. Place on a microwave-safe plate. Microwave on
HIGH for 10 to 12 minutes, or until the entire squash is
a darker shade of beige than before and it is tender
when pierced, turning the squash over after 6 minutes
and rotating the plate one-quarter turn. Let stand 5
minutes.
3. Cut the squash in half and spoon out the seeds. The
flesh will pull away from the peel easily.
4. Spoon the cooked squash into the bowl of a food
processor. Add the remaining ingredients and pulse the
processor on and off until mixture is pureed.

The rule for cooking a butternut squash in the microwave oven is to cook it on HIGH for 8 minutes per 1 pound, adding 4 minutes on HIGH for each additional pound and cooking it until the squash has turned a darker beige all over.

Breaded Zucchini Sticks

MAKES: *8 sticks (1 snack serving, or 2 side-dish servings)*
COOKING TIME: *2 minutes*

No cholesterol

15.1 grams fat per snack serving; 7.5 grams fat per side-dish serving

SERVING SUGGESTIONS:
Kids love these dipped in Basic Tomato Sauce (page 145) or plain.

1 small zucchini (4 ounces), scrubbed but not peeled
1 tablespoon olive, peanut, or vegetable oil
¼ cup flavored bread crumbs

1. Cut the zucchini in half crosswise and then quarter each half lengthwise to make eight sticks.
2. Pour the oil into a cereal bowl; put the bread crumbs in a small plastic bag.
3. Dip the zucchini sticks in the oil and then shake them in breading to coat.
4. Place the pieces around the outer edge of a 9-inch paper plate. Microwave on HIGH for 2 minutes. Let stand for 2 minutes.

Mixed Vegetable Platter with Lemon Sauce

MAKES: *8 to 10 servings*
COOKING TIME: *8 to 10 minutes*

No-cholesterol variation

0.1 gram fat per serving without sauce; 8.8 grams fat

1 medium acorn squash, with skin left on (about 1 pound)
1 head broccoli, cut into florets (2 cups)
3 large carrots, cut into 2-inch julienne strips
2 cups mushroom caps
1 recipe Lemon Sauce (recipe follows)

1. Place the whole squash in the microwave. Cook on HIGH for 1 minute. Cut in half, seed, and cut into ¼-inch slices.
2. Arrange squash slices around the edge of a 12-inch round microwave-safe platter, overlapping the slices slightly. Place the broccoli in a circle inside the squash; place the carrots in a circle inside the broccoli; place the mushrooms in the center.

per serving with 1 tablespoon sauce

SERVING SUGGESTIONS:
A great addition to holiday and company meals.

3. Sprinkle with 2 tablespoons water. Cover with plastic wrap turned back slightly on one side. Microwave on HIGH for 8 to 10 minutes, or until tender-crisp, rotating the dish after 4 minutes. Let stand 1 minute; uncover and serve with sauce on the side.

VARIATION NO-CHOLESTEROL MIXED VEGETABLE PLATTER (0.1 gram fat per serving): Serve without sauce or with Mustard Vinaigrette (page 311).

Lemon Sauce

MAKES: ⅔ *cup*
COOKING TIME: *2 minutes*

8.8 grams fat per tablespoon

SERVING SUGGESTIONS:
Serve over Mixed Vegetable Platter (page 227) or any other vegetable.

½ cup (1 stick) butter
2 tablespoons fresh lemon juice
2 tablespoons minced fresh parsley
2 tablespoons minced fresh dill
2 tablespoons minced fresh chives

Place all ingredients in a 4-cup glass measure. Microwave on HIGH for 1 to 2 minutes, or until butter melts, stirring once. Pour into a serving dish; serve warm.

Creamy Mashed Sweet Potatoes

MAKES: *4 servings*
COOKING TIME: *10 to 12 minutes*

No cholesterol

2 grams fat per serving

SERVING SUGGESTIONS:
Great with poultry or pork. To make a vegetarian meal, serve with Barley Pilaf (page 116) and extra yogurt.

1½ pounds sweet potatoes, peeled and cut into 2-inch pieces
½ cup nonfat yogurt
½ teaspoon grated nutmeg
¼ teaspoon freshly ground black pepper
¼ teaspoon salt
1 tablespoon brown sugar, honey, or molasses
1 teaspoon lemon juice

1. Place the sweet potatoes in a 2-quart microwave-safe casserole with ½ cup water. Cover tightly with a lid or plastic wrap turned back slightly. Microwave on HIGH for 10 to 12 minutes, or until tender, stirring once.
2. With a potato masher, mash the sweet potatoes with their cooking water until they are smooth. Stir in the remaining ingredients (or use a food processor for even faster preparation).

VARIATION CREAMY MASHED SWEET POTATOES WITH CINNAMON

AND ORANGE: Substitute cinnamon for nutmeg. Add 1 tablespoon orange juice and 1 teaspoon grated orange rind with spices.

Sweet-Potato Pie with Mandarin Oranges and Pecans

MAKES: *10 servings*
COOKING TIME: *15 to 20 minutes*

No-cholesterol variation

4.2 grams fat per serving

SERVING SUGGESTION: Make the day before and reheat in the microwave oven right before serving (6 to 10 minutes on HIGH) to take the pressure off of holiday entertaining.

A welcome addition to any holiday table, this crustless ''pie'' is simple to make.

2 pounds sweet potatoes, peeled and cut into 2-inch cubes
1 can (11 ounces) mandarin oranges in light syrup
2 tablespoons butter or margarine
2 tablespoons brown sugar
¼ teaspoon grated nutmeg
½ teaspoon ground cinnamon
1 teaspoon lemon juice
¼ cup coarsely chopped pecans, plus 16 halves for garnish

1. Combine the potato pieces and ½ cup water in a 2-quart microwave-safe casserole. Cover with a lid or plastic wrap turned back slightly on one side. Microwave on HIGH for 10 to 12 minutes, or until tender, stirring once after 5 minutes.
2. Meanwhile, drain oranges and reserve syrup.
3. Spoon the potato pieces into the bowl of a food processor or blender and process in two batches until pureed, or mash in a bowl.
4. Place the butter in a 1-cup glass measure and microwave on HIGH until melted. Stir into the potatoes, along with the reserved syrup, brown sugar, nutmeg, cinnamon, and lemon juice, until well blended.
5. Fold in the mandarin oranges and chopped pecans. Spoon the mixture evenly into a 10-inch microwave-safe pie plate. Smooth the top and garnish with pecan halves.
6. Cover with waxed paper and heat on MEDIUM for 3 to 5 minutes before serving. Cut into wedges and serve.

VARIATION NO-CHOLESTEROL SWEET POTATO PIE WITH MANDARIN ORANGES AND PECANS (1.8 grams fat per serving): Substitute 2 tablespoons nonfat plain yogurt for butter or margarine.

Peppers, Onions, and Basil

MAKES: *About 2 cups*
COOKING TIME: *6 to 8 minutes*

No cholesterol

1.9 grams fat per ¼ cup

SERVING SUGGESTIONS:
Serve on sandwiches or as a side dish with meat, fish, or poultry.

1 tablespoon olive oil
2 cups thinly sliced onion
2 garlic cloves, minced
4 green or red bell peppers (or 2 of each), cut into
   ¼-inch strips
¼ cup chopped fresh basil or 1 teaspoon dried
½ teaspoon dried oregano
¼ teaspoon salt
¼ teaspoon freshly ground black pepper

1. In a 2-quart microwave-safe casserole, combine the olive oil, onion, garlic and pepper.
2. Cover tightly with a lid or plastic wrap turned back slightly on one side. Microwave on HIGH for 6 to 8 minutes, or until the vegetables are tender, stirring after 4 minutes.
3. Stir in the remaining ingredients; cover again and microwave on HIGH for 1 minute. Serve warm or at room temperature.

NOTE Keeps for 1 week, refrigerated. To bring to room temperature, microwave on HIGH for 1 to 2 minutes; stir well.

Lightly Creamed Spinach

MAKES: *4 servings*
COOKING TIME: *6 to 7 minutes*

Low cholesterol

3.4 grams fat per serving

1 tablespoon olive or canola oil
1 small onion, finely chopped
1 tablespoon flour
¼ cup skim milk or low-fat milk
1 package (10 ounces) frozen spinach
⅛ teaspoon freshly ground black pepper
Pinch freshly grated nutmeg
1 teaspoon Maggi (Swiss vegetable sauce) or soy
   sauce

1. Combine the oil and onion in a 1½-quart microwave-safe casserole. Microwave on HIGH for 1 minute; stir in the flour until smooth. Add milk; stir until smooth.
2. Add the spinach. Cover tightly and microwave on HIGH for 3 minutes; stir to break up the spinach. Cover again; microwave on HIGH for 2 to 4 minutes more, or until the spinach is cooked. Season with the remaining ingredients and serve.

Whole Green Beans

MAKES: *4 servings*
COOKING TIME: *3 to 4 minutes*

0.2 gram fat per serving

NOTE

SERVING SUGGESTIONS:
Delicious served "au natural."
Cook during the standing time

VARIATIONS

of any meat or fish. Or cook earlier in the day, drizzle with a dressing, and chill. Serve right on the platter for a salad course.

If your microwave oven is large enough to hold a 12-inch round platter, these beans will come out perfectly without stirring and can be served right on the cooking platter.

1 pound fresh green beans, stems trimmed but point intact

1. Arrange the beans on a 12-inch microwave-safe platter, with the points toward the center. (A few will need to overlap; make these the thinner ones.) Add 2 tablespoons water.
2. Cover with plastic wrap turned back slightly. Microwave on HIGH for 3 to 4 minutes, or until tender-crisp.

You may cut the green beans into 1½-inch pieces and cook in a 2-quart casserole with ⅓ cup water. Cover tightly with a lid or plastic wrap turned back slightly. Microwave on HIGH for 5 to 8 minutes, stirring twice.

WHOLE GREEN BEANS WITH TOMATO VINAIGRETTE (6.2 grams fat per serving): Prepare Tomato Vinaigrette (page 309). Cook the beans and drain. Spoon the vinaigrette over the beans and chill until serving time. This makes a delicious and beautiful presentation.

STEAMED WHOLE GREEN BEANS WITH GINGER SAUCE AND MANDARIN ORANGES (1.7 grams fat per serving): Cook the beans as directed and drain. Drain the juice from 1 can (11 ounces) mandarin oranges and spoon into the center of the bean dish. Prepare Ginger Sauce (page 321); spoon the dressing over the beans and oranges. Chill until serving time. A nice side dish to serve with Gyozas (page 129); prepare the beans earlier in the day.

Steamed Asparagus

MAKES: *4 servings*
COOKING TIME: *4 to 6 minutes*

0.3 gram fat per serving

VARIATION

1 pound asparagus, ends snapped

1. Place the asparagus on a 10-inch round or 2-quart rectangular microwave-safe dish, with the tips pointing toward the center. Sprinkle with 2 tablespoons water.
2. Cover tightly with plastic wrap turned back slightly. Microwave on HIGH for 4 to 6 minutes, or until stalks can be pierced with a fork.

STEAMED ASPARAGUS WITH GINGER SAUCE (1.7 grams fat per serving): Drain asparagus after cooking and

SERVING SUGGESTIONS:
Serve warm as a vegetable side
dish or chilled as a salad.

drizzle with Ginger Sauce (page 321). Serve with grilled meats or fish.

Dilled Small Potatoes

MAKES: *4 servings*
COOKING TIME: *6 to 8 minutes*

No-cholesterol variation

6.1 grams fat per serving

SERVING SUGGESTIONS:
Great served with fish or
poultry.

1½ pounds small new or red potatoes (about 1½ to 2 inches in diameter)
2 tablespoons butter or margarine
2 tablespoons chopped fresh dill

1. Scrub the potatoes and peel a single strip around the middle of each. (This is not only decorative, it also eliminates the need to pierce the potatoes.)
2. Combine the potatoes and butter in a 2-quart microwave-safe casserole. Cover tightly with a lid or with plastic wrap turned back slightly. Microwave on HIGH for 6 to 8 minutes, or until tender, stirring after 3 minutes.
3. Sprinkle with dill and stir well to coat.

VARIATIONS NO-CHOLESTEROL DILLED SMALL POTATOES (0.1 gram fat per serving): Substitute ¼ cup water for butter. Drain the water before adding dill.

PARSLIED SMALL POTATOES: Substitute parsley for dill.

Steamed Broccoli

MAKES: *4 servings*
COOKING TIME: *6 to 8 minutes*

0.2 gram fat per serving

1 bunch broccoli (1 pound), 1 inch trimmed from the end

1. Slice the broccoli in half or in quarters lengthwise, depending on the size of the stalk.
2. Place the stalk ends toward the outside of a 2-quart rectangular or 10-inch round microwave-safe serving dish. Sprinkle with 2 tablespoons water.
3. Cover tightly with plastic wrap turned back slightly. Microwave on HIGH for 6 to 8 minutes, or until the stalks can be pierced with a fork.

VARIATIONS ITALIAN-STYLE BROCCOLI (6.8 grams fat per serving): Place 2 minced garlic cloves and 2 tablespoons olive oil in a 2-quart rectangular or 10-inch round microwave-safe serving dish. Cook on HIGH for 35 seconds. Add

Serve as a side dish or drizzle with a dressing, chill, and serve as a salad.

This is one of the best ways to cook broccoli. It stays tender-crisp while retaining its water-soluble vitamins.

the broccoli as indicated in step 1 of the basic recipe. Substitute 2 tablespoons wine vinegar for water. Cover and cook on HIGH for 6 to 8 minutes, or until tender. Uncover and sprinkle with 2 tablespoons grated Parmesan. To serve, spoon the garlic and pan juices over the broccoli.

BROCCOLI RABE (6.8 grams fat per serving): Substitute broccoli rabe for bunch broccoli, but don't split the stalks. Follow the instructions for Italian-Style Broccoli.

Broccoli Salad with Roasted Peppers

MAKES: *4 servings*
COOKING TIME: *6 to 8 minutes*

VARIATION

No cholesterol

9.5 grams fat per serving

SERVING SUGGESTIONS:
This is a nice side dish for grilled meats or fish.

1 recipe Steamed Broccoli (page 232)
1 small red onion, thinly sliced
¼ cup roasted pepper or pimiento strips
1 recipe Garlic, Rosemary, and Thyme Vinaigrette (page 310) or balsamic vinegar

1. Cook broccoli; drain and place in a serving bowl.
2. Add onion and roasted pepper. Add dressing and toss. Serve warm, at room temperature, or chilled.

BROCCOLI SALAD WITH ROASTED PEPPERS AND OLIVES (10.5 grams fat per serving): Add ¼ cup pitted, sliced black olives with onion and pepper.

Mixed Oriental Vegetable Platter

MAKES: *4 servings*
COOKING TIME: *3 to 5 minutes*

1 teaspoon light sesame oil or vegetable oil
1 large Bermuda onion, thinly sliced
1 medium zucchini, cut into thin 2-inch-long strips
1 medium bell pepper, cut into thin strips
¼ pound bean sprouts, washed and drained
¼ cup low-sodium soy sauce
1 tablespoon orange juice
1 teaspoon sherry or dry vermouth
1 teaspoon whole-grain Dijon mustard

No cholesterol

1 gram fat per serving

SERVING SUGGESTIONS:
Serve alongside chicken or
fish. Prepare the platter while
the chicken or fish is cooking,
then cook in the microwave
while putting the finishing
touches on the table.

1. On a 10- to 12-inch round microwave-safe plate, combine the sesame oil and onion.
2. Cover with plastic wrap turned back slightly. Microwave on HIGH for 1 minute.
3. Stir in the remaining vegetables.
4. In a small bowl, combine the remaining ingredients; stir well.
5. Pour half the sauce over the vegetables. Cover again and cook on HIGH for 2 to 4 minutes, or until the vegetables are tender-crisp.
6. Serve warm. Pass the remaining sauce at the table.

Provençale Ratatouille

MAKES: 4 servings
COOKING TIME: 15 to 21 minutes

No cholesterol

6.8 grams fat per serving

SERVING SUGGESTIONS:
Serve with grilled or roasted
meats or fish. Makes a
delicious vegetarian meal
when served with Pleated
Cheese Bread (page 38). Good
both warm and cold. This is
one of the few vegetable
dishes that benefit from being
reheated, so make it before
you cook the main dish and
reheat it right before serving.

1 tablespoon olive oil
2 garlic cloves, minced
1 medium onion, coarsely chopped
1 medium eggplant (about ½ pound), cut into
    ½-inch cubes
1 large red or green bell pepper, cut into ½-inch
    cubes
2 small zucchini (about ½ pound, total), cut into
    1-inch sticks
1 pound ripe tomatoes, ends removed, cut into thin
    wedges
1 teaspoon chopped fresh thyme or ¼ teaspoon dried
⅛ teaspoon freshly ground black pepper
¼ cup chopped fresh parsley
1 tablespoon fresh lemon juice

1. In a 3-quart microwave-safe casserole, combine the oil, garlic, and onion.
2. Cover tightly with a lid or with plastic wrap turned back slightly. Microwave on HIGH for 3 to 5 minutes, or until the onion is tender.
3. Stir in the eggplant and pepper. Cover again and cook on HIGH for 6 to 8 minutes, or until the eggplant and pepper are tender-crisp, stirring after 3 minutes.
4. Stir in the zucchini, tomato, thyme, and pepper. Cover again; cook on HIGH for 6 to 8 minutes, or until the zucchini is tender-crisp, stirring after 3 minutes. Sprinkle with parsley and lemon juice.
5. Let stand, covered, for 5 minutes before serving.

VARIATIONS   PROVENÇALE RATATOUILLE WITH OIL-CURED BLACK OL-

IVES (7.8 grams fat per serving): Stir in ¼ cup oil-cured black olives at the end of cooking time.

PROVENÇALE RATATOUILLE WITH FENNEL (6.8 grams fat per serving): Add 1 head fennel (½ pound), tops trimmed and stalks cut in half lengthwise and then into ½-inch sticks, along with the bell pepper.

New-Potato Salad

MAKES: *4 servings*
COOKING TIME: *5 to 9 minutes*

Low-cholesterol variation

15.1 grams fat per serving

SERVING SUGGESTIONS:
Serve with barbecued or grilled meats or fish, or on a salad plate with Turkey Salad (page 179).

The most time-consuming part of making potato salad is peeling the potatoes, so in the interest of saving time we suggest using small new potatoes and leaving the skins on.

VARIATION

The secret to a tasty potato salad is to let the potatoes marinate in oil and vinegar before adding the final seasonings.

1 pound small new potatoes, scrubbed and cut in half
¼ cup olive or canola oil
2 tablespoons vinegar
¼ teaspoon salt
¼ teaspoon freshly ground black pepper
1 tablespoon finely chopped green onion
½ cup thinly sliced celery
¼ cup mayonnaise
¼ cup plain yogurt

1. Place the potatoes in a 2-quart microwave-safe casserole. Add ¼ cup water.
2. Cover with a lid or with plastic wrap turned back slightly. Microwave on HIGH for 5 to 9 minutes, or until tender, stirring halfway through cooking.
3. Drain; toss with oil, vinegar, salt, and pepper, while still warm.
4. Let marinate for at least 30 minutes in the refrigerator.
5. Stir in the remaining ingredients and serve.

LOW-CHOLESTEROL NEW-POTATO SALAD (8.4 grams fat per serving): Substitute canola oil for olive oil, low-cholesterol mayonnaise for regular mayonnaise, and nonfat yogurt for regular yogurt.

Baked Potato and Spinach Salad with Creamy Ricotta-Chive Dressing

MAKES: *4 servings*
COOKING TIME: *12 minutes*

Low cholesterol

8.3 grams fat per serving

Great for days when you need a quick energy boost. The dressing, made with low-fat ricotta, adds needed protein to this delicious vegetarian meal.

4 baking potatoes (1½ pounds, total)
1 pound spinach, washed and dried, with leaves separated
2 medium tomatoes, sliced
8 ounces low-fat ricotta
3 tablespoons fresh lemon juice
2 tablespoons buttermilk or regular milk
1 tablespoon olive oil
¼ cup chopped chive
½ teaspoon salt
¼ teaspoon freshly ground black pepper

1. Wash the potatoes and pierce them with a fork on the top and bottom. Wrap each potato in a piece of paper towel. In the microwave oven, position them in a circle, leaving 1 inch between them. Microwave on HIGH for 12 minutes, or until the potatoes give slightly under your fingers right under the surface. Let stand for 5 minutes.
2. Meanwhile, line four salad plates with washed and dried spinach leaves. Tuck tomato slices between the leaves.
3. In a small bowl, whisk the remaining ingredients together.
4. Leaving the peel on, slice each potato crosswise, not quite through to the bottom. Spoon 1 teaspoon of dressing between each slice and place the potato in the center of the spinach leaves. Spoon the remaining dressing over the spinach. Serve with additional freshly ground pepper, if desired.

Wilted Greens Salad

MAKES: *4 servings*
COOKING TIME: *2 to 3 minutes*

9 grams fat per serving

SERVING SUGGESTIONS:
Great with fish or grilled poultry. Prepare the greens

1 pound spinach or romaine leaves, washed and dried
2 tablespoons sesame or vegetable oil
1 medium red onion, thinly sliced
¼ cup vinegar
1 tablespoon low-sodium soy sauce
¼ cup sesame seeds

1. Tear up the spinach or romaine leaves and place them in a salad bowl.
2. In a 2-cup glass measure, combine the oil and onion. Microwave on HIGH for 1 to 2 minutes, until onion is tender-crisp.

while the rest of the meal is cooking, and heat up the dressing right before serving.

3. Stir in the vinegar, soy sauce, and sesame seeds. Microwave on HIGH for 30 seconds to 1 minute, or until heated through. Pour over greens and toss.

Honeyed Pear and Lettuce Salad with Cheese Croustades

MAKES: *4 servings*
COOKING TIME: *15 minutes*

VARIATION

Low-cholesterol variation

10.3 grams fat per serving with 2 tablespoons dressing

SERVING SUGGESTIONS:
Serve with soup for a complete meal or by itself for a light lunch.

1 head romaine (½ pound), washed and torn into pieces
1 recipe Perfectly Poached Pears (page 238), chilled
1 recipe Cranberry Pepper–Honey Dressing (page 310)
1 recipe Cheese Croustades (page 67)

1. Arrange the lettuce on four salad plates.
2. Slice pears into ½-inch pieces lengthwise.
3. Arrange the pear slices on the lettuce and drizzle with the dressing.
4. Place two Cheese Croustades on each salad plate.

LOW-CHOLESTEROL HONEYED PEAR AND LETTUCE SALAD WITH HERBED CHEESE CROUSTADES (10 grams fat per serving with 2 tablespoons dressing): Spread croustades with Herbed Cheese Spread (page 316) instead of one of the suggested cheeses.

Coleslaw

MAKES: *8 servings*

11.2 grams fat per serving

SERVING SUGGESTIONS:
Great with any barbecued or fish meal.

1 small head cabbage (about 2 pounds), cut into quarters and halved crosswise
1 carrot, peeled and cut into 1½-inch chunks
1 green pepper, seeded and cut into quarters, then each quarter cut in half crosswise
½ cup low-cholesterol mayonnaise
½ cup low-fat yogurt
2 tablespoons cider vinegar
1 teaspoon salt
¼ teaspoon freshly ground black pepper

Some people insist on hand-slicing the cabbage into slivers, but when time is of the essence, we have been known to make this variety, in which all the cabbage is chopped in the food processor. The flavor is just as good, especially if you let it stand for at least 30 minutes before serving. Overnight refrigeration is also fine.

1. Place one-fourth of the cabbage in the bowl of a food processor. Pulse on and off three to four times, until chopped to the desired consistency.
2. Continue with the remaining cabbage (in three batches); scrape into a large bowl after each batch is chopped.
3. Chop the carrot and green pepper together, in the same manner as the cabbage. Scrape into the same bowl.
4. Combine the remaining ingredients in a small bowl; blend with the chopped vegetables. Cover and chill until serving time.

Spiced Plums

MAKES: *4 to 6 servings*
COOKING TIME: *2 to 4 minutes*

No fat

SERVING SUGGESTIONS:
Serve warm with cooking juices or let cool, covered, in their juice. Especially good served with Potato Virtiniai (page 131) or with cooked cereal at breakfast.

¼ cup white wine, apple juice, cranberry juice, or water
¼ cup sugar
1 teaspoon fresh lemon juice
1 cinnamon stick or ½ teaspoon ground cinnamon
¼ teaspoon ground nutmeg
1½ pounds ripe plums, halved and pitted

1. In a 1½- or 2-quart microwave-safe casserole, combine all the ingredients. Cover with a lid or with plastic wrap turned back slightly.
2. Microwave on HIGH for 2 to 4 minutes, until just tender but not overcooked, stirring once. Remove cinnamon stick.

Perfectly Poached Pears

MAKES: *4 servings*
COOKING TIME: *10 to 14 minutes*

No fat

SERVING SUGGESTIONS:
Serve warm or chilled with their liquid as a breakfast fruit course, a lunch or dinner side

4 firm ripe pears
1 lemon, quartered
¼ cup sugar
1 teaspoon vanilla

1. Keeping the stems intact, core each pear so that it retains its shape by cutting a cone out of the base with a grapefruit or other small knife.
2. Peel the pears and rub them with the cut lemon to prevent discoloration. Set them aside and reserve the lemon quarters.
3. In a 1½- or 2-quart microwave-safe casserole, combine the sugar, ¼ cup water, vanilla, and reserved lemon quarters.
4. Cover tightly with a lid or with plastic wrap turned

dish, or a delightful dessert, either plain or sauced.

Poaching pears in the microwave oven has two advantages: They preserve more of their natural nutrients, and they retain their lovely shapes.

VARIATIONS

back slightly. Microwave on HIGH for 2 minutes. Stir well to dissolve the sugar.

5. Place the pears on their sides in the casserole, positioning the thicker ends toward the outside. Re-cover the dish. Microwave on HIGH for 6 minutes.

6. Turn the pears over and baste them. Cover again and microwave on HIGH for 4 to 6 minutes, or until tender.

PERFECTLY POACHED PEARS WITH ORANGES: Substitute ½ cup white wine for the water and add 2 tablespoons orange-flavored liqueur or orange juice. Add the peeled segments of 2 medium oranges with the pears. Serve in glass dishes surrounded by oranges.

SPICED PINK POACHED PEARS: Substitute ½ cup red wine or cranberry juice for water. Add 1 teaspoon black peppercorns, 1 cinnamon stick or ¼ teaspoon ground cinnamon, and ¼ teaspoon ground nutmeg.

Pink Applesauce

MAKES: *2 to 2½ cups*
COOKING TIME: *10 to 14 minutes*

No fat

SERVING SUGGESTIONS: Serve warm or chilled as a side dish with roasted or grilled meats, with pancakes in place of syrup, or as a dessert.

NOTE

Cooking apples with their skins on adds flavor and a pretty pink hue. The amount of sugar you add will depend

2 pounds red-skinned cooking apples, washed and quartered
1 tablespoon fresh lemon juice
¼ to ½ cup sugar
½ teaspoon vanilla extract
1 teaspoon ground cinnamon (optional)

1. In a 2-quart microwave-safe casserole, combine the apples, ¼ cup water, and lemon juice.

2. Cover with a lid or with plastic wrap turned back slightly. Microwave on HIGH for 5 minutes; stir.

3. Cover again and cook on HIGH for 5 to 8 minutes, or until the apples are tender.

4. Spoon the apples into a food mill and puree, or force them through a sieve.

5. Stir in the remaining ingredients.

If you have large quantities of apples that you wish to preserve, cook 4 pounds at a time. Double the above ingredients; cook in a 4-quart microwave-safe casserole for 15 to 20 minutes, until tender. Freeze following the instructions on pages 326–28.

CHUNKY PINK APPLESAUCE: Core and peel the apples and slice them into ¼-inch pieces before cooking. When the apples are tender, stir in the remaining ingredients. Do not puree. This sauce has more texture.

ROSY GREEN APPLE SAUCE: Follow the instructions for making Chunky Pink Applesauce above, but use green apples (Granny Smith) and substitute red wine for water. (This will impart a rosy color to the apples.) Serve as a side dish with meats or eggs.

Chunky Apple and Pear Sauce

MAKES: *2 to 2½ cups*
COOKING TIME: *10 to 14 minutes*

No fat

SERVING SUGGESTIONS:
Serve warm, at room temperature, or chilled as a side dish with poultry, or top with frozen yogurt for dessert.

NOTE

1 pound ripe pears, peeled, cored, and thinly sliced
1 pound Macintosh apples, peeled, cored, and thinly sliced
2 to 4 tablespoons sugar, depending on taste
1 teaspoon ground cinnamon
¼ teaspoon grated nutmeg
1 teaspoon vanilla extract

1. Combine the pears and apple slices and ¼ cup water in a 2-quart microwave-safe casserole.
2. Cover with a lid or with plastic wrap turned back slightly. Microwave on HIGH for 10 to 14 minutes, or until fruit is tender, stirring once.
3. Stir in the remaining ingredients.

If you wish to cook larger amounts and/or freeze this sauce, follow the instructions in the note following Pink Applesauce (page 239).

Perfectly Poached Peaches

MAKES: *4 servings*
COOKING TIME: *3 to 5 minutes*

No fat

2 tablespoons peach or other fruit-flavored liqueur
1 teaspoon fresh lemon juice
1 teaspoon vanilla
4 firm ripe peaches (1 to 1½ pounds, total) washed, halved, and pitted

1. In a 2-quart flat-bottomed microwave-safe casserole, combine the liqueur, lemon juice, and vanilla; stir to mix.
2. Add the peaches. Cover tightly with a lid or with plastic wrap turned back slightly. Microwave on HIGH

Serve alongside grilled or poached poultry. For a dessert, spoon into tall goblets along with cooking juices, or use in Peach Melba (page 290).

Poaching with a splash of liqueur adds a wonderfully heady flavor to the perfectly ripened peaches.

for 2 minutes; turn the peaches over and rearrange them. Cover again and cook on HIGH for 1 to 3 minutes, or until the peaches are tender.

3. Let stand for a few minutes, uncovered. Slip the skins off with a sharp knife. Serve warm with some of the cooking juices, or chill.

Old-Fashioned Baked Apples

MAKES: *4 servings*
COOKING TIME: *6 to 7 minutes*

No fat

SERVING SUGGESTIONS:
A nice dessert for a soup meal or a side dish with pork.

We remember coming home for lunch on cold winter days to the comforting aromas of apples baking in the oven and a pot of soup simmering on top of the stove. You can create this cozy atmosphere in minutes by popping these apples into the microwave while putting together the ingredients for a soup.

4 medium-size tart baking apples (Rome, Granny Smith)
4 tablespoons raisins or chopped walnuts
4 tablespoons brown sugar
4 teaspoons orange juice, cranberry juice, or brandy
1 tablespoon fresh lemon juice
½ teaspoon ground cinnamon

1. Remove the apple cores, but do not cut all the way through to the bottoms.
2. Peel a 1-inch strip around the top of each apple.
3. Halfway down the apple, cut a ¼-inch-deep slit in the skin around the circumference; this will allow steam to escape while keeping the skin from splitting.
4. Place the apples in four 10-ounce microwave-safe custard cups or around the edge of a 9-inch round microwave-safe cooking dish.
5. Spoon 1 tablespoon of raisins or nuts, 1 tablespoon brown sugar, and 1 teaspoon orange juice into the cavity of each apple. Sprinkle with lemon juice and cinnamon.
6. Cover with plastic wrap turned back slightly. Microwave on HIGH for 6 to 7 minutes, repositioning the individual dishes halfway through cooking time.

VARIATION OLD-FASHIONED RASPBERRY BAKED APPLES: Substitute 4 tablespoons raspberry preserves for brown sugar. These are great served for breakfast along with muffins, biscuits, or toast.

Spring Rhubarb Sauce

MAKES: 2 cups
COOKING TIME: 3 to 6 minutes

No fat

SERVING SUGGESTIONS:
Serve with grilled or poached meats or fish. Also heavenly when spooned over vanilla ice cream or frozen yogurt.

Rhubarb is one of the first plants in our spring garden. The flavor of spring can be yours all year if you freeze pieces of rhubarb (see pages 326–27) and then use them for this sauce.

1 pound rhubarb, cut into ½-inch pieces
½ to ¾ cup sugar
2 tablespoons orange juice or water

1. In a 1½-quart microwave-safe casserole, combine all the ingredients, stirring well to mix.
2. Cover with a lid or with plastic wrap turned back slightly. Microwave on HIGH for 3 to 6 minutes, or until the rhubarb is tender.(Be careful not to overcook rhubarb, or it will become stringy and lose its beautiful fresh flavor.)
3. Chill, covered, until ready to serve.

NOTE Frozen rhubarb pieces will take 5 to 8 minutes to cook.

PLATTER MEALS

FIRST PEOPLE were asking us for meals that cooked in 30 minutes in the microwave, then it was 20, even 10! Platter meals were our answer.

These are complete meals that can be assembled on one plate because of the way that microwave ovens cook—from the outside to the inside. Here are the basics:

- Begin with an 11-inch round or 12- to 14-inch oval microwave-safe dish: One dish to cook on, serve from, and later cleanup.
- Place the denser or longer-cooking food (like the meat, fish, or chicken) on the outside, the faster-cooking food (like the vegetables) on the inside. They will all cook in the same amount of time!
- The size of the pieces the ingredients are cut into is important, so follow the recipes exactly. The proportion of ingredients must be balanced, too. Most of the recipes that follow call for approximately 1 pound of meat, chicken, or fish, 1 pound of starchy vegetable, and 2 cups of nonstarchy vegetables.

- The dish must be covered with a lid or plastic wrap so that steam from the food and added liquid can speed the cooking process.
- A dish towel is the best form of pot holder.

With a meal this simple we usually just make an ice cream pie, a combination conventional/microwave pie, or a simple cobbler for dessert.

Pacific Ocean Supper

MAKES: *4 servings*
COOKING TIME: *10 to 12 minutes*

Low cholesterol

4 grams fat per serving

This recipe is low in fat, which makes it low in calories—only 238 per serving! Yet it's as pretty as a picture, with the acorn-squash slices and spinach framing a platter of fish fillets.

1 acorn squash (about 2 pounds)
2 teaspoons sesame or salad oil
1 teaspoon minced fresh ginger
1 garlic clove, minced
1 pound fresh spinach leaves, washed and drained
2 tablespoons low-sodium soy sauce
1 pound thin fish fillets (flounder, whiting, or pollack)
2 green onions, thinly sliced
1 tablespoon sesame seeds, lightly toasted

1. Place the whole squash in the microwave. Cook on HIGH for 1 minute. Cut it in half and remove the seeds. With the skin on, cut the squash crosswise into ¼-inch-thick slices; set aside.
2. Place the oil, ginger, and garlic in the center of a 12-inch round microwave-safe platter. Cook on HIGH for 30 to 35 seconds.
3. Mound the spinach on top of the garlic mixture. (This will appear to be a large amount of spinach, but it will cook down.) Sprinkle lightly with 1 tablespoon soy sauce. Cover tightly with plastic wrap turned back slightly. Cook on HIGH for 2 minutes. Stir the spinach to coat it with the cooking juices. Spread the spinach in an even layer on the bottom of the platter, leaving a 1-inch space around the outer rim.
4. Arrange the squash slices around the outer rim of the platter, overlapping the slices, with green skin to the outside, to form a scallop pattern.
5. If the fillets are wider than 2 to 3 inches, cut them in half lengthwise. Fold the thinner ends of each fish fillet under the thicker centers in two-fold letter fashion. Place fish, seam side down, on top of the spinach.

6. Sprinkle the fillets with the remaining soy sauce; cover again and cook on HIGH for 10 to 12 minutes, or until the fish is done. Sprinkle with green onion and sesame seeds. Serve.

Mexican Chicken, Corn, and Potato Platter

MAKES: *4 servings*
COOKING TIME: *14 to 16 minutes*

Low-cholesterol variation

10.2 grams fat per serving

SERVING SUGGESTIONS:
Serve with taco sauce, chopped tomatoes, shredded lettuce, and taco chips, if desired.

2 cups cooked corn kernels or 1 package (10 ounces) frozen corn
1 can (4 ounces) mild green chilies, drained
2 green onions, thinly sliced
1 pound potatoes, washed but not peeled, cut into ⅓-inch-thick × 2½-inch-long pieces
½ teaspoon chili powder
1 pound skinless, boneless chicken breasts, cut into 1 × 2-inch strips
¼ cup Salsa Cruda (page 317)
4 ounces Monterey Jack cheese, grated

1. If using frozen corn, defrost it first by placing the package (nonmetal only) in the microwave oven and heating on HIGH for 2 minutes. (If package has metal on it, remove package and place corn in a 1-quart microwave-safe dish before heating.)
2. Remove the corn from the package and place it in the center of a 12-inch round or 11 × 15-inch oval microwave-safe platter.
3. Combine the chilies and onion with the corn and push the mixture to the center of the platter. Arrange the potato strips around the edge of the platter and sprinkle with chili powder.
4. Place the chicken pieces in a ring between the potatoes and corn, overlapping them onto the potatoes by about 1 inch. Spoon the Salsa over the chicken.
5. Cover tightly with plastic wrap turned back slightly. Microwave on HIGH for 12 to 14 minutes, or until the chicken is cooked through, rotating the platter one-quarter turn halfway through cooking.
6. Sprinkle the potatoes and chicken with cheese. Serve.

NOTE For 2 servings: Cut the amounts of all the ingredients in half and arrange as above on a 10-inch microwave-safe dinner plate. Cover as directed and microwave on HIGH for 5 to 6 minutes.

VARIATION Low-Cholesterol Mexican Chicken, Corn, and Potato Platter (6.2 grams fat per serving): Omit the cheese or substitute a low-cholesterol cheese.

Potato and Chicken Platter with Ginger Dressing

MAKES: *4 servings*
COOKING TIME: *8 to 10 minutes*

Low cholesterol

2.8 grams fat per serving

1 pound potatoes, scrubbed, cut into ¼ × 2½-inch julienne
1 pound skinless, boneless chicken breasts, cut into 1 × 2-inch strips
8 ounces bean sprouts
1 medium red or green bell pepper, seeded and thinly sliced
2 green onions (green parts only), cut into ½-inch pieces
1 tablespoon sesame seeds (black if available; see Note 1)
2 tablespoons low-sodium soy sauce
1 tablespoon grated fresh ginger
1 tablespoon orange juice
1 tablespoon brown sugar
1 teaspoon Dijon mustard (optional)

1. Arrange the potato pieces around the rim of a 12-inch round or 11 × 15 inch oval microwave-safe platter (see illustration). Place the chicken pieces in a ring inside the potatoes, overlapping the potatoes by about 1 inch.
2. Toss the bean sprouts with the bell pepper and place in the center of the platter. Sprinkle the green onion between the potato and the chicken. Sprinkle the sesame seeds on the chicken.
3. In a small bowl, combine the remaining ingredients and pour over the chicken and vegetables. Cover tightly with plastic wrap turned back slightly on one side. Microwave on HIGH for 8 to 10 minutes, or until the chicken is cooked through and the vegetables are tender-crisp, rotating the dish one-quarter turn once halfway through cooking time.

NOTE 1 Black sesame seeds are available at Asian grocery stores.

NOTE 2 To make 2 servings: Cut the amounts of all the ingredients in half and arrange as above on a 10-inch microwave-safe dinner plate. Cover tightly, with another microwave-safe plate or plastic wrap turned back slightly on one side. Microwave on HIGH for 4 to 5 minutes, or until done, rotating after 2 minutes.

Chicken with Sweet-and-Spicy Peanut Sauce

MAKES: *4 servings*
COOKING TIME: *About 10 minutes*

Low cholesterol

6 grams fat per serving

2 tablespoons smooth peanut butter
2 tablespoons low-sodium soy sauce
1 tablespoon catsup
1 tablespoon fresh lime juice
1 tablespoon brown sugar
⅛ teaspoon cayenne
1 pound red-skinned potatoes (about 3 medium),
   unpeeled, scrubbed, and cut in ¼ × 2½-inch
   julienne
1 pound skinless, boneless chicken breasts, sliced in
   ½-inch strips
¼ pound mushrooms, thinly sliced, crosswise
1 medium red bell pepper, diced
1 tablespoon fresh lemon juice
2 green onions, green parts only, cut in ½-inch strips

1. In a small bowl, combine the peanut butter and soy sauce. Stir in the catsup, lime juice, brown sugar, and cayenne. Set aside.
2. Arrange the potato strips in a double layer around the rim of a 12-inch round or 11 × 15-inch oval microwave-safe platter. Place the chicken strips in a ring inside the potatoes, overlapping the potatoes by about 1 inch.
3. Combine the mushroom and bell pepper in the center of the platter. Sprinkle with lemon juice and scallion.
4. Cover tightly with plastic wrap turned back slightly on one side. Microwave on HIGH for 9 to 11 minutes, or until the chicken is cooked and the vegetables are tender-crisp. Rotate the plate one-quarter turn once during cooking.
5. Uncover, and spoon the peanut sauce between the potato and chicken strips in a 1-inch ribbon. Cover again and let stand for 2 to 3 minutes to complete the cooking and warm the sauce.

NOTE For 2 servings: Cut the ingredient amounts in half and arrange as above on a 10-inch microwave-safe dinner plate. Cover as directed and microwave on HIGH for 5 to 6 minutes.

Meat Loaf Platter

MAKES: *4 servings*
COOKING TIME: *20 to 25 minutes*

13.3 grams fat per serving

Regular ground beef can contain up to 30 percent fat; lean ground beef and turkey have less fat but will still yield a moist, flavorful loaf.

3 green onions, thinly sliced
1 pound lean ground beef or ground turkey
¼ cup flavored dry bread crumbs
1 egg
½ cup catsup
2 large baking potatoes (about 1 pound, total), scrubbed but not peeled
1 tablespoon butter or margarine
2 tablespoons grated Parmesan
1 pound green beans, trimmed and cut into 1-inch pieces, or 1 package (10 ounces) frozen green beans, unthawed

1. In a large mixing bowl, combine the green onion, ground beef, bread crumbs, egg, and ¼ cup catsup.
2. Form the mixture into four individual meat loaves (each about 4 × 2½ × 1½ inches); set aside.
3. Cut the potatoes into ¼-inch-thick slices. Arrange the potato slices around the outer edge of a 12-inch round or 11 × 15-inch oval microwave-safe platter.
4. Place the butter in a microwave-safe custard cup; microwave on HIGH for 35 to 45 seconds to melt. Brush the potatoes with the butter; sprinkle with Parmesan.
5. Place the meat loaves in a ring on the platter inside the potato slices, leaving a space between the loaves. Spread the remaining catsup on top of the meat loaves.
6. Place the beans in the center of the platter. Cover with waxed paper, tucking the edges under the platter. Microwave on HIGH for 10 minutes. Stir the beans; cover again. Rotate the platter one half turn; microwave on HIGH for 10 to 12 minutes, or until the meat loaves are cooked through. Let stand for 5 to 10 minutes, covered, before serving.

VARIATION BARBECUED MEAT LOAF PLATTER (13.4 grams fat per serving): Substitute ½ cup barbecue sauce for catsup.

Oriental Beef, Potatoes, and Peppers

1 garlic clove, minced
1 tablespoon sesame seeds
1 tablespoon sesame or vegetable oil
1 pound potatoes, scrubbed but not peeled, cut into strips about ¼ inch wide and 2½ inches long
¾ pound top round steak, cut into strips about ¼ inch wide and 2 inches long (see Note 1)

MAKES: *4 servings*
COOKING TIME: *11 to 13 minutes*

12.2 grams fat per serving

This is a microwave version of a stir-fry dish. You won't have crispy vegetables because there is no dry heat in the microwave oven, but neither will you have to cook the ingredients in batches or add more than 1 tablespoon of fat.

The Japanese-inspired sauce gives this dish its interesting flavor, yet it is the type of sauce that kids just love to dip the potatoes into.

2 medium red or green bell peppers, seeded and cut into ½-inch squares
2 green onions, cut into ½-inch pieces
1 recipe Tonkatsu Sauce (page 317)

1. Place the garlic and sesame seeds in the center of a 12-inch round or 11 × 15-inch oval microwave-safe platter. Spoon oil over the garlic and sesame seeds. Microwave on HIGH for 1 minute. Place the potato strips on the platter and toss to coat with the sesame-garlic mixture. Arrange the potato strips in a ring around the outer 2 inches of the platter.
2. Place the beef strips inside the potatoes.
3. Toss the pepper and onion pieces together and spoon into the center of the dish. Spoon half of the Tonkatsu Sauce over the beef.
4. Cover tightly with plastic wrap turned back slightly. Microwave, on HIGH for 10 to 12 minutes, or until the potato is tender and the beef is cooked to the desired doneness, rotating the plate one-quarter turn halfway through cooking.
5. Remove the plastic wrap and pour the remaining sauce over the entire platter; toss to mix the vegetables and meat together.

NOTE 1   Place the beef in the freezer for 30 to 40 minutes; this will make slicing easier.

NOTE 2   For 2 servings: Cut the amounts of all the ingredients in half and arrange as above on a 10-inch microwave-safe dinner plate. Cover as directed and microwave on HIGH for 5 to 6 minutes.

Barbecued Pork and Potato Strips with Corn-and-Pepper Hash

1 pound potatoes, scrubbed but not peeled, cut into strips ¼ inch wide and 1½ inches long
1 pound boneless pork tenderloin, cut into strips ½ inch thick, 1 inch wide, and 2½ inches long
2 cups corn of 1 package (10 ounces) frozen corn, defrosted
½ medium bell pepper, seeded and diced
¼ teaspoon freshly ground black pepper
½ cup All-Purpose Barbecue Sauce (page 214)
2 green onions (green part only), cut into ½-inch pieces

MAKES: *4 servings*
COOKING TIME: *12 to 14 minutes*

Low-cholesterol variation

6 grams fat per serving

Three ounces of pork tenderloin have only 4 grams of fat and 79 milligrams of cholesterol. If you don't want to make your own barbecue sauce, you may substitute a commercially prepared sauce.

1. Arrange the potato strips around the rim of 12-inch round or 11 × 15-inch oval microwave-safe platter.
2. Place the pork strips inside the potatoes, overlapping the potatoes by about 1 inch. In the center of the platter, toss corn, bell pepper, and black pepper together.
3. Spoon the barbecue sauce in a 1-inch ribbon between the potato and pork strips. Sprinkle the green onion on top of the sauce.
4. Cover tightly with plastic wrap turned back slightly. Microwave on HIGH for 12 to 14 minutes, or until the pork is cooked through and the vegetables are tender-crisp, rotating one-quarter turn halfway through cooking.

NOTE   To make 2 servings: Cut all the ingredients in half and place on a 10-inch microwave-safe plate. Cover with another microwave-safe plate or plastic wrap turned back slightly; microwave on HIGH for 5 to 6 minutes.

VARIATION   Low-Cholesterol Southwestern Chicken and Potato Strips with Corn-and-Chili Hash (2 grams fat per serving): Substitute skinless, boneless chicken for the pork and Southwestern Chili Sauce (page 319) for the barbecue sauce. Combine ½ cup of the chili sauce with the corn mixture and spoon on the remaining amount in a ribbon between the corn and potatoes.

Glazed Pork, Potato, and Cabbage Platter

MAKES: *4 servings*
COOKING TIME: *14 to 16 minutes*

5.4 grams fat per serving

The apricot glaze gives this dish a distinctive flavor.

1 medium onion, thinly sliced
1 teaspoon butter or margarine
½ small head green cabbage, shredded (about 3 cups)
1 pound red potatoes, washed but not peeled, cut into strips about ¼ inch wide and 2½ inches long
1 pound boneless pork tenderloin or boneless chops, all fat removed, cut into strips ½ inch thick, 1 inch wide, and 2½ inches long
½ teaspoon paprika
½ cup apricot preserves
1 tablespoon coarse Dijon mustard
1 tablespoon brown sugar

1. Place the onion and butter on 12-inch round or 11 × 15-inch oval microwave-safe platter. Microwave,

uncovered, on HIGH for 1 to 2 minutes, or until the onion is slightly tender.

2. Add the cabbage and toss well to mix. Cover tightly with plastic wrap turned back slightly. Microwave on HIGH for 2 to 3 minutes, or until the cabbage has cooked down somewhat.

3. Push the cabbage mixture to the center of the platter. Arrange the potatoes in a ring around the outer 2 inches of the platter.

4. Place the pork strips between the cabbage and the potato, and sprinkle with paprika. Cover again and microwave on HIGH for 10 to 12 minutes, or until the pork is cooked through and the potato is tender.

5. Meanwhile, in a small bowl, combine the paprika, apricot preserves, mustard, and brown sugar.

6. Uncover the platter and spoon half of the apricot mixture over the pork. Cook, uncovered, on HIGH for 2 to 3 minutes to glaze. Pass the extra glaze at the table.

Parslied Potato, Fish, and Tomato Platter with Mustard-Horseradish Sauce

MAKES: *4 servings*
COOKING TIME: *12 to 14 minutes*

Low-cholesterol variation

10.7 grams fat per serving

1 pound potatoes, washed but not peeled, cut into ⅛-inch rounds
1 tablespoon chopped fresh parsley
1 pound fish fillets, ½ inch thick (flounder, sole, turbot, whiting)
4 fresh tomatoes, stems removed, cut into ½-inch cubes (about 2 cups)
1 tablespoon chopped fresh basil or 1 teaspoon dried
1 recipe Mustard-Horseradish Sauce (page 324)
Lemon wedges

1. Arrange the potato pieces around the outer rim of a 12-inch round or 11 × 15-inch oval microwave-safe platter. Sprinkle with parsley.

2. If the fillets are wider than 2 to 3 inches, cut them in half lengthwise. Fold the thinner ends of each fish fillet under the thicker centers in two-fold letter fashion. Place them, seam-side down, inside the ring of potato.

3. Spoon the tomato in the center of the platter and sprinkle with basil.

4. Spoon half of the Mustard-Horseradish Sauce evenly over the fish fillets. Stick a toothpick in the center of each fillet to keep the plastic wrap from touching the sauce.

5. Cover tightly with plastic wrap turned back slightly. Microwave on HIGH for 9 to 10 minutes, rotating the platter one-quarter turn halfway through cooking.
6. Serve with lemon slices and extra sauce.

NOTE For 2 servings: Cut the amounts of all ingredients in half and arrange as above on a 10-inch microwave-safe dinner plate. Cover as directed and microwave on HIGH for 4 to 5 minutes.

VARIATIONS DILLED POTATO, FISH, AND ZUCCHINI PLATTER WITH MUSTARD-HORSERADISH SAUCE: Substitute dill for parsley and 2 cups of cubed zucchini for tomatoes, or mix 1 cup zucchini and 1 cup tomatoes together.

LOW-CHOLESTEROL POTATO, FISH, AND TOMATO PLATTER WITH MUSTARD-HORSERADISH SAUCE (11 grams fat per serving): Substitute low-cholesterol mayonnaise for regular mayonnaise.

PARSLIED POTATO AND FISH PLATTER WITH MINTED PEAS AND MUSTARD-HORSERADISH SAUCE: Substitute 2 cups fresh peas or 1 package (10 ounces) frozen peas, defrosted, for tomatoes and 1 tablespoon chopped fresh mint for basil.

Salmon and Potato Platter with Dill Sauce

MAKES: *4 servings*
COOKING TIME: *About 10 minutes*

Low cholesterol

6.8 grams fat per serving

Salmon and potatoes can cook perfectly on the same plate. The secret is the arrangement and equal weight of the two ingredients.

1 pound potatoes, scrubbed and sliced ⅛ inch thick
1 pound salmon fillets, skinned and cut crosswise into pieces about 1½ × 3 inches
¾ pound zucchini, cut lengthwise into strips about ½ × 2 inches
¼ cup fresh lemon juice
1 cup nonfat yogurt
2 tablespoons white-wine vinegar
2 tablespoons chopped chives
½ teaspoon freshly ground black pepper
½ teaspoon salt
½ cup chopped fresh dill
Dill sprigs, for garnish

1. Arrange the potato pieces around the edge of a 12-inch round or 11 × 15-inch oval microwave-safe platter.
2. Place the salmon pieces end to end in a ring inside

the potatoes. Mound the zucchini in the center of the platter. Sprinkle all the ingredients with lemon juice.
3. Cover tightly with plastic wrap turned back slightly. Microwave on HIGH for 8 to 10 minutes, or until the salmon is cooked through and the potatoes are tender, rotating one-quarter turn halfway through cooking.
4. Meanwhile, in a small bowl, combine the remaining ingredients, except the dill sprigs. After removing the platter from the microwave oven, uncover and drizzle the yogurt sauce between the potatoes and salmon. Garnish with dill sprigs.

VIDEO MEALS

The BURGEONING of video stores and cable television has created a whole new way of eating. It's not just popcorn at the movies anymore (but check out our popcorn recipe on page 270). Now we can eat our dinner, or at least a hefty snack, while enjoying our favorite flick.

As we undertook to develop recipes for this new category of dining, there were a few stipulations: Preparation must be simple. One course is usually enough. Eating should not take attention away from the movie. To that end, we felt that the food must be hand-held and should not require a knife or fork. That led us to come up with all kinds of hot sandwiches—from heroes, to Middle Eastern pitas, to dough-encased calzones.

We've included a few lighter snacks and even a frozen dessert on a stick. For more elaborate sweets, try the ice-cream pies (pages 283–85), which are easy to make in advance. We think all of these recipes will make your movie watching more fun.

To Prepare the Whole Meal

- Make the dessert and put it in the freezer at least an hour before serving, or make a simple ice-cream sauce.
- Do all the chopping and cooking beforehand, and assemble the meal when you're ready to turn on the tube.

Oven-Crisped "Buffalo Chicken Wings" with Celery and Herb Sauce

MAKES: *4 servings*
COOKING TIME: *20 minutes*

6.6 grams fat per serving

SERVING SUGGESTION:
Have lots of cold drinks on hand when serving these spicy wings.

Our wings have less fat because they cook in the microwave and crisp in a hot oven, and our sauce uses nonfat yogurt—no blue cheese.

2 pounds chicken wings
Hot sauce (optional)
1 cup nonfat plain yogurt
¼ cup chopped fresh herbs (parsley, chives, dill) or 1 tablespoon dried mixed herbs (1 teaspoon each)
Celery sticks

1. Preheat the conventional oven to 500° F.
2. Cut off the tips from the chicken wings. Cut the wings at the joints. Place the wings in a 2-quart rectangular microwave-to-oven baking dish. Microwave on HIGH for 10 minutes, or until cooked through, turning over and rearranging the pieces after 5 minutes. Drain off the cooking juices.
3. Transfer the dish to the preheated oven. Bake for 10 minutes, or until crisp, turning over once during cooking. Sprinkle with hot sauce at the end of cooking, if desired.
4. Meanwhile, in a small bowl combine the yogurt and herbs. Serve the wings with celery; pass more hot sauce for sprinkling over the wings.

Calzones

MAKES: *4 servings*
COOKING TIME: *25 minutes*

25.3 grams fat per serving

DOUGH

2 cups unbleached all-purpose flour
1 package fast-rising yeast
½ teaspoon baking powder
½ teaspoon sugar
½ teaspoon salt
2 tablespoons olive oil
1 tablespoon cornmeal

FILLING

4 ounces shredded mozzarella cheese
¼ cup grated Parmesan
1 cup ricotta
1 tablespoon chopped fresh basil or parsley, or 1 teaspoon dried oregano plus 1 teaspoon dried parsley

1 egg
2 tablespoons olive oil
2 tablespoon cornmeal
2 cups Tomato Pizza Sauce (page 48)

1. Place the flour, yeast, baking powder, sugar, and salt in the bowl of a food processor. Pulse on and off a few times to mix well.
2. Pour ¾ cup warm water into a 1-cup glass measure. Heat the water to 130° F in a microwave oven using the food sensor that comes with the oven, inserting the sensor end into the water. (If you have no food sensor, heat the water on HIGH for 1 to 1½ minutes, or use very hot tap water.)
3. With the processor running, pour the water and 2 tablespoons oil into the bowl through the feed tube. Process until a soft dough forms. (Add 1 or 2 table-spoons additional warm water if needed.) Scoop out the dough and place it on a counter that has been sprinkled with 2 tablespoons flour. Push the dough down, fold it over, and turn it about twenty times, until it is shiny and elastic.
4. Place the dough in a 1-quart microwave-safe bowl that has been greased with 1 teaspoon oil. Turn the dough to coat with the oil. Cover the bowl with a piece of waxed paper and set it in a 3-quart microwave-safe bowl holding 2 cups of hot tap water. Microwave on WARM (10 percent power) for 2 minutes. Let stand, covered, for 10 minutes or until almost doubled. (If your microwave oven doesn't have a WARM power setting, place the bowl in the hot water and cover it with a cookie sheet for 30 minutes.)
5. Meanwhile, preheat the conventional oven to 450° F and position the oven rack to the bottom.
6. Prepare a rectangular 10 ½ × 15 ½ × 1-inch black or shiny cookie sheet by greasing the bottom with 1 tablespoon olive oil and sprinkling it evenly with the

cornmeal. Set aside.

7. In a small bowl, combine the mozzarella, Parmesan, and ricotta cheeses and the basil.

8. Divide the dough into four equal balls. Roll or press into four ovals approximately 8 × 6 inches each. Divide the filling into quarters, spooning each quarter onto one side of a dough oval, leaving a ¾-inch border.

9. Combine the egg and 1 teaspoon of water in a small bowl and brush around the outer edge of the dough. Fold the dough over the filling and press together around the outer edges.

10. Place the calzones on the prepared cookie sheet and brush with a little olive oil. Bake for 12 to 14 minutes, or until golden brown.

11. While the calzones are baking, cook the sauce in the microwave oven.

12. Let the calzones stand for 5 minutes before eating. Serve with warm Pizza Sauce for dipping.

VARIATION MEXICALI CALZONES (25.3 grams fat per serving): Substitute part-skim Monterey Jack cheese for mozzarella. Add 1 or 2 chopped Refrigerator Pickled Jalapeño Peppers (page 314), if desired. Serve with 2 cups Mexican Tomato Sauce (page 319).

Pepper Steak Hero

MAKES: *4 servings*
COOKING TIME: *4 minutes*

12.6 grams fat per serving

1 teaspoon canola or olive oil
¾ pound very lean (90 percent lean) ground round
2 tablespoons coarsely ground black peppercorns
½ teaspoon salt
½ pound mushrooms, sliced
1 teaspoon fresh lemon juice
4 club rolls (4 to 6 inches each), split and toasted
1 cup shredded lettuce (optional)
1 tomato, thinly sliced (optional)

1. Heat the oil in a 10-inch frying pan on the conventional range until a drop of water sputters.

2. Form the meat into four 4 × 2 × ¾-inch patties. Press ½ teaspoon coarsely ground peppercorns into each side and sprinkle lightly with salt.

3. Fry for about 2 minutes on the first side and 1 minute on the second side for rare. Add 1 minute on the second side for medium and 2 minutes for well done.

4. Meanwhile, place the mushrooms and lemon juice in a 1-quart microwave-safe casserole. Microwave, uncovered, on HIGH for 3 minutes, or until just heated through, stirring once.

5. Place a meat patty and one-quarter of the mushrooms on each toasted roll. Top with shredded lettuce and sliced tomatoes, if desired.

Chicken or Turkey Club Sandwich

MAKES: *4 servings*
COOKING TIME: *4 minutes*

Low-cholesterol variation

15 grams fat per serving

Thelma remembers going with a friend to a hotel dining room for lunch, where they ordered club sandwiches. They could hardly stretch their mouths around the towering concoctions, but somehow they imagined that this was how fine ladies dined.

These sandwiches are best when we poach the chicken just for them. We leave out the middle piece of bread.

1 recipe Poached Boneless Chicken Breasts (page 185) or 1 pound thinly sliced turkey breast
8 slices bacon
8 slices good-quality white sandwich bread, toasted
4 tablespoons mayonnaise
8 thin slices tomato
8 lettuce leaves (iceberg or romaine)
Potato chips and/or Refrigerator Bread-and-Butter Pickle Chips (page 313)

1. After cooking the chicken breasts, place them in the refrigerator to cool slightly while cooking the bacon.
2. Place four slices of bacon at a time on a microwave roasting rack or on a pie plate lined with paper towel. Cover with a paper towel; microwave on HIGH for 2½ to 4 minutes, or until crisp.
3. Remove the bacon from the rack and pour off the fat or throw away the paper towels that have absorbed the grease. Repeat the process.
4. Cut each chicken breast into four thin crosswise slices.
5. Spread one side of each piece of toast with 1 tablespoon mayonnaise. Top with sliced chicken, 2 slices of bacon, 2 slices of tomato, and 2 pieces of lettuce.
6. Place the remaining toast, with the mayonnaise side down, on top of the lettuce.
7. Stick a toothpick 1 inch from each corner of the sandwich to hold it together. Cut the sandwich in half both crosswise and lengthwise to form four squares. Pile onto a large plate with a handful of chips.

VARIATION LOW-CHOLESTEROL CHICKEN OR TURKEY CLUB SANDWICH (10 grams fat per serving): Use low-cholesterol mayonnaise and eliminate the bacon.

Chicken Cutlet Hero with Peppers

MAKES: *4 servings*
COOKING TIME: *16 minutes*

15.5 grams fat per serving

SERVING SUGGESTIONS:
Serve with Refrigerator
Bread-and-Butter Pickle Chips
(page 313) and potato chips.

We pile on the hot peppers to add a little extra excitement to our video watching.

4 hero rolls (6 to 8 inches long), split and toasted
1 recipe Lightly Breaded Chicken Cutlets, Milan Style (page 185)
1 recipe Sizzled Peppers and Onions (page 209)
Chopped Refrigerator Pickled Jalapeño Peppers (page 314) or cherry peppers.

Top each toasted roll with a freshly cooked breaded chicken cutlet. Spoon peppers and onions on top. Add chopped hot peppers to taste.

Mideastern Chicken Pita Pockets

MAKES: *4 servings*
COOKING TIME: *6 to 8 minutes*

Low cholesterol

8.3 grams fat per serving

SERVING SUGGESTIONS:
Serve with Greek olives and
anchovies, if desired.

4 large pita pockets
1 recipe Poached Boneless Chicken Breasts (page 185)
1 large tomato, thinly sliced
½ head lettuce, shredded
1 medium Spanish onion, thinly sliced
Yogurt Sauce (page 318)

1. Toast the pita. Cut each pita in half crosswise.
2. Cut the chicken into thin slices.
3. Divide the slices from one piece of chicken between the two halves of one toasted pita. Tuck in some tomato, lettuce, and onion.
4. Spoon 1 tablespoon sauce inside each half.

Couch-Potato Fajitas

MAKES: *4 servings*
COOKING TIME: *21 to 25 minutes*

Low cholesterol

3.6 grams fat per serving

4 baking potatoes (6 to 8 ounces each), scrubbed
1 teaspoon canola, olive, or vegetable oil
1 medium onion, thinly sliced
1 garlic clove, minced
1 red or green bell pepper, sliced in ¼-inch strips
¾ pound skinless, boneless chicken breast, sliced into
   ¼-inch strips
2 tablespoons chopped fresh cilantro (optional)
1 tablespoon fresh lime juice
1 teaspoon chili powder
¼ teaspoon salt
Nonfat yogurt
Salsa Cruda (page 317) or purchased salsa

1. Pierce the potatoes with a fork on the top and bottom. Place in a microwave in a circle, end to end, on a piece of paper towel, leaving a 1-inch space between them.
2. Microwave on HIGH for 15 to 20 minutes, or until tender, turning over once during cooking and removing any that are done after 15 minutes. Let stand.
3. In a 9-inch microwave-safe pie plate, combine the oil, onion, and garlic. Microwave on HIGH for 35 seconds.
4. Add the pepper, chicken, lime juice, and chili powder, and salt. Cover with waxed paper and microwave on HIGH for 6 to 8 minutes, or until the chicken is cooked through, stirring after 4 minutes. Sprinkle with cilantro.
5. Cut the potatoes in half. Spoon the chicken mixture over the potato halves. Serve with yogurt and salsa.

Video Nachos Grandes

MAKES: *2 snack-size servings*
COOKING TIME: *3 to 5 minutes*

27 grams fat per serving using Intense Chili; 19 grams fat using Vegetarian Chili

20 corn tortilla chips
1 cup Intense Chili or Vegetarian Chili (page 155, 111)
4 ounces grated Monterey Jack cheese
Refrigerator Pickled Jalapeño Peppers (page 314), cut
   into rings
Tomato Salsa (page 317)

1. On a 10- or 12-inch microwave-safe platter, place the corn chips in a single layer.
2. Spoon a generous teaspoonful of chili on each chip.

Serve with guacamole and crudités, if desired.

These are easy to cook and eat on the same dish.

We give instructions for a large tray for two. If you want more, get a few trays ready and pop them in the microwave oven whenever you need them.

Sprinkle with cheese. Top with pepper rings.
3. Microwave, uncovered, on MEDIUM for 3 to 5 minutes to melt the cheese.
4. Serve with salsa.

DON'T FORGET THE POPCORN

Make and serve Popcorn in a Bag (page 270; 0.3 grams fat per cup), right from the brown paper bag in which it was popped, or pour it into a bowl and toss it with some of the following toppers:

MELTED BUTTER (4.3 grams fat per cup): Put 2 tablespoons butter in a 1-cup glass measure. Microwave on MEDIUM (to prevent spatters) for 1 minute to melt.

CAJUN SEASONING: To melted butter add ⅛ teaspoon cayenne and 3 to 4 drops hot-pepper sauce.

CHILI SEASONING: To melted butter add 2 teaspoons chili powder and ⅛ teaspoon ground cinnamon.

Chocolate-Covered Bananas

MAKES: 6
COOKING TIME: *3 to 5 minutes*

10 grams fat per serving

3 firm ripe bananas
6 ounces semisweet chocolate pieces
1 tablespoon canola or vegetable oil
Coarsely chopped nuts, sprinkles, or granola (optional)

1. Peel the bananas and cut them in half crosswise. Insert a wooden skewer into the center of each banana securely.
2. Place the skewered bananas on a cookie sheet that has been lined with waxed paper. Freeze for at least an hour, or until frozen solid. (The chocolate will slide off if bananas are not frozen completely.)
3. When the bananas are frozen, place the chocolate and oil in a 1-quart microwave-safe bowl or 4-cup glass

Serve with video meals, at
picnics, or for snacks.

*When Marcia's youngest
daughter Mae was teething,
Marcia would freeze a banana
half for her and give it to her
(without chocolate coating, of
course) to cool her gums while
the rest of the family enjoyed
their treats. Everyone was
happy.*

measure. (The measure works especially well because
the handle allows you to get the perfect angle for
twirling.)

4. Microwave the chocolate mixture on MEDIUM for 2
minutes; stir. Microwave on MEDIUM for 1 to 2 minutes
more, or until melted and smooth, stirring every 30
seconds to check and prevent overcooking.

5. Hold the bowl or measure at an angle to let the
chocolate run into the side, for easy dipping. Roll each
banana in the chocolate and twirl to remove the excess
coating (see Note).

6. Roll the banana in the nuts, if desired. Place on a
lined cookie sheet and return to the freezer. When the
coating is set, wrap each banana in waxed paper, plastic,
or foil and keep in the freezer until ready to eat. (Keeps
2 to 3 weeks.)

NOTE   Work quickly to keep the chocolate from hardening. If
it becomes too hard to twirl, place the bowl of melted
chocolate in the microwave oven. Heat on HIGH for 30
seconds and stir well.

OFFICE MEALS

OFFICE LUNCHES

We know how important lunch is to you. It's the meal that has to last through the afternoon and then some, because the day isn't over when you leave the office. Without a doubt, a homemade brown-bag lunch fits the bill—it's tastier and more healthful than a mysterious sandwich from the coffee wagon.

And a homemade lunch doesn't have to be prepared in the morning. An office microwave and a stop at a nearby salad bar on the way to work are all you need to have a hot meal in minutes.

Choose a midday meal that is nutritious (a complex carbohydrate like a Potato with Herbed Topping), not too heavy (Tofu Soup), and simple to prepare (Warm Pear Slices Topped with Cheese). You may even want to invest in a few accoutrements to make office lunching more fun and efficient:

- Buy a high-quality (stylish?!) insulated bag and thermos for carrying your raw materials. (To keep things really cold, wet a washcloth and squeeze it out the night before. Roll it up and then put it in a plastic sealable bag in the freezer. Stick it in your insulated bag to keep foods chilled.)

- Store such things as colorful paper napkins and a good pepper grinder in your desk.
- Discover a favorite mug. It can be a workhorse throughout the day, for everything from coffee to mineral water with lime.
- Choose paper plates good for microwave heating. Look for the molded fiber type, rather than the foam or plastic variety. They're better because they won't melt from the heat of the food.

NOTE   The recipes on pages 266–68 highlight calcium-rich dairy products and average about 150 calories per serving.

Fish and Vegetable Packet

MAKES: *1 serving*
COOKING TIME: *1½ to 3 minutes*

Low cholesterol

0.5 gram fat per serving

The mint and lemon add flavor without extra calories.

1 flounder or sole fillet (4 ounces)
2 or 3 leaves fresh mint, chopped
2 ounces mushrooms or zucchini, sliced
1 small tomato, sliced
1 lemon slice
Salt and pepper

AT HOME:

1. Cut a 12-inch square of parchment paper or non-stick microwave cooking paper. Place the fish fillet in the center, turning the thinner edges of the fillet under the middle to make a 4-inch-long piece.
2. Top with mint, vegetables, and lemon and sprinkle with salt and pepper. Pull up the edges of the paper together and secure with a nonmetallic tie or ribbon.

AT THE OFFICE:

Place the packet in the microwave oven and cook on HIGH for 1½ to 3 minutes.

Chicken and Potato Packet

MAKES: *1 serving*
COOKING TIME: *3 to 4 minutes*

Low cholesterol

2.9 grams fat per serving

1 serving skinless, boneless, chicken breast (3 ounces), cut into 2-inch strips
1 green onion, thinly sliced
⅛ teaspoon paprika
1 teaspoon fresh lemon or lime juice
1 small red potato, scrubbed with the skin on, cut into ⅛-inch slices (cut right before cooking.)
2 tablespoons Salsa Cruda (page 317) or purchased salsa

AT HOME:

1. Cut chicken and place in a freezer-quality plastic bag (to keep juice from leaking) along with the onion, paprika, and lemon juice.
2. Cut a 12-inch square of parchment or nonstick microwave cooking paper.

AT THE OFFICE:

1. Cut the potato. Overlap the potato slices to form a circle in the center of the parchment square. Place the chicken pieces, along with the onion, over the potatoes. Pour the juices from the bag over the chicken.
2. Pull the corners of the paper together and twist the top to secure. Microwave on HIGH for 3 to 4 minutes, or until the chicken is cooked. Top with salsa and enjoy.

VARIATION CHICKEN AND POTATO PACKETS WITH CHUTNEY: Substitute 2 tablespoons of your favorite chutney (pages 330–33) for the salsa.

Cheese-Topped Broccoli

MAKES: *1 serving*
COOKING TIME: *3 minutes*

Low cholesterol

4.5 grams fat per serving

8 ounces broccoli (about ¼ head), florets cut into bite-size pieces, stalks peeled and cut into ½-inch slices
1 teaspoon fresh lemon juice or water
1 ounce fat-reduced cheese (such as mozzarella or Monterey Jack), thinly sliced or grated

TOPPINGS

Red-pepper flakes (optional)
Black olive slices (optional)
Fresh thyme leaves (optional)
Freshly ground black pepper (optional)

AT THE OFFICE:

1. Place the broccoli pieces on a 9- or 10-inch paper plate and sprinkle with lemon juice or water.
2. Microwave on HIGH for 2 minutes, or until tender-crisp
3. Sprinkle with cheese and microwave on HIGH for 30 seconds to 1 minute, or until the cheese is melted. Top with optional toppings.

Olive Burrito

MAKES: *1 serving*
COOKING TIME: *Less than 1 minute*

Low cholesterol

4.5 grams fat per serving

2 ounces low-fat ricotta or cottage cheese
1 flour tortilla (7-inch diameter)
2 teaspoons prepared salsa
2 green or black pitted olives, thinly sliced

AT HOME:

1. Spread ricotta on tortilla; top with salsa and olives.
2. Roll up tortilla. Wrap.

AT THE OFFICE:

Place on a 9-inch paper plate. Microwave on HIGH for 30 to 45 seconds, or until heated through. Let stand 1 minute before eating.

Southwestern Zucchini Boats

MAKES: *1 serving*
COOKING TIME: *1 to 2 minutes*

Low cholesterol

2.4 grams fat per serving

1 small (¼ pound) zucchini, halved lengthwise
2 ounces low-fat ricotta or cottage cheese
2 teaspoons prepared salsa
Freshly ground black pepper, to taste

AT HOME:

Scoop the pulp from the zucchini to make a ¼-inch shell. Spoon the ricotta into the zucchini shells and season with salsa and pepper. Wrap.

AT THE OFFICE:

1. Unwrap the zucchini and place on a 9-inch paper plate.
2. Microwave on HIGH for 1 to 2 minutes, or until the cheese is heated through and the zucchini is tender-crisp.

White Pita Pizza

MAKES: *1 serving*
COOKING TIME: *about 1 minute*

Low cholesterol

4.6 grams fat per serving

1 pita (7-inch diameter), split in two circles
1½ ounces low-fat ricotta cheese
1 teaspoon chopped fresh basil or ¼ teaspoon dried
Freshly ground black pepper to taste
½ ounce grated low-fat mozzarella cheese

AT HOME:

Spread the pita on the cut side with ricotta; sprinkle with basil, pepper, and mozzarella. Wrap.

AT THE OFFICE:

1. Place the pita on a 9-inch paper plate.
2. Microwave on HIGH for 45 seconds to 1½ minutes. Let stand 1 minute before eating.

VARIATIONS

PESTO PITA PIZZA (335 grams fat per serving): Combine 1 teaspoon pesto with the ricotta before spreading on the pita.

VEGETABLE PITA PIZZA (2.6 grams fat per serving): Top the ricotta with ¼ cup thinly sliced mushrooms, zucchini, or fresh roasted pepper slices.

Warm Pear Slices Topped with Cheese

MAKES: *1 serving*
COOKING TIME: *1 to 2 minutes*

7.9 grams fat per serving

1 pear, cored but not skinned, cut into 12 wedges
1 ounce blue, brie, or raclette cheese, cut into ¼-inch slices

AT THE OFFICE:

1. On a 9-inch paper plate, place the pears in a pinwheel (with the narrow ends pointing toward the center).
2. Arrange the cheese slices in the center on top of the pears, where the pear tips meet. Microwave on HIGH for 1 to 2 minutes, or until the cheese has softened. Let stand for 1 minute.
3. Eat with a slice of good-quality whole-grain bread.

Potato with Herbed Topping

MAKES: *1 serving*
COOKING TIME: *3 to 5 minutes*

Low cholesterol

0.2 gram fat per serving

2 tablespoons low-fat yogurt
1 teaspoon chopped fresh herbs (such as parsley,
   chives, tarragon, or chervil)
1 medium baking potato
Freshly ground black pepper to taste

AT HOME:

Combine the yogurt and herbs in a container.

AT THE OFFICE:

1. Pierce the potato once with a fork on both top and bottom. Place on a 9-inch paper plate.
2. Microwave on HIGH for 3 to 5 minutes, or until the potato is tender when pierced with a fork or it gives slightly when squeezed. (Caution: Potato will be hot; hold it with a cloth or paper towel.)
3. Cut the cooked potato in half. Spread both halves with herbed yogurt and season with pepper.

VARIATION

POTATO WITH VEGETABLE TOPPING (2.5 grams fat per serving): Omit the yogurt and herbs. Top the cooked potato with 2 tablespoons mixed grated low-fat mozzarella and Monterey Jack cheese and ½ cup cooked vegetables. Microwave on HIGH for 45 seconds to 1 minute, or until the cheese is melted.

Open-Face Sandwich

MAKES: *1 serving*
COOKING TIME: *30 seconds*

Low cholesterol

7.5 grams fat per serving

1 piece Italian or French bread or roll (6 inches
   long), cut in half lengthwise
1 slice smoked turkey
1 tablespoon bottled Italian pepper salad, drained
1 slice part-skim-milk mozzarella cheese (1 ounce)

AT HOME:

Top one piece of bread with the turkey, then the pepper salad, and lastly the cheese. Cover with the second piece of bread. Wrap.

AT THE OFFICE:

Place the assembled sandwich on a paper plate or paper towel. Microwave on HIGH for 30 seconds, or until cheese is melted.

• 1 slice turkey breast, thinly sliced tomato, and 1 slice part-skim-milk Muenster or Monterey Jack cheese (6.5 grams fat per serving).
- ½ cup drained bean salad (from a salad bar), thinly sliced tomato, and 1 slice part-skim-milk Muenster or Monterey Jack cheese (7.5 grams fat per serving).
- Rye bread spread with 1 teaspoon Dijon-style mustard, 1 slice smoked turkey, and 1 slice part-skim-milk Swiss cheese (6.5 grams fat per serving).
- ½ bagel, 2 slices tomato, and 1 slice part-skim-milk cheese (mozzarella, Muenster, or Monterey Jack) (6.5 grams fat per serving).
- 1 piece toast, 2 slices tomato, 1 slice part-skim-milk cheese (mozzarella, Muenster or Monterey Jack) (5.6 grams fat per serving).
- ½ pita (6-inch diameter), split lengthwise. Top with ⅓ cup bean sprouts, 2 ounces thinly sliced tofu, 4 thinly sliced mushrooms, and 1 slice part-skim-milk Monterey Jack cheese (8.5 grams fat per serving).

Tofu Soup

MAKES: *1 serving*
COOKING TIME: *1½ to 2 minutes*

No cholesterol

4 grams fat per serving

Tofu makes a quick meatless-protein lunch. We like to serve it in a soup for our midday pick-me-up.

1 square (4 ounces) tofu, cut into ¼-inch cubes
1 thinly sliced green onion
2 mushrooms, sliced
1 packet low-sodium vegetable broth or miso soup

AT HOME:

Place tofu and sliced vegetables in a small container, or wrap.

AT THE OFFICE:

1. Combine the broth packet and water in a large (12-ounce) cup or soup bowl.
2. Add the tofu and vegetables; microwave on HIGH for 1½ to 2 minutes, or until heated but not boiling. (Boiling will cause a spillover.) Stir well and enjoy.

VARIATION   TOFU SOUP WITH BEAN SPROUTS: Substitute 2 tablespoons bean sprouts for the mushrooms.

Popcorn in a Bag

MAKES: *6 cups*
COOKING TIME: *3 minutes*

No cholestrol

0.3 gram fat per cup

Keep a supply of brown sandwich bags, popcorn, and a ⅓-cup measure in your desk for this high-fiber, low-calorie (23 calories per cup) pick-me-up. (Prepackaged purchased popcorn is generally much higher in calories, fat, and additives.) At the end, you may add salt and melted butter if you wish. We prefer to add some grated Parmesan (at 8 calories per teaspoon) or a few drops of Tabasco or chili powder.

In addition to the equipment above, you'll need a 650-watt or higher microwave. *Don't attempt this with lower-wattage ovens.* To make sure that your popcorn is fresh, keep it in a tightly sealed jar.

This basic formula for microwave popping works only for this amount of popcorn; if you don't want it all, share it with a coworker.

⅓ cup popping corn

1. Place the popcorn in a brown sandwich-size paper bag. (Do not use a recycled bag.) *Do not add oil.* Fold the top of the bag over twice, to close lightly but firmly.
2. Microwave on HIGH for 2½ to 3 minutes, or until popping has begun to slow down but has not completely stopped (about 2 seconds between pops), listening carefully during the last minute. Do not attempt to pop unpopped kernels—they will burn! If the popcorn hasn't popped within 3 minutes, either the corn is too old or the wattage isn't high enough.

WARM DRINKS

WARM SPICED CRANBERRY COCKTAIL: Pour cranberry juice into a microwave-safe mug. Add a dash of cinnamon and a pinch of nutmeg. Heat on HIGH for 1 to 2 minutes, watching that it doesn't boil over.

TOMATO-MINT SOUP: Pour tomato juice into a microwave-safe mug. Add a chopped mint leaf and a dash of cayenne. Heat on HIGH for 1 to 2 minutes, watching that it doesn't boil over.

SPICED APPLE JUICE: Pour apple juice into a microwave-safe mug. Add ½ teaspoon fresh lemon juice and a lemon slice, along with a dash of cinnamon and nutmeg. Heat on HIGH for 1 to 2 minutes, watching that it doesn't boil over.

GINGERED TOMATO-ORANGE DRINK: Combine about ¾ cup tomato juice with ¼ cup orange juice in a microwave-safe mug; add a pinch ground ginger. Heat on HIGH for 1 to 2 minutes, watching that it doesn't boil over.

DESSERTS

Sundaes at the ice-cream parlor, silky puddings, and gingerbread with real whipped cream; these are just a few of the delights that haunt our dessert memories. Many of our childhood food recollections revolve around desserts, because that was the whole point of eating dinner! This explains why many of the desserts in this chapter are based on those childhood favorites.

Sweets were part of celebrations. Recitals, graduations, school concerts, and other rites of passage were marked by a stop at the local ice-cream parlor. Ice cream was piled into tall glasses and topped with hot fudge, hot butterscotch, or gooey walnut sauce. Now you can scoop up a memory swiftly by keeping ice cream in the freezer and making one of the sauces in two to ten minutes. For special occasions, we have designed more sophisticated variations on this theme by blending customized ice creams and spooning them into crusts for ice cream pies.

When we were growing up, most of the desserts we had at home were fruit-based, because our mothers wanted us to eat well. We have come to appreciate them as adults and have put new twists on them for our own children. The microwave oven can poach fruits quickly and lock in their precious flavors. But to make authentic cobblers, with fluffy biscuit toppings, we turn to the toaster oven to brown the crusts before popping them on the fruit base—another example of two everyday appliances working well together.

To Prepare the Whole Meal

Pick the dessert that fits into your time schedule:

- A dessert that is served chilled or frozen, or one that requires standing time, should be prepared before the meal. Ice cream pies may be frozen for up to a month in advance if wrapped tightly.
- Many of the warm desserts are quick enough to be cooked after dinner if there has been some premeasuring or chopping in advance.
- Warm sauces can be premeasured and cooked right before serving. If making more than one (for an ice cream party, for example), it is best to make them in advance and reheat them just before serving.

Fruit Cobblers

Fruit cobblers are similar to deep-dish pies but a little easier and quicker to prepare because of the quick biscuit topping. We call for a combination method of toaster oven and microwave to achieve the perfect balance of golden crisp crust and quickly cooked fruit. The toaster oven is preferred over the conventional oven for the biscuits, because preheating is a quick 5-minute process. The fruit will taste fresher because of the shorter cooking time possible in the microwave. The waxed-paper covering is especially important here, as a tighter cover would cause a boil.

Cobblers have a special place in Thelma's memories. The first cobbler she ever tasted was made by her friend Becky's Aunt Grace, who was a secretary in Thelma's small New England high school. On special days she would send Becky a message in home room telling her to stop by her office to pick up a cobbler that she had baked for her. Thelma remembers the first time she shared some with her—it was heavenly! In return for these marvelous cobblers, she and Becky would give Aunt Grace driving lessons (she had just purchased her first car). Grace was anxious to learn how to drive, and at sixteen they were eager to share their newly learned skill with her. There was no doubt in their minds who got the better deal, although they did give Aunt Grace a lot of thrills. Fortunately, everyone is still around to tell the tales and appreciate our "modern cobblers."

Rhubarb Cobbler

MAKES: *6 servings*
COOKING TIME: *20 minutes*

Low-cholesterol variation

6.6 grams fat per serving

SERVING SUGGESTIONS:
Top with frozen yogurt, vanilla yogurt, or ice cream.

½ cup plus 1½ tablespoons sugar
1 cup plus 1 tablespoon flour
½ teaspoon baking powder
½ teaspoon baking soda
¼ teaspoon salt
3 tablespoons butter, cut into three pieces
½ cup buttermilk
½ teaspoon ground cinnamon
1 pound rhubarb, cut into ½-inch pieces
½ teaspoon grated orange zest

1. Preheat the toaster oven to 400° F.
2. In the bowl of a food processor, place 1 tablespoon sugar, 1 cup flour, and the baking powder, baking soda, and salt. Pulse on and off quickly two to three times to mix.
3. Add the butter. Pulse two to three times until the butter is cut into the flour to resemble a coarse meal.
4. Pour in the buttermilk; pulse on and off four to five times, or until a soft dough forms.
5. Butter the small baking sheet that fits in the toaster oven.
6. Using a spoon, drop the dough onto the tray in six evenly spaced mounds.
7. Combine 1½ teaspoons sugar and ¼ teaspoon cinnamon in a small bowl and sprinkle on top of the mounds.
8. Bake for 20 to 25 minutes, or until golden.
9. Meanwhile, place the rhubarb in an 8-inch round glass cake dish. Stir in the remaining ½ cup sugar, 1 tablespoon flour, ¼ teaspoon cinnamon, and orange rind.
10. Cover with waxed paper. Microwave on HIGH for

8 to 10 minutes, stirring once, or until the rhubarb is tender.

11. Spoon each serving into a bowl and top with a biscuit. Serve warm, as is or with a topping.

VARIATIONS Low-Cholesterol Rhubarb Cobbler (5 grams fat per serving): Substitute ½ recipe Old-Fashioned Biscuits Made Light (page 55) for the recipe above (steps 1–8). Prepare rhubarb and bake as directed in steps 9–11.

Other Fruit Cobblers: Follow the basic recipe, but substitute 3 cups blueberries, sour pitted cherries, raspberries, peeled and cubed peaches, or peeled, cored, and sliced apples for rhubarb. Add only ¼ cup sugar to these less-tart fruits or berries. Substitute grated lemon rind for orange rind. Microwave on HIGH for 6 to 8 minutes, or until slightly softened and heated through, stirring after 3 minutes.

New-Fangled Vanilla Pudding

MAKES: *4 servings*
COOKING TIME: *6 to 8 minutes*

Low-cholesterol variation

4.1 grams fat per serving

Kids help

⅓ cup granulated sugar
3 tablespoons cornstarch
2 cups milk
1 tablespoon vanilla
Whipped cream (optional)

1. Combine the sugar and cornstarch in a 4-cup glass measure.
2. Stir in the milk and vanilla. Microwave, uncovered, on HIGH for 3 minutes; stir.
3. Microwave on HIGH for 3 to 5 minutes more, or until boiling and thickened, stirring each minute to keep it smooth. Pour into individual serving dishes. Cover and chill in refrigerator until serving time. Top with whipped cream, if desired.

VARIATIONS

We've created a microwave version of vanilla pudding that requires only about 6 minutes of cooking time, with a stir or two. For a real treat, top this simple but luscious pudding with whipped cream.

Low-Cholesterol New-Fangled Vanilla Pudding (0.2 gram fat per serving): Substitute evaporated skim milk for regular milk. Omit the whipped cream.

NEW-FANGLED CHOCOLATE PUDDING (5.4 grams fat per serving): Add ⅓ cup unsweetened cocoa powder to the sugar and cornstarch. Reduce the vanilla to 1 teaspoon.

NEW-FANGLED BUTTERSCOTCH PUDDING (10 grams fat per serving): Eliminate the granulated sugar. Place 2 tablespoons butter and ½ cup brown sugar in a 2-cup glass measure. Microwave, uncovered, on HIGH for 1 to 3 minutes, or until the butter and sugar are melted and blended together, stirring every 30 seconds. Stir in the cornstarch and only 1 teaspoon vanilla. Stir the milk in slowly to make the mixture as smooth as possible. There will be some lumps, but these will smooth out when cooked. Follow the basic cooking instructions.

Chocolate Bread Pudding

MAKES: *4 servings*
COOKING TIME: *12 to 14 minutes*

Low-cholesterol variation

11.7 grams fat per serving

SERVING SUGGESTIONS: Serve warm, at room temperature, or chilled. Spoon into goblets and top with whipped cream, Pastry Cream (page 278), Quick Raspberry Sauce (page 282), Warm Berry Sauce (page 282), or Hint-of-Lemon Ice Cream (page 279).

Bread cubes in a silken dense chocolate sauce make this old-fashioned dessert a satisfying and delicious favorite.

1½ cups milk
4 ounces semisweet chocolate pieces
2 large eggs
½ cup sugar
1 teaspoon vanilla
6 slices good-quality white bread, ½ inch thick, cut into 1-inch cubes (about 4 cups)
½ teaspoon ground cinnamon
¼ teaspoon ground nutmeg

1. Combine the milk and chocolate in a 4-cup glass measure.
2. Microwave on HIGH for 2½ to 3½ minutes, or until the chocolate melts but the milk doesn't boil, stirring twice.
3. Meanwhile, in a mixing bowl, beat the eggs and sugar together. Stir in the vanilla. Slowly pour half the warm milk mixture into the egg mixture, stirring constantly.
4. Pour the mixture back into the 4-cup glass measure.
5. Microwave on MEDIUM for 2 minutes, stirring once.
6. Stir in the bread cubes. Let stand for 5 minutes, occasionally pushing top bread cubes into the sauce.
7. Pour the bread mixture into a 1-quart microwave-safe casserole. Sprinkle the top with cinnamon and nutmeg.
8. Cover with waxed paper. Microwave on MEDIUM for 10 to 12 minutes, or until a knife inserted 1 inch from the center comes out clean, rotating the pudding

one-quarter turn twice. Let stand directly on the counter for 10 minutes. Unmold, if desired.

VARIATIONS DOUBLE CHOCOLATE BREAD PUDDING: Substitute purchased chocolate pound cake for bread cubes.

LOW-CHOLESTEROL CHOCOLATE BREAD PUDDING (5.9 grams fat per serving): Substitute skim milk for whole and 4 egg whites for the eggs.

Cream Puffs

MAKES: *4 servings*
COOKING TIME: *Microwave time: 2 minutes; baking time: 35 to 40 minutes*

12 grams fat per serving

SERVING SUGGESTIONS:
Use as containers for ice cream, whipped cream, or Pastry Cream (page 278), or as edible cups for a stew.

3 tablespoons butter
½ cup flour
1 teaspoon sugar
2 eggs

1. Preheat the conventional oven to 400° F.
2. Grease a cookie sheet.
3. Pour ½ cup water into a 4-cup glass measure; add the butter.
4. Microwave on HIGH for 1½ to 3 minutes, or until boiling.
5. Remove from the oven and stir once or twice to remove any excess bubbles. (This prevents the mixture from boiling over when other ingredients are added.)
6. Add the flour and sugar to water-and-butter mixture all at once. Stir quickly with a wooden spoon until a smooth batter forms and then pulls away from the sides of the cup.
7. Still using the wooden spoon, beat in the eggs one at a time, beating well after each addition.
8. Spoon four 3-inch mounds onto the greased cookie sheet.
9. Bake for 10 minutes at 400° F. Reduce the oven temperature to 350° F and bake for 25 to 30 minutes more, or until puffed and browned.
10. Cut off the top third of each cream puff and spoon out the soft insides. Allow to cool or serve warm.

NOTE To make 8 puffs: Double the ingredients and microwave cooking time. Conventional cooking time remains the same.

Filled Cream Puffs Topped with Hot Fudge Sauce

1 recipe Cream Puffs (page 277)
Vanilla ice cream, Pastry Cream (page 278),
    Strawberry "Sorbet" (page 287), or frozen yogurt
Hot Fudge Sauce (page 280)

Spoon filling of your choice into puffs. Replace cover and spoon Hot Fudge Sauce over the top.

Pastry Cream

MAKES: 2 cups
COOKING TIME: 6 to 7 minutes

3.7 grams fat per ¼ cup serving

SERVING SUGGESTIONS:
Serve this delicious cream warm, spooned over berries, fresh or poached fruits, or Chocolate Bread Pudding (page 276). Chill the cream and spoon it into Cream Puffs (page 277).

1½ cups milk
¼ cup sugar
4 large egg yolks, beaten
¼ cup flour
1 tablespoon vanilla, sherry, or rum

1. Pour the milk into a 4-cup glass measure.
2. Microwave on HIGH for 3 minutes, or until hot but not boiling.
3. Meanwhile, in a 2-quart microwave-safe casserole, beat the sugar into the egg yolks until well blended. Stir in the flour.
4. Gradually add the heated milk to the egg mixture, beating constantly.
5. Microwave on HIGH for 1 minute; beat with a whisk. Continue to cook on HIGH for 2 to 3 minutes more, or until thickened, beating every 30 seconds.
6. Stir in the vanilla.
7. Serve warm or chill until needed (see Note).

NOTE   When chilling, place a piece of plastic wrap or waxed paper directly on the cream to prevent a skin from forming.

Customized Cinnamon Ice Cream

MAKES: 1 quart
COOKING TIME: 1 minute

1 quart vanilla or French vanilla ice cream, frozen yogurt, tofu "ice cream," or nonfat frozen "ice cream"
1½ teaspoons ground cinnamon

1. Remove the ice cream cover; place the paper or plastic carton in the microwave oven and heat on DEFROST for 30 seconds to 1 minute, or until the ice cream is soft enough to spoon easily.

7.1 grams fat per ½ cup ice cream; 2.8 grams fat per ½ cup ice milk; 3.1 grams fat per ½ cup frozen yogurt

2. Spoon the ice cream into a large bowl and fold in the cinnamon.
3. Spoon into a container that has a tight-fitting cover and refreeze for at least an hour to harden.

NOTE

To make ½ gallon: Place ½ gallon ice cream in a paper or plastic container in the microwave oven. Microwave on LOW for 2 to 3 minutes, or on DEFROST for 1 minute, to soften. Double the ingredients to be folded in.

VARIATIONS

SERVING SUGGESTIONS:
Great spooned over baked apples or apple tarts and pies, or topped with Hot Fudge Sauce (page 28).

Customizing ice cream is quick, fun, and delicious when the microwave oven is used as a softening tool. We share with you some of our favorite flavors and encourage you to use your imagination and taste preferences to develop your own signature flavors.

GINGER ICE CREAM: Substitute 1½ teaspoons ground ginger for cinnamon. Serve with Perfectly Poached Pears (page 238) or warm Chocolate Bread Pudding (page 276). Garnish with chopped crystallized ginger, if desired.

CANDY BAR ICE CREAM (12 grams fat per ½ cup serving): Substitute a 6-ounce Snickers, Heath, or Milky Way bar or a candy bar of your choice, chopped into ½-inch chunks, for cinnamon. Serve with Hot Fudge Sauce (page 280) or Butterscotch Sauce (page 280).

CHOCOLATE CHIP–TEQUILA ICE CREAM (9 grams fat per ½-cup serving): Substitute 4 ounces semisweet chocolate chips, or white chocolate pieces, ⅓ cup tequila, and 2 tablespoons lime juice for cinnamon. A great way to finish a Mexican-style meal. Rim the serving dish with salt if desired, and garnish with a twist of lime.

HINT-OF-LEMON ICE CREAM: Substitute 2 tablespoons fresh lemon juice and 1 tablespoon grated lemon rind for cinnamon. Serve with Chocolate Bread Pudding (page 276), Fresh Peach Sauce (page 281), or Warm Berry Sauce (page 282).

Ice-Cream Sauces

Every kid has been to or heard about those wonderful ice-cream parlors where ice-cream sundaes were made to order behind marbled counters and enjoyed on curlicued wrought-iron chairs. Wood's Ice Cream Parlour in Thomaston, Connecticut, was one of those, and these sauces bring back memories to Thelma of a good report card, or a passing performance in the band concert. Serve them swirled over your favorite ice cream in a tall glass, maybe even topped with whipped cream and a cherry.

Hot Fudge Sauce

MAKES: 1½ cups
COOKING TIME: 3 to 5 minutes

1.7 grams fat per 1 tablespoon

6 ounces semisweet chocolate pieces
½ cup half-and-half
¼ cup light corn syrup
1 teaspoon vanilla

1. In a 4-cup glass measure, combine the chocolate, half-and-half, and corn syrup.
2. Microwave, uncovered, on HIGH for 2 minutes; stir.
3. Microwave on HIGH for 1 to 3 minutes more, or until smooth, stirring each minute. Stir in the vanilla.

NOTE   If made in advance, reheat on MEDIUM for 2 to 3 minutes.

Butterscotch Sauce

MAKES: 1½ cups
COOKING TIME: 7 to 11 minutes

2.6 grams fat per tablespoon

1 cup sugar
¼ cup corn syrup
1 tablespoon hot water
¼ cup (½ stick) butter
½ cup half-and-half

1. In a 4-cup glass measure, combine the sugar, corn syrup, and water.
2. Microwave, uncovered, on HIGH for 1 minute; stir well.
3. Microwave on HIGH for 4 to 7 minutes, or until the mixture reaches a light golden, butterscotch color, stirring once.
4. Meanwhile, cut the butter into four pieces. Add to the warm sugar mixture, stirring until melted. Stir in the half-and-half.
5. Microwave on MEDIUM for 2 to 3 minutes, or until well blended. Let stand for 5 minutes, until the sauce becomes slightly thicker and a deeper gold.

NOTE   If made in advance, reheat on MEDIUM for 2 to 3 minutes.

Warm Walnut Sauce

MAKES: 1½ cups
COOKING TIME: 4 to 6 minutes

5 grams fat per tablespoon

From a favorite ice cream parlor of Thelma's in Thomaston, Connecticut. We add brandy to warm the spirit.

⅔ cup light brown sugar
¼ cup (½ stick) butter
¼ cup half-and-half
2 tablespoons light corn syrup
1 cup coarsely chopped walnuts
1 teaspoon vanilla

1. In a 4-cup glass measure, combine the sugar, butter, half-and-half, and corn syrup.
2. Microwave, uncovered, on HIGH for 2 minutes; stir.
3. Microwave on HIGH for 1 to 3 minutes more, or until boiling.
4. Stir in the nuts and vanilla. Microwave on HIGH for 1 minute.

VARIATION

BRANDY-WALNUT SAUCE: Add 3 tablespoons brandy when adding nuts and vanilla. This is one of our all-time favorite ice-cream toppers.

Brown Sugar–Caramel Sauce

MAKES: ¾ cup
COOKING TIME: 3 to 4 minutes

1.1 grams fat per tablespoon

SERVING SUGGESTION:
Serve over Customized Cinnamon Ice Cream (page 278).

½ cup firmly packed dark brown sugar
½ cup heavy cream
2 tablespoons light corn syrup

1. In a 4-cup glass measure, combine all the ingredients and whisk to blend.
2. Microwave, uncovered, on HIGH for 2 minutes, then whisk to blend well.
3. Microwave on HIGH for 1 minute more, or until slightly thickened and caramel-colored. Whisk well until the boiling stops. The sauce will thicken as it cools.

NOTE

The sauce can be made up to 2 days in advance and refrigerated. To bring to room temperature, microwave on HIGH for 1 minute.

Fresh Peach Sauce

¼ cup sugar
1 tablespoon fresh lemon juice
1 teaspoon vanilla
3 perfect ripe peaches, peeled, pitted, and thinly sliced

No fat

When Thelma worked at
Wood's Ice Cream Parlour,
                    VARIATION

she discovered the secret of
their peach sauce for ice
cream—the freshest, ripest
peaches available in a simple
vanilla syrup.

1. In a 4-cup glass measure, combine the sugar, lemon juice, vanilla, and ¼ cup water.
2. Microwave, uncovered, on HIGH for 2 to 4 minutes, or until boiling rapidly.
3. Stir in the peaches. Chill for at least 30 minutes before serving.

FRESH PEACH SAUCE WITH PEACH SCHNAPPS: Add 2 tablespoons peach schnapps with the vanilla.

Warm Berry Sauce

MAKES: *2 cups*
COOKING TIME: *4 to 5 minutes*

No fat

2 cups fresh ripe berries
2 tablespoons raspberry or currant jam
2 tablespoons fruit-flavored liqueur (optional)
1 tablespoon fresh lemon juice

Place all the ingredients in a 4-cup glass measure. Microwave on HIGH for 4 to 5 minutes, or until just heated through, stirring once.

Quick Raspberry Sauce

MAKES: *1 cup*
COOKING TIME: *1 to 2 minutes*

No fat

SERVING SUGGESTIONS:
Spoon over ice cream, frozen
yogurt, or poached fruits.

1 cup raspberry preserves
2 tablespoons fruit-flavored liqueur
1 teaspoon vanilla

Place all the ingredients in a 4-cup glass measure. Microwave on HIGH for 2 to 3 minutes, or until preserves are melted. Stir well.

Customized Ice-Cream Pies

There is no easier way to please a crowd, especially a mixed group of children and adults, than to serve one of these ice-cream pies. After preparing a few of these recipes, you may wish to create your own version to please family and friends. All of these pies may be stored in the freezer for a month.

Snickers Ice-Cream Pie with Hot Fudge Sauce

MAKES: *10 servings*
COOKING TIME: *Less than 10 minutes*

23.9 grams fat per serving

1 recipe Cookie-Crumb Crust (using chocolate wafers) for a 10-inch pie (page 286)
½ gallon Snickers Ice Cream (see Candy Bar Ice Cream, page 279), softened but not refrozen
Hot Fudge Sauce (page 280)

1. Refrigerate the crust for 15 minutes to chill.
2. Spoon the ice cream into the prepared crust.
3. Freeze for at least 1 hour or overnight, until frozen solid.
4. Serve with Hot Fudge Sauce.

Lemon Ice-Cream Pie with Warm Berry Sauce

MAKES: *10 servings*
COOKING TIME: *Less than 10 minutes*

19.7 grams fat per serving

1 recipe Cinnamon-Nut Crumb Crust (page 286)
½ gallon Hint-of-Lemon Ice Cream (page 279), softened but not refrozen
1 lemon, thinly sliced
Warm Berry Sauce (page 282)

1. Refrigerate the crust for 15 minutes to chill.
2. Spoon the ice cream into the prepared crust.
3. Freeze for at least 1 hour or overnight, until frozen solid.
4. Right before serving, garnish with lemon slices.
5. Serve with Warm Berry Sauce, another fruit sauce, or fresh fruit.

Chocolate Chip–Tequila Pie

1 recipe Graham-Cracker Crumb Crust (page 285) or Tortilla Chip Crust (page 286)
½ gallon Chocolate Chip–Tequila Ice Cream (page 279), softened but not refrozen
1 lime, thinly sliced

MAKES: *10 servings*
COOKING TIME: *Less than 10 minutes*

18.7 grams fat per serving

SERVING SUGGESTION:
Serve with sliced fresh strawberries.

1. Refrigerate the crust for 15 minutes to chill.
2. Spoon the ice cream into the prepared crust.
3. Freeze for at least 1 hour or overnight, until frozen solid.
4. Right before serving, garnish with lime slices.

Mud Pie

MAKES: *10 servings*
COOKING TIME: *Less than 10 minutes*

20.4 grams fat per serving

SERVING SUGGESTION:
Serve with dollops of whipped cream.

1 recipe Cookie-Crumb Crust (using chocolate wafers) (page 286)
½ gallon good-quality purchased vanilla or coffee ice cream, softened but not refrozen
1 recipe Hot Fudge Sauce (page 280)

1. Refrigerate the crust for 15 minutes to chill.
2. Spoon the ice cream into the prepared crust.
3. Freeze for at least 3 hours or overnight, until frozen solid. (If the ice cream isn't solidly frozen, the sauce will slide off when you try to spread it on.)
4. Meanwhile, make the Hot Fudge Sauce and let it stand until it reaches room temperature.
5. Spread ¾ cup fudge sauce evenly over the pie and freeze again until ready to serve (at least 2 hours).
6. Serve with remaining Hot Fudge Sauce. To heat, pour into a 2- or 4-cup glass measure. Microwave on MEDIUM for 1 to 2 minutes.

Pumpkin Ice-Cream Pie in Ginger Crust

MAKES: *10 servings*
COOKING TIME: *Less than 10 minutes*

18.5 grams fat per serving

1 recipe Cookie-Crumb Pie Crust (using gingersnaps) for a 10-inch pie (page 286)
1 teaspoon ground cinnamon
1 teaspoon ground ginger
¼ teaspoon ground cloves
1 can (8 ounces) pumpkin-pie filling
½ gallon purchased vanilla ice cream

1. Refrigerate the crust for 15 minutes to chill.
2. Meanwhile, mix the cinnamon, ginger, and cloves into the pumpkin pie filling.
3. When the crust has chilled, soften the ice cream in the microwave on the DEFROST setting for 1 minute.
4. Fold the pumpkin mixture into the softened ice

SERVING SUGGESTION:
A nice addition to the
Thanksgiving dessert table.

cream. Spoon into the prepared crust immediately.
5. Freeze for at least 3 hours or overnight, until frozen solid.

Low-Cholesterol Ice Milk Pie in Honey-Graham Crust

½ gallon any flavor ice milk
1 recipe Low-Cholesterol Honey-Graham Crust
(page 286)

1. Spoon the ice milk into the prepared crust.
2. Freeze for at least 3 hours or overnight.

MAKES: *10 servings*
COOKING TIME: *Less than 10 minutes*

VARIATION

Low cholesterol

6.5 grams fat per serving

SERVING SUGGESTIONS:
Serve with Warm Berry Sauce
(page 282), Quick Raspberry
Sauce (page 282), or any fresh
berries or sliced fruit.

LOW-CHOLESTEROL FROZEN YOGURT PIE (7.6 grams fat per serving): Substitute nonfat frozen yogurt for ice milk.

Graham-Cracker Crumb Crust

MAKES: *Crust for a 9-inch pie;
10 servings*
COOKING TIME: *3½ to 4 minutes*

6.9 grams fat per serving

Low-cholesterol variation

¼ cup (½ stick) butter or margarine
1⅓ cups crushed graham crackers
2 tablespoons sugar

1. Place the butter in a 9-inch microwave-safe pie plate. Microwave on MEDIUM for 2 to 3 minutes, or until melted (see Note).
2. Add the crumbs and sugar. Stir to mix well. With the back of a spoon, press the mixture against the sides and bottom of the plate to form an even crust.
3. Microwave on HIGH for 1½ to 2 minutes, or until set.
4. Allow to cool before filling.

Butter or margarine is melted on the MEDIUM setting to prevent excess spattering and popping.

SERVING SUGGESTION:
A quick crust for ice-cream pies (pages 283–85).

VARIATIONS CINNAMON-NUT CRUMB CRUST (8.2 grams fat per serving): Substitute ⅓ cup finely ground nuts for ⅓ cup of the graham-cracker crumbs. Add ½ teaspoon ground cinnamon.

COOKIE-CRUMB CRUST (6.9 grams fat per serving): Eliminate the sugar. Substitute 1⅓ cups vanilla wafers, chocolate wafers, or gingersnaps for the graham crackers. If using gingersnaps, add 1 teaspoon ground ginger to the crumbs.

TORTILLA CHIP CRUST (8.1 grams fat per serving): Substitute tortilla corn chips for graham crackers. Makes a salty-sweet crust for Chocolate Chip–Tequila Pie. (For the adventuresome palate.)

10-INCH CRUST: Increase the butter to 5 tablespoons. Increase the crumbs to 1½ cups and the sugar to 3 tablespoons. Follow the basic cooking times.

LOW-CHOLESTEROL HONEY-GRAHAM CRUST (2.1 grams fat per serving): Combine 1½ cups graham-cracker crumbs with 4 tablespoons honey in a pie plate until the crumbs stick together. Press into pie pan.

Sorbet

The freezer helps one take advantage of fresh fruit by turning it into a frozen dessert called *sorbet* quickly and easily.

French sorbets are similar to American ices in that they are a frozen combination of fresh fruit, fruit juices, and sweeteners. Unlike ice creams, no milk or eggs are included. Because of this, and because additional juices are added, they must be stirred during freezing to prevent ice crystals from forming. Our sorbets are predominantly made of fruit, with relatively little fruit juice, so no stirring is needed during freezing. Like French sorbets, they are best eaten immediately after they are made.

NOTE If the sorbet is frozen too hard to scoop, microwave on DEFROST for 1 to 3 minutes, or until soft enough to scoop.

Strawberry Sorbet

MAKES: *8 servings*
COOKING TIME: *1 minute*

Low cholesterol

0.2 gram fat per serving

SERVING SUGGESTION:
Serve a scoop on breakfast cereal for a delicious change of pace.

1 bag (16 ounces) frozen unsweetened strawberries
2 tablespoons sugar
½ cup low-fat plain yogurt
1 tablespoon triple sec or frozen orange juice

1. Place the bag of frozen strawberries in the microwave oven and heat on DEFROST for 1 minute, or until partially defrosted.
2. Pour into the bowl of a food processor and chop into small pieces by pulsing on and off eight to ten times.
3. Add the remaining ingredients and process until smooth.
4. Serve immediately as a soft cream or spoon into a container and return to freezer for scooping later.

Strawberry-Banana Sorbet

MAKES: *8 servings*
COOKING TIME: *30 seconds*

0.1 gram fat per serving

SERVING SUGGESTION:
Serve garnished with mint leaves.

A perfectly ripened banana makes this wonderful concoction smooth and creamy.

1 bag (8 ounces) frozen unsweetened strawberries
2 tablespoons sugar
1 ripe banana

1. Place the strawberries in the microwave oven and heat on DEFROST for 30 seconds, or until partially defrosted.
2. Pour into the bowl of a food processor and chop into small pieces by pulsing on and off six to eight times.
3. Add remaining ingredients and process until smooth.
4. Serve immediately as a soft cream or spoon into a container and return to freezer for scooping later.

Mango Sorbet

MAKES: *8 servings*

Low cholesterol

0.1 gram fat per serving

SERVING SUGGESTIONS:
Serve at breakfast scooped onto fresh fruit salad, or as a dessert or snack later in the day.

2 ripe mangoes (2 pounds), peeled and seeds removed
2 tablespoons sugar
½ cup nonfat plain yogurt
2 tablespoon orange-flavored liqueur (triple sec) or orange juice
1 teaspoon vanilla

1. Cut the mangoes into 1-inch chunks and place on a dish.
2. Put the mango in the freezer for 1 hour, or until partially frozen (see Note).
3. Place the partially frozen mango pieces in the bowl of a food processor along with the remaining ingredients and pulse on and off until a smooth cream is formed.
4. Serve immediately as a soft cream or spoon into a container and return to freezer for scooping later.

NOTE   If the mango is frozen hard, microwave for 1 minute on DEFROST to defrost partially.

Peach Sorbet

MAKES: *8 servings*

No cholesterol

0.1 gram fat per serving

SERVING SUGGESTION:
Serve a double peach treat by topping with ripe fresh peach slices.

4 peaches

1. Poach peaches as in Perfectly Poached Peaches (page 240).
2. Reserve cooking juices. Quarter each peach half and place the pieces on a plate. Place in the freezer for at least 1 hour to freeze partially.
3. Place the frozen peach pieces and reserved cooking juices in the bowl of a food processor and pulse on and off until a smooth cream is formed.
4. Serve immediately as a soft cream or spoon into a container and return to freezer for scooping later.

Sorbet Sandwiches

0.3 gram fat per sandwich

When whipping up one of the sorbets, use half of the batch for these yummy mini-sandwiches. Kids and adults adore them.

Line a cookie sheet with twenty-five vanilla, chocolate, or lemon wafers. Top each with a well-rounded teaspoon of sorbet; push another wafer on top and freeze for at least 1 hour, or until set. At this time you may wish to transfer them to a plastic freezer bag and return to the freezer. These keep for about 1 month.

Country Kitchen Apple Pie with a New Twist

MAKES: *10 servings*
COOKING TIME: *16 to 24 minutes*

15 grams fat per serving

SERVING SUGGESTIONS:
Serve warm, at room temperature, or chilled, with Customized Cinnamon Ice Cream (page 278) or a slice of cheddar cheese.

This pie has a flaky crust and fresh-tasting fruit because it is baked in the microwave and then browned in a conventional oven.

2 recipes Basic Pastry (page 172)
6 cups tart apples, peeled, cored, and cut into ¼-inch slices
½ to ¾ cup sugar
1 tablespoon fresh lemon juice
1 tablespoon cornstarch
1 teaspoon ground cinnamon

1. Make the pastry dough and chill.
2. Preheat the conventional oven to 425° F.
3. On a lightly floured surface, roll out one pie-dough ball into a 12-inch circle. Place the rolled dough into a 9-inch microwave-safe pie plate to form a bottom crust.
4. In a large mixing bowl, toss together the apples, sugar, lemon juice, cornstarch, and cinnamon.
5. Roll out the top crust in the same manner as the bottom crust.
6. Spoon the filling evenly into the bottom crust.
7. Place the top crust over the apples. Cut a few decorative slashes in the upper crust to vent the steam.
8. Tuck the upper crust under the lower crust. Flute the edges or press with a fork.
9. Microwave on HIGH for 8 to 12 minutes, or until the juices start to bubble through the slits in the crust, rotating one-quarter turn after 4 minutes.
10. Transfer to the preheated conventional oven. Bake for 8 to 12 minutes, or until the crust is golden brown.

NOTE   If using frozen fruit, defrost before mixing with the other ingredients.

VARIATIONS   RHUBARB PIE: Substitute the following rhubarb filling for the apple filling: In a large mixing bowl, combine 4 cups rhubarb, cut into ½-inch pieces, 1¼ cups sugar, and ¼ cup all-purpose flour. Mix well and spoon into the crust.

FRESH BERRY OR CHERRY PIE: Substitute the following berry or cherry filling for the apple filling: In a large mixing bowl, combine 2 tablespoons cornstarch, ¼ cup water or fruit juice, and 1 tablespoon fresh lemon juice. Stir into the fruit.

Chocolate Custard Sauce

MAKES: 1½ cups
COOKING TIME: 4 to 6 minutes

4.9 grams fat per ¼ cup

SERVING SUGGESTIONS:
Serve with fresh berries or poached pears.

A childhood favorite. Grandmother didn't make the white-chocolate variety, but we love it.

1 cup milk
1 ounce semisweet chocolate pieces, or chocolate chopped into ½-inch pieces
3 tablespoons sugar
3 egg yolks, lightly beaten
1 teaspoon vanilla or rum extract

1. In a 4-cup glass measure, combine the milk, chocolate, and sugar. Microwave on HIGH for 3 to 4 minutes, or until the chocolate is melted.
2. Add the egg yolks slowly, in a steady stream, whisking constantly.
3. Microwave on HIGH for 1 minute; whisk to blend. If the sauce is still not thick enough, microwave on HIGH for 30 seconds more and beat until smooth.
4. Stir in the vanilla. Cool to room temperature. Press a sheet of plastic wrap directly on the sauce to prevent a "skin" from forming.

NOTE The sauce can be stored in the refrigerator for up to 3 days.

VARIATION WHITE CHOCOLATE CUSTARD SAUCE (4.9 grams fat per ¼ cup): Substitute white chocolate pieces for semisweet chocolate pieces.

Peach Melba

MAKES: 4 servings

No-cholesterol variation

7.1 grams fat per serving

SERVING SUGGESTIONS:
Cook Perfectly Poached Peaches (page 240) during

1 recipe Perfectly Poached Peaches (page 240), or 1 package Freezer-Poached Peaches (page 337), defrosted
4 scoops vanilla ice cream
1 recipe Quick Raspberry Sauce (page 282) or Melba Sauce (page 338), defrosted
Fresh mint (optional)

Place the peaches, cut sides up, in four dessert dishes. Top each with a scoop of ice cream and 2 tablespoons of sauce. Garnish with mint if desired.

peach season. Store them in the freezer, along with the other ingredients for this dessert, for year-round serving.

No-Cholesterol Peach Melba (3 grams fat per serving): Substitute nonfat frozen yogurt for ice cream.

Pineapple Rings Filled with a Light Pineapple Mousse

MAKES: *6 servings*
COOKING TIME: *11 minutes*

15 grams fat per serving

SERVING SUGGESTIONS:
Sprinkle pineapple mixture with chopped nuts or raspberries.

Lightly poached pineapple pieces are frozen and then whirred into an airy mousse that is mounded on top of green-rimmed pineapple slices.

1 pineapple (3 to 4 pounds)
2 tablespoons rum
1 tablespoon fresh lemon juice
¼ cup sugar
1 packet (1 tablespoon) unflavored gelatin
½ teaspoon ground cardamom
1 cup heavy cream
A few pineapple leaves for garnish

1. With a sharp knife, cut about 1 inch off the top and bottom of the pineapple. Set aside the top leaves for garnish.
2. Cut the remaining pineapple into six crosswise disks, approximately ¾ inch wide.
3. Cut the flesh from each pineapple disk, leaving a ½-inch ring. Cover the rings and refrigerate for filling later.
4. Slice the flesh into ½-inch cubes, removing the core while cutting. (You should have about 4 cups of fruit.)
5. In a 10-inch microwave-safe pie plate, combine the rum, lemon juice, and sugar. Microwave on HIGH for 2 to 3 minutes, stirring after 1 minute to dissolve the sugar. Stir in the pineapple.
6. Cover with waxed paper and microwave on HIGH for 6 to 8 minutes, stirring once after 3 minutes, until the pineapple is cooked through. Set aside.
7. In a large microwave-safe mixing bowl, mix 3 tablespoons of water with the gelatin. Stir. Microwave on HIGH for 35 to 45 seconds, or until dissolved. Stir the pineapple mixture and cardamom into the gelatin.
8. Cover and speed-chill in the freezer for ½ hour, or refrigerate for 1 hour.
9. Whip the heavy cream and fold into the chilled pineapple mixture. Let chill for 3 hours, or overnight.
10. To serve: Divide the pineapple mixture between six reserved rings, which have been placed on individual serving plates. Garnish with a few pineapple leaves.

Nectarines Poached in Sake with Green-Tea Custard

MAKES: *4 servings*
COOKING TIME: *18 minutes*

8.6 grams fat per serving

We had always poached fruits in the microwave oven using the conventional method of removing the skins before cooking. Then we discovered that leaving the skins on the nectarines not only made peeling a breeze but also left a rosy glow on the fruit after the skin is pulled off.

When Marcia met her husband Koji, we learned more about Oriental flavorings, and specifically that sake was an interesting substitute for wine in poaching. The idea for Green-Tea Custard also came from their many trips to Japan.

¼ cup sake
1 tablespoon fresh lemon juice
2 tablespoons sugar
½ teaspoon ground cinnamon
4 star anise (optional) (see Note)
4 large nectarines, halved and pitted
1 recipe Green-Tea Custard (recipe follows)
4 shiso leaves (see Note) or mint leaves

1. In a 2-quart microwave-safe casserole, combine the sake, lemon juice, sugar, cinnamon, and star anise; stir well. Add the nectarines, cut sides down.
2. Cover with a lid or with plastic wrap turned back slightly. Microwave on HIGH for 2 minutes. Turn the nectarines over. Cover again and microwave on HIGH for 1½ to 2 minutes, or until tender. Let stand for 2 minutes.
3. Gently slide off peels, cover and chill for at least 1 hour.
4. Strain the poaching liquid into a 2-cup glass measure. Reserve the star anise for garnish.
5. Re-cover the nectarines and return to refrigerator.
6. Microwave the poaching liquid on HIGH for 3 to 4 minutes to reduce to a 2-tablespoon glaze. Cover and refrigerate the glaze until serving time. (Both may be refrigerated up to 3 days.)
7. To serve: Arrange two nectarine halves, cut sides down, on each of four dessert plates. Spoon Green-Tea Custard Sauce around the nectarines. Garnish with a shiso leaf. Brush the nectarines with the glaze.

NOTE   You can find star anise and shiso leaves in specialty and Asian markets.

Green-Tea Custard

MAKES: *About 2 cups*
COOKING TIME: *6 minutes*

1½ cups milk
2 Chinese or Japanese green-tea bags (see Note)
4 large egg yolks
¼ cup sugar
2 tablespoons flour

1. Pour the milk into a 4-cup glass measure. Microwave on HIGH for 3 minutes, or until almost boiling.

8.6 grams fat per ½ cup

If you've ever been to Japan, you've probably noticed that everything—from cakes to ice cream—is flavored with green tea. At first, to the Western eye, the resulting green tint looks strange—like something that would only be reserved for St. Patrick's Day here. But the tea lends a very delicate flavor, and the light green color is really very pleasing, especially for summer desserts.

2. Immerse the tea bags in the hot milk and let steep for 5 minutes.
3. Meanwhile, in a 2-quart microwave-safe casserole, beat the egg yolks and sugar with a wire whisk until well blended. Stir in the flour.
4. Gradually pour the heated milk into the egg mixture, beating constantly.
5. Microwave on HIGH for 1 minute; beat with a whisk. Microwave on HIGH for 2 to 3 minutes more, until thickened, beating every 30 seconds.
6. Place a piece of plastic wrap directly on the cream, to prevent a skin from forming. Chill until serving time or up to 3 days.

NOTE   Available in specialty and Asian markets.

Gratin of Warm Berries with Lemon or Orange Sherbet

MAKES: *4 servings*
COOKING TIME: *Less than 5 minutes*

Low-cholesterol variation

5 grams fat per serving

¼ cup orange-flavored liqueur (triple sec)
2 tablespoons unsalted butter
2 tablespoons sugar
1 tablespoon grated orange rind
2 cups berries (a mixture of what is available; we like ½ cup each blueberries, red raspberries, black raspberries, and strawberries, sliced)
1 pint lemon or orange sherbet
Long threads of orange rind
Mint leaves

1. In a 2-quart microwave-safe casserole, combine the liqueur, butter, sugar, and grated rind. Microwave on HIGH for 1½ to 2 minutes, or until the butter is melted, stirring to dissolve the sugar.
2. Gently fold in the berries to coat.
3. Cover with waxed paper. Microwave on HIGH for 1 to 2 minutes, or until just slightly heated.
4. Place a scoop of sherbet on each of four serving dishes. Spoon the berries and juices around the sherbet and garnish with orange strips and mint leaves.

VARIATION   LOW-CHOLESTEROL GRATIN OF WARM BERRIES WITH LEMON OR ORANGE SHERBET (1.9 grams fat per serving): Eliminate the butter.

Strawberry-Rhubarb Compote

MAKES: *4 cups*
COOKING TIME: *8 to 10 minutes*

0.1 gram fat per ½ cup

SERVING SUGGESTIONS:
Serve as a dessert with cookies or over frozen yogurt or ice cream. Or try our favorite ways—with chocolate cake or as a filling for Cream Puffs (page 277). Don't forget the whipped cream!

1 pound rhubarb, cut into ½-inch pieces
½ cup sugar
1 teaspoon grated orange rind
2 tablespoons orange-flavored liqueur (triple sec) or orange juice
1 pint strawberries, hulled and sliced

1. Combine all the ingredients except the strawberries in a 2-quart microwave-safe casserole or 4-cup glass measure. Cover with a lid or with plastic wrap turned back slightly. Microwave on HIGH for 5 minutes.
2. Stir in the strawberries. Cover again and microwave on HIGH for 3 to 5 minutes, or until the rhubarb is tender. Chill.

Conventional Cakes

Each of the following three cakes can be quickly mixed in the food processor and then baked conventionally in just 25 to 30 minutes. Meanwhile, the microwave can be humming with a fragrant soup or stew. By coordinating your kitchen appliances in this way, you can turn out a complete meal in less than an hour.

Mom's Mystery Cake

MAKES: *8 servings*
COOKING TIME: *30 to 35 minutes*

No-cholesterol variation

19 grams fat per serving

1 cup all-purpose flour
1 cup brown sugar
1 teaspoon baking soda
1 teaspoon ground cinnamon
1 teaspoon ground nutmeg
1 cup grated carrot
½ cup chopped walnuts
½ cup applesauce
¼ cup plain yogurt
½ cup vegetable oil
1 egg, lightly beaten

1. Preheat the conventional oven to 350° F.
2. Grease the bottom of an 8-inch round baking pan.

A great snack or brunch cake. Sprinkle with confectioners' sugar or spread with Cream-Cheese Frosting (page 296).

We call this Mom's Mystery Cake because whenever we've served it to friends who haven't tasted it before, they say, "This is delicious—what's in it? Can I have the recipe?"

Line the bottom of the pan with a piece of waxed paper cut to fit. Grease the paper and sprinkle with about 1 teaspoon flour, tapping the sides of the pan to distribute the flour evenly.

3. In the bowl of a food processor, combine the flour, sugar, baking soda, cinnamon, and nutmeg. Pulse on and off two to three times to blend.

4. Add the remaining ingredients and pulse on and off four to five times, or until the flour just disappears. Do not overprocess.

5. Pour the batter into the prepared pan and smooth the top with a rubber spatula.

6. Bake in the conventional oven for 30 to 35 minutes, or until a toothpick inserted near the center comes out clean.

7. Cool on a wire rack for 5 minutes before removing from the pan. Finish cooling on the rack.

VARIATION   NO-CHOLESTEROL MYSTERY CAKE (18 grams fat per serving): Substitute canola oil, if available, for vegetable oil, nonfat yogurt for regular, and 2 egg whites for whole egg.

Old-Fashioned Gingerbread

MAKES: *8 servings*
COOKING TIME: *25 to 30 minutes*

No-cholesterol variation

8 grams fat per serving

SERVING SUGGESTIONS:
Serve warm with real whipped cream, Spring Rhubarb Sauce (page 242), Warm Berry Sauce (page 282), or vanilla ice cream or frozen yogurt.

1 cup all-purpose flour
½ cup brown sugar
2 teaspoons ground ginger
1 teaspoon ground cinnamon
¼ teaspoon ground cloves
¼ teaspoon freshly ground black pepper
½ teaspoon salt
1 teaspoon baking soda
1 tablespoon unsweetened cocoa
½ cup molasses
¼ cup plain yogurt
¼ cup vegetable oil
1 egg, lightly beaten

1. Preheat the conventional oven to 350° F.

2. Grease the bottom of an 8-inch round baking pan. Line the bottom of the pan with a piece of waxed paper cut to fit. Grease the paper and sprinkle with about 1 teaspoon flour, tapping the sides of the pan to distribute the flour evenly.

3. In the bowl of a food processor, combine the flour, sugar, ginger, cinnamon, cloves, pepper, salt, baking soda, and cocoa. Pulse on and off two to three times to blend.

4. Add the remaining ingredients and pulse on and off four to five times, or until the flour just disappears. Do not overprocess.

5. Pour the batter into the prepared pan and smooth the top with a rubber spatula.

6. Bake in the conventional oven for 25 to 30 minutes, until a toothpick inserted near the center comes out clean.

7. Cool on a wire rack for 5 minutes before removing from the pan. Finish cooling on the rack.

VARIATION

No-Cholesterol Gingerbread (7.2 grams fat per serving): Substitute nonfat yogurt for regular, canola oil for vegetable oil, and 2 egg whites for whole egg. Serve with Spring Rhubarb Sauce, Warm Berry Sauce, or frozen nonfat yogurt.

Cream-Cheese Frosting

MAKES: *Enough to frost 1 cake layer serving 8*
COOKING TIME: *About 1 minute*

5.5 grams fat per serving

SERVING SUGGESTIONS: Spread on Old-Fashioned Gingerbread (page 295) or Mom's Mystery Cake (page 294).

4 ounces cream cheese
2 tablespoons butter
¼ cup confectioners' sugar
½ teaspoon vanilla
1 teaspoon fresh lemon juice
½ teaspoon lemon zest

1. In a 1-quart microwave-safe bowl, combine the cream cheese and butter.

2. Microwave on DEFROST for 35 seconds to 1 minute to soften.

3. Beat in the remaining ingredients until smooth. Spread on cake.

Glazed Chocolate Cake

MAKES: *8 servings*
COOKING TIME: *25 to 30 minutes*

No-cholesterol variation

Low-fat variation

13.7 grams fat per serving

1 cup all-purpose flour, plus extra for flouring pan
¼ cup unsweetened cocoa
1 cup brown sugar
¾ teaspoon baking soda
½ teaspoon salt
⅓ cup vegetable oil
¼ cup plain yogurt
1 teaspoon vanilla
1 egg, lightly beaten
1 recipe Chocolate Glaze (recipe follows)

1. Preheat the conventional oven to 350° F.
2. Grease the bottom of an 8-inch round baking pan. Line the bottom of the pan with a piece of waxed paper cut to fit. Grease the paper and sprinkle with about 1 teaspoon flour, tapping the sides of the pan to distribute the flour evenly.
3. Pour ½ cup water into a 2-cup glass measure; stir in the cocoa. Microwave on HIGH for 1½ to 2 minutes, until just boiling. Stir well to dissolve the cocoa.
4. Meanwhile, combine the flour, sugar, baking soda, and salt in the bowl of a food processor. Pulse on and off two to three times to blend.
5. Pour in the remaining ingredients, including the water-cocoa mixture (but excluding the Chocolate Glaze), and pulse on and off four to five times, or until the flour just disappears. Do not overprocess.
6. Bake in the conventional oven for 25 to 30 minutes, or until a toothpick inserted near the center comes out clean.
7. Cool on a wire rack for 5 minutes before removing from the pan. Finish cooling on the rack.
8. Transfer the cake to a serving plate and coat with the glaze.

VARIATIONS NO-CHOLESTEROL CHOCOLATE CAKE (9.7 grams fat per serving): Substitute canola oil for vegetable oil, nonfat yogurt for regular, and 2 egg whites for whole egg. Omit the glaze; sprinkle with confectioners' sugar instead. Serve with Strawberry "Sorbet" (page 287), Spring Rhubarb Sauce (page 242), or Quick Raspberry Sauce (page 282).

LOW-FAT CHOCOLATE CAKE (7 grams fat per serving): Prepare pan by spraying with nonstick vegetable spray.

Substitute ½ cup applesauce for oil, nonfat yogurt for regular, and 2 egg whites for the whole egg. Sprinkle with confectioners' sugar. Serve with Strawberry Sorbet (page 287), Spring Rhubarb Sauce (page 242), or Quick Raspberry Sauce (page 282).

Chocolate Glaze

MAKES: *Enough to glaze 1 cake layer serving 8*
COOKING TIME: *2 to 4 minutes*

3 grams fat per serving

¼ cup light cream or half-and-half
4 ounces semisweet chocolate pieces
1 tablespoon vanilla or brandy

1. In a 2-cup glass measure, combine all the ingredients.
2. Microwave on HIGH for 2 to 4 minutes, stirring after 1½ minutes and checking every 30 seconds thereafter to see if the chocolate has become soft and spreadable. (Stirring often is necessary to redistribute heat to ensure even melting.)
3. Remove from the oven and stir for 2 minutes, just until well blended, thickened, and smooth.
4. Pour the warm glaze over the top of the cake. With a rubber spatula, spread it lightly down the sides.
5. Chill until set.

Peanut Brittle

MAKES: *About 2 pounds*
COOKING TIME: *8 to 12 minutes*

7.7 grams fat per ounce

SERVING SUGGESTIONS:
Eat while watching videos, or crush and sprinkle over vanilla ice cream that has been topped with warm Butterscotch Sauce (page 280).

We remember crunching on large round pieces of peanut brittle that we purchased at the candy counter of our local

2 cups sugar
½ cup light corn syrup
3 tablespoons warm water
2 tablespoons unsalted butter
1 teaspoon vanilla
2 cups roasted peanuts
1 teaspoon baking soda

1. Lightly grease a cookie sheet.
2. In a 3-quart microwave-safe casserole, combine the sugar, corn syrup and water, stirring well to mix.
3. Microwave, uncovered, on HIGH for 4 to 6 minutes, or until boiling; stir. Microwave on HIGH for 4 to 6 minutes more, or until the syrup reaches 290° F, or the beginning of the hard-crack stage (see Note).
4. When the bubbling stops, stir in the butter, vanilla, and nuts; blend well. Stir in the baking soda. (This will make a light, airy brittle.)
5. Pour immediately onto the greased cookie sheet. Let

cool for about 30 minutes; break into pieces.
6. Store in an airtight container.

movie theater on Saturdays. When we reminisce about those days, we whip up a batch of this candy, rent a video, turn down the lights, and munch away.

NOTE   If using a regular candy thermometer, test the temperature of the syrup outside of the oven. (It will take 2 minutes to register accurately.) For an accurate reading, don't let the thermometer touch the bottom of the dish. A microwave candy thermometer can be left in the dish during cooking.

If you don't have a candy thermometer, drop a small amount of syrup into a glass of ice water. The syrup will separate into threads that are hard and brittle.

Fruit-Granola Pinwheels

MAKES: *1 serving*
COOKING TIME: *2 minutes*

8.5 grams fat per serving

Kids help

SERVING SUGGESTION:
A great fruit snack for children.

This paper-wrapped "pie" is easy for children ten and up to make.

1 medium apple, pear, plum, nectarine, or peach,
   washed but not peeled
¼ cup granola
1 tablespoon orange juice
1 teaspoon butter or margarine
Dash cinnamon (optional)
Length of colorful, nonmetallic ribbon
Frozen vanilla yogurt (optional)

1. Cut a 12-inch square of parchment paper (see Note). Cut the fruit lengthwise into ¼-inch slices and remove seeds.
2. Sprinkle 2 tablespoons granola in a 6-inch circle in the center of the paper.
3. Arrange the fruit in a pinwheel on top of the granola.
4. Sprinkle with the remaining granola and orange juice.
5. Cut the butter into four pieces and place on top of the granola. Add the cinnamon.
6. Pull the corners of the parchment paper together and twist the top to secure. Tie with the ribbon.
7. Microwave on HIGH for 2 minutes.
8. Untie the ribbon and top with frozen yogurt, if desired. Eat right from the packet.

NOTE   If you don't have any parchment paper, substitute two sheets of waxed paper placed on a paper plate.

THE WELL-STOCKED PANTRY, REFRIGERATOR, AND FREEZER

Where the kitchen pantry is well stocked and the kitchen utensils are adequate one may confidently exclaim, "Ah, a cook lives here."

The Unprejudiced Palate, ANGELO PELLEGRINI

THIS IS one of our favorite chapters because it contains all the elements that give a home cook his or her signature touch. A crock of herbed olives on the table or a pair of homemade bread-and-butter pickles skewered to a sandwich—these are the touches that show people you care about the details of eating.

They are the condiments you want to have on hand for emergencies, or to add spark to an otherwise humdrum meal. They are recipes best prepared in advance, perhaps on a lazy Saturday morning in the kitchen.

We promise that the time you'll spend on them will

pay off for weeks to come. One cooking session will turn out the likes of Garlic-Ginger Vinegar and Walnut-Flavored Oil for sensational salads, a Cranberry Chutney to elevate turkey sandwiches, and a Basic Tomato and Pepper Sauce that can be pulled out of the freezer for that super last-minute pasta dish.

In addition, we offer suggestions on how to keep your pantry, refrigerator, and freezer efficiently stocked with store-bought items. This will help you avoid that "quick trip" to the grocery store—the errand that ends up taking twenty minutes and costing you more than the rest of the meal combined. We've found that such time management makes our lives a little more graceful around mealtime.

PANTRY TIPS
- Keep the room as dark and cool as possible to extend the shelf life of herbs, spices, and oils.
- Potatoes, onions, and winter squash will keep best in a dark, cool place when well ventilated and out of plastic bags.

    Potatoes should never be refrigerated because their starch will convert to sugar and give them a sweet flavor. If stored in a warm place they will shrink. When exposed to light, potatoes will develop a green skin. This can be removed and the potato still eaten. Sprouts should be also removed before potatoes are cooked.
- Store oils and vinegars in containers with tight-fitting lids to avoid spoilage. Store oils in metal or glass containers away from the light. Store vinegars in glass bottles or jars. Use both within 2 months.
- *All baking supplies should be stored in airtight containers to keep out the moisture that causes deterioration.*
- FLOURS: All-purpose flour keeps for 6 months at room temperature and for several years in the freezer. Whole-wheat and other grain flours keep for several months if stored in a cool, dark, dry area. If the temperature exceeds 70° F, refrigerate for 8 to 10 months or freeze for several years.

    CORNMEAL: Keeps for 6 months in a cool, dry place. Warm and damp conditions cause mold to grow and insects to hatch, so if the temperature exceeds 70° F, refrigerate for up to a year or freeze for several years.

BAKING POWDER AND SODA: Keep for 18 months at room temperature.

NONFAT DRY MILK: Keeps in a cool dry place for 6 months, in the refrigerator for a year, and in the freezer for several years.

HONEY: Keep in a cool, dry place. Honey will start to crystallize if it is refrigerated or becomes old. Heating it in the microwave oven can restore it to a liquid state. Remove the lid or—if the jar is more than half full, or plastic—transfer to a glass measure. Heat on HIGH for 2 to 2½ minutes per cup, stirring once.

CHOCOLATE: Keeps for a year if stored at room temperature. If it becomes too cold, a bloom (white coating) will form, which will disappear when chocolate is heated.

NUTS: Keep a month at room temperature, 6 months in the refrigerator, up to a year in the freezer.

DRY YEAST: Store in the refrigerator and use by the date marked on the package.

- Keep track of how long you have had dry spices and herbs by labeling them. When they are past their prime (older than one year), they add little flavor and should be tossed. You can replace each teaspoon of dried herbs with 1 to 2 tablespoons of chopped fresh herbs.
- Dried beans should not be kept for more than a year. After a year they will begin to darken and harden and will require a longer cooking time. Store them in airtight containers.
- All rice should be stored in a tightly sealed container to keep out dust and moisture. If stored in a cool area, white rice should keep for up to a year. Brown rice will keep for 8 months. It can also be stored in the freezer for up to 2 years.
- Other grains should be stored in tightly sealed containers and will keep in a cool, dry area for 8 months. If the pantry gets warm, transfer them to the refrigerator or the freezer. Grains can be frozen for up to a year before their flavors deteriorate.
- Keep items organized so that you know what's there at a glance.
- Keep a pad of paper and a pencil handy to write down

items as they are used up. Replace them during your regular shopping trips.

HOW TO CUSTOMIZE TAKEOUT AND PACKAGED FOODS

- PIZZA: Add Olivada (page 314) or Pesto (page 335).
- FRESH or COOKED PASTA DISHES: Top with Basic Tomato and Pepper Sauce (page 336). (The aroma of the garlic alone will excite the palate!)
- BREADS or BREAD STICKS: Make Tomato Pizza Sauce (page 48) or Olivada (page 314) for a low-cholesterol dip or spread that can be used in place of butter.
- COOKED CHICKEN, MEAT, or FISH DISHES: Serve with Tomato, Plum, or Peach Chutney (page 333 and 331), Corn Salsa (page 334), or All-Purpose Barbecue Sauce (page 214). Try serving the following as flavorful whole-grain side dishes: Multigrain Pancakes (page 20), Couscous (page 124), or Bulghur Pilaf (page 118).
- COLD SLICED MEATS: Make Yogurt Sauce (page 318) and serve with toasted pita bread; or add Sizzled Peppers and Onions (page 209) and serve on toasted hero rolls. Serve Refrigerator Bread-and-Butter Pickle Chips (page 313), Refrigerator Cucumber Pickles (page 313) or Refrigerator Pickled Jalapeño Peppers (page 314) alongside.
- SOUPS: Add Aïoli (page 104), Pistou (page 75), Pesto (page 335), or Olivada (page 314).
- SALAD GREENS: Make Wilted Greens Salad (page 236) or toss with one of the dressings (pages 307–11).
- ICE CREAM: Top with one of the ice-cream sauces (pages 280–83) or Peanut Brittle (page 298).
- POUND CAKE or ANGEL CAKE: Serve with Warm Berry Sauce (page 282), Quick Raspberry Sauce (page 282), or Hot Fudge Sauce and a side of fruit sorbet (page 287), if desired.

Flavored Vinegars and Oils

Flavored vinegars are something that we have been making over the years. When a stew, salad, or soup didn't quite taste right we would splash a few drops of vinegar in to perk up the flavor. Now we sprinkle flavored vinegars over meats, fish, poultry, fruits, and cooked vegetables. Not only do they enhance the flavor of the food; they also eliminate the need for high-fat sauces.

The flavorants depend on what we have growing in our gardens and our particular food fancies at the time. Here we offer a selection of our favorites and encourage you to make some of your own concoctions. A few guidelines:

- Place whole pieces of foods like garlic, peppers, and fruit on wooden skewers to keep them from floating to the top of the jar. This will allow them to flavor the entire bottle of vinegar.
- Make small amounts, since most flavored vinegars keep for only 2 months. This also provides you with an opportunity to try new combinations.
- Allow 2 weeks' steeping time for most of the vinegars. Steeping is best done in a dark area.
- Save those 16-ounce soda bottles—they are just the right size for each one of these recipes.

Walnut-Flavored Oil

MAKES: *1¼ cups*
COOKING TIME: *5 to 6 minutes*

No cholesterol

14 grams fat per tablespoon

SERVING SUGGESTIONS:
This oil will contribute a toasted-nut flavor to breads, salad dressings, or fish. The nuts, which are later removed from the oil, may be sprinkled on salads or ground up to coat fish and chicken fillets before cooking.

1 cup walnut pieces (halves, quarters, etc.)
1½ cups safflower or canola oil

1. Line a 9- or 10-inch microwave-safe plate with paper towel.
2. Scatter the walnuts over the paper towel, leaving the center area open. (This will eliminate any need to stir.) Microwave on HIGH for 5 to 6 minutes, rotating the plate once. (You will know the nuts are toasted when you smell a toasted-nut aroma in the kitchen; be sure not to let them burn.)
3. Put the toasted nuts in the bowl of a food processor; pulse on and off four or five times to chop coarsely.
4. Combine the nuts and oil in a glass jar with a cover; stir well. Cover and store in a cool spot or in the refrigerator for 3 days, shaking the jar every so often to mix. Strain through a fine sieve. Store in a metal container or a jar kept away from the light for up to 2 months.

TO SHELL WALNUTS
OR PECANS IN
THE MICROWAVE OVEN

Place 2 cups nuts and ¼ cup water in a microwave-safe casserole. Cover tightly with a lid or with plastic wrap, turned back slightly to vent steam. Microwave on HIGH for 2 to 3 minutes. Drain, dry, and cool slightly before shelling.

Chili Oil

MAKES: *1 cup*
COOKING TIME: *3 to 4 minutes*

No cholesterol

13.5 grams fat per tablespoon

SERVING SUGGESTIONS:
A lively addition to breads, vegetables, poultry, stir-fries, and fish dishes.

1 cup light olive oil
¼ cup crushed red-pepper flakes

Pour the oil into a 2-cup glass measure. Mix in the pepper. Microwave on HIGH for 3 to 4 minutes, or until hot but not boiling; stir well. Let cool and pour into a small jar. Cover and store in a cool spot or in the refrigerator for 3 days, shaking the jar every so often to mix. Strain through a fine sieve. Store in a metal container or a jar kept away from the light for up to 2 months.

Garlic, Rosemary, and Thyme Vinegar

MAKES: *1½ cups*
COOKING TIME: *3 to 5 minutes*

No fat

SERVING SUGGESTIONS:
Add a little to tomato sauces, gravies, stews, and salads, or dab right onto fish.

2 garlic cloves, peeled
10 black peppercorns
4 sprigs rosemary
4 sprigs thyme or oregano
1½ cups red-wine vinegar

1. Pierce the garlic with a wooden skewer and place in a 16-ounce bottle or jar. Add the peppercorns and herb sprigs.
2. Pour the vinegar into a 4-cup glass measure. Microwave on HIGH for 3 to 5 minutes.
3. Pour the vinegar into the bottle over the garlic and herbs; seal. Let stand in a dark place for 2 weeks, removing the garlic after 2 days.

Garlic-Ginger Vinegar

MAKES: *1½ cups*
COOKING TIME: *3 to 5 minutes*

3 garlic cloves, peeled
3 slices fresh ginger
10 peppercorns
1½ cups rice vinegar or white vinegar

1. Pierce garlic and ginger on a wooden skewer. Place in a 16-ounce bottle or jar. Add the peppercorns.
2. Pour the vinegar into a 4-cup glass measure. Mi-

No fat

SERVING SUGGESTIONS:
Good on meats and
vegetables; adds zest to
stir-frys, salads, and rice.

crowave on HIGH for 3 to 5 minutes, or until hot but
not boiling.
3. Pour vinegar into the jar over the skewered garlic
and ginger; seal. Let stand in a dark place for 2 weeks,
removing the garlic and ginger after 2 days.

Cranberry-
Pepper Vinegar

MAKES: _1½ cups_
COOKING TIME: _3 to 5 minutes_

No fat

SERVING SUGGESTIONS:
Delicious when splashed on
fresh or poached fruits,
especially pears. Dot meats
with it or add to oil for a salad
dressing.

½ cup fresh of frozen cranberries, plus 10 to skewer
10 peppercorns
1½ cups balsamic or red-wine vinegar
½ teaspoon vanilla

1. Pierce 10 cranberries on a wooden skewer; place
skewer in a 16-ounce jar or bottle along with peppercorns.
2. Pour the vinegar into a 4-cup glass measure. Add
the remaining cranberries. Microwave on HIGH for 3 to
5 minutes, or until mixture is hot but not boiling and
the cranberries have popped.
3. Pour the mixture through a fine mesh strainer, then
pour into the bottle over the skewered cranberries;
seal. Store in a dark place for 2 weeks.

Cumin–
Hot Pepper
Vinegar

MAKES: _1½ cups_
COOKING TIME: _3 to 5 minutes_

No fat

SERVING SUGGESTIONS:
Try this in soup, on a salad,
or with fish or chicken cutlets.
It's even good sprinkled on
corn chips.

2 jalapeño peppers, cut in half lengthwise
1 tablespoon cumin seeds
4 sprigs thyme or oregano
1½ cups white-wine vinegar

1. Pierce the peppers on a wooden skewer and place in
a 16-ounce bottle or jar. Add cumin seeds and thyme.
2. Pour the vinegar into a 4-cup glass measure. Microwave on HIGH for 3 to 5 minutes, or until hot but
not boiling.
3. Pour the vinegar into the bottle. Seal with a top or
cork. Store in a dark place for 2 weeks.

Quick Raspberry Vinegar

MAKES: ¼ to ⅓ cup
COOKING TIME: 2 minutes

No fat

SERVING SUGGESTIONS:
Use in Raspberry-Honey Dressing (page 309) or in other salad dressings in place of plain vinegar. Drizzle a few drops over fresh or cooked fruit, cooked vegetables or grilled poultry.

1 package (10 ounces) frozen raspberries
2 tablespoons red-wine vinegar

1. Remove the raspberries from their package. If they are in a metal container, place them in a microwave-safe bowl. Otherwise, leave them in their paper or plastic container.
2. Microwave on DEFROST for 2 minutes. Let stand for 5 minutes.
3. Drain the raspberry juice into a 1-cup glass measure or a small bowl (you should get about ¼ cup), and reserve the raspberries for another use. Add the vinegar to the juice and stir.
4. Pour the vinegar into a bottle. Seal with a top or cork.

Walnut Dressing

MAKES: ½ cup

No cholesterol

9 grams fat per tablespoon

SERVING SUGGESTIONS:
Toss with 6 cups mixed greens to serve four people. Also good spooned over grilled fish or poultry.

⅓ cup Walnut-Flavored Oil (page 304)
2 tablespoons balsamic or wine vinegar
¼ teaspoon salt
⅛ teaspoon freshly ground black pepper

Combine all ingredients in a small bowl and mix well.

Cumin-Chili Dressing

MAKES: 1 cup

⅓ cup olive oil
1 tablespoon fresh lime juice
1 tablespoon Cumin–Hot Pepper Vinegar (page 306)
½ teaspoon ground cumin
1 can (2-ounces) chopped mild green chilies, drained
¼ teaspoon salt
⅛ teaspoon freshly ground black pepper.

No cholesterol

4.5 grams fat per tablespoon

SERVING SUGGESTIONS:
Toss with 2 cups cooked corn, sliced zucchini, canned and drained black beans, or sliced fresh tomatoes. Serve as a side dish with grilled meats or fish.

Combine all ingredients in a small bowl and mix well. Toss with cooked vegetables and chill.

Oriental Dressing

MAKES: ½ *cup (enough for a salad for 4 or 1 pound of meat)*

No cholesterol

1.7 grams fat per tablespoon

SERVING SUGGESTIONS:
Toss with cooked or grated raw vegetables for a vegetable side dish. Spoon over poultry or fish before cooking; serve cooking juices as a flavorful sauce spooned over rice.

2 tablespoons orange juice
2 tablespoons Garlic-Ginger Vinegar (page 305)
2 tablespoons low-sodium soy sauce
1 tablespoon sesame oil
1 tablespoon Dijon mustard with seeds
1 teaspoon grated fresh ginger

Combine all ingredients in a small bowl and mix well.

Sake-Lime Dressing

MAKES: ¾ *cup*
COOKING TIME: *5 to 6 minutes*

No cholesterol

3.7 grams fat per tablespoon

1 garlic clove, minced
3 tablespoons sesame oil
½ cup chopped almonds
¼ cup sake
¼ cup fresh lime juice
2 tablespoons low-sodium soy sauce
1 tablespoon Dijon mustard
1 teaspoon chopped fresh ginger

1. Place garlic, sesame oil, and almonds in a 2-cup glass measure. Microwave on HIGH for 1½ minutes; stir.

SERVING SUGGESTIONS:
Spoon over warm or chilled
meat or vegetable salads.

Microwave for 30 seconds to 1 minute more, or until
nuts are slightly toasted.
2. Add remaining ingredients, stirring well to blend.
Microwave on HIGH for 2 to 3 minutes to warm
through.

Raspberry-
Honey Dressing

MAKES: ¾ cup

No cholesterol

4.5 grams fat per tablespoon

SERVING SUGGESTIONS:
Spoon over fresh or poached
fruits to make flavorful salads.
Makes a nice topping for
grilled poultry.

¼ cup Quick Raspberry Vinegar (page 307)
1 tablespoon fresh lemon juice
1 teaspoon Dijon mustard
¼ cup olive oil
2 tablespoons honey

Combine all ingredients in a small bowl and mix well.

Tomato
Vinaigrette

MAKES: ¾ cup

No cholesterol

6 grams fat per tablespoon

SERVING SUGGESTIONS:
Good over fish fillets, chicken
cutlets, or mixed greens.

1 tablespoon Dijon mustard
3 tablespoons white-wine vinegar
⅓ cup olive or canola oil
¼ teaspoon salt
⅛ teaspoon freshly ground black pepper
1 large ripe tomato, chopped into ¼-inch cubes
2 green onions, thinly sliced

1. In a small bowl, combine mustard, vinegar, oil, salt,
and pepper.
2. Stir in tomato and green onion. Stir well before
serving.

Cranberry Pepper–Honey Dressing

MAKES: ¾ cup
COOKING TIME: *1 minute*

No cholesterol

4.5 grams fat per tablespoon

SERVING SUGGESTIONS:
Drizzle over salads containing fruit or mixed greens and nuts.

¼ cup Cranberry-Pepper Vinegar (page 306)
1 tablespoon fresh lemon juice
1 teaspoon Dijon mustard
1 teaspoon chopped fresh thyme or ¼ teaspoon dried
¼ cup olive oil
2 tablespoons honey

In a 2-cup glass measure whisk all ingredients together. Microwave on HIGH for 1 minute. Whisk again and serve.

Garlic, Rosemary, and Thyme Vinaigrette

MAKES: ⅓ cup

No cholesterol

7.6 grams fat per tablespoon

SERVING SUGGESTIONS:
Toss with salad greens or steamed vegetables. Drizzle over fish or grilled poultry to boost their flavor.

1 tablespoon Garlic, Rosemary, and Thyme Vinegar (page 305)
1 tablespoon fresh lemon juice
3 tablespoons olive oil
¼ teaspoon salt
⅛ teaspoon freshly ground black pepper

Combine all ingredients in a small bowl and mix well.

Mustard Vinaigrette

MAKES: ⅔ cup

No cholesterol

2.3 grams fat per tablespoon

SERVING SUGGESTIONS:
Spoon over vegetables or use as a salad dressing.

This tangy dressing is low in both cholesterol and calories (only 17 calories per tablespoon). It will keep in the refrigerator for 2 weeks.

1 tablespoon olive oil
2 tablespoons Dijon mustard
3 tablespoons wine vinegar or cider vinegar
2 tablespoons chopped fresh parsley
Pinch freshly grated nutmeg
Pinch freshly grated black pepper

Combine all of the ingredients with ¼ cup water in the bowl of a food processor or blender. Pulse on and off three to four times to blend well. Chill.

Large Garlic-Thyme Croutons

MAKES: *24 croutons*
COOKING TIME: *About 5 minutes*

No cholesterol

2.3 grams fat per crouton

These may be stored for up to 2 days in an airtight container.

1 2-inch-diameter loaf French bread (or Italian bread cut in half lengthwise)
¼ cup olive oil
1 garlic clove, finely minced
½ teaspoon freshly ground black pepper
½ teaspoon dried thyme leaves

1. Cut the bread into ¼-inch-thick slices, to make 24 pieces.
2. Line the bottom of a 2-quart (12½ × 7-inch) rectangular microwave-safe dish with a paper towel. Place the bread on top of the paper. (It will just fit.) Microwave on HIGH for 2 minutes. The bread should be dried at this point but not colored. If it is not dried, cook on HIGH for 30 seconds to 1 minute more, checking carefully to make sure the bread doesn't burn. Set aside.
3. Combine the oil and garlic in a 1-cup glass measure. Microwave on HIGH for 1 minute.
4. Remove the paper towel from the dish and reposition the pieces of bread by moving the outside pieces to the inside and the inside pieces to the outside. Spoon or brush the oil-garlic mixture evenly over the bread.

Sprinkle with the pepper and thyme. Microwave on HIGH for 1 to 2 minutes, or until the croutons are crisp.

VARIATION   LARGE GARLIC CROUTONS: Eliminate thyme.

REFRIGERATOR TIPS • Store eggs in the carton in the main part of the refrigerator, not in the door. They will keep for 2 to 3 weeks. After hard-boiling eggs, let them sit in the refrigerator for a few days. This will make them easier to peel.

• Store fresh herbs in an open plastic bag (they'll rot in a sealed bag) in the refrigerator for 1 week to 10 days. If it appears that you won't be using them in that time, chop and freeze parsley and thyme in well-sealed plastic bags, and freeze whole basil and sage leaves in similar bags. Their flavor, though not fresh, will be better than that of their dried counterparts. Cilantro is best chopped and cooked right away.

• Keep one or two sticks of margarine or butter in the refrigerator at all times and freeze additional quantities for up to a year, defrosting upon need. Wrapped and covered tightly, butter keeps 2 weeks and margarine keeps 6 months.

• Replenish lemons every 3 weeks. Lemon juice always perks up a dish, as does grated lemon peel.

• Store tofu, once opened, in the refrigerator covered with water in a tightly sealed container. The water should be drained and new water added every few days. It will keep for up to 1 week. If purchased fresh, unpackaged tofu should be used in 2 to 3 days.

• Store miso (fresh soybean paste), once opened, in the refrigerator, making sure that it is resealed well. It will keep for 3 to 6 months.

• Store chutneys, fruit butters, and relishes, once opened, in the refrigerator. They will keep for at least a week.

Refrigerator Zucchini Pickles

6 small zucchini (1½ pounds), washed and cut in half crosswise
1 garlic clove, peeled and thinly sliced
1 medium onion, peeled and thinly sliced crosswise
2 heads fresh dill flowers, or 1 teaspoon dried dill
1½ cups white vinegar
½ cup sugar

MAKES: *48 pickles*
COOKING TIME: *About 5 minutes*

No fat

This recipe uses about one-third as much salt as the average pickle recipe. It is best made with young zucchini for a crisp, seedless pickle, so choose zucchini that are about 6 inches long and ¼ pound each.

3 tablespoons pickling spices
1 teaspoon salt
¼ teaspoon cream of tartar

1. Cut each zucchini half into lengthwise quarters, making 48 pickles.
2. Combine the remaining ingredients in a 2-quart (preferably flat-bottomed) microwave-safe casserole. Microwave on HIGH for 2 minutes; stir. Microwave for 2 to 3 minutes more, or until simmering; stir.
3. Place the zucchini in the hot brine; cover and refrigerate (see Note). Let stand for 24 hours to develop full flavor, turning the zucchini over once or twice.

NOTE If you plan to keep these longer than a few days, place them in a plastic container with a cover. They will be good for at least a month.

Refrigerate the brine and continue to add to it all summer long.

VARIATION REFRIGERATOR CUCUMBER PICKLES: Substitute 1 pound unpeeled Kirbie or small cucumbers for the zucchini.

Refrigerator Bread-and-Butter Pickle Chips

MAKES: *1 quart*
COOKING TIME: *3 to 5 minutes*

No fat

These are the "chips" of choice to be served with our sandwiches and soups. They will keep in the refrigerator for about a month.

1½ cups cider vinegar
1½ cups brown sugar
2 tablespoons pickling spices
½ teaspoon cream of tartar
1 tablespoon salt
1 cinnamon stick
1 pound unpeeled Kirbie or small cucumbers, cut into ¼-inch slices
1 large onion, peeled and thinly sliced

1. In a 4-cup glass measure, combine the vinegar, sugar, pickling spices, cream of tartar, salt, and cinnamon. Microwave on HIGH for 3 to 5 minutes, but don't allow the mixture to boil. Stir well to dissolve the sugar.
2. Meanwhile, layer the cucumber and onion slices alternately in a 1-quart jar. (You may purchase one especially for this purpose or use a mayonnaise jar.)
3. Pour the hot liquid over the cucumbers. Push the cinnamon stick down into the jar.

Kirbies, or small cucumbers, can be found in many markets almost year-round nowadays.

4. Cover the jar tightly while contents are still hot. Let cool to room temperature and refrigerate for at least 24 hours before serving. Shake the jar two or three times during the first 24 hours.

VARIATION   ZUCCHINI BREAD-AND-BUTTER PICKLE CHIPS: Make these when zucchini is abundant. Follow the recipe above, substituting zucchini for cucumbers.

Refrigerator Pickled Jalapeño Peppers

MAKES: *24 pickles*
COOKING TIME: *3 to 4 minutes*

No fat

SERVING SUGGESTIONS:
Sprinkle on Pizza (page 46), serve as a relish, or slice onto your next tuna salad sandwich —you'll never miss the mayo.

There's always a ready supply of pickled jalapeño peppers in our refrigerator (They keep for at least a month.) Save

1½ cups white vinegar
1 large onion, thinly sliced
1 garlic clove, peeled and crushed
2 teaspoons salt
¼ teaspoon cream of tartar
1 bay leaf, crushed
24 medium jalapeño peppers, washed, with stems on

1. Place all the ingredients, except the peppers, in a 4-cup glass measure. Microwave on HIGH for 3 to 4 minutes, or until the liquid bubbles but *does not boil.* Stir well to dissolve the salt.
2. Meanwhile, arrange the peppers in a clean 1-quart jar with a screw top. Pour the warm liquid over the peppers, pushing the peppers down under the lip of the jar and making sure they are all covered. (If the liquid doesn't completely cover the peppers, add a little more vinegar to cover.)
3. Cover tightly with lid. Let cool to room temperature and refrigerate for at least 24 hours before serving.

VARIATION   SOUTHWESTERN REFRIGERATOR PICKLED JALAPEÑO PEPPERS: Add 1 teaspoon cumin seed to the liquid mixture.

1-quart mayonnaise jars. They just hold these pickles.

Hot peppers are supposed to increase your metabolism temporarily, helping you to burn more calories.

Olivada

¼ pound Greek or Italian olives packed in oil, pitted (about 15)
2 tablespoons fresh lemon juice
1 tablespoon olive oil

MAKES: 1/2 cup

No cholesterol

2.6 grams fat per tablespoon

SERVING SUGGESTIONS:
Serve as a spread for bread, or
place a dollop on Hearty Corn
Chowder (page 70) or
Fisherman's Catch (page 102)
to add a little extra zest.

Called "poor man's caviar" by
some, this spread originated
along the Mediterranean.
Made with full-flavored black
or purple olives, not the
canned variety, it is a great
no-cholesterol spread that can
be substituted for butter on
bread at dinner.
   When packed in a crock, it
makes a nice hostess gift and
keeps, refrigerated, for about
a month.

1/2 teaspoon paprika
1/4 teaspoon dried thyme leaves
1/8 teaspoon dried rosemary leaves

Place all ingredients in the bowl of a food processor.
Pulse on and off until all ingredients are finely chopped
and blended. Pack into a covered crock or jar.

Herb Butter

MAKES: 1/2 cup
COOKING TIME: 1 minute

4.1 grams fat per teaspoon

SERVING SUGGESTIONS:
Serve on grilled vegetables and
fish.

1/2 cup (1 stick) butter or margarine
4 tablespoons fresh herbs (basil and chives are good,
   but any combination can be used)
1/4 teaspoon freshly ground black pepper or dash
   cayenne

1. Place the butter in a small microwave-safe bowl.
Microwave on MEDIUM for 40 to 45 seconds to soften.
Stir in the herbs and pepper.
2. Spoon onto a piece of waxed paper and form into a
roll about 1 inch in diameter. Place in the freezer to
harden (at least 1 hour).
3. To serve, cut into thin slices.

Herbed Cheese Spread

MAKES: 1½ cups

Low cholesterol

1.9 grams fat per tablespoon

SERVING SUGGESTIONS:
This versatile condiment can be spread on toasted bread, served up as a dip for vegetable crudités, or spooned over pasta.

1 container (15 ounces) low-fat ricotta or cottage cheese
1 garlic clove
1 tablespoon fresh lemon juice
¼ cup thinly sliced green onion tops
¼ cup chopped fresh parsley
¼ teaspoon dried thyme leaves
Dash cayenne

1. Spoon the cheese into a colander; allow the excess water to run off while you chop the herbs.
2. Place the metal blade in position in the bowl of a food processor and put the cover in place. Start the processor and add the garlic through the feed tube. With a rubber spatula, push the minced garlic to the bottom of the processor bowl.
3. Add the cheese and the remaining ingredients. Pulse the processor on and off three to four times until well mixed. Spoon into a crock, cover, and refrigerate up to 1 week.

VARIATION HERBED CHEESE OVER PASTA: To serve as a pasta topping, cook the desired amount of pasta on top of the stove. Before draining it, reserve 1 tablespoon pasta cooking water for each bowl of pasta you plan to serve. Place 1 tablespoon cooking water in each serving bowl. Spoon the drained pasta into the bowl or bowls. Spoon ¼ cup cheese spread on top of the pasta and toss with pasta and water. Sprinkle with grated Parmesan.

Sauces

A good sauce adds flavor and dimension to whatever is being served. Sauces cooked in the microwave are virtually foolproof because they don't need constant stirring and won't burn on the bottom. The reason for this is that microwave energy begins heating all sides of the sauce rather than just the bottom, as is the case when sauces are cooked on a burner. The shorter cooking time prevents those natural flavors from cooking away.

Most of these sauces are made for a specific recipe, but just in case you have any left over, we've provided serving suggestions to help use them up. See each recipe for storage time in the refrigerator.

Balsamic Peppercorn Sauce

MAKES: ¾ *cup*

No fat

SERVING SUGGESTIONS:
This zippy sauce is great with poached fish or chicken, either warm or chilled. Spoon over thin slices of beef or fresh oysters and clams.

¼ cup chopped chives or thinly sliced green onion tops
2 tablespoons chopped fresh parsley
1 tablespoon freshly ground black pepper
¼ cup balsamic or Garlic, Rosemary, and Thyme Vinegar (page 305)
¼ cup dry red wine

Combine all ingredients in a small bowl and mix well. Keeps 1 week in the refrigerator.

Salsa Cruda

MAKES: *About 2 cups*

No fat

SERVING SUGGESTIONS:
Serve with nachos and tacos as well as with steamed chicken cutlets, fish, and eggs.

There are many good salsas on the market, but when tomatoes are in season we love to make our own in just minutes.

2 medium-size ripe tomatoes, stemmed and quartered
1 medium onion, peeled and quartered
2 jalapeño peppers, halved (remove seeds if you want a milder salsa)
1 tablespoon fresh lime or lemon juice
½ teaspoon salt
1 tablespoon chopped fresh cilantro (optional)

Place all the ingredients in the bowl of a food processor and chop to desired consistency, or chop by hand. Keeps refrigerated for 2 to 3 days.

Tonkatsu Sauce

MAKES: *About ⅔ cup*

No fat

½ cup catsup
2 tablespoons low-sodium soy sauce
1 tablespoon brown sugar
2 teaspoons Worcestershire sauce
2 teaspoons minced fresh ginger
2 teaspoons fresh lemon juice

SERVING SUGGESTIONS:
Serve with meat sandwiches,
or add to beef or pork platter
meals (page 348).

Combine all ingredients in a small bowl and mix well.
Keeps for 2 weeks in the refrigerator.

Mint Sauce

MAKES: *1 cup*
COOKING TIME: *2 minutes*

No fat

SERVING SUGGESTIONS:
Serve with lamb, grilled
poultry, and fish.

*Fortunately, mint grows like a
weed in our garden, so we can
enjoy this sauce from early
spring until the first snowfall.*

2 tablespoons sugar
½ cup finely chopped fresh mint leaves
½ cup cider vinegar

1. Combine the sugar with 3 tablespoons water in a
1-cup glass measure. Microwave on HIGH for 1 to 2
minutes, or until the water boils; stir to dissolve.
2. Add the mint and vinegar; stir well. Let stand ½
hour to develop the flavor. Store in a covered jar in the
refrigerator for up to 2 weeks. Shake well before
serving.

Yogurt Sauce

MAKES: *1 cup*

No cholesterol

0.3 gram fat per tablespoon

SERVING SUGGESTIONS:
Delicious as a sandwich sauce
or a dipping sauce for crudités.

1 cup nonfat yogurt
1 teaspoon fresh lemon juice
1 teaspoon olive oil
1 garlic clove, finely minced
½ teaspoon cumin powder
¼ cup chopped fresh parsley
¼ teaspoon salt
¼ teaspoon freshly ground black pepper
Dash hot-pepper sauce

Combine all the ingredients in a small bowl and mix
well. Keeps for 2 to 3 days in the refrigerator.

VARIATION   YOGURT SAUCE WITH MINT: Substitute chopped fresh
mint for parsley.

Mint Raita

MAKES: 2 cups

No cholesterol, no fat

SERVING SUGGESTIONS:
Use as a salad dressing or a
dip for crudités. Spoon onto
sandwiches as a flavorful
spread in place of mayonnaise.

*This is a refreshing Indian
sauce; the fresh mint really
gives it character.*

1 cucumber, peeled, seeded, and grated (about 1 cup)
1 cup nonfat plain yogurt
1 tablespoon chopped fresh mint
½ teaspoon ground cumin
Dash cayenne

Combine all the ingredients in a small bowl and mix
well. Chill. Keeps for 2 days in the refrigerator.

Mexican Tomato Sauce

MAKES: 2 cups
COOKING TIME: 6 minutes

No cholesterol

0.4 gram fat per tablespoon

SERVING SUGGESTIONS:
A versatile enchilada-type
sauce. Spoon over Tamales in
the Round (page 153), Polenta
(page 120), or chili-flavored or
regular pasta.

1 tablespoon olive oil
2 garlic cloves, minced
1 onion, coarsely chopped
1 can (28 ounces) crushed tomatoes
2 fresh jalapeño peppers, seeded and finely chopped,
   or 2 Refrigerator Pickled Jalapeño Peppers (page
   314)

1. Combine the oil, garlic, and onion in a 2½-quart
microwave-safe casserole. Microwave on HIGH for 1
minute.
2. Stir in the tomatoes and peppers. Cover with lid or
with plastic wrap turned back slightly on one side.
Microwave on HIGH for 5 minutes, stirring after 3
minutes, or until heated through. Keeps about 1 week
in the refrigerator.

Southwestern Chili Sauce

1 can (8 ounces) tomato sauce with onion
1 can (4 ounces) peeled chopped mild green chilies
¼ teaspoon ground cumin
¼ teaspoon dried oregano
⅛ teaspoon cayenne

MAKES: *About 1½ cups*

No fat

SERVING SUGGESTIONS:
Use in place of Enchilada
Sauce in Tamales in the
Round (page 153), as a dip for
chips or crudités, or with
scrambled eggs or omelets.

Combine all the ingredients in a medium bowl and mix well. Keeps about 1 week in the refrigerator.

Quick Piperade

MAKES: *About 2 cups*
COOKING TIME: *5 to 7 minutes*

No cholesterol

1.7 grams fat per ¼ cup

SERVING SUGGESTIONS:
Use as a topping for fish, omelets, or scrambled eggs.

*From Basque country
comes this lively
red-and-green-pepper
condiment, redolent of olive
oil, garlic, and onions. It is
most often served with
omelets.*

1 tablespoon olive oil
1 large onion, coarsely chopped
1 garlic clove, minced
1 green bell pepper, cut into narrow strips
1 red bell pepper, cut into narrow strips
2 medium tomatoes, chopped into ½-inch cubes
2 tablespoons chopped fresh parsley
¼ teaspoon salt
¼ teaspoon freshly ground black pepper

Combine all the ingredients in a 2-quart microwave-safe casserole. Cover with waxed paper. Microwave on HIGH for 5 to 7 minutes, or until the peppers are tender-crisp, stirring after 3 minutes. Keeps 1 week in the refrigerator.

Warm Tomato Salsa

MAKES: *1 cup*
COOKING TIME: *7 to 8 minutes*

No cholesterol

0.9 gram fat per tablespoon

1 tablespoon vegetable oil
1 garlic clove, minced
1 small onion, chopped
*3 medium tomatoes, peeled and coarsely chopped, or
    1 cup canned tomatoes, coarsely chopped*
1 jalapeño pepper, coarsely chopped
1 teaspoon fresh lemon juice or vinegar
¼ teaspoon salt
¼ teaspoon freshly ground black pepper
Dash hot-pepper sauce (optional)
2 tablespoons chopped fresh cilantro

Serve as a topping for chili and tortillas or as a dip for nachos.

Unlike many salsas, this one is cooked, which allows the flavors of the ingredients to develop even more.

1. In a 4-cup glass measure, combine the oil, garlic, and onion. Microwave on HIGH for 2 to 3 minutes, or until the onion is tender.
2. Stir in the tomato, jalapeño, lemon juice, salt, pepper, and hot-pepper sauce. Microwave, uncovered, on HIGH for 5 minutes, stirring once. Stir in cilantro. Keeps 1 week in the refrigerator.

Honey-Sherry Onion Marmalade

MAKES: *1 cup*
COOKING TIME: *6 to 7 minutes*

No cholesterol

0.9 gram fat per tablespoon

SERVING SUGGESTIONS:
Delicious served on the side with meat, fish, or poultry.

This sweet-and-sour spread can take the place of a high-fat sauce.

1 tablespoon olive or canola oil
2 medium red onions, ½ pound peeled and thinly sliced
2 tablespoons honey
1 tablespoon sherry
1 tablespoon balsamic or wine vinegar

1. Combine the oil and onion in a 1-quart microwave-safe casserole or measure. Cover tightly with a lid or with plastic wrap turned back slightly. Microwave on HIGH for 3 minutes, stirring once.
2. Stir in the remaining ingredients and microwave on HIGH for 3 minutes more. Let stand 3 minutes. Serve warm, at room temperature, or chilled. Keeps 1 week in the refrigerator.

Ginger Sauce

MAKES: *½ cup*

No fat

SERVING SUGGESTIONS:
Spoon over cooked fish fillets, chicken cutlets, or vegetables.

¼ cup low-sodium soy sauce
1 tablespoon orange juice
1 teaspoon rice vinegar
1 tablespoon grated fresh ginger
1 teaspoon Dijon mustard

Place all the ingredients in a small jar and shake well. Keeps 1 week in the refrigerator.

Plum Sauce

MAKES: *2 cups*
COOKING TIME: *8 to 10 minutes*

No cholesterol

0.1 gram fat per tablespoon

SERVING SUGGESTIONS:
Serve warm or chilled with chicken or ham.

1 teaspoon canola or vegetable oil
2 garlic cloves, minced
1 pound California, Santa Rosa, or Nubiana plums, pitted and coarsely chopped
2 tablespoons low-sodium soy sauce
2 tablespoons orange juice
¼ cup brown sugar
½ teaspoon ground cinnamon
¼ teaspoon freshly ground black pepper

1. Combine the oil and garlic in a 1-quart microwave-safe casserole or glass measure. Microwave on HIGH for 35 to 45 seconds to soften but not brown.
2. Add remaining ingredients; cover tightly with a lid or plastic wrap turned back slightly and cook on HIGH for 8 to 10 minutes, or until plums are cooked.
3. Spoon mixture into the bowl of a food processor and puree. Serve warm, at room temperature, or chilled. Keeps refrigerated, when covered, for up to 2 weeks.

Cranberry Sauce

MAKES: *2 cups*
COOKING TIME: *4 to 7 minutes*

No fat

1 package (12 ounces) fresh cranberries
¼ cup orange juice
½ cup sugar (add up to ½ cup more if you like a sweeter sauce)

Combine all the ingredients in a 2-quart microwave-safe casserole. Cover with waxed paper (see Note). Microwave on HIGH for 4 to 7 minutes, or until the berries have popped, stirring after 2 minutes. Serve warm or chilled. Keeps 1 month in the refrigerator.

NOTE This prevents spatters without causing a boilover, the way a lid or plastic wrap would.

VARIATIONS CRANBERRY-PINEAPPLE SAUCE: At the end of cooking, stir in 1 can (16 ounces) unsweetened pineapple chunks, drained, reserving ¼ cup juice. Substitute the ¼ cup reserved pineapple juice for orange juice.

CRANBERRY-ORANGE SAUCE: Peel and thinly slice, crosswise, 6 large naval oranges; remove seeds. Add to cranberry sauce at the end of cooking.

SERVING SUGGESTIONS:
Serve warm or cold with poultry, soups, stews, warm salads, or even with ice cream. It is also delicious served with Tomato-Beef Soup (page 107), or grilled or roasted turkey.

Cooked fresh cranberry sauce is best made in the microwave oven: It's quicker and tastier this way, with much less mess and fuss.

Buy cranberries when they are available in the fall and freeze them right in the bags. When using frozen cranberries in a microwave dish, add 1 minute to the cooking time.

They are also a delicious addition to bran muffins (and make a nice change from raisins). Defrost them first: 1 cup takes about 1 minute on DEFROST.

Apricot-Raspberry Sauce

MAKES: *1 cup*
COOKING TIME: *4 to 6 minutes*

No fat

SERVING SUGGESTIONS:
Serve this flavorful and easy-to-make fruit sauce with grilled or steamed poultry.

1 pound ripe apricots, pitted and halved
1 tablespoon raspberry vinegar

1. Place the apricots in a 2-quart microwave-safe casserole. Cover with a lid or with plastic wrap turned back slightly. Microwave on HIGH for 4 to 6 minutes, or until tender.
2. Spoon apricots into the bowl of a food processor. Add the raspberry vinegar and puree. Keeps for 1 week in the refrigerator.

Creole Sauce

MAKES: *4 cups*
COOKING TIME: *8 to 12 minutes*

No cholesterol

0.2 gram fat per tablespoon; 0.9 gram fat per ¼ cup

SERVING SUGGESTIONS:
Serve with Chicken Breasts (page 185) for a fast dinner that goes well with rice, or

1 medium onion, peeled and quartered
1 garlic clove, peeled
1 celery stalk, cut into 2-inch pieces
1 medium green bell pepper, seeds removed, cut into 2-inch pieces
1 tablespoon olive or vegetable oil
½ teaspoon freshly ground black pepper
½ teaspoon paprika
½ teaspoon cayenne
½ teaspoon dried basil leaves
1 can (14½ ounces) stewed tomatoes
1 can (8 ounces) tomato sauce
½ teaspoon sugar
½ teaspoon Tabasco
1 bay leaf

spoon it over yesterday's meat loaf to add pizzazz. We especially like it served with scrambled eggs or omelets and grits for breakfast.

This spicy, chunky pepper-and-tomato sauce brings taste buds to attention at many New Orleans brunch tables.

1. Place the onions, garlic, celery, and bell pepper in the bowl of a food processor. Pulse on and off five to six times, until coarsely chopped.
2. Scrape mixture into a 2-quart microwave-safe casserole. Add the oil, black pepper, paprika, cayenne, and basil. Cover with waxed paper. Microwave on HIGH for 3 to 4 minutes, or until the vegetables are tender but not browned.
3. Meanwhile, place the tomatoes in the food processor bowl and pulse two to three times, until coarsely chopped.
4. Add the tomatoes to the casserole, along with the remaining ingredients. Cover again and microwave on HIGH for 5 to 8 minutes, or until the flavors are blended, stirring after 3 minutes. Remove the bay leaf. After cooling, the sauce may be sealed and stored up to 1 week in the refrigerator. Freeze any leftover sauce for later use.

Mustard-Horseradish Sauce

½ cup mayonnaise
2 tablespoons Dijon mustard
2 teaspoons horseradish
1 teaspoon fresh lemon juice
1 teaspoon grated lemon rind

Combine all ingredients in a small bowl and mix well. Keeps 2 weeks in the refrigerator.

VARIATION

MAKES: *About ½ cup*

Low-cholesterol variation

5.1 grams fat per teaspoon

SERVING SUGGESTIONS:
Try on any type of fish, warm or chilled. Also makes a great potato topper, sandwich spread, or dip.

LOW-CHOLESTEROL MUSTARD-HORSERADISH SAUCE (5.2 grams fat per teaspoon): Substitute low-cholesterol mayonnaise for regular.

Raspberry-Mint Sauce

MAKES: *1 cup*
COOKING TIME: *4 minutes*

No-cholesterol variation

1.5 grams far per teaspoon

SERVING SUGGESTIONS:
Use as a basting sauce and/or
a condiment with grilled or
poached poultry or fish.

VARIATION

*This fresh and fruity barbecue
sauce is brought to attention
by the addition of fresh mint.
It will bring simple fish or
chicken to new heights.*

1 garlic clove, minced
2 tablespoons unsalted butter
¼ cup catsup
¼ cup firmly packed light brown sugar
2 tablespoons raspberry vinegar
1 tablespoon Dijon mustard
1 cup fresh or thawed frozen raspberries
2 tablespoons chopped fresh mint

1. Combine garlic and butter in a 4-cup glass measure. Microwave on HIGH for 1 minute.
2. Stir in the catsup, sugar, vinegar, and mustard. Microwave on HIGH for 2 minutes; stir well. Microwave on HIGH for 1 minute more.
3. Stir in raspberries and mint. Keeps 1 week in the refrigerator.

NO-CHOLESTEROL RASPBERRY-MINT SAUCE (0.9 gram fat per tablespoon): Substitute 1 tablespoon canola or olive oil for butter.

FREEZER TIPS

- Store all frozen foods in tightly sealed, moisture- and vaporproof containers. When packaging your own food, use heavy-duty foil, self-sealing freezer bags, or plastic containers with tight-fitting lids and label each package with the date. The shrink-wrap film on meats in self-serve counters allows air to enter the package and is not suitable for storage beyond 2 weeks. Overwrap to keep longer.
- When packaging solid foods, leave as little air space as possible to avoid freezer burn.
- Stews and soups need about ¼-inch head space to expand upon freezing. These keep for 3 months.
- Frozen berries, peaches, pears, pineapple, and melon keep for up to a year.
- Frozen peas, corn, and spinach, without sauces, keep for 10 months when home-frozen, 8 months when purchased.

- 1-pound packages of ground beef or turkey keep for 2 to 3 months.
- Homemade sausage patties keep for 2 months, but freezing alters flavors.
- 1-pound packages of skinless, boneless chicken breasts, and chicken pieces keep for 6 months.
- Store-bought baked yeast breads and rolls keep for 6 months, home-baked for 3 months. Frozen bread dough keeps for 1 month. Baked pies keep for 2 months.
- Homemade cakes and quick breads keep for 2 months.
- Frozen cooked food keeps for 3 months.
- Ice cream and frozen desserts keep for 2 months.
- All the storage times given are for 0° F or below. At this temperature, properly wrapped food will be safe to eat. It will also have good flavor and texture and contain all (or nearly all) the nutrients it had when fresh. Check the temperature with a freezer thermometer or outdoor thermometer. If no thermometer is available, use this rule of thumb: If the freezer can't keep ice cream brick-solid, the temperature is above the recommended level. Do not store food for more than 1 week in a freezer whose temperature is above the recommended level.

FREEZING IN THE FAST LANE:
FRUITS, VEGETABLES, AND CONDIMENTS

Foods prepared for freezing in the microwave oven will have a flavor, color, texture, and nutritive value superior to those of foods prepared by the conventional (top-of-the-stove) method. Since the microwave oven works most efficiently on small quantities, we work in batches, chopping one while another is cooking. The method is efficient and the finished results excellent.

When packaging fruits and vegetables for freezing, four principles apply to microwave preparation:

- *Package the produce in heavy-duty plastic bags, freezer containers, or paper boxes, but do not use metal twist ties.* Microwaves penetrate plastic and paper just as easily as glass. Metal twist ties, however, will cause a reflection back and forth between the ends, which will result in a sparking, called *arcing*.

    We prefer plastic bags to rigid containers for most fruits and vegetables because of the "doughnut" theory (below). And foods frozen in plastic bags won't require as much stirring or breaking up while they are defrosting).

- *Combine similar sizes and/or shapes in one container.* When food is heated in the microwave, the outside surfaces become hot before the inside. It is therefore best to cut all the vegetables or fruits that you plan to freeze together into uniform shapes so that the microwaves have more or less the same distance to travel in each piece. This will ensure even defrosting.

  Pair corn kernels with lima beans, for example, or red and green pepper pieces, or peas with cubed carrot. Green beans freeze and defrost most evenly when cut into 1-inch lengths.

  Separate broccoli florets and Swiss chard or spinach leaves from their stems. (A 2-inch broccoli floret with stem is optimum.) Stems and leaves or florets together will defrost unevenly, with the floret defrosting first. Save the stems of broccoli and greens for tasty additions to stir-fry dishes.

  Wash and dry strawberries and blueberries, and cut up rhubarb into ½-inch pieces. Place the rhubarb in 1-pound portions in sealable freezer bags.

- *After filling the bags, lay the contents flat and form a doughnut shape with your fist.* Well, here it is—the secret to all microwave cooking (not exactly, but it works to a great degree). Because microwave energy heats from outside to inside, and because round-sided foods heat more evenly than those with angles, a round container or shape with two surface areas is ideal for even heating. Enter the doughnut shape.

  To create this shape with frozen foods in a bag, push the food toward the edges so that the least amount is in the center. (This allows quicker and more even defrosting.) The "hole" can be created before or after the bag is sealed.

  The degree to which the food holds its doughnut shape will depend on its moisture—spinach leaves will do better than corn. But even a loosely formed "doughnut" will be better than none. The size or uniformity of the hole is not as important as the fact that the sides are formed into fairly equal widths and thicknesses, with no thin edges.

  Fruit pieces in syrup will not work as well in a bag. The extra liquid makes it harder to form the hole in the center, and the syrup tends to seep into the corners of the bag. A precooked tomato sauce, on the other hand, although very liquid, can be manipulated by hand during the defrosting process to equalize the heat from the outside edges to the inside without damaging the contents.

But for fruit that has a lot of liquid, and any food that is very liquidy, plastic containers are the alternative. When you are ready to defrost, you should plan to run hot water over the freezer container first and then remove the contents to a microwave-safe dish. This will avoid any possible overheating in the corners.

- *Package in 1- or 2-cup portions.* Condiments such as chutneys, fruit butters, salsas, and relishes should be frozen in 1-cup portions. (A 1-quart freezer bag holds 1 cup.) Items that are used as part of a main dish, such as tomato sauces, pesto, or applesauce, can be packaged in 1-cup portions to serve one or two, or 2-cup portions to serve four. (A 2-quart freezer bag holds 2 cups.)

The doughnut shape can be formed before or after sealing the bag. The microwave oven is most efficient (i.e., cooks fastest and most evenly) with smaller amounts of food. We therefore recommend that you limit each bag or box to no more than 2 cups.

Fruit Butters

Apple butter is the best-known member of the fruit-butter clan, but we have found that many fruits make these tasty spreads for pancakes or toast. Fruit butters are made with ripe fruit that is cooked to a soft, buttery consistency. This early-American method of putting up fruit for the winter has a decidedly modern-day benefit in that it provides a fat-free substitute for butter. Choosing fruit at its peak sweetness will enable you to keep added sugar on the low side, too.

Marcia remembers her grandmother making fruit butters. In those days, they required long cooking over a low flame, and constant stirring. With less time and more things to do with our hands, we prefer to cook them in the microwave oven. Cooking time is reduced by a third, and only two stirs are required.

Keep in mind that that 3 cups of chopped fruit should be cooked in a 3-quart casserole to prevent boilovers.

Apple Butter

MAKES: *About 3 cups*
COOKING TIME: *16 to 20 minutes*

No fat

The lemon gives this spread a nice spark. Spooned into an earthenware crock, it makes a lovely hostess gift.

2 pounds apples (about 6 medium), washed and cut into eighths
½ cup brown sugar
1 teaspoon grated lemon peel
¼ teaspoon ground cinnamon

1. Place the apples in a 2-quart microwave-safe casserole. Cover with a lid or with plastic wrap turned back slightly. Microwave on HIGH for 8 to 10 minutes, or until apples are tender. Press through a colander or food mill.
2. Return apples to casserole and stir in sugar, lemon peel, and cinnamon. Microwave, uncovered, on HIGH for 8 to 10 minutes more, until very thick, stirring once.

NOTE Even though this recipe can be made in larger amounts, we prefer to start one batch cooking, while cutting and preparing the next. Little cooking time is actually saved by doubling up.

VARIATION PEAR BUTTER: Substitute pears for apples. Substitute ¼ teaspoon ground ginger for cinnamon.

Cherry Butter

MAKES: *4 cups*
COOKING TIME: *40 minutes*

No fat

SERVING SUGGESTIONS:
This is wonderful when spread on Basic Irish Soda Bread (page 64), either of the shredded-wheat breads (pages 41–42), or Old-Fashioned Biscuits Made Light (page 55).

3 pounds (about 7 cups) sweet dark cherries, stemmed and pitted
½ cup packed dark brown sugar
1 teaspoon ground cinnamon

1. In a food processor fitted with the steel blade, combine the cherries and sugar in two batches, until finely chopped.
2. Place the cherry mixture in a 4-quart microwave-safe casserole. Cover with a lid or with plastic wrap turned back slightly. Microwave on HIGH for 20 to 25 minutes, stirring after 10 minutes; stir well.
3. Microwave, uncovered, on HIGH for 20 to 25 minutes, or until very thick.
4. Store in a crock in the refrigerator or freeze in 1-cup portions.

VARIATION CHERRY-RHUBARB BUTTER: Substitute 1½ pounds rhubarb, cut into 1-inch pieces, for half the cherries.

RHUBARB BUTTER: Substitute 3 pounds (about 8 cups) rhubarb, cut into 1-inch pieces, for cherries. Follow recipe, but because rhubarb tends to be tarter than cherries, add an additional ¼ to ½ cup sugar.

Chutney

The origin of the word *chutney* or *chatni* is a word in Sanskrit that means "to lick." Chutney is a spicy condiment usually made from fruits. We were first introduced to this wonderful food by Indians living in this country and later encountered it on travels to India. We have since learned to make our own interesting fruit combinations to give as gifts and add a touch of interest to otherwise simple meals.

Even if you are bringing prepared foods home, you can whip up one of these condiments in a short time. Keep the extras on hand for those days when lunch is no more than opening a can of tuna fish and downing a glass of milk. The tomato chutney, in particular, will transform that plebeian fare into a midday pleasure.

These chutneys are fat- and cholesterol-free and weigh in at around 16 calories per tablespoon! This makes them ideal condiments and healthful alternatives to butter or margarine, which everyone tells us we should cut back on.

Chutneys store well in the refrigerator, tightly covered, for 3 to 4 weeks.

TO FREEZE ANY CHUTNEY

- Divide the chutney into 1-cup portions. Place in sealable freezer bags and freeze until ready to use. Chutney will keep for up to 9 months in the freezer.
- To Defrost: Unseal freezer bag halfway. Microwave the bag and its contents on DEFROST or LOW for 4 minutes, or until the pieces break up but some ice crystals remain. Let stand for 5 minutes, or until the ice crystals disappear. Pour into a serving dish.

Cranberry Chutney

1 medium onion, coarsely chopped
1 cup brown sugar
¼ cup cider vinegar
1 tablespoon grated fresh ginger
½ teaspoon salt

MAKES: *3 cups*
COOKING TIME: *13 to 15 minutes*

No fat

SERVING SUGGESTIONS:
Try serving this flavorful alternative to cranberry sauce with roasted or grilled poultry—it is wonderful! We also like to slather it on turkey sandwiches after Thanksgiving.

1 package (12 ounces) fresh cranberries, rinsed and
   picked over
½ pound Granny Smith apples, cored but not peeled,
   cut into ½-inch cubes
½ teaspoon ground allspice
¼ teaspoon freshly ground black pepper
⅛ teaspoon cayenne

1. In a 3-quart microwave-safe casserole, combine the onion, sugar, vinegar, ginger, and salt. Microwave on HIGH for 3 minutes; stir until sugar dissolves.
2. Stir in the remaining ingredients. Cover with waxed paper (see Note) and cook on HIGH for 10 to 12 minutes, or until cranberries pop, stirring after 5 minutes.
3. Let stand for 10 minutes. Serve warm or chilled.

NOTE   This will allow excess steam to escape and prevent the cranberry mixture from boiling over.

VARIATION   GOOSEBERRY CHUTNEY: Substitute gooseberries for cranberries in the summer, when fresh cranberries are not available.

Peach Chutney

MAKES: *2 cups*
COOKING TIME: *3 minutes*

No fat

SERVING SUGGESTIONS:
Serve with grilled poultry or fish. Delicious on cream-cheese sandwiches.

1 garlic clove, minced
2 teaspoons minced fresh ginger
2 tablespoons cider vinegar
½ cup dark brown sugar
1 pound firm ripe peaches, peeled, pitted, and
   coarsely chopped
½ cup golden raisins
1 tablespoon fresh lime juice
2 teaspoons coarse Dijon mustard
¼ teaspoon salt
⅛ teaspoon cayenne

1. In a 4-cup glass measure combine garlic, ginger, vinegar, and sugar. Cover with waxed paper and microwave on HIGH for 3 minutes, stirring once.
2. Stir in remaining ingredients. Cover again and microwave on HIGH for 8 minutes, stirring once. Pour into a serving crock and chill.

•   Refrigerated chutneys can be stored in tightly covered containers for up to a week.

Mango Chutney

MAKES: *2 cups*
COOKING TIME: *11 minutes*

No fat

SERVING SUGGESTIONS:
This chutney, inspired by the tropics, is perfect with grilled meat or as a yogurt topper.

½ cup dark-brown sugar
2 tablespoons cider vinegar
2 teaspoons minced fresh ginger
1 garlic clove, minced
2 ripe mangoes (1 pound each), peeled, pitted, and coarsely chopped
½ cup golden raisins
1 tablespoon fresh lime juice
2 teaspoons coarse Dijon mustard
¼ teaspoon salt
⅛ teaspoon cayenne

1. In a 4-cup glass measure, combine the brown sugar, vinegar, ginger, and garlic. Microwave on HIGH for 3 minutes; stir to dissolve the sugar.
2. Stir in remaining ingredients. Cover with plastic wrap turned back on one side. Microwave on HIGH for 8 minutes, stirring once.
3. Pour into a serving crock and chill.

Rhubarb Chutney

MAKES: *3 cups*
COOKING TIME: *8 to 10 minutes*

No fat

SERVING SUGGESTIONS:
Serve with any poultry or grilled meat.

This chutney is one of our favorites because it signals spring and tells us that our garden is once again alive with exciting ingredients and fresh flavors.

1 pound rhubarb, cut into ½-inch pieces
¾ cup sugar
½ cup golden raisins
¼ cup white or cider vinegar
1 tablespoon grated fresh ginger
1 garlic clove, minced
1 teaspoon salt
½ teaspoon allspice
½ teaspoon cayenne

1. Place all the ingredients in a 2-quart microwave-safe casserole or 4-cup glass measure. Cover tightly with a lid or with plastic wrap turned back slightly. Microwave on HIGH for 5 minutes; stir.
2. Cover again and microwave on HIGH for 3 to 5 minutes, or until rhubarb is tender. Chill.

VARIATION MINTED RHUBARB CHUTNEY: During the second half of cooking time, add 2 tablespoons chopped fresh mint leaves.

Plum Chutney

MAKES: *4 cups*
COOKING TIME: *14 to 16 minutes*

No fat

SERVING SUGGESTIONS:
Serve with a simple fish fillet or chicken cutlet, or with Potato Virtiniai (page 131).

½ cup cider vinegar
½ cup sugar
1 tablespoon grated fresh ginger
1 garlic clove, minced
½ teaspoon ground cinnamon
½ teaspoon ground allspice
½ teaspoon salt
¼ teaspoon freshly ground black pepper
2 pounds plums, pitted and cut into eighths
1 jalapeño pepper, seeded and minced
½ cup raisins

1. In a 2-quart microwave-safe casserole or glass measure, combine all ingredients except the plums, jalapeño pepper, and raisins. Cover tightly with a lid or with plastic wrap turned back slightly. Microwave on HIGH for 4 minutes; stir until the sugar dissolves completely.
2. Add the remaining ingredients and stir well. Cover again and microwave on HIGH for 10 to 12 minutes, or until the plums are tender, stirring once. Chill.

Tomato Chutney

MAKES: *4 cups*
COOKING TIME: *18 to 28 minutes*

No fat

SERVING SUGGESTIONS:
Serve with eggs, sausage, and grilled meats or alongside cold leftover meats and fish. Serve a dollop on baby corn cakes or cream cheese and crackers for a quick and fabulous appetizer.

½ cup cider vinegar
1 medium onion, chopped
1 cup brown sugar
½ teaspoon ground cinnamon
½ teaspoon salt
⅛ to ¼ teaspoon cayenne (depending on taste)
½ teaspoon dried thyme leaves
1 can (28 ounces) peeled tomatoes, drained and chopped (about 2½ cups), or 1½ pounds fresh tomatoes, peeled, seeded, and chopped (see Note)
½ pound apples (1 large), cored but not peeled, cut into ¼-inch cubes (about 1½ cups)

1. Combine all the ingredients in a 2-quart microwave-safe casserole. Cover with waxed paper. Microwave on HIGH for 18 to 20 minutes, or until the apples are tender and the flavors are blended, stirring twice.
2. Cool and refrigerate. Serve chilled or at room temperature.

NOTE Process the tomatoes in a food processor, briefly (with

This is a favorite condiment of family and friends. We found that canned tomatoes actually

make a more consistently delicious chutney than fresh, so it can be prepared year-round. The flavor improves after a day or two, so make it in advance and keep some on hand.

just one or two pulses) until chunky, instead of chopping, but be careful not to puree.

TOMATO-WALNUT CHUTNEY: Add ½ cup coarsely chopped walnuts at the end of cooking.

• If you don't have any fresh herbs, add 1 tablespoon of chopped parsley to each teaspoon of dried herbs to enhance their flavor.

Corn Salsa

MAKES: *4 cups*
COOKING TIME: *About 10 minutes*

No cholesterol

0.2 gram fat per tablespoon; 0.8 gram fat per ¼ cup

SERVING SUGGESTIONS:
Serve warm, cold, or at room temperature with eggs, grilled meats, poultry, or fish.

1 tablespoon vegetable oil
1 onion, coarsely chopped
3 cups uncooked corn kernels (from about 4 ears), or 2 cans (12 ounces each) corn kernels, drained
½ pound ripe tomatoes, peeled, seeded, and coarsely chopped
½ pound green or red bell peppers, seeded and cut into ¼-inch cubes (1 cup)
1 jalapeño pepper (3 inches long), finely chopped (and seeded if you like your salsa less hot)
¼ cup fresh lime juice
½ teaspoon ground cumin
½ teaspoon salt
½ teaspoon freshly ground black pepper

1. In a 2-quart glass measure or microwave-safe casserole, combine the oil and onion. Microwave on HIGH for 1 minute. Stir in corn and tomato. Cover tightly with lid or plastic wrap turned back slightly. Microwave on HIGH for 6 to 7 minutes, or until the corn is cooked, stirring after 3 minutes.
2. Add the remaining ingredients; stir well. Cover again and microwave on HIGH for 2 to 3 minutes more to develop flavor. Freeze in 1-cup self-sealing freezer bags (see Note).

NOTE To defrost: Place each 1-cup bag in microwave oven. Heat on DEFROST for 3 minutes, or until the pieces break apart but some ice crystals remain. Let stand 5 minutes.

PEELING TOMATOES IN THE MICROWAVE

To peel ½ pound tomatoes: Pour 1 cup water in a 4-cup glass measure or 1-quart microwave-safe bowl. Microwave on HIGH for 2½ to 3½ minutes, or until simmering. Add tomatoes and let stand in water 1 minute. Drain, peel, and seed.

Pesto

MAKES: *About 2 cups*

4.5 grams fat per tablespoon

SERVING SUGGESTIONS:
Pesto makes an exciting pasta sauce. We also like to serve a few spoonfuls on grilled fish or lamb or toss it with 2 cups of cooked fresh peas. Try serving over baked potatoes, too.

This is a pesto to be made for the freezer, as you clear the garden of all the last leaves of basil, mint, or spinach. If you

VARIATIONS

don't have a garden, take advantage of your market's supply. You'll be glad you did in the dead of winter.
   Traditionally, the puree contains basil, pine nuts, garlic, cheese, and olive oil, but if it is made specifically for freezing and serving later, it is best to make it without the cheese. Stirring in freshly grated cheese right before serving adds an enormous flavor boost.

2 cups firmly packed fresh basil leaves, stems removed
¼ cup pine nuts or walnuts
2 garlic cloves, peeled
½ cup olive oil
½ cup grated Parmesan
2 tablespoons grated Romano or additional Parmesan

1. In the bowl of a food processor or blender, combine the basil, nuts, and garlic; chop finely.
2. With the blender or processor motor going, slowly pour in oil. Continue to blend until a fine paste forms.
3. Spoon into small plastic freezer bags. Place the bags on a cookie sheet and freeze. Once frozen, pile up the flattened bags. Keeps for up to 1 year.
4. To serve: Place a bag of pesto in the microwave oven and heat on DEFROST for 3 to 4 minutes, or until pliable. Scrape into a food processor bowl. Add the grated cheeses. Blend until a smooth paste is formed.

MINT PESTO: Substitute mint leaves for basil leaves.

SPINACH PESTO: Substitute spinach leaves for basil leaves and walnuts for pine nuts.

Pear and Pepper Relish

MAKES: 6 cups
COOKING TIME: 21 to 25 minutes

No fat

SERVING SUGGESTIONS:
This condiment is a wonderful accent for grilled meats, poultry, and fish.

The inspiration for this relish comes from Thelma's New England childhood, when her neighbor's pear trees produced more fruit than the family could eat. Back then everyone was still canning, but we have

NOTE

since found that freezing is easier and keeps the relish tastier.

1 large onion, minced
3 garlic cloves, minced
2 tablespoons grated fresh ginger
¾ cup cider vinegar
½ cup brown sugar
2 pounds firm pears, peeled, cored, and coarsely chopped (see Note)
1 green bell pepper, coarsely chopped
1 red bell pepper, coarsely chopped
1 medium jalapeño pepper, seeded and minced
1 teaspoon grated lemon rind
½ teaspoon ground nutmeg
½ teaspoon ground cloves

1. Place the onion, garlic, ginger, vinegar, and sugar in a 2-quart microwave-safe casserole. Microwave on HIGH for 5 minutes; stir well to dissolve the sugar.
2. Add the remaining ingredients; stir well. Cover with waxed paper and microwave on HIGH for 16 to 18 minutes, stirring after 6 minutes. Let cool. Refrigerate the amount that you plan to use within a week; freeze the rest according to the instructions on page 326.

We use the food processor to speed the chopping but chop only 1 pound of pears at a time to keep from overprocessing them.

Basic Tomato and Pepper Sauce

MAKES: Generous 6 cups
COOKING TIME: 13 minutes

Low cholesterol

0.3 gram fat per tablespoon;
1.2 grams fat per ¼ cup

2 tablespoons olive oil
4 garlic cloves, minced
1 onion, chopped
4 pounds ripe tomatoes, peeled, seeded, and coarsely chopped (4 cups)
1 pound bell or long mild peppers, seeded, cut in half crosswise, and then cut into ¼-inch strips
1 can (6 ounces) tomato paste
1 cup fresh basil leaves, chopped
¼ cup grated Parmesan
1 teaspoon salt
½ teaspoon freshly ground black pepper

1. Combine oil, garlic, and onion in a 3-quart microwave-safe casserole. Microwave on HIGH for 2 minutes.

*This is a great sauce to make
when the tomato and pepper
crops are bursting from the
garden. Freeze it in 2-cup
portions for later meals.*

2. Stir in tomato and pepper. Cover with waxed paper and microwave on HIGH for 8 minutes, stirring after 4 minutes. Stir in the remaining ingredients. Cover again and microwave on HIGH for 3 minutes; stir well.
3. Package in generous 2-cup quantities in self-sealing freezer bags; freeze. To defrost, place the bag of sauce in the microwave oven and heat on HIGH for 3 minutes.

Freezer Poached Peaches

MAKES: *32 peach halves*
COOKING TIME: *12 minutes*

No fat

SERVING SUGGESTIONS:
Serve as a side dish with grilled meats or as a dessert with frozen yogurt or in Peach Melba (page 290).

Peeling the peaches after poaching rather than before saves time and leaves each peach half with a beautiful rosy glow.

1 cup sugar
2 tablespoons fresh lemon juice
2 tablespoons vanilla
16 firm ripe peaches, cut in half lengthwise and pitted

1. In a 3-quart microwave-safe casserole, combine sugar, lemon juice, vanilla, and 1 cup water. Cover tightly with a lid or with plastic wrap turned back slightly on one side. Microwave on HIGH for 2 to 3 minutes; stir until sugar dissolves.
2. Place 8 peach halves, cut sides down, in syrup, forming a circle around outside of dish. Cover; microwave on HIGH for 2 minutes. Turn peaches over and cook, covered, for 2 minutes more. With a slotted spoon, remove to a plate. Repeat with remaining peach halves.
3. Slip skins off one batch of peaches while remaining peaches are poaching. After skins are removed from all peaches, place peaches back in syrup to cool for 1 hour.
4. Pack peach halves flat in sealable freezer bags, four halves to a bag, dividing syrup among bags. Freeze flat until ready to use. To defrost, unseal freezer bag halfway. Place in microwave oven and heat on DEFROST or LOW for 3 minutes. Let stand in bag for 5 minutes, until all ice crystals have disappeared.

*TO EXTRACT
MORE JUICE FROM
CITRUS FRUIT*

• Place one lemon, one orange, or one lime in microwave oven. Heat on HIGH for 30 seconds.

Melba Sauce

MAKES: *2 cups*
COOKING TIME: *8 to 10 minutes*

No fat

SERVING SUGGESTIONS: Use in Peach Melba (page 290) or spoon over frozen yogurt.

4 cups raspberries
⅔ cup currant jelly
2 tablespoons raspberry-flavored or other fruit-flavored liqueur (optional)

1. In a 2-quart microwave-safe casserole, combine berries and jelly. Cover tightly with a lid or plastic wrap turned back slightly on one side. Microwave on HIGH for 8 to 10 minutes, or until berries are softened and the mixture begins to boil. Slightly crush berries with a fork; stir in liqueur. Let cool before freezing.
2. Divide sauce into ½-cup portions; pour into sealable freezer bags and freeze. To defrost, place a ½-cup bag in the microwave oven. Heat on DEFROST for 1 minute. Open bag and squeeze contents into a 1-cup glass measure. Microwave on HIGH for 1 to 2 minutes, until completely defrosted.

NOTE If you don't care for seeds, strain sauce through a fine-mesh strainer.

INDEX

Halibut, Choucroute with, 200
Ham:
    barbecuing in combination
        with microwave, 211
    on the Bone, 162
    Bone, Pea Soup with, 79
    Frizzled, 27
    Salad from Holiday Ham,
        164
Harissa, 124
Harvest Red Cabbage, 222
Hawaiian:
    Barbecue Sauce, 215
    Pork Loin, Barbecued, 210
Hearty:
    Corn Chowder, 70
    Italian Sausage-and-Bean
        Soup, 78
Herb(ed)(s):
    Beer Bread, 64
    Bread Stuffing, 175
    Butter, 315
    Cheese Spread, 316
    storing, 302, 312
    -Topped Tomatoes, 221
Heros:
    Beef, 162
    Chicken Cutlet, with Pep-
        pers, 259
    Pepper Steak, 257
Hoagies, Meatball, 158
Home Fries, 30
Honey(ed):
    Bran Muffins, 56
    Mustard Barbecue Sauce,
        215
    Mustard Glazed Turkey
        Drumsticks, 213
    Pear and Lettuce Salad with
        Cheese Croustades, 237
    Sherry Onion Marmalade,
        321
    storing, 302
Horseradish-Mustard Sauce,
    324
Hot:
    Cocoa, Old-Fashioned, 33
    Fudge Sauce, 280
    Italian-Style Turkey Sau-
        sage, 181
    Sweet-and-Sour Sauce, 216

Ice cream, 326
    Candy Bar, 279

Chocolate Chip–Tequila,
    279
Customized Cinnamon, 278
Ginger, 279
Hint-of-Lemon, 279
see also Sorbet
Ice-cream pies, 282–85
    Chocolate Chip–Tequila,
        283
    Lemon, with Warm Berry
        Sauce, 283
    Low-Cholesterol Ice-Milk, in
        Honey-Graham Crust,
        285
    Mud, 284
    Pumpkin, in Ginger Crust,
        284
    Snickers, with Hot Fudge
        Sauce, 283
Ice-cream sauces, 279–82
    Brandy Walnut, 281
    Brown Sugar–Caramel, 281
    Butterscotch, 280
    Fresh Peach, 281
    Hot Fudge, 280
    Quick Raspberry, 282
    Warm Berry, 282
    Warm Walnut, 281
Intense Chili, 155
Irish:
    Brown Bread, 65
    Soda Bread, 64
Italian:
    Broccoli, 232
    Broccoli Soup, 94
    Bruschetta, 66
    Calzones, 255
    Chicken Cutlets Parmigiana,
        190
    Hearty Sausage-and-Bean
        Soup, 78
    Lightly Breaded Chicken
        Cutlets Milan Style, 189
    Meatball-Noodle Soup, 92
    Ricotta-Filled Dumplings,
        133
    Turkey Sausages, 181
    see also Pasta

Jalapeño (peppers):
    Corn Muffins, 62
    Cumin–Hot Pepper Vine-
        gar, 306
    Pizza, 47

Refrigerator Pickled, 314
Japanese Pot Stickers (Gyozas),
    129
Jelly doughnuts, heating in
    microwave, 17
Juice:
    extracting from citrus fruit,
        337
    thawing frozen concentrate,
        21

Lamb:
    Basic Stew, 167
    Gravy, 165
    Leg of, 164
    Mideastern Pita Pockets, 166
    Shepherd's Pie, 165
Lasagna Packages, Individual,
    142
Legumes, 110
    Lentil Soup, 76
    Lentil Stew (Dal), 112
    see also Bean(s)
Lemon(s):
    Hint-of-, Ice Cream, 279
    Honey Cream-Cheese
        Spread, 34
    Ice-Cream Pie with Warm
        Berry Sauce, 283
    Mustard Grilled Chicken,
        212
    Sauce, 228
    -Scented Blueberry Muffins,
        58
    -Scented Cranberry Bread,
        60
    -Scented Cranberry-Bread
        French Toast, 25
    storing, 312
Lentil:
    Soup, 76
    Stew (Dal), 112
Lettuce and Pear Honeyed
    Salad with Cheese Crous-
    tades, 237
Lightly Breaded Chicken Cut-
    lets Milan Style, 189
Lime-Sake Dressing, 308
Linguine, 144
    with Red-Pepper Sauce, 141
    with White Clam Sauce, 139
Linsenpuree (German Lentil
    Puree), 113
London Broil, Marinated, 207